Anime, Philosophy and Religion

Edited by
Kaz Hayashi
Bethel University, St. Paul MN USA
William H. U. Anderson
Concordia University of Edmonton, Alberta, Canada

Series in Philosophy of Religion

Copyright © 2024 by the Authors.

All rights reserved. No part of this publication may be reproduced, stored in a retrieval system, or transmitted in any form or by any means, electronic, mechanical, photocopying, recording, or otherwise, without the prior permission of Vernon Art and Science Inc.

www.vernonpress.com

In the Americas:
Vernon Press
1000 N West Street, Suite 1200
Wilmington, Delaware, 19801
United States

In the rest of the world:
Vernon Press
C/Sancti Espiritu 17,
Malaga, 29006
Spain

Series in Philosophy of Religion

Library of Congress Control Number: 2023943643

ISBN: 978-1-64889-933-1

Also available: 978-1-64889-762-7 [Hardback]; 978-1-64889-800-6 [PDF, E-Book]

Product and company names mentioned in this work are the trademarks of their respective owners. While every care has been taken in preparing this work, neither the authors nor Vernon Art and Science Inc. may be held responsible for any loss or damage caused or alleged to be caused directly or indirectly by the information contained in it.

Cover design by Vernon Press. Cover image by jsks from Pixabay. Background designed by pikisuperstar / Freepik.

Every effort has been made to trace all copyright holders, but if any have been inadvertently overlooked the publisher will be pleased to include any necessary credits in any subsequent reprint or edition.

To My Brother Jonathan Hayashi

Anime makes me smile more than reality

Table of contents

	List of Contributors	xi
	Acknowledgments	xv
	Introduction William H. U. Anderson *Concordia University of Edmonton*	xvii
Chapter 1	**History of Anime: Periods, Genres and Industry** Barışkan Ünal *Journalist and Independent Researcher*	1
Chapter 2	**Spatial Trialectics and Indian Spiritual Philosophy in Tezuka's *Buddha* and Morishita's *Buddha: The Great Departure*** A. P. Anupama *VIT-AP University* Amar Ramesh Wayal *VIT-AP University*	61
Chapter 3	**Metamodernity, American Transcendentalism and Transhumanism in Japanese Anime** Steven Foertsch *Baylor University*	73
Chapter 4	**(Re)Making the Monsters of Everyday Life: Minzokugaku and Yuki Urushibara's *Mushishi*** Drew Richardson *University of California Santa Cruz*	99

Chapter 5	**The Refashioned Tengu: Tradition and Contemporary Romance in *Black Bird***	117
	Tara Etherington *University of Toronto*	
Chapter 6	**Where is the Real Me? Encountering Transhumanism and Cybernetic Divinity in *Serial Experiments Lain***	133
	Anik Sarkar *Salesian College Siliguri*	
Chapter 7	**Philosophy, Soul, Politics and Power in *Dragon Ball Z***	153
	Issei Takehara *Independent Researcher*	
Chapter 8	**The *Avatar* Aminated Series: A Queer Reading of Embodied Power**	181
	Martin Lepage *Independent Researcher*	
Chapter 9	**The Pokédex, Knowledge Production and the Technocratic Colonial Project in Pokémon**	201
	Devon P. Levesque and D. Y. Turner *Queen's University*	
Chapter 10	***The Promised Neverland*: Exploitation of the Religious "Others"**	223
	Michelle Chan *Hong Kong Shue Yan University*	
Chapter 11	**Machines to Pray for Us: The Mechanization of Religious Labor in Ichikawa Haruko's *Hōseki no Kuni***	243
	Christopher Smith *University of Florida*	
Chapter 12	**Dragon Ball: Love and Renewed Life**	257
	Alberto Oya *Instituto de Filosofia da Nova*	

Chapter 13	*Isekai* **Typological Themes and Jesus Parallels**	271
	Graham Lee *Independent Researcher*	
	Bibliography	289
	Index	325

List of Contributors

William H. U. Anderson did his Ph.D. in Biblical Studies and Theology in Postmodern Literary Critical Circles at the University of Glasgow in Scotland. Bill is a Professor of Pop Culture, Philosophy and Religion at Concordia University of Edmonton in Alberta, Canada. He is the author of *Qoheleth and Its Pessimistic Theology: Hermeneutical Struggles in Wisdom Literature* (1997) and *Scepticism and Ironic Correlations in the Joy Statements of Qoheleth?* (2010). He has worked interdisciplinarily throughout his academic career and this is his fifth edited volume with Vernon Press in the Philosophy of Religion Series. His next book with VP is *Space, Philosophy and Ethics* slated for 2024.

Anupama A. P. earned her Ph.D. in Film Studies in the Department of Humanities and Social Sciences from the National Institute of Technology in Tiruchirappalli, India. She was awarded a UNESCO research fellowship in connection with her Ph.D. in Film Studies. Her research interests include Film Studies, Space Studies, Semiotics, Spectatorship Studies and Cyberpunk. She has presented several research papers at various International Conferences and published papers and book chapters around the world. She is an Assistant Professor of English, at the School of Social Sciences and Humanities at VIT-AP University, Amaravati, Andhra Pradesh, India.

Dr. Michelle Chan did her Ph.D. in English at Royal Holloway, University of London. She is an Assistant Professor of English at Hong Kong Shue Yan University in Hong Kong. Her research focuses mainly on Children's Literature, Picture Book Narratives, Victorian Literature and Fantasy Literature.

Tara Etherington achieved her Ph.D. in English at the University of Exeter, U.K., specializing in cultural reading practices of Japanese manga. Tara is the Executive Director, Centre for Entrepreneurship at the University of Toronto in Canada. Her primary research and teaching interests include Cultural Studies, Visual Culture, and Hybridity as a literary method of social critique. Her current research focuses on the uses of hybridity in manga to question prevailing social and cultural discourses on gender, sexuality and identity that transcend Japanese readerships.

Steven Foertsch is a doctoral candidate in the Sociology of Religion program at Baylor University and a research assistant at the Institute for Studies of Religion (ISR). His research focuses on ideology and the intersection between Politics and Religion, Deviance, Social and Political Philosophy, and New Age groups.

Kaz Hayashi did his Ph.D. in Old Testament at Baylor University. He is an Associate Professor of Old Testament at Bethel University in St. Paul, Minnesota, USA. He has a passion for biblical archaeology and historiography and has been on several digs in Israel. Kaz was born and raised in Japan and has a passion for anime.

Graham Lee has an M.A. in Philosophy from the University of Houston and most recently, was a graduate fellow with the Elizabeth D. Rockwell Center on Ethics and Leadership of the Hobby School of Public Affairs at the University of Houston.

Martin Lepage received his Ph.D. in Religious studies at Université du Québec à Montréal in 2017 and has been an independent researcher ever since. His research interests include Contemporary Religiosities, Queer Studies, Gender Studies, Intersectionality and epistemologies and methodologies in Social Sciences and Humanities.

Devon P. Levesque is a doctoral candidate in History at Queen's University in Kingston, Ontario, Canada. He studies Medieval Political Philosophy and Religion in the Mediterranean region.

Alberto Oya is a Research Fellow (*Investigador Doutorado Contratado*) at the IFILNOVA – *Instituto de Filosofia da Nova* (Universidade Nova de Lisboa in Portugal) and a Senior Member of ArgLab—Lisbon Mind, Cognition and Knowledge Research Group. He is the author of *Unamuno's Religious Fictionalism* (2020) and has published extensively around the world.

Drew Richardson is a Ph.D. candidate in the Department of History at the University of California Santa Cruz and a visiting research fellow at Kokugakuin University (2020-22). He also serves as the co-director for curriculum development in the Okinawa Memories Initiative. His dissertation project examines media and place-making practices in native Japanese Ethnography, Folklore and Monsters.

Anik Sarkar is an Assistant Professor of English at Salesian College, Siliguri. His research interests and areas include the Dystopian Novel, Surveillance, Posthumanism, Film Studies and Popular Culture. He is a contributor to books such as *Science Fiction in India* (2022) and *Indian Feminist Ecocriticism* (2022). He is the author of the forthcoming book *Fabulating Ecologies* (2023).

Christopher Smith received a Ph.D. in Japanese Literature from the University of Hawaii at Mānoa and is currently an Assistant Professor of Modern Japanese Literature at the University of Florida, where he teaches courses on modern Japanese Literature, Japanese Culture, Manga and Anime. His research focuses on Postwar Japanese Literature, particularly contemporary literature (Heisei-Reiwa), as well as Japanese Pop Culture, including Manga and Anime. He recently published a translation of *Tanaka Yasuo's Somehow, Crystal* with Kurodahan Press.

Issei Takehara did his M.A. in History and Philosophy of Science and Medicine at the University of Western Ontario in Canada. He teaches Japanese professionally online, while working on various interdisciplinary studies. His expertise is in the comparative studies of the Philosophy of Medicine in Early Modern Periods between the West and the East.

D. Y. Turner is a Ph.D. candidate studying Canadian history at Queen's University. Her current research centers upon Canadian Publishing History and seeks to interrogate the semblances of national history as they are portrayed over time and across multiple authors. Her interests also include East Asian History, Historiography and Historical Theory.

Barışkan Ünal did her Ph.D. on the image of the journalists in American cinema at Gazi University in Ankara, Turkey. She is a journalist in Turkey with more than twenty years of experience. She is currently an editor at a news agency in Turkey and worked as Washington's Chief Correspondent for six years. Barışkan has published countless news reports and analyses on several issues, as well as academic articles in peer-reviewed journals and book chapters. Her interests are Cinema, Film Analysis, Journalism, Digital Media and Communication Studies.

Amar Ramesh Wayal is an Assistant Professor of English in the School of Social Sciences and Humanities at VIT AP University, Andhra Pradesh, India. He was awarded a doctoral research fellowship from the Indian Council of Social Science Research (2017-2018) and a research fellowship from Shastri Indo-Canadian Institute (2019) in connection with a Ph.D. thesis on North American Native writing. His research interests include North American Native Studies, Canadian Studies, Post-Colonial Literature, Translation Studies and Discourse Analysis. He has presented several research papers at various International Conferences and published papers and book chapters internationally.

Acknowledgments

I would like to thank every contributor who has expanded my education through their chapters. The Reviewers make these edited volumes possible: Thank you! As usual, Chris Legerme compiled the bibliography (and all it cost me was a curry at New Asian Village!).

Introduction*

William H. U. Anderson
Concordia University of Edmonton

Anime is exploding on the worldwide stage! Anime has been a staple in Japan for decades, with a strong connection to manga. So why has anime become a worldwide sensation? A cursory explanation is the explosion of online streaming services that specialize in anime, like Funimation and Crunchyroll. Even more general streaming services like Netflix and Amazon have gotten in on the game.

I won't provide a detailed history of anime, definitions and genres here in the Introduction because Chapter 1, by Turkish journalist Dr. Barışkan Ünal, is a comprehensive history of anime which the reviewer said of it:

---

* Excursus on the use of internet sources in pop culture and anime studies. I wasn't sure where to put this but I guess upfront in a footnote is as good a place as any. As a traditional biblical scholar, I still cringe every time I see an internet source in an academic document. But there is no way to navigate pop culture or anime studies without referencing from the internet. Interestingly enough, one of the reviewers made a comment regarding a submission that the author had no need to defend Anime as a discipline—since it is well-established in academia now. I have also come to realize that many of the fandoms are very serious about, and have a deep knowledge of, the primary sources in pop culture and anime. They know the stories, plots, characters and development, arcs and background inside and out, backwards and frontwards. They have much to contribute to an intellectual discussion which may be employed and documented by serious academics. Moreover, many of the internet contributors have Ph.D.s and or are professional researchers. Having said all that, what internet sources demand from scholars is that they double down on rigorous critical engagement. The only courses I allow internet sources are in my pop culture and film courses where one of the learning objectives is: "**To vet internet sources for veracity, quality and substance**". Internet sources can be valid and good; just as peer-reviewed sources may not be that good. It is a part of the scholarly engagement, analysis and assessment ("handling") to determine what is good content or not. But it is a lot harder work and takes a lot more time, e.g., cross-referencing with legitimate scholarly sources on correlated subject matter, statistics and details. Like anime itself, anime scholarship can be very serious and still fun!

This piece of scholarship is a genuine contribution to the Anglophone study of anime. I am familiar with no comprehensive overview that accomplishes so much within this number of pages. That the author ties together both the "content" and "production" aspects of the history of anime lends this chapter a refreshing buoyancy that, if lacking, would seriously weigh down such a lengthy chapter. I heartily recommend its publication, and I applaud the author for this useful and enjoyable work. . . . . I believe that the piece itself will be worth the price of the book![1]

Sold! Chapter 1 lays the foundation for the rest of the book. Here in the Introduction, I want tersely to pull together the many aspects that make anime so popular these days, as well as demonstrate why it deserves the respect of scholars.

Anime is exotic to Western eyes and culture. That is one of the reasons anime has gained worldwide popularity. This strange aesthetic draws the audience in only to find it is deeper and more sophisticated than its surface appearance. The beautiful artwork and style is just so cool. This relates both to the aforementioned "exotic" nature of it and its pure aesthetic. *Akemi's Anime World* provides an excellent treatment of anime art style basic drawing techniques. Here those exotic artistic stylings are visualized: the face and big eyes with the purpose of highlighting emotions (the eyes are the window of the soul); body proportion including highly sexualized exaggeration of women's anatomy; punk and gothic hair and clothing.[2]

Anime has often been criticized for both its Western and White characteristics. I think there are a variety of reasons for this. One is Japan's obsession with Western culture (probably because it is exotic to their Eastern culture).[3] Secondly, it's obsession with Christianity. This is ironic since only

---

[1] I became aware of Dr. Ünal's erudition in her co-authored chapter in my previous book and thought she, as a journalist, would be perfect to write Chapter 1 of this book. Barışkan Ünal and Şeyma Balcı, "Working Women and Rape Myths in Turkish Cinema between 1923-1996", in *Film, Philosophy and Religion*, ed. William H. U. Anderson (Wilmington: Vernon Press, 2019), 281-323.

[2] "Akemi's Anime World", *waybackmachine*: https://web.archive.org/web/20070707043344/http:/animeworld.com/howtodraw/faces.html#top. This is such a helpful internet source which aids the reader's visual and affectual understanding of the art of anime, especially if they are not artists or non-specialists.

[3] See the comment by Anno's protégé regarding the employment of Christian iconography in *Neon Genesis Evangelion* in note 33 of this Introduction.

around 1.5% of the population is Christian.[4] Christian themes can be found in many anime. For example, the *Seven Deadly Sins*[5] (also found in *Fullmetal Alchemist*) or the quest for the "Holy Grail" in *Fate/Zero*.[6] However, this is not a reverse form of "Orientalism" (the portrayal of the East in "white terms") because it is intra-cultural, i.e., it is Japanese artists who have made these artistic choices, including blue eyes and hairstyles.

Anime has amazing music! Anison, a combination of "anime" and "song", is the genre designation of anime music. Anison is a mixed genre primarily related to pop music. But it plays a very important role in anime—acting as the theme music for the openings and endings—a significant part of the attraction going far beyond the anime in Japanese pop culture. Indeed, anison is popular in karaoke.[7] While I love the music from *Honey and Clover*, I adore the music from *Persona 5* and the vocals of Lyn.[8] There are numerous live concerts often performed in cosplay and with sets based on specific anime series like *Persona 5*.[9] My Musicology friend, Dr. Jamie Meyers-Riczu, has introduced me to Ludomusicology or the "Study of Videogame Music" (my son's favorite genre of music). There is often a close relationship between many video games and anime. Indeed, *Persona 5* is just one of many anime that is based on an original video game. But the music in *Persona 5* is so sophisticated as a mix of rock, jazz and pop of the highest quality in both composition and performance.

Anime has many great stories and relatable characters with which the audience can relate and find some affinity. There are often great action and

---

[4] "Japan: Religious Affiliations in 2019", *Statista*: https://www.statista.com/statistics/237609/religions-in-japan/.

[5] *Seven Deadly Sins*: Directed by Tensai Okamura with Screenplay by Shōtarō Suga based on the manga by Nakaba Suzuki (JNN 2014-2015).

[6] *Fate/Zero*: Directed by Ei Aoki with Screenplay by Akira Hiyama and Akihiro Yoshida (Tokyo MX 2011-2012).

[7] "The Growing Anison Scene in Japan", *Trends in Japan*: https://web-japan.org/trends/11_culture/pop160713.html.263-83.

[8] *Persona 5: The Animation*: Directed by Masashi Ishihama with Screenplay by Shinichi Inotsume, Kazuho Hyodo and Noboru Kimura (Tokyo MX 2018-2019). N.B. The openings and endings of P5 are really remarkable artwork with amazing music by Shoji Meguro and vocals by Lyn which perfectly capture the spirit of the series. See Opening "Wake Up, Get Up, Get Out There" https://www.youtube.com/watch?v=0jm8nnHqx80 and Ending "Infinity" https://www.youtube.com/watch?v=0jm8nnHqx80. The "Best of Persona 5" featuring Lyn can be found at https://www.youtube.com/watch?v=joVwwQlu134.

[9] Cf. Kaz Hayashi, "Holograms and Idols: The Image of God and Artificial Transcendence in the Cultural Phenomenon of the Japanese Vocaloid Hatsune Miku", in *Technology and Theology*, ed. William H. U. Anderson (Wilmington: Vernon Press, 2019), 263-83.

fight scenes. Martial arts are a staple of anime and they are often combined with supernatural powers. *Naruto* would be an example of this combination.[10]

Humor plays an important role in anime, even in serious storylines. While *Avatar: The Last Airbender* is disputed as a legitimate anime (since its provenance is not Japan), there are so many serious scenes that perfectly set up a surprise gag. What is interesting to me, is that the joke makes you laugh but doesn't dimmish the seriousness of the situation and or dialogue. The power of a joke, is the power to tell the truth. Funny faces are a staple of anime, too and *Fullmetal Alchemist* is a classic example.[11]

Sex sells! And anime knows that! All kinds of sexual expressions are found in anime and it is rife with fetishism. Fan Service is also what makes anime attractive.

> [F]an Service refers to scenes designed to excite or titillate the viewer. This can include scantily-clad outfits, cleavage shots, panty shots, nude scenes (shower scenes especially), etc. Some broader definitions also include things like cool mecha, big explosions, battle scenes, etc. Basically, if it has little plot-redeeming value, but makes the viewer sit up and take notice, it's probably fan service in one form or another.[12]

Fan Service may attract viewers (primarily male) but it is also the source of negative criticism. Anime is often charged with male sexism, misogyny, and the objectification and exploitation of women.[13] Along with this, its proclivity for ephebophilia and unapologetic sexualization or representation of teenage/underage sex. *Neon Genesis Evangelion* (NGE or Eva) would be a classic example of this with Shinji and Misato.[14] What is unusual about this relationship is that it is an adult 29-year-old woman who is the predator of a 14-year-old boy. This aspect, as one might expect, has been severely criticized

---

[10] *Naruto*: Directed by Hayato Date with Screenplay by Katsuyuki Sumisawa and Junki Takegami based on the manga by Masashi Kisimoto (TXN TV Tokyo 2002-2007).

[11] *Fullmetal Alchemist*: Directed by Seiji Mizushima with Screenplay by Shō Aikawa based on the manga by Hiromu Arakawa (JNN 2003-2004).

[12] "Fan Service", *Urban Dictionary*: https://www.urbandictionary.com/define.php?term=fan%20service.

[13] "Evangelion, Misogyny, and Sexuality: The Women of Evangelion in Relation to Shinji and the Audience", *controlaltdelete-my-existence*: https://www.tumblr.com/controlaltdelete-my-existence/640625310518427648/evangelion-misogyny-and-sexuality-the-women-of.

[14] *Neon Genesis Evangelion*: Directed with Screenplay by Hideaki Anno (TV Tokyo 1995-1996). There were several later spinoffs: films, OVA (Original Video Animations) and video games.

Introduction

for its inappropriateness. The creator, writer and director of NGE, Anno Hideaki, has explicitly identified himself with Shinji and there is speculation that this is a reflection of his own fantasies.

Anime is also popular because it provides a platform for discussing personal problems. Japan is an honor and shame culture. So talking about one's problems is just not cool. This is one theory for the high suicide rate in Japan, i.e., because people feel like they can't talk about their problems, they kill themselves as an act of escape.[15] There are also a lot of "Daddy Issues" in anime, e.g., NGE and *Honey and Clover*.[16]

Anime is often didactic. Common themes are "Loss of Innocence" and "Coming of Age" in Slice of Life, of which, *Honey and Clover* would be a classic example.[17] Anime teach a lot of personal and life lessons. The *Dragon Ball* series is inundated with these life lessons on how to be a better person (warrior), the fallacies of selfishness and self-service, and the value of service to others.[18]

While it is impossible to provide a comprehensive treatment of subject matter of anime, there are common ones. *Ki* literarily means "air, atmosphere, mind and heart" but has a wider reference to the "psychic" or "supernatural". This is often combined with martial arts and battle, e.g., *Dragon Ball*. Anime often portrays the supernatural as "natural" or "normal". Indeed, the audience must apply a "Suspension of Disbelief" since the characters view the supernatural as an everyday part of life, e.g., see Chapter 12 on "Dragon Ball: Love and Renewed Life". Other subject matter involves ghosts, demons and angels, heaven and hell. A common thread in these anime is not to misuse power and to protect those who are not as powerful. Goku in *Dragon Ball* would be a prime example, as demonstrated in Chapter 7 of "Philosophy, Soul, Politics and Power in Dragon Ball Z".

The centrality of the honor and shame culture in Japan is crucial for understanding many of the themes in context. Interestingly enough, both manga and anime are—on the one hand, popular and mainstream—and on the other, viewed as "rebellious" and treated with shame by Japan's very traditional culture. This dichotomy is powerfully portrayed in the Slice of Life

---

[15] Andrew Chambers, "Japan: Ending the Culture of the 'Honorable' Suicide", *The Guardian* 03rd August 2010.
[16] *Honey and Clover*. Directed by Ken'ichi Kasai with Screenplay by Yōsuke Kurodo based on the manga by Chica Umino (Fuji TV 2005).
[17] Slice of Life is a subgenre of anime which is primary set in the real world and has to do with day to day life including relationships and romance.
[18] *Dragon Ball*: Directed by Minoru Okazaki and Daisuke Nishio with Screenplay by Toshiki Inoue and Takao Koyama (Fuji TV 1986-1989).

anime *Kakushigoto: My Dad's Secret Ambition*.[19] The premise of the show is that a young manga writer/illustrator, Kakushi Gotō, is widowed and left to be a single father to his dearly loved daughter Hime. Not wanting to shame his daughter by his profession, he walks her to school in a suit and tie, only to go to his studio and change into his "work clothes" with all the fun and laidback shenanigans surrounding the manga/anime business and his team.

NEET is a common theme in anime. NEET is a British acronym for "Not in Education, Employed or Training". The causes of this social phenomenon are not completely known. The most common theories relate to mental health issues brought on by economics, unemployment, under-employment and under-paid culture. One anime that tried to mitigate the effects of this phenomenon is *Eden of the East*.[20] Notice the biblical/religious name and Eden's association with creation, new life and paradise. The biblical or religious association follows into two films, *The King of Eden* and *Paradise Lost*, the latter having a clear association with Milton as a piece of Christian literature.[21] The premise of the anime is that 20,000 NEET save the world against terrorism by way of their technical skills. The literary intent appears to be that NEET have skills and are valuable to society, perhaps as a means of providing NEET with support and self-esteem.

Depression and Suicide are common themes in anime. There are around seventy suicides every day in Japan and around 25,000 per year.[22] One cultural explanation is that suicide does not have the stigma that Western/Christian cultures do, and consequently, it is seen as an "honorable" way to resolve life circumstances or escape shame. But the cognitive dissonance of this may be found in *Welcome to the N.H.K.*, a black comedy (an anime I'll pick up on again once I've put more pieces together).

Another associated or interrelated theme is *hikikomori*. *Hikikomori* literally means "pulling inward" or "being confined" but has come to describe a growing population of around a million younger Japanese men. The primary descriptor would be "recluses"—young men who cut themselves off from society and social situations—and spend most of their days home alone,

---

[19] *Kakushigoto: My Dad's Secret Ambition*: Directed by Yūta Murano with Screenplay by Takashi Aoshima based on the manga by Kōji Kumeta (Tokyo MX 2020).
[20] *East of Eden*: Directed and Screenplay by Kenji Kamiyama (Fuji TV 2009).
[21] *The King of Eden*: Directed by Kenji Kamiyama with Screenplay by Kenji Kamiyama et al. (Crunchyroll 2009) and *Paradise Lost*: Directed by Kenji Kamiyama with Screenplay by Kenji Kamiyama et al. (Crunchyroll 2010).
[22] "Number of Suicides Increase in 2022", *Nippon.com* 27th March 2022: https://www.nippon.com/en/japan-data/h01624/#:~:text=The%20number%20of%20suicides%20in, from%20the%20National%20Police%20Agency.

Introduction xxiii

indulging in *otaku*. *Otaku* culture tends to be fanatical regarding computers, technology, pop culture, manga and anime.[23] *Otaku* may be analogous to the currently cool "nerd" in the West; but one definitely doesn't want to become a weeaboo![24] *Hikikomori* tend to be NEET. There are, again, many complicated factors to explain it. One explanation is the rise of technology and the ability to isolate oneself. *Hikikomori* tend have a very unhealthy diet and addictive personalities, both physiological (smoking and alcohol) and behavioral (video "gaming" addiction). They tend to stay up all night and sleep all day. Some scholars have suggested the *otaku* relates to the "appeal of the spiritual in a post-religious world, in which personal identity and meaning in life may be crafted from popular cultural texts".[25] In other words, *hikikomori* are searching for a metaphysical solution outside of traditional religion.

Welcome to the N.H.K. is an anime that fully encompasses NEET, *hikikomori*, *otaku*, depression and suicide.[26] Each episode is entitled "Welcome to . . . ." and is based on a character, personal problems (including anxiety), *otaku*, sexual repression (often related to porn/hentai) and *hikikomori* or all of the above. Satō, the 22-year-old protagonist who has been a *hikikomori* for 4 years, inadvertently ends up in a suicide pact. And here's where the cognitive dissonance comes in since he is pretty uncomfortable with the idea standing at the end of the cliff with the group. Misaki, a mysterious girl who takes an interest in Satō, has taken it upon herself to "save him" from being a *hikikomori*. She sets up regular "Table Talks" to educate him away from that lifestyle. She is, of course, deeply in love with him but not transparent with him regarding herself. As one would expect, existentialism is the background based in Eastern religion (as in a lot of anime). But there is a lot of philosophy and Christianity too. Issues like determinism are discussed and this is Satō's excuse for being a *hikikomori* ("it's not my fault"). Misaki employs Nietzsche and Ubermensch as a counter. Theodicy ("God/Life is Not Fair") is bluntly brought up with Misaki discoursing on it. In Episode 29, "Welcome to God", she argues that 90% of life is

---

[23] "Otaku: Japan's Anime-Obsessed Enthusiasts", NBC News 20th August 2006: https://www.nbcnews.com/id/wbna14415584.

[24] While *otaku* are cool nerds, weebs (shortened version of weeaboo) are not. Weebs also have a broader interest in Japan (Japanophiles) but are considered extreme to the point of being laughable. "Weeaboo vs. Otaku: Here's the Difference!", *linguablog* 15th April 2023: https://linguaholic.com/linguablog/weeaboo-vs-otaku/.

[25] Katherine Buljan and Carole M. Cusack, *Anime, Religion and Spirituality* (Sheffield: Equinox Publishing, 2015), 1.

[26] *Welcome to the N.H.K.*: Directed by Yūsuke Yamamoto with Screenplay by Satoru Nishizono based on the manga by Tatsuhiko Takimoto (Chiba TV 2006).

misery and that if God exists, he must be evil based on the evidence of obvious evil and suffering in the world.[27]

Kawaii and Moe are important themes in anime. Kawaii can be rendered "cute" or "adorable". Kerr has gone so far as to claim that Japan is a "Culture of Cuteness". She further argues that it relates to Japan's serious and strict traditional culture.[28] Moe is used to "describe a euphoric response to fantasy characters or representations of them" or "strong feelings towards anime/manga characters and video games".[29] There is a correlation here between kawaii and fetish (including the sexualization of children), perhaps best represented by "Hello Kitty" (a children's anime) in cosplay.[30] Again, the theme of sexual hangups may be related to a stifling traditional culture in Japan. Ironically, embarrassment is also a theme in anime. So there seems to be a lot of cognitive dissonance within Japanese culture and *otaku* related to anime specifically. One might also wonder if these cultural strictures are the etiology of the ubiquitous theme of "teen problems with adults".[31] Often these relate to the inflexibility and hypocrisy of adult society in relation to young people. These are highlighted in *Persona 5*, which also exhibits common settings for these anime in high schools and cafes.

Anime, like a lot of pop culture forms, has a lot to say about philosophy and religion. In many ways, coming back to *Neon Genesis Evangelion*, it is the perfect cultural expression for dealing with most of the issues above. While it has been psychoanalyzed to death, NGE is a deeply philosophical work obsessed with religion.

Neon Genesis Evangelion, in 1995, was a watershed in anime and a game changer. It set the standard and style which led the way to a new future and explosion of anime. This included aesthetics, themes, content and tone. In many ways, it's very postmodern in its use of deconstructed tropes, antiheroes and archetypes. The anime is definitely a case of "Art Reflecting the Artist". It is well-known that NGE was a platform for the creator Hideaki Anno to express his issues with mental health in a Japanese cultural context. Indeed,

---

[27] *Welcome to the N.H.K.*, Episode 29, entitled "Welcome to God".
[28] Hui-Ying Kerr, "What is Kawaii—and Why Did the World Fall for the 'Cult of Cute'?", *The Conversation* 23rd November 2016: https://theconversation.com/what-is-kawaii-and-why-did-the-world-fall-for-the-cult-of-cute-67187.
[29] Patrick W. Galbraith, "Moe: Exploring Virtual Potential in Post-Millennial Japan", *Electronic Journal of Contemporary Japanese Studies*: https://www.japanesestudies.org.uk/articles/2009/Galbraith.html.
[30] A picture is worth a thousand words. See "Hello Kitty Cosplay" images at https://www.pinterest.com/liz26donovan/hello-kitty-cosplay/.
[31] Of course, it may be argued that teen problems with parents and adults is "universal".

Introduction

part of the controversy regarding the original ending was that it essentially was a psychoanalytical representation of Anno's struggles that didn't really wrap up the series and tie up loose ends. That lead to an alternative ending.[32] What NGE then became was a matrix for "dealing" with serious and widespread Japanese problems and philosophy. Of course, religion has a prominent place in NGE too as abundantly evidenced in the ubiquitous and famous iconography of Christian crosses in the series.[33] There is also Kabbalah and, of course, Eastern religions like Buddhism and Taoism with an emphasis on existentialism. Both the iconography and terminology (e.g., Adam, angels, Tree of Life and Sephiroth from Kabbalah, etc.) reveal its deeply religious interest (if not obsession). The name of the anime is a dead giveaway from the Greek: Neon ("new"), Genesis (Bible book and "beginnings") and Evangelion from the root meaning "angel" [EVA] and "evangelize"). My own view is that existentialism inevitably leads to metaphysics, and like Anno's mental health issues reflected in the anime, so too are his struggles with metaphysics and religion. Notwithstanding, NGE became a matrix to start "dealing" with serious and widespread Japanese problems, philosophy and metaphysics (religion). This approach became widespread in anime post-NGE and reflected in many different subgenres outside of apocalyptic *mecha*. NGE also came in the context of the Japanese culture of "honor and shame". It was one of the first to deal with depression, guilt, family dysfunction, sex (fetish) loneliness and suicide—along with the relationship with science, technology and fantasy—all common themes in anime thereafter. NGE heavily employed Mind Screw: Everything you know is wrong—relying on symbolism, surrealism and absurdism to disorient the audience—creating existential angst (probably reflecting Anno's state of mind and many who felt trapped in Japanese culture).

---

[32] *The End of Evangelion*: Directed with Screenplay by Hideaki Anno and Kazuya Tsurumaki (Toei Company 1997).

[33] In an interview, Anno's protégé Kazuya Tsurumaki, said of Christianity and crosses in the series that "There are a lot of giant robot shows in Japan, and we did want our story to have a religious theme to help distinguish us. Because Christianity is an uncommon religion in Japan we thought it would be mysterious. None of the staff who worked on *Eva* are Christians. There is no actual Christian meaning to the show, we just thought the visual symbols of Christianity look cool. If we had known the show would get distributed in the US and Europe we might have rethought that choice". Owen Thomas, "Amusing Himself to Death", *waybackmachine*: http://www.akadot.com/article/article-tsurumaki2.html.

[T]he series slowly descended into its madness at the end of the show, so by the time you got to the end, you were emotionally attached with these characters as they spiraled into depression.[34]

As will be seen in Chapter 1 of the "History of Anime", NGE provided the "fringe benefit" of leading the way in the relationship of franchising and merchandizing as a part of the larger anime industry. Again, the influence of NGE cannot be underestimated in anime.[35]

Like NGE, *Persona 5* (one of my favorite animes) also has a strong psychoanalytical and metaphysical fabric. Jung is the background to the story and plot of *Persona 5* along with existentialism.[36] While Jungian psychology is the background, it is expressed in metaphysics in *Persona 5*. The persona is the "mask" that human beings wear to hide their shadow (true dark side) in social situations. Ren, whose alter-ego is the "Joker", is successful because he is aware of his dark side and harnesses its power for good.[37] It is this realistic awareness that is his strength. The Metaverse—where Ren and his team (The Phantom Thieves) do their work to "save souls" and make the world a better place—is the metaphysical realm representing the Human Psyche and Collective Unconscious. The Palaces represent the houses where the Personal (Individual) Unconsciousness resides in the Metaverse and the Shadows are self-protective. In the palaces, there is treasure: the negative side of people. The Palaces are also "prisons of our own making" and make us "prisoners of our own minds". Mementos in the series represents the metaphysical location of all human souls represented by the Tokyo Subway (with chains and bars along the way) and traveled by Morgana's "Navigator". Of course, the Personal

---

[34] "How Evangelion Impacted the Industry?", *TV Tropes*: https://tvtropes.org/pmwiki/posts.php?discussion=kqk9rhs9hw4ro10t9gvf63x2&page=1.

[35] Theo Kogod, "Neon Genesis Evangelion: 10 Undeniable Ways That It Changed Mecha Anime Forever", *CBR.com*: https://www.cbr.com/neon-genesis-evangelion-changed-mecha-anime/#strong-women.

[36] Benjamin Carpenter, "'I Am Thou...', Thou Art Free: *Persona 5 and Existentialism*", *Medium* 26th December 2018: https://benjaminjjcarpenter.medium.com/i-am-thou-thou-art-free-persona-5-and-existentialism-62476b0da22d; Alex Tisdale, "Persona Takes Jungian Psychology and Runs with It", *Inverse* 27th October 2016: https://www.inverse.com/gaming/22672-persona-carl-jung-psychology-matthew-fike-interview#:~:text='Persona'%20Takes%20Jungian%20Psychology%20and,accuracy%20is%20hit%20or%20miss.&text=Atlus's%20Persona%20series%20is%20very,visual%20representations%20of%20its%20concepts and Coleman Gailloreto, "The Jungian Psychology Concepts Which Inspired The Persona Franchise", *Screenrant* 10th April 2020: https://screenrant.com/persona-games-jungian-psychology-concepts-themes-inspiration-details/. N.B. How the series understands and applies Jungian psychology is questionable in certain places.

[37] My son Liam particularly noted this to me.

Introduction xxvii

Unconsciousness is at odds with Collective Unconscious and that leads to denial and cognitive dissonance which is seen throughout the *Persona 5* series.

The big theme in *Persona 5* is "redemption". Or as *Heroes Wiki* puts it: The Phantom Thieves of Hearts' goal is to steal "the corrupt hearts of 'evil' adults in order to change and reform society for the better".[38] This, in turn, reflects the Japanese theme of teens' problems with adults in terms of hypocrisy but also as a call for justice and a better society.

Interestingly enough, one of the main places the protagonist, Ren, goes for advice/counsel is a church. Ren's confidant and tactical advisor, Hifumi Togo, plays shogi with the priest there (she is a shogi champion). The ostensible reason they meet there is because it is quiet and meditative. But the iconography is intentional—including when Yusuke (an artist and team member aka "Fox")—goes to the church for inspiration which becomes the series of paintings called "The Anguish of Original Sin". The primary message is based in Christian Theology and its primary theme is "balance". Life is a "mixed bag" with evil and good, hate and love, ugly and beauty: understanding this leads to more love, peace and joy (Gospel).

Anime is art that reflects its cultural milieu and expresses its cultural milieu. Japan is an Eastern culture with Eastern religion as its background. Consequently, one shouldn't be surprised that existentialism is the philosophical background of much anime. One of my favorite animes is *Honey and Clover*. It's such a beautiful anime (Slice of Life) with a beautiful story and beautiful characters who struggle with real-life problems and have a lot of fun with a sense of humor. The music also beautifully accompanies the series. While there are many anime that have existentialism as their philosophical background and deal with existential angst, *Honey and Clover* does so masterfully. The anime has a university setting with characters at various stages from sophomore to "college and careers" (those who act as a senpai or "senior" with more experience). Existentialism is found in the iconography of the anime related to *direction, meaning and purpose in life*. There is the "Weather Vane" leitmotif which is always "blowing around" with the implication of "where am I going in life?". Then there is the "Bicycle Wheel" leitmotif or the "Wheel of Life", i.e., life is a journey that may not have meaning, purpose or even answers. This is played out in the protagonist Yūta's literal bicycle trip (a kind of Japanese version of the Australian "Walk About") to find out just such answers (or not). Yūta, like many university students, has

---

[38] "Phantom Thieves of Hearts", *Heroes Wiki*: https://hero.fandom.com/wiki/Phantom_Thieves_of_Hearts#:~:text=Sick%20of%20the%20deception%2C%20hypocrisy,Kazuya%20Makigami%20and%20Futaba%20Sakura.

no real interest in academics but rather likes to "build things". He eventually finds his raison d'être restoring and renovating temples. But to abandon higher (university) education for menial, manual labor has the potential to bring shame to himself and his family. Yūta settles for his "calling" and existential philosophy that life is a journey and "living in the moment". But Shinobu, a mysterious fellow student in love with the female protagonist Hagu (an auteur artist), advises her after having a serious hand injury, that "It's absurd to think your life won't have a meaning unless you leave some [art] work behind. Just living is enough". This echoes French existentialist philosopher Sartre, or at least popular existential answers to the questions of *direction, meaning and purpose in life.*

Part of the excitement of editing books is the submissions for chapters. They come from different countries with different subject matter and perspectives (angles). The close relationship between manga and anime will be felt throughout the book. This book, like my last one on film, only has a rather loose structure to the order of the chapters. It begins with a historical overview (C1), provides one technical approach (C2), and then has three chapters loosely related to Cultural Studies (3-5). While the focus of this book is anime, anime's close relationship with manga is inescapable. Chapter 6 is one of two chapters related to transhumanism (along with Chapter 3). Chapters 7-9 have "power" as their main theme. The book ends with religion as the main theme from a variety of points of view (10-13). The last two chapters conclude with love and Jesus parallels with *isekai* (12-13).

Another fringe benefit of editing books is the people you meet along the way. The co-editor of this volume, Dr. Kaz Hayashi, wrote a chapter in my book *Technology and Theology* entitled "Holograms and Idols: The Image of God and Artificial Transcendence in the Cultural Phenomenon of the Japanese Vocaloid Hatsune Miku". I knew I had this book on anime slated, and I asked him if he'd like to join me as co-editor. Kaz was born in Japan (Japanese is his first language) and is a big anime fan. Coincidentally, he is trained as a biblical scholar and has a Ph.D. in Old Testament, like me. We both have a passion for biblical archaeology and Kaz has been on many digs in Israel (I just like to go there and view the results). He has enriched my mind and my soul. I have been able to introduce him, through this volume, to another Japanese scholar Issei Takehara who wrote Chapter 7 "Philosophy, Soul, Politics and Power in Dragon Ball". I sign off my emails to them with the Japanese war cry used at anime parties "BANZAI"!

BANZAI!
Billy Sensei
July 2023

Chapter 1

History of Anime: Periods, Genres and Industry

Barışkan Ünal

Journalist and Independent Researcher

ABSTRACT: Anime, a form of animation from Japan, has a distinctive place in film studies. This is not only because of its visual style but also because of its narrative, media-mix, the industry itself, and its whole subculture. Anime's increasing appeal to a global audience has led to it becoming part of the academic discussion since the 1990s. While many articles and books regarding the history of anime usually focus on specific genres, periods, films, media-mix or industry aspects separately, anime and its unique position in film studies may be better grasped by looking at its history in a broad perspective. Therefore, this chapter approaches anime and its history by discussing developments of both genres and techniques, as well as different periods and changes in the industry. The chapter starts with a discussion of what anime is and why it is appealing. After discussing anime's roots, I will explore its history and different genres—from Tezuka's approach to Miyazaki's unique visual and narrative style, from umbrella genres *shōjo* and *shōnen* to specific genres *mecha, isekai,* and from anime companies such as Toei, Studio Ghibli, to *otaku* culture and the effect of digitalization. Since anime is such a large phenomenon, it is impossible to cover it all in one chapter. Therefore, the goal here is to provide a historical sketch covering over a century by highlighting notable developments in genres, periods, films, directors, the state of the industry and correlated subculture.[1]

KEYWORDS: Anime, Anime Industry, Cinema, Film, Genre, History, *Isekai*, Japan, Japanese Animation, Mecha, Miyazaki, Periods, Tezuka, Toei, TV Series, Shōjo, Shōnen, Studio Ghibli.

---

[1] Thanks to Gülbin Yıldırım, Mark Armamentos and Dr. Shaun James Kilpatrick for proofreading this chapter.

***

What is Anime?

Anime, in its most general sense, is moving drawings in which imaginations are brought to life. If anime means the collection of imaginative drawings by certain techniques that give a sense of moving images, then, why is it called *anime*, rather than animation or cartoon?

This is the first question that appears in almost everyone's mind when they encounter the term "anime", since anime and animation are similar yet different in many ways. They are similar in meaning because anime is actually a Japanese abbreviation for animation used by the Japanese to define all types of animation. However, it also specifically refers to a Japanese genre of animation.[2] It is not clear when the term was coined, but according to Hu, the term *anime* appeared in the literature in the 1970s.[3] In Japan, animation has been called different names, such as *senga*, *kuga*, *anime-shon*, *manga-eiga*, *dōga*, *ugoku manga*, *anime manga*, *komikku eiga*, *manga fuirumu*, and *bideo ge-mu anime*.[4]

While in Japan, anime can refer to animation in general, there are clear differences between traditional Western animation and Japanese anime. Western cartoons were for adults in movie theatres to begin with but were later designed for children as Saturday Morning Cartoons for decades. This change occurred due to the influence of the Hays Code, budget cuts in animation studios caused by the emergence of television, and the demand for children's programs on television.[5] Because of that, anime differs markedly from Western cartoons (animations) in both visual style and narrative form.

---

[2] David Bordwell and Kristin Thompson, *Film Sanatı* [*Film Art: An Introduction*], trans. Ertan Yılmaz and Emrah Suat Onat (Ankara: Deki, 2011), 386; Jonathan Clements, *Anime: A History* (London: British Film Institute, 2013), 11; Tze-yue G. Hu, *Frames of Anime of Anime: Culture and Image-Building* (Hong Kong: Hong Kong University Press, 2010), 101; Gilles Poitras, "Contemporary Anime in Japanese Pop Culture", *Japanese Visual Culture: Explorations in the World of Manga and Anime*, ed. Mark W. MacWilliams (New York: An East Gate Book, 2008), 48; Dani Cavallaro, *Anime Intersections: Tradition and Innovation in Theme and Technique* (Jefferson: McFarland, 2007), 2 and Robin E. Brenner, *Understanding Manga and Anime* (London: Libraries, 2007), 29.
[3] Hu, *Frames of Anime*, 102.
[4] Clements, *Anime*, 10 and Hu, *Frames of Anime*, 101.
[5] Julian Lawrence, "Cartoons Have Always Been for Adults but Here's How They Got Tangled Up with Kids", *The Conversation* 03rd February 2020: https://theconversation.com/cartoons-have-always-been-for-adults-but-heres-how-they-got-tangled-up-with-kids-130421.

History of Anime 3

Anime has an adult audience typically. It typically has a more well-structured storyline and complex narrative style than Western animation. Its detailed and striking visual style and characters drawings were unique and had more depth than Western cartoons. Therefore, as Napier states, defining anime simply as Japanese cartoons or animation "minimizes the variety of the form" and "gives no sense of the depth and variety that make up" anime.[6]

This point raises another ambiguity about defining anime. The core of this ambiguity lies in anime's transmedia reach, or media-mix, which is "a practice of releasing interconnected products for a wide range of media platforms and commodity types".[7] Anime does not only correspond to one type of product but refers to all types of media productions, such as films, TV series, Original Video Animation (OVA), and original net animation (ONA), as well as other aspects such as merchandising and anime-related events, and conventions.[8] Therefore, scholars use different terms to define anime, such as "medium",[9] "format",[10] "genre", "a phenomenon of popular culture",[11] "cultural phenomenon and a genre",[12] "medium-genre",[13] "style of animation popular in Japanese films",[14] "a part of mainstream Japanese pop culture",[15] and "media-form".[16] It

---

[6] Susan J. Napier, *Anime from Akira to Princess Mononoke: Experiencing Contemporary Japanese Animation* (New York: Palgrave, 2001), 6.

[7] Marc Aaron Steinberg, "The Emergence of the Anime Media Mix: Character Communication and Serial Consumption" (Ph.D. Dissertation: Brown University, 2009), 4. See also Rayna Denison, *Anime: A Critical Introduction* (London: Bloomsbury Publishing, 2015), "Introduction", olb and Thomas LaMarre, *The Anime Machine: A Media Theory of Animation* (Minneapolis: University of Minnesota Press, 2009), xiv.

[8] Bordwell and Thompson, *Film*, 386; Napier, *Anime from Akira to Princess Mononoke*, 5; Denison, *Anime*, "Introduction", olb and Brenner, *Understanding Manga and Anime*, 29.

[9] Paul Wells, *Understanding Animation* (London: Routledge, 1998), 6; Susan J. Napier, *Anime from Akira to Howl's Moving Castle: Experiencing Contemporary Japanese Animation* (New York: Palgrave, 2005), xi; Marc Steinberg, *Anime's Media Mix: Franchising Toys and Characters in Japan* (Minneapolis: University of Minnesota Press, 2012), 17 and Clements, *Anime*, 14.

[10] Brenner, *Understanding Manga and Anime*, 30.

[11] Napier, *Anime from Akira to Howl's Moving Castle*, 3.

[12] Denison, *Anime*, "Introduction", olb.

[13] Hu, *Frames of Anime*, 2.

[14] Miyazaki Hayao, "Anime", *Britannica*: https://www.britannica.com/art/anime-Japanese-animation.

[15] Mark W. MacWilliams, "Introduction", *Japanese Visual Culture*, 13.

[16] Stevie Suan, "Repeating Anime's Creativity Across Asia", in *Trans-Asia as Method: Theory and Practices*, eds. Jeroen de Kloet et al. (London: Rowman&Littlefield International, 2020), 143.

is difficult to describe anime easily since its meanings depends on context, and it comprises diverse media productions with commercial and cultural angles.[17]

However, one clear thing is that anime has impacted audiences not only in Japan but around the globe for decades. Some audiences grew up with anime and continue to be fans of it, while others first encountered it as adults. Every new generation of audiences has new tastes, and animators have added new perspectives and angles to anime. For this reason, even after decades, anime continues to attract new people and create a passionate fanbase around the world. This leads to another question which is why anime has remained so appealing to so many people for as long as it has.

What Makes Anime So Appealing?

The answer to this question is found in anime's distinct visual styles, characters and themes—with its "anime-esque elements"[18] —that separate it from Western animation and cartoons. Regarding narratives, unlike cartoons and Western animation, anime does not only deal with basic themes that aim to teach and entertain children. Rather, it addresses various issues and uses more universal themes and narratives. Anime ranges from romance to drama and adventure, from science fiction (sci-fi) to dark fantasy. It also targets different demographics from children to adult content. There is even pornographic anime.

Audiences can encounter genres and subgenres that are specific to anime such as *mecha* (mechanized robots) and *isekai* (fantasy otherworld). Anime targets certain demographics, such as *shōnen* (young boys) and *shōjo* (young girls). As Poitras describes, the audience watches "something very different from the song-and-dance numbers, wacky antics, situation comedies, and bloodless action that are the common fare of Western animation".[19] Stories may not provide straight or moral black-and-white solutions or ends. In this sense, anime does not only provide entertainment but also conveys discourses and ideologies, and discusses the problems of the contemporary

---

[17] Ian Condry, *The Soul of Anime: Collaborative Creativity and Japan's Media Success Story* (Durham: Duke University Press, 2013), 87; Napier, *Anime from Akira to Howl's Moving Castle*, 251 and 291; Denison, *Anime*, "Introduction" and "Textual and Technical Definition of Anime", olb.
[18] Suan, "Repeating Anime", 146. Suan defines anime-esque elements as a kind of "models", which are constantly cited in different combinations when producing anime. These elements appear regularly, have built up over time, and each having a history.
[19] Poitras, "Contemporary Anime", 48.

world in its narratives.[20] Therefore, anime can provide unique animation experiences that classic Western animation cannot provide because of its unique style and narratives in relation to various audiences and demographics.

In addition, anime is *"stateless"* in both its universal themes and also its character drawings, as Napier suggests.[21] Anime characters are less stereotyped more multidimensional than those in Western animation.[22] They may not represent classic binary good-evil or hero-villain prototypes; they are stateless with their big eyes and a range of hair colors, like green and blue. That anime characters appear free of cultural, ethnic stereotypes and characteristics allow audiences from different backgrounds and regions to easily identify with anime characters. Since anime characters range from realistic to broadly grotesque and from human to icons or animals,[23] the audiences also have endless alternatives or opportunities to identify themselves and take a journey with unique protagonists, e.g. in the genre of *isekai*.

Anime also seems to have limitless imagination and creative expressions beyond that of Western animation. Through "moving drawings",[24] anime has the ability to give "movement and life to inert materials" through moving drawings with strikingly detailed visual representations.[25] As Cavallaro indicates, anime's "most distinctive attribute is the uncompromising madness of its images" and its passion for details and pictorial signs which are no less textual.[26] He further adds that "No detail is ever too trivial or diminutive: even a discarded can, a lowly desktop computer . . . . can be lovingly designed and hence capable of exuding a palpable charm of its own".[27] As it presents more

---

[20] Annalee Newitz, "Anime Otaku: Japanese Animation Fans Outside Japan", *Bad Subjects* 13 (April 1994): 12; Napier, *Anime from Akira to Howl's Moving Castle*, 292 and 11.
[21] The term "stateless" is borrowed from Napier in *Anime from Akira to Princess Mononoke*, 24.
[22] Antonia Levi, *Samurai from Outer Space: Understanding Japanese Animation* (Chicago: Open Court, 2000), 20; Laura Pope Robbins, "Bringing Anime to Academic Libraries: A Recommended Core Collection", *Collection Building*, 33.2 (2014): 34; Napier, *Anime from Akira to Howl's Moving Castle*, 33 and 10; Hu, *Frames of Anime*, 3 and MacWilliams, "Introduction", 13.
[23] Napier, *Anime from Akira to Howl's Moving Castle*, 25 and Cavallaro, *Anime Intersections*, 175.
[24] This is a particular stress of Thomas LaMarre, "From Animation to Anime: Drawing Movements and Moving Drawings", *Japan Forum* 14.2 (2002): 359.
[25] Napier, *Anime from Akira to Howl's Moving Castle*, 294.
[26] Cavallaro, *Anime Intersections*, 1.
[27] Ibid., 176.

"striking visual dynamic imagery"[28] than animation, emotions and expressions are more vivid in anime.[29] In particular, the big eyes of characters not only represent the style of anime, but also function as a key to reflect emotions clearly, strongly and dramatically,[30] like "windows or gateways to character's the soul".[31] Or as Levi describes them: "Those eyes could glisten with hope, blur with tears, or melt with love".[32]

Visual projections of anime are also "stateless". Although anime constitutes some elements from Japanese culture and history, it takes place in diverse places from Japanese and European cities to apocalyptic worlds and unknown galaxies. Therefore, as Lu states, "through its suggestion of racial mixing and cultural blurring, anime neutralizes itself".[33] Or as Napier suggests, it offers "an extremely heterogeneous kind of cultural self-representation" and "a space for identity exploration in which the audience can revel in a safe form of Otherness unmatched by any other contemporary medium".[34] Therefore, anime enables the audience to enter unique imaginary worlds in which they can identify with various richly designed characters and be in different places, worlds and times with rich visual images.

There is another reason why anime is so appealing. As Wells states, it "is everywhere".[35] It crosses sectors, media platforms, and national boundaries, and circulates transnationally. Anime media-mix ranges from both popular and art-house films to TV series, from videos to webisodes, from huge merchandise to video games, from contemporary art and fashion to fun conventions.[36] LaMarre notes that the relationship and convergence of this different media-mix "serve to reinforce a sense that the underlying condition

---

[28] J. Jeffery Timbrell, "1963 Astro Boy" in *Anime Impact: The Movies and Shows that Changed the World of Japanese Animation*, ed. Chris Stuckmann (Mango Publishing, 2018), olb.

[29] Napier, *Anime from Akira to Howl's Moving Castle*, xi and Poitras, "Contemporary Anime", 62.

[30] Condry, *The Soul of Anime*, 103; Cavallaro, *Anime Intersections*, 175 and Brenner, *Understanding Manga and Anime*, 40-42.

[31] Hayao, "Anime", wp and Levi, *Samurai from Outer Space*, 11.

[32] Levi, *Samurai from Outer Space*, 11.

[33] Amy Shirong Lu, "The Many Faces of Internationalization in Japanese Anime", *Animation* 3.2 (2008): 172.

[34] Napier, *Anime from Akira to Howl's Moving Castle*, 27.

[35] Wells, *Understanding Animation*, 1.

[36] Condry, *The Soul of Anime*, 1, 85, 204; Denison, *Anime*, "Introduction", olb; Wells, *Understanding Animation*, 1; Napier, *Anime from Akira to Howl's Moving Castle*, 23; LaMarre, *The Anime Machine*, xiv; MacWilliams, "Introduction", 6 and Cavallaro, *Anime Intersections*, 2.

for Japanese animations is general circulation and acceleration".[37] Hence, anime provides its audience a range of experiences and even creates a society or community, an "anime world".

In summary, anime is appealing because it is different in striking visuals, character design and narrative style from the classic children's animation of the West in many ways. With the help of these features, anime presents diverse imagery and offers both realistic and fantasy worlds in which the audience can face reality and escape from reality concurrently. It provides the audience freedom for limitless imagination as well as discovering different identities, times and spaces. As Hu indicates, anime provides "a buffer living space in which fantasy, art, and technology can co-exist satisfactorily".[38] Therefore, the response of Napier to the question of "Why anime?" summarizes all these different aspects discussed above by saying: "anime helps to fill a basic human need for the different" and "opens a world that sometimes seems more 'real' than our own".[39] In this regard, Wells suggests that it "is arguably the most important creative form of the twenty-first century".[40]

In saying so, anime has come a long way since its inception. As it has constantly changed and developed in terms of content, form, production and merchandising with the emergence of various studios, directors, and genres, looking at the history of anime can allow us to better understand the nature of anime and why it is appealing and so popular.

Roots of Anime and Early Days

Although anime had started to shine in post-Second World War (WWII) Japan, its root and inspirations can be traced back to the Japanese traditional arts, Western animations, and developments in the photography and film industries.

Anime shows influences from traditional Japanese arts ranging from the picture-scrolls (*Emakimono*) of the Kamakura period (1185-1333), picture-card storytelling (*Kamishibai*) of the early Shōwa period (1926- 1989), all the way to the woodblock print image (*Ukiyo-e*) and the projected pictures (*Utsushi-e* or Edo anime) of the Edo period (1603-1868).[41] It is also inspired by

---

[37] LaMarre, *The Anime Machine*, xviii.
[38] Hu, *Frames of Anime*, 158.
[39] Susan Napier, "Why Anime?", *Japan Spotlight* (March/April, 2004): 23.
[40] Wells, *Understanding Animation*, 1.
[41] Nobuyuki Tsugata, "A Bipolar Approach to Understanding the History of Japanese Animation", in *Japanese Animation: East Asian Perspective*, eds. Masao Yokota and Tze-yue G. Hu (Jackson: University Press of Mississippi, 2013), 25; Takuji Okuno, "Roots of Cool Japan: From the Japanese Traditional Edo Culture to Anime and Manga", *Kwansei Gakuin University Social Sciences Review* 19 (2014): 3; Guido Tavassi, *Storia*

Japanese traditional performing arts, such as Kabuki, puppet theatre (*Bunraku*), *Nō* theatre and *Kyōgen* stage-acting, as well as by legends, novels, and even ancient plays and recited tales.[42] Furthermore, the effect of modern manga (Japanese comic books)—whose origin also goes back to at least the Edo period and which rose in the nineteenth century—is indisputable since it provides diverse themes, narratives, characters and inspirations to most anime.[43] All of these arts—with a focus on visuals and pictocentricism—are reflected in Japanese anime. As the cultural and technological exchange between the Japanese, European and American cultures increased in the Meiji era (1868-1912)—the appearance of Western cartoons in Japan around 1909-1910 and the emergence of photography and cinema—also influenced the birth of anime.[44] Anime thus emerged as a hybrid art which carries both traditional and Western influences.

The Early Pioneer Years of Anime

Animated works started to appear in Japan around 1915-1917. Three artists are seen as the founding pioneers of Japanese animation: Ōten Shimokawa (cartoonist), Jun-ichi Kōuchi (cartoonist) and Seitarō Kitayama (a western-style artist). While all completed their first animated films in 1917, Shimokawa's *The Doorman* is considered the first anime.[45] These early works were two-five minute short films, "mainly animated versions of Japanese folk tales or slapstick cartoons of the day".[46] As anime were called *manga films*,

---

Dell'Animazione Giapponese: Autori, arte, industria, successo dal 1917 a oggi [A History of Japanese Animation. Authors, Art, Industry, Success from 1917 to Today] (Latina: Tunue, 2021), 8; Poitras, "Contemporary Anime", 49; Denison, *Anime*, "Chapter 4", olb; Napier, *Anime from Akira to Howl's Moving Castle*, 4; LaMarre, *The Anime Machine*, 13; Hu, *Frames of Anime*, 26, 28 and Clements, *Anime*, 489.

[42] Hu, *Frames of Anime*, 33-35 and Poitras, "Contemporary Anime", 61.

[43] Susan Napier, "When the Machines Stop Fantasy, Reality, and Terminal Identity in Neon Genesis Evangelion and Serial Experiments: Lain", in *Robot Ghosts Wired Dreams: Japanese Science Fiction from Origins to Anime*, eds. Christopher Bolton, Istvan Csicsery-Ronay Jr. and Takayuki Tatsumi (Minneapolis: University of Minnesota Press, 2007), 105; MacWilliams, "Introduction", 6 and 10; Poitras, "Contemporary Anime", 61; Hu, *Frames of Anime*, 112; Condry, *The Soul of Anime*, 21; Cavallaro. *Anime Intersections*, 174 and Napier, *Anime from Akira to Howl's Moving Castle*, 19.

[44] Poitras, "Contemporary Anime", 49; Napier, *Anime from Akira to Howl's Moving Castle*, 4; Cavallaro, *Anime Intersections*, 4; MacWilliams, "Introduction", 6 and 11; Hu, *Frames of Anime*, 22-23; Napier, *Anime from Akira to Howl's Moving Castle*, 16 and Condry, *The Soul of Anime*, 95.

[45] *The DoorMan*: Directed by Ōten Shimokawa (Tenkatsu 1917). The Japanese title is *Imokawa Mukuzo Genkanban no Maki*.

[46] Tsugata, "A Bipolar Approach", 25.

manga eiga in this period, early works were not the same anime as known today.[47] However, early animators improved anime through trial-and-error drawings and used cutout animation techniques. Cel-animation was introduced to the industry in the 1920s.[48] Pioneering animators also worked with film studios such as Tenkatsu, Kobayashi Shōkai and Nikkatsu Kitayama (an early pioneer). Kitayama set up an animation film department within the Nikkatsu Corporation and later opened his own studio named the Kitayama Film Studio in 1921. He specialized in anime and used a variety of techniques.[49] Unfortunately, many early works did not survive the 1923 earthquake and resulting fires. These pioneers were followed by the second generation.

The Second Generation of Anime

Sanae Yamamoto (1898-1981), Noburo Ōfuji (1908-1961) and Yasuji Murata (1896-1966) were a part of this second generation.[50] The first anime to have an international presence, and bring international acclaim to a director, was *The Thief of Baghdad Castle* by Ōfuji in 1926.[51] Ōfuji introduced new techniques by making the film by using cutting and pasting colored paper (*chiyogami*),[52] which also made the film look "uniquely Japanese".[53]

Another important development that took place in the 1920s is the Japanese government's decision to use anime for educational purposes. As a result, animators produced works not just for children but also for the general public with educational and instructional content.[54] In this period, two prominent animation studios were also set up: P.C.L. (Photo Chemical Laboratories), Shashin Kagaku Kenkyūsho and J. O. Company.

---

[47] Yasuo Yamaguchi, "The Evolution of the Japanese Anime Industry", *Nippon* 20th December 2013: https://www.nippon.com/en/features/h00043/ and Jaqueline Berndt, "Anime in Academia: Representative Object, Media Form, and Japanese Studies", *Arts* 7.4 (2018): 6.
[48] "Celluloid Animation".
[49] Tsugata, "A Bipolar Approach", 26; Hu, *Frames of Anime*, 60 and LaMarre, *The Anime Machine*, xxix.
[50] Yasushi Watanabe, "The Japanese Walt Disney: Masaoka Kenzo", trans. Sheuo Hui Gan, in *Japanese Animation: East Asian Perspective*, 98.
[51] *The Thief of BaghdadCastle*: Directed by Noburō Ōfuji (Jiyu Eiga Kenkyusho 1926). The Japanese title is *Baguda-jou no Touzoku*.
[52] Akiko Sano, "*Chiyogami*, Cartoon, Silhouette the Transitions of Ōfuji Noburō", in *Japanese Animation: East Asian Perspective*, 87 and Yamaguchi, "The Evolution", wp.
[53] Clements, *Anime*, 105.
[54] Clements, *Anime*, 69 and Denison, *Anime*, "Chapter 4: 4 Early Anime Histories", olb.

Japan's Fifteen Years War during 1931-1945

Japan's Fifteen Years War during 1931-1945 impacted the development of anime. The fact that foreign films were gradually banned from screening provided an opportunity for more locally produced short animated films. Some Japanese film companies, such as Tōhō (founded in 1932) and Shochiku (founded in 1895), started to produce animations.[55] Cel-animation became the highest-profile form of animation and hand-painted anime has been a commonly used technique in the industry.[56] During this period, Kenzo‑Masaoka produced the first talkie animation in Japan and led the industry to transform the use of celluloid in animation. He produced high-quality works, and trained young animators and opened a way for them to produce collectively. For this reason, he is recognized as "The Father of Japanese Animation".[57] Furthermore, war-related anime propaganda films with military sponsorship took the stage in this period. *Momotaro's Divine Sea Warriors*, a thirty-seven-minute film that features animal-like characters in military attire taking up arms, was funded largely by the Imperial Navy.[58] In compliance with the military's propagandistic discourses, the film implies that the Japanese military was "the incoming savior of the Pacific Islands' colonized natives".[59] Hu says that "metaphorically speaking, Momotarō was Japan's silhouette wartime mascot as opposed to America's Mickey Mouse".[60]

Late 1930s Onward

From the late 1930s onwards, anime was called *manga doga* (moving images), and during the Occupation period (1945–1952), the term *anime shon* started to spread.[61] During this period, new important anime studios emerged. Shin Nihon Dōga Sha (New Japan Animation Company), later renamed as Nihon Manga Eiga Kabushiki Kaisha (Japan Manga Film Corporation), was founded by about 100 animators led by Kenzō Masaoka and Sanae Yamamoto and with

---

[55] Tsugata, "A Bipolar Approach", 26 and Tavassi, *Storia*, 12.
[56] Denison, *Anime*, "Chapter 4: 4 Early Anime Histories", olb; Poitras, "Contemporary Anime", 58; Hu, *Frames of Anime*, 63 and LaMarre, *The Anime Machine*, 24.
[57] Tze-yue G. Hu, "Animating for 'Whom' in the Aftermath of a World War" in *Japanese Animation: East Asian Perspective*, 116; Tsugata, "A Bipolar Approach", 27 and Watanabe, "Masaoka Kenzo", 99.
[58] *Momotaro's Divine Sea Warriors:* Directed by Mitsuyo Seo with Screenplay by Mitsuyo Seo (Shōchiku Dōga Kenkyūsho 1945). The Japanese title is *Momotarō umi no Shinpei*.
[59] Hu, *Frames of Anime*, 68.
[60] Ibid.
[61] Berndt, "Anime in Academia", 6.

History of Anime

the support of General Headquarters of the Allied occupation in 1945.[62] The Tōhō Kyōiku Eiga Sha was set up in 1948 for new educational film productions. However, the most important development in this period was the establishment of Tokyo Motion Picture Distribution Company (Toei), a new film conglomerate resulting from the merger of the Toyoko and Oizumi film production companies in 1951. Considerable anime works were produced during the Occupation (1945-1952).[63] However, in the 1950s, as American animation films, such as *Snow White*, *Pinocchio* and *Bambi*, started to be screened in Japan again.[64] These movies with sound effects amazed both Japanese audiences and animators, which caused audiences to start searching for better quality anime products.[65]

Rise of Anime with Toei Company and Television in 1950s and 1960s

Anime "as a commercial art form", especially feature-length films, actually started to rise "organically and voluntarily" after the postwar period of Japan in the 1950s and 1960s.[66] Denison touches upon three factors in the 1950s that were "necessary to the birth of what we now think of as anime": the recovery of the Japanese economy and the rise of commercial culture, the expansion of Japan's animation industry during and after the Occupation period, and the rise of television.[67]

Toei Animation

On the industrial side, in 1956, Toei purchased Nihon Dōga-sha and renamed it Toei Dōga (now Toei Animation). As Japan's first large-scale studio devoted entirely to making animated films,[68] Toei has always had a special place and role in the development of the genre. First, with its goal of becoming the

---

[62] Later, it is renamed as Nihon Manga Eiga Kabushiki Kaisha/Japan Manga Film Corporation.
[63] Hu, "Animating", 116.
[64] *Snow White:* Directed by David Hand with Screenplay by Ted Sears based on *Snow White* by The Brothers Grimm (Walt Disney 1937); *Pinocchio:* Directed by Ben Sharpsteen and Hamilton Luske with Screenplay by Ted Sears based on *The Adventures of Pinocchio* by Cario Collodi (Walt Disney 1940) and *Bambi:* Directed by David Hand with Screenplay by Perce Pearce based on *Bambi, a Life in the Woods* by Felix Salten (Walt Disney 1942).
[65] Bordwell and Thompson, *Film*, 383; Hu, *Frames of Anime*, 175-76; Tsugata, "A Bipolar Approach", 28 and Denison, *Anime*, "Chapter 4: 4 Early Anime Histories", olb.
[66] Napier, *Anime from Akira to Howl's Moving Castle*, 16 and Hu, *Frames of Anime*, 103, respectively.
[67] Denison, *Anime*, "Chapter 4: 4 Early Anime Histories", olb.
[68] Tsugata, "A Bipolar Approach", 28.

"Disney of the East",[69] it quickly established itself as a major player and focused on the highest quality feature-length films and TV series that targeted not just children but also general audiences.[70] Therefore, Toei produced serious anime films, and it produced Japan's first color-animated feature, *The Legend of the White Snake* in 1958.[71] The film is also the second animated feature film from Japan, and the first anime screened in the U.S.[72] Potrais states that the film "would prove to be an inspiration for many who later joined the Japanese animation industry in the 1960s and 1970s, as well as proving that locally made animated features were a viable commercial product".[73] Second, with its high-quality training programs, the company has trained many animators. Hayao Miyazaki, Osamu Tezuka, Isao Takahata, Yasuri Mori, Leiji Matsumoto and Yoichi Kotabe started their career in Toei and later became well-known animators, some of whom even went on to establish Japan's current animation studios. By both producing quality works and training promising anime creators since its foundation, Toei has become one of the most important anime studios in the industry.

Role of Television for Anime in the 1950s and 1960s

In the 1950s, as television gradually became a popular for entertainment in Japan, anime companies saw it as a new medium to sell their works. This new medium, however, came with the challenge of adapting visuals and narratives of anime works for TV standards. Therefore, beginning in the 1960s and for the next decades, TV was the largest influence on anime industry.[74] In 1960, the first anime broadcast on TV was *Three Tales*, three anime adaptations of famous stories.[75]

In 1962, the first anime series on TV was *Otogi Manga Calendar*, educational anime.[76] The turning point for the anime industry, however, came with the

---

[69] Yamaguchi, "The Evolution", wp.

[70] Colin Odell and Michelle Le Blanc, *Studio Ghibli: The Films of Hayao Miyazaki and Isao Takahata* (Herts: Kamera Books, 2015), 16; Denison, *Anime*, "Chapter 4: 4 Early Anime Histories", olb and Napier, *Anime from Akira to Howl's Moving Castle*, 16.

[71] *The Legend of the White Snake*: Directed by Taiji Yabushita with Screenplay by Taiji Yabushita and Shin Uehara based on *Legend of the White Snape* (Toei 1958). The Japanese title is *Hakujaden*.

[72] Clements, *Anime*, 232.

[73] Poitras, "Contemporary Anime", 49-50.

[74] Clements, *Anime*, 299 and Poitras, "Contemporary Anime", 50.

[75] *Three Tales*: Directed by Keiko Kozonoe and story by Hirosuke Hamada et al. (NHK 1960). The Japanese title is *Mitsu no Hanashi*. Poitras, "Contemporary Anime", 67.

[76] *Otogi Manga Calendar:* Directed by Ryūichi Yokoyama (Otogi Production 1961-1962). The Japanese title is Otogi Manga Karenda. Poitras, "Contemporary Anime", 50.

phenomenal rise of Osamu Tezuka and his *Astro Boy* series.[77] In 1961, Tezuka, the "god of Japanese comics (manga *No Kamisama*)", established his own animation production studio after Toei, named Tezuka Osamu Production (later Mushi Productions). His aim for his company was to "become the Disney of the Orient".[78] In 1963, his *Astro Boy* series began airing on TV and became the most important turning point in Japanese animation history. Not only it was the first successful Japanese animation series on TV, but it also left an immeasurable mark on the anime industry with its novel technical approach, narrative style, and merchandising strategy. Therefore, *Astro Boy* is considered the "birth"[79] of modern anime as known today and started "a new age in Japanese animation".[80]

Tezuka, Astro Boy in 1963 and the Impact on the Anime Industry

Regarding this revolutionary technical approach, Tezuka created a prototype and new anime technique that has dominated the anime industry ever since. Before Tezuka, full animation movies required twenty-four drawn animated frames per second. That means making anime films involves creating thousands of celluloids, which takes considerable time.[81] Tezuka also proposed *Astro Boy* as 30-minute episodes. This was much longer than an American animation series which was usually around 5-10 minutes in that period.[82] In fact, he even undersold the series to have his offer accepted by the TV station.[83] Hence he needed to find creative ways, with limited staff, to reduce costs and to produce weekly episodes on time. So, he used "limited animation", with roots in early 1940s commercial animation. Tezuka radically limited the number of drawn frames to the minimum required, used more still images, reused some frames by storing (bank system), and created a sense of movement by implementing certain techniques, such as Pull-Cel.[84] This

---

[77] *Astro Boy*. Directed by Osamu Tezuka with Screenplay by Yoshiyuki Tomino based on a manga of the same name in 1952 by Osamu Tezuka (Mushi Production 1963-1966). The Japanese title is *Tetsuwan Atomu*.
[78] Hu, *Frames of Anime*, 11 and Steinberg, *Anime's Media Mix*, 40.
[79] Napier, *to Princess Mononoke*, 16; Denison, *Anime*, "Chapter 4: 4 Early Anime Histories", olb; Condry, "Contemporary Anime", 100; Hu, *Frames of Anime*, 11 and 98; Yamaguchi, "The Evolution", wp and Tsugata, "A Bipolar Approach", 29.
[80] Clements, *Anime*, 269.
[81] Poitras, "Contemporary Anime", 58 and Steinberg, *Anime's Media Mix*, 39.
[82] Tsugata, "A Bipolar Approach", 29.
[83] Steinberg, *Anime's Media Mix*, 39.
[84] Condry, *The Soul of Anime*, 104; Hu, *Frames of Anime*, 99; Yamaguchi, "The Evolution", wp; Denison, *Anime*, "Television and the Birth of 'Anime' in Japan", olb; Tsugata, "A Bipolar Approach", 28 and Clements, *Anime*, 273.

technique gradually came to dominate the industry because it allowed animators to produce much faster.[85] As such, this style is sometimes called "Tezuka's Curse" since it "dramatically reduced the quality of Japanese anime in comparison to works made in the US".[86] It also led to a low-budget and a low-income industry which consequently led to low wages in the industry.

In terms of its different narrative style, *Astro Boy* is about the adventures of a little android boy, built by a scientist as a replacement for his dead son. At first, it sounds like a story for children similar to *Pinocchio*, but it has a deeper and more elaborate narrative structure. Its narrative provides meaningful discussion about technology, robots, the meaning of being human, friendship and love. In fact, by featuring a humanoid robot and questioning the developments of technology, *Astro Boy* also helped with the emergence of one of the main genres in anime: humanoid robots and giant robots. Besides, as Tsugata highlights, unlike American animations, characters in *Astro Boy* are fully developed.[87] Unlike *Pinocchio*, "*Astro Boy* is not trying to become a real boy; he is alive, from the very beginning to the very end. It is humanity that has trouble seeing the truth about him".[88] In opposition to Western animation, in which emotions of characters were not presented in depth in that period, the large eyes of *Astro Boy* characters show emotions better and deeper, which affected audience perceptions. Because of that, large-eye characters became one of anime's signature features. By setting *Astro Boy* in a sci-fi space, it made it an easier sell overseas because it wasn't set in a certain region. "This concept came to form an important element in the articulation of many later anime" by reducing Japanese elements to be able to sell anime abroad.[89]

On the commercial side, *Astro Boy* was a turning point for the beginning of the media-mix and character merchandising in anime.[90] According to Steinberg, the reason behind this is "Tezuka's Curse". Despite reducing costs through the methods described above, since Tezuka was still unable to produce *Astro Boy* for less than the amount agreed to by the TV station, he needed sponsorship and made an agreement with Meiji Seika, a chocolate manufacturer. As *Astro Boy* quickly became a cultural icon in Japan, posters of the Astro Boy character on the Meiji chocolates became popular. In this way,

---

[85] Hu, *Frames of Anime*, 99; Denison, *Anime*, "Introduction", olb and LeMarre, *The Anime Machine*, 33-38.
[86] Hiroki Azuma, *Otaku: Japan's Database Animals*, trans. Jonathan E. Abel and Shion Kono (Minneapolis: University of Minnesota Press, 2009), 11.
[87] Tsugata, "A Bipolar Approach", 29.
[88] Timbrell, "1963 Astro Boy", olb.
[89] Clements, *Anime*, 285.
[90] Steinberg, *Anime's Media Mix*, 43; LaMarre, *The Anime Machine*, 300 and Denison, *Anime*, "Chapter 4: 4 Early Anime Histories", olb.

History of Anime

the TV series transformed character merchandising into "a part of the basic business model for all the TV anime that followed".[91] Thus, merchandising became a common practice that "was embedded at the very core of anime as a media-mix system" and guaranteeing "that anime would develop as a transmedia system".[92] Therefore, Steinberg says that *Astro Boy* is "one of the major reasons the country is today known as the 'Empire of Characters'".[93] Besides, the series was the first Japanese character marked with a copyrighted song, and Tezuka was the first Japanese producer to sell licenses and collect royalties, a core element of his business model.[94]

Moreover, *Astro Boy* is not only important for being the first popular animated television series domestically, it was the first anime that was dubbed, exported and introduced on American television in the same year.[95] Thus, anime was ushered into the global presence. Since the release of *Astro Boy*, anime has been gradually more popular in Japan and abroad.[96] Some of the most famous other works broadcast internationally are *Gigantor*, *8 Man*, and *Speed Racer*.[97] *Astro Boy* also showed that manga series could successfully transform into anime shows on TV and could become big hits.[98] With all of its novelties, the series became one of the most influential anime of all time.

Tezuka's Mushi Production followed *Astro Boy* with the color series *Kimba the White Lion*, which also became a major hit in this period.[99] Tezuka always made himself distinct with his themes and characters and was inspired by all

---

[91] Yamaguchi, "The Evolution", wp.
[92] Steinberg, *Anime's Media Mix*, 40.
[93] Ibid., 41.
[94] Ibid., 40.
[95] MacWilliams, "Introduction", 14.
[96] Chris Stuckmann, "Introduction", in *Anime Impact*, olb.
[97] Poitras, "Contemporary Anime", 50. *Gigantor*: Directed by Yonehiko Watanabe with Screenplay by Kinzo Okamoto based on the manga *Tetsujin 28-go* by Mitsuteru Yokoyama (TCJ 1963). The Japanese title is *Tetsujin Nijūhachi-gō*; *8 Man*: Directed by Haruyuki Kawajima based on the manga of the same name by Kazumasa Hirai (TCJ 1963-1964). The Japanese title is *Eitoman* and *Speed Racer*: Directed by Hiroshi Sasagawa with Screenplay by Jinzō Toriumi based on the manga of the same name by Tatsuo Yoshida (Tatsunoko Productions 1967-1968). The Japanese title is *Mahha GōGōGō*.
[98] Tsugata, "A Bipolar Approach", 29.
[99] *Kimba the White Lion*: Directed by Eiichi Yamamoto with Screenplay by Osamu Tezuka (Mushi Production 1964). The Japanese title is *Janguru Taitei*. Napier, *Anime from Akira to Princess Mononoke*, 16 and Poitras", Contemporary Anime", 64.

types of sources, such as Asian and European history, fairy tales, myths, films and novels.[100]

After *Astro Boy* animated TV series became part of regular TV programming in Japan.[101] The famous "timeless" animated TV series *Sazae-san* has the tittle of the longest-running TV series in Japan, airing from 1969 to present.[102] In this period, Toei also developed productions such as *Gulliver's Travels Beyond the Moon* as a full length animation.[103] Takahata, one of the foremost directors, made his first feature film *Horusu: Prince of the Sun* in 1968.[104] Miyazaki, who would later be called the greatest anime director, took part as the designer in the film. The film is seen as "pivotal in the history of cel-animation as an art form".[105] Besides, Notable auteur Ōfuji's *The Whale* and *The Phantom Ship* were screened at the Cannes and Venice film festivals in 1953 and 1956, respectively.[106] Both films, which were silhouette animations using color cellophane, were praised for their uniqueness.[107]

While anime shows were generally made for children in the 1960s,[108] they started to widen their audiences in the next decade. Anime works for theatres and TV started to grow and diversify in terms of creativity and genres.

Emergence and Development of Genres in the 1960s and 1970s

Economic development in Japan, and the success of *Astro Boy* in the country and abroad, made way for the anime industry to expand in the 1960s and 1970s. According to Eiji, during this period, the anime industry was helped

---

[100] Susanne Phillipps, "Characters, Themes, and Narrative Patterns in the Manga of Osamu Tezuka", *Japanese Visual Culture*, 68.

[101] MacWilliams, "Introduction", 13 and Tsugata, "A Bipolar Approach", 30.

[102] *Sazae-san*: Directed by Kenji Kodama based on the manga of the same name by Machiko Hasegawa (TCJ 1969-present). MacWilliams, "Introduction", 3 and Clements, *Anime*, 308.

[103] *Gulliver's Travels Beyond the Moon*: Directed by Masao Kuroda and Sanae Yamamoto with Screenplay by Shinichi Sekizawa and Hayao Miyazaki based on Jonathan Swift *Gulliver's Travels* (Toei 1965). The Japanese title is *Garibā no Uchū Ryokō*.

[104] *Horusu: Prince of the Sun*: Directed by Isao Takahata with Screenplay by Kazuo Fukazawa (Tokyo: Toei 1968). The Japanese title is *Taiyō no Ōji Horusu no Daibōken*.

[105] Odell and Le Blanc, *Studio Ghibli*, 43.

[106] *The Whale*: Directed by Noburō Ōfuji (Chiyogami Eiga-sha 1952). The Japanese title is *Kujira*. *The Phantom Ship*: Directed by Noburō Ōfuji (Chiyogami Eiga-sha 1956). The Japanese title is *Yureisen*.

[107] Tsugata, "A Bipolar Approach", 27 and Sano, "Ōfuji Noburō", 87.

[108] Poitras, "Contemporary Anime", 60.

History of Anime

along by a high literacy rate and a burgeoning publishing and film industry.[109] Condry further emphasizes that a diverse catalog of manga allowed animators to construct and diversify genres and themes to reach new audiences.[110]

The Rise of Science Fiction in Anime

The first and emerging genre was science fiction in this period. *Astro Boy* started this trend as a major genre in anime that has continued to grow ever since. One of sci-fi's major appeals is that animators have the freedom to create endless fantasy worlds through their imaginations. What might be impossible to reproduce in live-action films—with regard to setting and technical restrictions—sci-fi anime could deliver. Furthermore, those fantasy worlds could be created without the huge costs associated with sets and special effects required for live-action films.[111] Thus, sci-fi anime enables audiences to watch and imagine fantasy worlds more creatively and vividly than live-action films or on TV. In addition to this visual distinctiveness, the fact that the fantasy spaces are "stateless"[112] in anime, along with complex storylines, can take the audience away from their daily world, realities and surroundings. All these reasons make sci-fi anime more reasonable to produce market-wise—and to reach not only children—but a wide demographic audience.

Space Opera and Steampunk

Two other popular sub-genres of sci-fi to grow in this period were *space opera* and *steampunk*. While space opera mixes intergalactic stories with romance, steampunk takes place in alternative histories, such as "the steam-powered technology of the Industrial Revolution era in anachronistically advanced directions".[113]

The first space opera anime television series was *Space Battleship Yamato*, directed by Leiji Matsumoto in 1974.[114] The feature film of the same name

---

[109] Oguma Eiji, "An Industry Awaiting Reform: The Social Origins and Economics of Manga and Animation in Postwar Japan", *The Asia-Pacific Journal: Japan Focus* 15.9 (2017): 1.
[110] Condry, *The Soul of Anime*, 91.
[111] Poitras, "Contemporary Anime", 50.
[112] Napier, *Anime from Akira to Howl's Moving Castle*, 24.
[113] "All Aboard the Steampunk Anime Train! Choo-Choo!", *MyAnimeList* 14th January 2016: https://myanimelist.net/featured/1299/Top10BestSteampunkAnimeLetOffSomeSteam_.
[114] *Space Battleship Yamato* [TV Series]: Directed by Leiji Matsumoto with Screenplay by Eiichi Yamamoto, Keisuke Fujikawa and Maru Tamura (NNN 1974-1975). The Japanese title is *Uchu Senkan Yamato*.

came out in 1977 and was directed by Noburo Ishiguro. It is also an example of steampunk. Yamaguchi says that "challenging the idea of anime as simply children's entertainment, this series and its film became a social phenomenon, tremendously popular with millions of young adults".[115] *Galaxy Express 999*, a space opera, was also produced first as TV series in 1978 and then as a film in 1979.[116] It was Rintora's first film, who also worked on the first colored film *Hakujaden* and then with Tezuma for *Astro Boy*.

Robots and Mecha

Mecha is arguably the most popular subgenre in science fiction anime. The concept involved humanoid robots, artificial intelligence, and giant robots. Astro Boy was the first humanoid robot to attract audiences. The remote-controlled robot in *Gigantor* became part of the next development. In the 1970s, that robot turned into giant robots controlled by a human pilot inside of the machine in *Mazinger Z*.[117] These robots were especially distinguished by "their giant size", and mecha became a distinct genre, especially with *Mazinger Z*.[118] *Getter Robo* added another dimension to giant robots by showing that separate modules can slot together to form a super-robot.[119]

Some directors in this period, such as Yoshiyuki Tomino, Ryosuke Takahashi, Hideaki Anno and Shoji Kawamori, focused on developing sci-fi and especially mecha narratives.[120] For example, Tomino, who previously worked under Tezuka, wanted to inject more realistic and mature themes into giant robot shows.[121] His *Mobile Suit Gundam* targeted adults with its complex

---

[115] Yamaguchi, "The Evolution", wp.
[116] *Galaxy Express 999* [TV series]: Directed by Nobutaka Nishizawa with Screenplay by Hiroyasu Yamaura, Keisuke Fujikawa and Yoshiaki Yoshida based on the manga of the same name by Leiji Matsumoto (Toei 1978-1981); *Galaxy Express 999* [film]: Directed by Rintaro with Screenplay by Shiro Ishimori (Toei 1979). The Japanese title is *Ginga Tetsudō Surī Nain*.
[117] *Mazinger Z*: Directed by Tomoharu Katsumata based on the manga of the same name by Go Nagai (Toei 1972-1974). The Japanese title is *Majingā Zetto*.
[118] Ryusuke Hikawa, Koichi Inoue, Daisuke Sawaki and Matt Alt, *Japanese Animation Guide: The History of Robot Anime* (Mori Building Co., 2013), 13; LaMarre, *The Anime Machine*, 111 and Clements, *Anime*, 342.
[119] *Getter Robo*: Directed by Tomoharu Katsumata with Screenplay by Shun'ichi Yukimuro based on the manga by Ken Ishikawa and Go Nagai (Toei 1974-1975). The Japanese title is *Gettā Robo*. Cf. Clements, *Anime*, 343.
[120] Ryusuke Hikawa, "Preface: Beginning", *Japanese Animation Guide*, 3.
[121] Clements, *Anime*, 351.

storylines.[122] By its huge success, *Gundam* "highlighted a wider shift from an emphasis on children's shows toward the inclusion of more adult-oriented themes".[123] It also left an important mark in anime history by introducing realistic robots, "what was once an almost magical, fantastical icon into a simple, functional weapon or tool".[124] It also divided *mecha* genre into two sub-genres: S*uper Robots* and *Real Robots*.[125] As a result, the audiences of *Astro Boy* were growing up. These new robot styles and narrative changes toward more mature themes increased the interest in mecha among young audiences. There was also a technical reason regarding the increase of *mecha*: robots and giant machines with heavy outlines and stiff movements were easier to animate than the flexible human body.[126]

The Rise of Franchising and Merchandising

Mazinger Z and *Gundam* also had an important impact on the development of anime's media-mix during this period. Cheap robot toys for children became a big seller stemming from the TV series *Mazinger Z*. "This helped launch a new interest in animated TV series about giant robots on the part of toy companies eager to capitalize on children's fascination with robot action figures".[127]

Gundam also left a mark by influencing the direction of the anime franchise industry.[128] It is a shifting example of the importance of market research and understanding audience expectations. At first, *Gundam* followed the same strategy with *Mazinger Z*, but its cheaply-made toys failed to captivate its young adult (*seinen*) audience, who preferred more intricate and better-crafted products. A serious and unexpected consequence of this ill-conceived marketing plan was that the series was abruptly ended. However, after redesigning the toys for their audience and making them with better quality materials, the rebroadcast of *Gundam* attracted large numbers of viewers and

---

[122] *Mobile Suit Gundam*: Directed by Yoshiyuki Tomino with Screenplay by Yoshiyuki Tomino (Nagoya TV 1979-1980). The Japanese title is *Kidō Senshi Gandamu*. Cf. Clements, *Anime*, 351; Poitras, "Contemporary Anime", 52; Denison, *Anime*, "Japanese Anime Diversifies: New Markets, New Genres", olb and Condry, *The Soul of Anime*, 126.
[123] Condry, *The Soul of Anime*, 126.
[124] Clements, *Anime*, 351.
[125] "The History of Anime: Part 2", *Evolution* 26th January 2021: https://evolutionninjapan.wordpress.com/2021/01/26/the-history-of-anime-1970-to-2010s/; Clements, *Anime*, 351; Poitras, "Contemporary Anime", 52; Denison, *Anime*, "Japanese Anime Diversifies: New Markets, New Genre", olb and Condry, *The Soul of Anime*, 126.
[126] Bordwell and Thompson, *Film*, 393.
[127] Condry, *Soul of Anime*, 120.
[128] Denison, *Anime* "Japanese Anime Diversifies: New Markets, New Genre", olb.

achieved remarkable success in merchandising.[129] Additionally, the diverse modular features and transformative capabilities of robots in *Getter Robo* opened doors for innovative merchandising through the introduction of "not one but three-in-one toy" packages.[130]

When toy companies saw the potential market of anime audiences, it expanded the relationship and cooperation between anime producers and toy companies.[131] The downside of this was that toy companies increased their influence on anime productions. Another downside arose as toy sales turned into "a significant barometer" for the success of the shows, and anime shows turned into "a vehicle" to sell toys.[132] However, both anime and toy companies, working together, were able to diversify their products and sell to a variety of audiences and customers.

The anime industry's main strategy to keep growing and appealing to audiences was to develop "anime formulas or clichés".[133] These are associated with certain genres and target particular demographics.[134] The result is that it transforms audiences into devoted fans of anime.

Core Target Audiences and Genres: Shōnen and Shōjo

The core target audience for the anime market has been adolescents. The main "demographic umbrella genres" are *Shōnen* (young boys) and *Shōjo* (young girls).[135] Each target audience requires certain anime formulas and codes; even though those formulas develop and change in time. For example, mecha generally aims to target young boys or adult males and it is a *shōnen* genre.

The *Shōjo* genre emerged in this period of the 1960s. The primary subgenre was Magical Girl (*Mahō Shōjo*). The first manga to have this form was *Himitsu*

---

[129] Poitras, "Contemporary Anime", 52.
[130] Clements, *Anime*, 343.
[131] Condry, *The Soul of Anime*, 120 and 122.
[132] Poitras, "Contemporary Anime", 52 and Tsugata, "A Bipolar Approach", 29.
[133] Manuel Hernández-Pérez, "Discussing 'Genre' in Anime through Neon Genesis Evangelion", in *Anime Studies: Media-Specific Approaches to Neon Genesis Evangelion*, eds. José Andrés Santiago Iglesias and Ana Soler Baena (Stockholm: Stockholm University Press, 2021), 191. Tropes would probably be a better term.
[134] Ibid.
[135] Jaqueline Berndt, "Introduction: Shōjo Mediations", in *Shōjo Across Media. East Asian Popular Culture*, eds J. Berndt, K. Nagaike and F. Ogi (London: Palgrave Macmillan, 2019), 5; Denison, *Anime*, "Anime's Categories", olb and Clements, *Anime*, 314.

no Akko-Chan in 1962.[136] *Little Witch Sally* is considered the first magical girl anime in 1966.[137] In fact, it was the latter that led anime to divide as *shōnen* and *shōjo* as demographic umbrella genres.[138] After that, anime films and series on *shōjo* genre increased and matured in the 1970s. The memorable *shōjo* examples from this period were *Candy* and *Heidi: Girl of the Alps*.[139]

Even though the characteristics of *shōjo* girls have changed in anime in line with the target audience and periods, in the classic *shōjo*, young girls (*bishōjo*) are drawn with specific features. First, they are neither child nor adult, but in-between.[140] Second, they are sweet, cute (*kawaii*), and attractive, but not purely sexy. They are often passive or dreamy,[141] as well as both strong and vulnerable. In terms of their physical appearance, they have wide eyes, long hair, as well as child style clothing and behaviors. What is more, *shōjo* characters are differentiated base on whether the target audience are men and adolescent males or girls. In anime that targets men, *shōjo* protagonists combine sexuality and child-like cuteness: they are often hypersexualized and are in need of protection.[142] They are also known as *Moe* characters (which are dealt with in more detail below). On the other hand, in anime for girls, characters emphasize cuteness and are not overly sexualized.[143] Moreover,

---

[136] Tim Lyu, "History of Magical Girls (Sailor Moon, Puella Magi Madoka Magica, Cardcaptor Sakura + MORE", *YouTube*: https://www.youtube.com/watch?v=VtFR8o9n4LA. Himitsu no Akko-chan.

[137] *Little Witch Sally*. Directed by Toshio Katsuta and Hiroshi Ikeda based on the manga by Mitsuteru Yokoyama (Toei 1966-1968). The Japanese title is *Mahō Tsukai Sarī*.

[138] The term *shōjo* is not only limited to anime. Its root goes back to school girls in Meiji period. As Deborah mentions, it is "a media image of idealized girlhood that was formed in the late nineteenth and early twentieth centuries in Japan". Deborah Shamoon, "Miura Ira: Shōjo", *Japanese Media and Popular Culture*: https://jmpc-utokyo.com/keyword/shojo/. Cf. Berndt, "Shōjo Mediations", 5; Denison, *Anime*, "Anime's Categories", olb and Clements, *Anime*, 314.

[139] *Candy Candy*. Directed by Hiroshi Shidara and Tetsuo Imazawa with Screenplay by Noboru Shiroyama based on the novel by Keiko Nagita under the pen name Kyoko Mizuki (Toei 1976-1979). The Japanese title is *Kyandi*. *Heidi: Girl of the Alps*: Directed by Isao Tahakata with Screenplay by Isao Matsuki (Fuji TV 1974). The Japanese title is *Arupusu no Shōjo Haiji*.

[140] Napier, *Anime from Akira to Howl's Moving Castle*, 192.

[141] Ibid., 150 and 154.

[142] Akiko Sugawa-Shimada, "Grotesque Cuteness of Shōjo Representations of Goth-Loli in Japanese Contemporary TV Anime", *Japanese Animation Guide*, 207; Freda Freiberg, "Miyazaki's Heroines", *Sense of Cinema* (July 2006): https://www.sensesofcinema.com/2006/feature-articles/miyazaki-heroines/; Anna Lindwasser, "How Anime Has Evolved Though the Years", *Ranker* 28th June 2018: https://www.ranker.com/list/how-anime-has-changed-and-evolved/anna-lindwasser.

[143] Akiko Sugawa-Shimada, "Grotesque Cuteness", 207.

since anime's most important characters are female, *shōjo* characters can be seen almost in any anime works regardless of genre, such as in *shōnen* anime.[144] However, since the anime market had to appeal to a wide range of audiences, adult variations of *shōnen* and *shōjo* also emerged as *seinen* that are aimed at adult men, and *Josei* that targets adult women during this period.

Further Developments in the Industry

In line with marketing strategy, anime producers gradually increased their focus on different genres. They were mostly aimed at either adolescents or adults, such as *Triton of the Sea*, directed by Tomino and based on a manga by Tezuka.[145] In this period, anime in the cinema began trending, as well.[146] Many films were often adaptations of TV series or manga, such as *Space Battleship Yamato*.[147] Although the global market was dominated by American cartoons and animations, small Japanese companies showed their potential to compete with Hollywood, and anime continued appearing overseas, such as *UFO Robot Grendizer*.[148] Anime also started "appearing in the underground of Western culture, often untranslated or translated by fans".[149]

On the industrial side, animators such as Rintaro, Yoshikazu Yasuhiko, Yoshiyuki Tomino, and Yoshinori Kanada "sought to develop artistic appeal in a different direction from the aesthetics of movement, by working within the confines of limited animation, cell recycling, and the bank system".[150] By the late 1960s, animators were adding impressionistic sounds to distract their audiences from the absence of emotions in the images.[151]

Although the volume of anime expanded rapidly, outsourcing remained a constant problem in the industry. In the 1960s, work was subcontracted offshore, especially to South Korea.[152] In the 1970s, Sunrise Anime Studio and

---

[144] Napier, *Anime from Akira to Howl's Moving Castle*, 12, 148 and Denison, *Anime*, "Chapter 3", olb.
[145] *Triton of the Sea*: Directed by Yoshiyuki Tomino with Screenplay by Yoshiyuki Tomino based on the manga of the same name by Osamu Tezuka (Asahi Broadcasting Company 1972). The Japanese title is *Umi no Toriton*.
[146] Napier, *Anime from Akira to Howl's Moving Castle*, 18.
[147] *Space Battleship Yamato*: Directed by Toshio Masuda and Noboru Ishiguro with Screenplay by Eiichi Yamamoto (Toei 1977). The Japanese title is *Uchii Senkan Yamato*.
[148] Bordwell and Thompson, *Film*, 393. *UFO Robot Grendizer*: Directed by Tomoharu Katsumata with Screenplay by Go Nagai based on the manga by Go Nagai (Toei 1975). The Japanese title is *Yūfō Robo Gurendaizā*.
[149] Brenner, *Understanding Manga and Anime*, 11.
[150] Azuma, *Otaku*, 12.
[151] Clements, *Anime*, 279.
[152] Hu, *Frames of Anime*, 139 and Clements, *Anime*, 330.

History of Anime 23

Madhouse Inc. were set up by former Mushi Pro animators, including Rintaro, in 1972. Pierrot Anime Studio was established in 1979. General economic conditions led all studios to cut back in the 1970s.[153] Japan Animation Film Association (JAFA) was founded in 1971 to promote animation culture in Japan and has held annual or bi-annual film festivals ever since (it was renamed Japan Animation Association or JAA in 1978). Festivals provided exhibiting space for independent animations.[154] In addition, the magazine *Animage* was first produced in July 1978.

Summary of Anime in the 1960s and 1970s

In summary, the 1960s and the 1970s were an era of changes and a turning point for the anime industry regarding narratives, visuals, genres, techniques, target audiences, franchising and merchandising.

The Rise of Miyazaki, Takahata and Studio Ghibli in the 1970s and 1980s

Miyazaki and Takahata have made "an indelible mark" in the history of anime.[155] First, starting from their first films and TV series in the 1970s, they mixed different genres—such as drama, sci-fi, and fantasy—and used diverse sources from manga to Western and Japanese stories and mythologies for inspiration. What is more, they focused on presenting social messages in their works by highlighting problems and concerns about the future of the earth, the environmental crises, the effect of industrialization and technology, as well as ethics, war and human dignity. In this regard, their works were different than others in both narrative and visual style. Odell and Le Blanc describe their works as being full of "gods and monsters, love and loss, jubilation and despair, the horrors of war, childhood wonder, the passion of life, the heart-soaring, euphoric, whimsical, terrifying, compassionate".[156] Therefore, Azuma defines their anime style as "expressionist".[157] Seeing realism as "a major ideological backbone of their aspirations", Hu also says that

> While other anime or Western productions have focused on such themes as ecology and nature preservation, what makes the anime of Miyazaki and Takahata unique is that such clichéd themes are presented in the dialectical motif of realism and fantasy and are

---

[153] Clements, *Anime*, 304.
[154] Hu, *Frames of Anime*, 107.
[155] Ibid., 111.
[156] Odell and Le Blanc, *Studio Ghibli*, 13.
[157] Azuma, *Otaku*, 12.

targeted at localized audiences. Yet, these themes are universal and have a global dimension.[158]

Second, perhaps the most important development of this period was the setting up of Studio Ghibli with producer Toshio Suzuki in 1985. This proved to be a turning point for their careers and the anime industry as a whole. The company partnered with Disney for its us distribution in 1996—which increased the company's and anime's recognition abroad—leading it to become one of the most recognized and acclaimed anime studios worldwide.[159] Its global success proved that anime is not only "for children or fanatics only in Japan", but reaches a much broader audience.[160]

Miyazaki started his career at Toei Dōga as a trainee animator in 1963, where he partnered with Takahata. After moving from Toei, they worked for various studios throughout the 1970s. Their first series together was *Lupin III* in 1971. Their first film, *Panda! Go, Panda!*, was directed by Takahata with the screenplay by Miyazaki.[161]

In 1978, Miyazaki went on to do his first solo TV series *Future Boy Conan*, a post-apocalyptic sci-fi and steampunk, and which is widely seen "as the prototype for his later films".[162] In 1979, he had his first directorial debut with the action comedy *Lupin III: Castle of Cagliostro*. This film inspired later filmmakers.[163]

In the 1980s, Miyazaki's unique style became more apparent with his second anime film *Nausicaä of the Valley of the Wind*.[164] *Nausicaä* is the first film that came to characterize later films by Miyazaki and Studio Ghibli. The film

---

[158] Hu, *Frames of Anime*, 119 and 126.
[159] Denison, *Anime*, "Chapter 7", olb; Odell and Blanc, *Studio Ghibli*, 14 and Hu, *Frames of Anime*, 105.
[160] Tsugata, "A Bipolar Approach", 31.
[161] *Lupin III*: Directed by Hayao Miyazaki, Isao Takahata and Masaaki Ōsumi with Screenplay by Gisaburō Sugii et al. (Yomiuri 1971-1972). The Japanese title is *Rupan Sansei*. *Panda! Go, Panda!*: Directed by Takahata Isao with Screenplay by Miyazaki Hayao (NHK 1972). The Japanese title is *Panda Kopanda*.
[162] *Future Boy Conan*: Directed by Hayao Miyazaki with Screenplay by Akira Nakano, Stoshi Kurumi and Sōji Yoshikawa (NHK 1978). The Japanese title is *Mirai Shonen Conan*. Hu, *Frames of Anime*, 111.
[163] *Lupin III: Castle of Cagliostro*: Directed by Hayao Miyazaki with Screenplay by Hayao Miyazaki and Haruya Yamazaki based on the manga *Lupin III* by Monkey Punch (Toho 1979). The Japanese title is *Rupan Sansei Cagliostro no Shiro*.
[164] *Nausicaä of the Valley of the Wind*: Directed by Hayao Miyazaki with Screenplay by Hayao Miyazaki (Toei 1984). The Japanese title is *Kaze no Tani no Nausicaä*. Cf. Michael Ray, "Hayao Miyazaki", *Britannica*: https://www.britannica.com/biography/Miyazaki-Hayao.

History of Anime

presents the devastating consequences of global pollution a thousand years in the future. It shows how a young girl hero called Nausicaä saves humanity by bonding with nature and animals, then sacrificing herself to save the world.

While *Nausicaä* has apocalyptic themes like others of the period, it does not provide the dark tone and imminent destruction of humanity and the planet seen in later anime, but presents "a vision of hope and rebirth",[165] which reflects Miyazaki's different approach to anime genres. In the same period, Miyazaki's first film with Studio Ghibli called *Laputa: Castle in the Sky* was released.[166] This film is centered around the themes of technology and nature.

Since Miyazaki distinguished his style of anime in the sci-fi, mecha and steampunk genres by adding a more humanistic side and deeper social aspects to his storyline, this film is seen as "one of the first modern Steampunk classics".[167] The 1988 film *My Neighbor Totoro* also carries a message saying that "respect for the environment can lead to harmony and reward".[168] The film went on to become very successful and merchandise sales of Totoro toys were huge. The film's character Totoro later became the mascot and logo for Studio Ghibli.

With his highly distinctive narrative and visual style, Miyazaki's films have attracted attention worldwide, and he has been called the greatest anime director of all time. As "wonderfully inventive", Miyazaki created detailed fantasy worlds in which unrealistic things feel so realistic that the audience members came to feel they were believable.[169] Odell and Le Blanc state that

> Miyazaki often fools us by establishing his films ostensibly in the real world and then demanding that we reject our notions of physics, biology and geography, albeit in a manner that is consistent with the world he is drawing us into, even if it appears to be familiar to us.[170]

Napier says that Miyazaki is an exceptional fantasy world builder who used empowered female protagonists, believable children, as well as apocalyptic

---

[165] Napier, *to Princess Mononoke*, 29.
[166] *Laputa: Castle in the Sky.* Directed by Hayao Miyazaki with Screenplay by Hayao Miyazaki (Toei 1986). The Japanese title is *Tenkuˉ no Shiro Rapyuta*.
[167] Jeff Vandermeer and S. J. Chambers, *The Steampunk Bible: An Illustrated Guide to the World of Imaginary Airships, Corsets and Goggles, Mad Scientists, and Strange Literature* (New York: Abrams Image, 2011), 182.
[168] *My Neighbor Totoro:* Written and directed by Hayao Miyazaki (Toei 1988). The Japanese title is *Tonari no Totoro*. Odell and Le Blanc, *Studio Ghibli,* 23.
[169] Odell and Le Blanc, *Studio Ghibli,* 20.
[170] Ibid.

elegiac or utopian visions.[171] Besides, as a "social and cultural filmmaker",[172] Miyazaki's works present rich social and cultural connotations. While his works mainly follow the classic narrative structure with an optimistic conclusion, they also often present unconventional and inconclusive ends as well.[173] In his films, the boundary between good or evil blurs, and he draws original complex characters. Although his young female characters are *shōjo* in the general sense, one of his signatures is creating young, strong and independent heroines who are more independent, assertive, active, mature and "crusaders".[174] They are also more caring and feminine than *shōjo* characters.[175]

As Freiberg points out, even though *kawaii* (cute) culture is commonly associated with consumerism, Miyazaki links his *shōjo* characters with social criticism, Environmentalism and reverence for nature.[176] Therefore, as Napier states, Miyazaki's *shōjo* characters "offer blueprints for a better identity that seems to combine both the nurturing aspects of the feminine and the strength and independence associated with the masculine".[177]

Nostalgia for childhood or yearning for a lost past also play out across Miyazaki's films.[178] Miyazaki's other distinction is that he has always preferred traditional animation techniques, cel-animation and full animation. Drawing the majority of the frames in each film himself, Miyazaki says that "I believe that the tool of an animator is the pencil".[179] His films present detailed and visually striking backgrounds with beautiful coloration, as well as attractive music and skillful sound effects.[180]

Takahata and Miyazaki mostly worked together under Ghibli. They had both similarities and differences. In some cases, Takahata's style was "completely

---

[171] Susan Napier, *Miyazakiworld: A Life in Art* (New Haven: Yale University Press, 2018), xii.
[172] Hu, *Frames of Anime*, 123.
[173] Hu, *Frames of Anime*, 122 and Odell and Le Blanc, *Studio Ghibli*, 20.
[174] Freiberg, "Miyazaki's Heroines", wp and Napier, *Anime from Akira to Howl's Moving Castle*, 154.
[175] Freiberg, "Miyazaki's Heroines", wp.
[176] Ibid.
[177] Napier, *Anime from Akira to Howl's Moving Castle*, 150.
[178] Napier, *MiyazakiWorld*, xii.
[179] Ligaya Mishan, "Hayao Miyazaki Prepares to Cast One Last Spell", *The New York Times Style Magazine* 23rd November 2021: https://www.nytimes.com/2021/11/23/t-magazine/hayao-miyazaki-studio-ghibli.html.
[180] Hiroshi Yamanaka, "The Utopian 'Power to Live': The Significance of the Miyazaki Phenomenon", *Japanese Visual Culture*, 239.

History of Anime

opposite to Miyazaki's".[181] While the running themes of Takahata's films were similar to Miyazaki's, those themes usually take place in the real world as opposed to Miyazaki's fantasy worlds.[182] Often adapting literary works and focusing on "animated versions of the realistic world",[183] Takahata had an interest in exploring growing up and the boundaries between childhood and adulthood. For example, the 1970s series *Heidi: Girl of the Alps* and *Anne of Green Gables* are based on novels by Western authors and focus on little orphan girls and their daily life.[184]

According to Minakawa, the success of *Heidi* at home and abroad even created a new genre of "masterpiece anime" based on works of children's literature.[185] Perhaps his most famous film is *Grave of the Fireflies*, which is about the consequences and human sufferings of WWII in the eyes of children.[186] Unlike Miyazaki, he experimented with different approaches to animation and storytelling techniques, but both directors used real-voice acting to increase the sense of reality.[187] Takahata's *Grave of the Fire Flies* is a such an example.

Along with the rise of Miyazaki, Takahata and Studio Ghibli, there are other developments in the 1980s that led the anime industry to another turning point.

The Boom in Anime and Otaku Culture in the 1980s

As the "boom in anime in Japan"[188] started in the late 1970s, the industry developed further in many aspects in the 1980s. Genres and target audiences varied, technological progress impacted the availability of anime both in Japan and overseas, and internationally acclaimed works increased.

On the industrial side, new anime studios emerged. Kyoto Animation was founded in 1981, Gainax in 1984 by co-founder Hideaki Anno, Studio Ghibli in

---

[181] Odell and Le Blanc, *Studio Ghibli*, 21.
[182] Ibid., 21-30.
[183] Tsugata, "A Bipolar Approach", 153.
[184] *Anne of Green Gables*: Directed by Isao Takahata with Screenplay by Isao Takahata (Nippon Animation 1979). The Japanese title is *Akage no an*.
[185] Clements, *Anime*, 342.
[186] *Grave of the Fireflies*: Directed by Isao Takahata with Screenplay with Isao Takahata based on a semi-autobiographical short story of the same name by Akiyuki Nosaka (Toho 1988). The Japanese title is *Hotaru no Haka*.
[187] Odell and Le Blanc, *Studio Ghibli*, 40 and Hu, *Frames of Anime*, 121.
[188] Tsugata, "A Bipolar Approach", 81 and Denison, *Anime*, "Chapter 4", olb.

1985, and Production I.G. in 1987. Many small, independent studios started to produce works for television and other markets.[189]

Sci-Fi Genre

In the sci-fi genre, Gainax's first work *Royal Space Force: Wings of Honneamise* grabbed the audiences' attention.[190] It was also the first anime underwritten by the giant toy manufacturing company Bandai Visual. Mecha's domination in anime films and series, with its links to *shōnen*, continued. Noboru Ishiguro's *Superdimensional Fortress Macross* and Mamoru Oshii's film *Patlabor* are examples.[191] According to Denison, this genre even transformed into "a transnational genre" with the exportation of some popular series. Along with giant robots, much smaller robots (more like anthropomorphic tanks), also emerged with *Armored Trooper Votoms*.[192] In the mid-1980s, while the super robot genre faded, the "real robot" genre became popular.[193]

Cyberpunk

Cyberpunk, a subgenre of sci-fi, also appeared in this period. This genre focuses on dystopian futures, mainly technological ones, in which people and machines struggle. Bolton et al. mention that cyberpunk mixes the main themes of postmodernist sci-fi both in Japan and the West, which is "the breakdown of ontological boundaries, pervasive virtualization, the political control of reality, as well as their artistic media".[194]

---

[189] Poitras, "Contemporary Anime", 53.

[190] *Royal Space Force: Wings of Honneamise*: Directed by Hiroyuki Yamaga with Screenplay by Hiroyuki Yamaga (Toho 1987). The Japanese title is *Ōritsu Uchūgun: Oneamisu no Tsubasa*.

[191] *Superdimensional Fortress Macross*: Directed by Noboru Ishiguro with Screenplay by Kenichi Matsuzaki (MBS 1982-1983). The Japanese title is *Chōjikū Yōsai Makurosu*. *Patlabor*: Directed by Mamoru Oshii with Screenplay by Kazunori Ito based on the manga by Masami Yuki (Studio Deen 1988-1989). The Japanese title is *Kidō Keisatsu Patoreibā*.

[192] Poitras, "Contemporary Anime", 53. *Armored Trooper Votoms*: Directed by Ryōsuke Takahashi with Screenplay by Sōji Yoshikawa and Jinzō Toriumi (TV Tokyo 1983-1984). The Japanese title is *Sōkō Kihei Votoms*.

[193] "History of Anime", wp.

[194] Christopher Bolton, Istvan Csicsery-Ronay Jr. and Takayuki Tatsumi, "Introduction. Robot Ghosts and Wired Dreams: Japanese Science Fiction from Origins to Anime", in *Robot Ghosts Wired Dreams*, ix.

The first film was Ishiguro's *Megazone 23*, and the first series was Katsuhito Akiyama's *The Bubblegum Crisis*.[195] The most important cyberpunk anime film of the period was Katsuhiro Ōtomo's first film *Akira* in 1988.[196] Stuckmann says that it "is so mind-bogglingly gorgeous that one struggles to comprehend the skill required to produce it".[197] The film was produced by the participation of several anime companies and is "one of the most lavishly produced anime films" which cost more than many contemporary productions.[198] In the film, set in a dystopic future in Tokyo, a young man named Tetsuo develops uncontrollable psychic powers by encountering a mutated child by mistake, and his power destroys the city. The film presents universal themes and "a fusion of contemporary art; anime, manga, cinema, digital graphics, and cyberpunk narrative".[199] Since its director Ōtomo "was part of a generation of Japanese artists and writers shaped by this history and by 1960s counter-culture",[200] the film discusses social and political issues in society on the connotative level. Hence, with its technical style, rich and striking imagery, and complex and challenging narratives, the film became a masterpiece and a cult classic. This was not only in Japan but also in the U.S.A. and Europe after its wide theatrical distribution in 1990. It marked "the beginning of a Japanese renaissance in long-form theatrical anime" for more adult and crossover audiences,[201] and played "the monumental role in bringing anime into popular focus and consolidating its fan base" [202] and led to the anime boom in the West.[203]

Akira attracted large numbers of new anime fans, and transformed into "a more solid subculture" in the 1980s in the US.[204] For this reason, *Akira* is also regarded as "the origin or ground zero of anime's spread to North America";

---

[195] *Megazone 23*: Directed by Noboru Ishiguro with Screenplay by Hiroyuki Hoshiyama (Studio AIC 1985). The Japanese title is *Megazōn Tsū Surī*. *The Bubblegum Crisis*: Directed by Katsuhito Akiyama (chief director) et al. with Screenplay by Toshimichi Suzuki (AIC 1987-1991). The Japanese title is *Baburugamu Kuraishisu*.
[196] *Akira*: Directed by Katsuhiro Ōtomo with Screenplay by Katsuhiro Ōtomo and Izo Hashimoto based on the manga of the same name by Katsuhiro Ōtomo (Tokyo Movie Shinsha 1988). However, he produced a segment of *Neo Tokyo* (1987) before this film.
[197] Stuckmann, "Introduction", olb.
[198] Christopher Bolton, *Interpreting Anime* (Minneapolis: University of Minnesota Press, 2018), 25 and Clements, *Anime*, 410.
[199] Bolton et al, "Introduction", ix.
[200] Bolton, *Interpreting Anime*, 31.
[201] Ibid., 17.
[202] Cavallaro, *Anime Intersection*, 173.
[203] Napier, *Anime from Akira to Howl's Moving Castle*, 5 and 41; Bolton, *Interpreting Anime*, 17.
[204] Bolton, *Interpreting Anime*, 26 and Brenner, *Understanding Manga and Anime*, 11.

although anime series began broadcasting on American television channels in the 1960s. Moreover, with this exceptional work, Ōtomo has inspired many up-and-coming manga and anime artists ever since. *Akira* left an indelible mark in anime history and its emergence popularity on the global level.

Social Issues in 1980s Anime

Since Japan is the only country that suffered from atomic bombing, apocalyptic themes and technology-related fears became an important aspect in anime, as seen in *Akira*.[205] So, autobiographical stories related directly to World War II also emerged as a subgenre in this period. Examples are Keiji Nakazawa's *Barefoot Gen* and Takahata's *Grave of the Fireflies*.[206] The striking imagery in *Barefoot Gen* presents the horror of the Hiroshima bombing in a way that live-action films can never reproduce. This type of anime continued to be produced until *Rail of the Star* in 1993.[207]

Another important anime film about social issues in this period was Miyazaki's *Nausicaä*. As previously mentioned, is considered to be one of the greatest animated films of all time. Another stylistic and artistic anime is *Angel's Egg*, Oshii's first experimental art movie.[208] With its visual storytelling, it presents the influence of surrealism and symbolism.

Music became a significant part of the industry starting in the late 1970s.[209] Noburo Ishiguro's *Superdimensional Fortress Macross*, a science fiction series, is also important to mention in this regard. Music was the major part of the series.

Anime for a more mature audience (*seinen* and *josei*) expanded. For example, the romantic comedy *Maison Ikkoku* provided a taste of soap opera and romance by following several years of the characters' lives.[210]

---

[205] Napier, *to Princess Mononoke*, 29 and Brenner, *Understanding Manga and Anime*, 6.
[206] *Barefoot Gen*: Directed by Mori Masaki with Screenplay with Keiji Hakazawa based on the manga of the same name by Keiji Nakazawa (Kyodo Eiga 1983). The Japanese title is *Hadashi no Gen*.
[207] *Rail of the Star*: Directed by Toshio Hirata with Screenplay by Hideo Asakura and Tatsuhiko Urahata (Madhouse 1993). The Japanese title is *O-Hoshisama no Rail*. Odell and Le Blanc, *Studio Ghibli*, 72 and Robbins, "Bringing Anime", 4.
[208] *Angel's Egg*. Written and directed by Mamoru Oshii (Studio Deen 1985). The Japanese title is *Tenshi no Tamago*.
[209] Poitras, "Contemporary Anime", 52.
[210] *Maison Ikkoku*: Directed by Kazuo Yamazaki, Takashi Annō and Naoyuki Yoshinaga with Screenplay by Tokio Tsuchiya, Kazunori Itō and Hideo Takayashiki based on manga series written and illustrated by Rumiko Takahashi (Fuji TV 1986-1988). The Japanese title is *Mezon Ikkoku*.

Rise in Shonen in the 1980s

In the 1980s, *shōnen* rose in popularity with *Dragon Ball* and then *Dragon Ball Z*. Together, they became one of the most successful anime franchises and the highest-grossing media-mix in Japan in the 1980s.[211] The martial arts genre also began with *Dragon* Ball.

The sports anime genre appeared with *Captain Tsubasa* in 1981, although *Star of Giants* is seen as the first sports anime in the 1960s.[212] By focusing on a theme of a school soccer team, *Captain Tsubasa* set a standard for this genre. While *shōjo* stagnated slightly in the 1980s, it was still popular and mixed with *shōnen*.[213]

Mamoru Oshii's first debut *Urusei Yatsura*, a fantasy comedy TV series, provided both *shōnen* and *shōjo* elements with its narrative about a lecherous boy and an alien princess who only wears a tiger-striped bikini and has magical powers.[214] With this mixed approach, the TV series became "a pioneering work in the magical girlfriend genre".[215]

Furthermore, in this period, women's presentation in anime expanded from *shōjo* to pornography. The term *hentai* (perverse) is used to describe pornographic anime. A popular example is *Urotsukidōji: Legend of the Overfiend*, a horror erotic anime OVA, a format of straight-to-video anime and film.[216]

---

[211] *Dragon Ball*: Directed by Minoru Okazaki and Daisuke Nishio with Screenplay by Toshiki Inoue and Takao Koyama based on the manga of the same name by Akira Toriyama (Toei 1986-1989). The Japanese title is *Doragon Bōru*. *Dragon Ball Z*: Directed by Daisuke Nishio and Shigeyasu Yamauchi with Screenplay by Atsushi Maekawa et al. (Toei 1989-1996). The Japanese title is *Doragon Bōru Zetto*.
[212] *Captain Tsubasa*: Directed by Hiroyoshi Mitsunobu with Screenplay by Saburô Ebinuma et al. based on the manga of the same name by Yōichi Takahashi (TV Tokyo 1983-1995). The Japanese title is *Kyaputen Tsubasa*. *Star of the Giants*: Directed by Tadao Nagahama with Screenplay by Ikki Kajiwara based on sports manga by Ikki Kajiwara (Yomiuri Television 1968-1971). The Japanese title is *Kyojin no Hoshi*. Clements, *Anime*, 102 and 314. Clements states that sports genre appeared in cartoons in Japan in the 1920s.
[213] Denison, *Anime*, "Chapter 4", olb.
[214] *Urusei Yatsura*: Directed by Mamoru Oshii with Screenplay by Takao Koyama, Kazunori Ito and Michiru Shimada based on a manga of the same name by Rumiko Takahashi (Kitty Films 1981-1986). The Japanese title is *Urusei Yatsura*.
[215] Napier, *Anime from Akira to Howl's Moving Castle*, 198.
[216] *Urotsukidōji: Legend of the Overfiend:* Directed by Hideki Takayama with Screenplay by Noboru Aikawa (Shochiku 1989). The Japanese title is *Choujin Densetsu Urotsukidouji*.

OVA and Merchandising Expansion

In the 1980s, anime merchandising expanded its reach to target adults with spin-off music, tickets to public events, gadgets, decorations and figurines.[217] On the technological side, "arguably anime's greatest transformation" was the arrival of commercial videotape.[218] New technological developments led the industry to produce OVAs ("Original Video Animation").

Later, anime made for TV and theatre started to be released in OVA format as well. In 1983, Oshii's *Dallos* became the first anime series to release directly to OVA in 1983.[219] OVA boosted the popularity and accessibility of anime products worldwide, and it opened the way to preserve the artistic heritage and allowed young animators to watch, re-watch, and analyze previous works frame by frame.[220] It also gave the opportunity to Western audiences to watch anime works without censorship and later with English-subtitles. The more this format became a "crucial fan technology", the more it turned into "a means for testing concepts and promoting innovation".[221] As a result, it transformed the level of ownership, distribution, exhibition and access to anime.[222] Additionally, finding and watching OVAs strengthened the ties among fans by organizing collective watching and fan clubs. These changes led to another important factor in the development of anime: *otaku*.

Otaku

Originally the term *otaku* meant an "obsessive geek".[223] But it transformed to be used to describe hardcore anime/manga fans. While *otaku* developed as "a subculture" in the late 1970s and early 1980s, it appealed to a larger audience by the end of 1980s.[224] Also, although it originated in Japan, the impact of

---

[217] Clements, *Anime*, 483.

[218] Ibid., 352 and 355.

[219] *Dallos*: Directed by Mamoru Oshii with Screenplay by Hisayuki Toriumi and Mamoru Oshii (Discotek 1983-1984). The Japanese title is *Darosu*.

[220] Clements, *Anime*, 355 and 368.

[221] Denison, *Anime*, "Chapter 4", olb and Poitras, "Contemporary Anime", 54, respectively.

[222] Clements, *Anime*, 355.

[223] Laurie Cubbison, "Anime Fans, DVDs, and the Authentic Text", *The Velvet Light Trap* 56 (2005): 45 and *Brenner, Understanding Manga and Anime*, 29.

[224] Azuma, Otaku, 3; Ito Mizuko, "Introduction", in *Fandom Unbound: Otaku Culture in a Connected World*, eds. Mizuko Ito, Daisuke Okabe and Izumi Tsuji (New Haven: Yale University Press, 2012), xi; Melek Ortabaşı, "National History as Otaku Fantasy: Satoshi Kon's Millennium Actress", *Japanese Visual Culture*, 278; "Otaku", *Anime News Network*: https://www.animenewsnetwork.com/encyclopedia/lexicon.php?id=22; Azuma, *Otaku*, vii; LaMarre, *The Anime Machine*, xvii; Napier, *to Princess Mononoke*, 7 and Stuckmann, "Introduction", olb.

otaku culture has reached far beyond.²²⁵ It became both a Japanese and transnational movement—with "arguably the most wired fandom on the planet"—and "a sort of international fellowship of 'geeks' bound by their intense absorption in these popular media".²²⁶ However, it had a negative connotation until the 1990s, especially after the murderer of four girls was labeled as *otaku* in the media. *Otaku* was also regarded as a "male club" until recently. Mizuko states that views about *otaku* change based on those inside and outside the subculture:

> For some, it evokes images of sociopathic shut-ins out of touch with reality. For others, and increasingly, it suggests a distinctive style of geek chic: a postmodern sensibility expressed through arcane knowledge of pop and cyber culture and striking technological fluency.²²⁷

Activities of *otaku* diverse from producing fanzines to *doujinshi*, organizing conventions to fansubbing.²²⁸ Mizuko describes "*otaku* culture" as "a constellation of fannish cultural logics, platforms, and practices" that cluster around anime, manga, video games, as well as merchandizing and events.²²⁹ With the rise of *otaku* culture, some anime films and TV series were produced only for *otaku*s, such as Anno's 1988 directorial debut *Gunbuster*, "the first OVA made by and for *otaku*".²³⁰ Furthermore, anime clubs, and activities of *otaku*, such as fansubbing and fan subtitling, played an important role in increasing awareness of anime, and contributed to anime's global success; first among youth, then among adults from different demographics.²³¹ *Otaku* also became a major economic force. Annual conventions and cosplaying (costume play), which allow fans to bond with their favorite anime characters,

---

²²⁵ Azuma, *Otaku*, 10.
²²⁶ Thomas Lamarre, "An Introduction to Otaku Movement", *Entertext* 4.1 (2004/5): 175; Hu, *Frames of Anime*, 162; Mizuko, "Introduction", xi and Ortabaşı, "Otaku Fantasy", 279.
²²⁷ Mizuko, "Introduction", xi.
²²⁸ *Doujinshi* is a self-published works of fans derived from anime or manga.
²²⁹ Mizuko, "Introduction", xi.
²³⁰ *Gunbuster:* Directed by Hideaki Anno with Screenplay by Hideaki Anno and Toshio Okada (Gainax 1988-1989). The Japanese title is *Toppu o Nerae!* Matthew Roe, "Hideaki Anno: A Career Retrospective", *Anime News Network* 01st October 2021: https://www.animenewsnetwork.com/watch/2021-10-01/hideaki-anno-a-career-retrospective/.178 012.
²³¹ Newitz, "Anime Otaku", 2; Poitras, "Contemporary Anime", 64; Condry, *The Soul of Anime*, 1-2 and 161; Napier, *to Princess Mononoke*, 6; Stuckmann, "Introduction", olb; Denison, *Anime*, "Chapter 6", olb; Brenner, *Understanding Manga and Anime*, 12 and Clements, *Anime*, 410.

have been regularly organized for *otaku*.[232] Azuma sees *otaku* culture "as the site that most sensitively registers social transformations".[233] However, LaMarre emphasizes that despite being called a "community", there is no strict boundaries to define *otaku* community. "Otaku activities are more like a distributed collective force of desire than an established, definable community".[234]

Summary of Anime in the 1980s

In summary, the 1980s saw important changes and developments in anime. Despite these developments, anime was still seen as a "cheap form of animation", and production of TV animation series started to decrease in the second half of 1985.[235] However, the 1980s can still be seen as a period "filled with minds eager to explore and experiment, which led to the explosion of new genres and innovations in the anime industry", and anime's presence in the global stage increased.[236]

Darker Tones in Anime in the 1990s

Despite a decade-long financial crisis in Japan during the 1990s—anime expanded its audience and increased its visibility around the world—since it was not overly expensive to produce.[237] While anime always had diverse narratives and styles, "darker tones"[238] and more psychological and philosophical tones seemed to increase in anime in the 1990s after *Akira*. Napier argues that it "inaugurated an infinitely darker vision of technology in relation to human identity".[239]

---

[232] Bordwell and Thompson, *Film*, 393; Poitras, "Contemporary Anime", 64; Condry, *The Soul of Anime*, 1 and Okuno, "Roots of Cool Japan", 2.
[233] Thomas LaMarre et al., "The Animalization of Otaku Culture", *Mechademia* 2.1 (2007): 184.
[234] Thomas Lamarre, "Otaku Movement", in *Japan After Japan: Social and Cultural Life from the Recessionary 1990s to the Present*, eds. Tomiko Yoda, Harry Harootunian, Rey Chow and Masao Miyoshi (Durham: Duke University Press, 2006), 359.
[235] Hu, *Frames of Anime*, 2; Yamaguchi, "The Evolution", wp and Tsugata, "A Bipolar Approach", 31.
[236] "History of Anime", wp.
[237] Poitras, "Contemporary Anime", 55; LaMarre, *The Anime Machine*, xxii and Napier, *Anime from Akira to Howl's Moving Castle*, 18.
[238] Napier used the term "darker" to define the change in anime. It is borrowed from Napier, *Anime from Akira to Princess Mononoke*, 87; Napier, "When Machines", 104 and Napier, *Anime from Akira to Howl's Moving Castle*, xv.
[239] Napier, "When Machines", 104.

Darker Tone in Mecha: Neon Genesis Evangelion

Neon Genesis Evangelion is a good example of this trend in anime.[240] It distinguished itself from others anime series and redefined the *mecha* genre with its complex story, character development and "darker tone". NGE was a personal reflection of its creator Hideaki Anno and delved deeper into philosophical questions.[241] Unlike classic *shōnen* heroes, Anno created flawed and passive characters who deal with severe pathological fears and existential crises.[242] He also added adult-oriented issues in the theme, such as sexual shame.[243] Even the end of the series differentiates from other mecha anime series by focusing on the psychological states of characters rather than war and victory between giant robots, and it "significantly thwarts viewers' expectations, with the protagonist failing to become the legend promised by the opening song of the series".[244]

Although it originally targeted specifically *otaku*, the series became a major phenomenon and massive commercial success in Japan.[245] Since it was produced at a time when the anime industry and real robot genre were declining, its success led to a "rebirth of the anime industry".[246] Therefore, it is also considered one of the most "groundbreaking anime series ever created" and "perhaps the most critically acclaimed anime TV series of the decade, energizing the entire industry with its large adult following".[247] With this TV series, Anno was recognized as "one of the minds that shaped Japanese entertainment and pop culture".[248]

Anno also directed *Nadia: The Secret of Blue Water*, a steampunk anime.[249] Tomino Yoshiyuki continued directing some *Gundam* series or film in the

---

[240] *Neon Genesis Evangelion*: Directed by Hideaki Anno with Screenplay by Hideaki Anno (Gainax 1995-1996). Japanese title is *Shinseiki Ebangerion*.
[241] "The Evolution of Japanese Animation", *Sotheby's* 14th December 2021: https://www.sothebys.com/en/articles/the-evolution-of-japanese-animation.
[242] Roe, "Hideaki Anno", wp; Tsugata, "A Bipolar Approach", 31; "The Evolution of Japanese Animation", wp. and "History of Anime", wp.
[243] Roe, "Hideaki Anno", wp.
[244] Selen Çalık Bedir, "Combinatory Play and Infinite Replay: Underdefined Causality in the *Neon Genesis Evangelion* Anime Series and Games", *Anime Studies*, 297.
[245] Tsugata, "A Bipolar Approach", 31.
[246] "The Evolution of Japanese Animation", wp. and "History of Anime", wp.
[247] Napier, "When Machines", 108 and Poitras, "Contemporary Anime", 56, respectively.
[248] Roe, "Hideaki Anno", wp.
[249] *Nadia: The Secret of Blue Water*. Directed by Hideaki Anno and Shinji Hicguchi with Screenplay by Hisao Ōkawa and Yasuo Tanami (NHK 1990-1991). The Japanese title is *Fushigi no Umi no Nadia*.

1990s, such as *Mobile Suit Gundam F91*, *Victory Gundam*, as well as other works such as *Brain Powerd*.[250]

Darker Tone in *Sci-fi:* Ghost in the Shell

The cyberpunk sci-fi subgenre developed and became more sophisticated with a "darker" and more philosophical tone in the 1990s. Oshii's *Ghost in the Shell* is considered a masterpiece in this regard.[251] The film is set in a dystopic future. The female cyborg protagonist continually questions the soul as she searches for a mysterious artificial intelligence program. Bolton et al. says that in the history of robot anime, ambivalence extended to "each new step in the process of imagining virtual creatures, from boy robots to the super robots of the 1970s, the real robots of the 1980s, the cyborgs of the 1990s".[252] With its appealing philosophical storyline and visual richness, the film was influential beyond anime, inspiring many other films, such as the *Matrix*.[253] Enhancing public awareness and appreciation of anime, it drew in a new generation of fans, and expanded its popularity worldwide.[254] It also raised interest in Oshii's other works, especially after the film became a hit in the US.[255]

Shōjo Gets Darker in the 1990s

The *shōjo* genre had a similar evolution in this period. Napier argues that there was a transformation to darker tones.[256] In this period, unlike their counterparts in previous decades, the *shōjo* characters generally dealt with "far tougher issues, including their own neuroses and dark pasts".[257] The magical girls became "more independent and erotically delineated" and they

---

[250] *Mobile Suit Gundam F91*: Directed by Yoshiyuki Tomino with Screenplay by Tsunehisa Ito and Yoshiyuki Tomino (Shochiku 1991). The Japanese title is *Kidō Senshi Gandamu Fōmyura Nainti Wan*; *Victory Gundam*: Directed by Yoshiyuki Tomino with Screenplay by Akira Okeya et al. (TV Asahi 1993-1994). The Japanese title is *Kidō Senshi Vikutorī Gandamu*; *Brain Powerd*: Directed by Yoshiyuki Tomino with Screenplay by Akemi Omode et al. (Wowow 1998). The Japanese title is *Buren Pawādo*.
[251] *Ghost in the Shell*: Directed by Mamoru Oshii with Screenplay by Kazunoi Itō based on the manga of the same name by Masamune Shirow (Shochiku 1995). The Japanese title is *Kōkaku Kidōtai*.
[252] Bolton et al, "Introduction", ix.
[253] Stuckmann, "Introduction", olb. *The Matrix*: Directed by The Wachowskis with Screenplay with The Wachowskis (Warner Bros 1999).
[254] Robbins, "Bringing Anime", 5; Brenner, *Understanding Manga and Anime*, 11 and Tsugata, "A Bipolar Approach", 31.
[255] Tsugata, "A Bipolar Approach", 31.
[256] Napier, *Anime from Akira to Howl's Moving Castle*, xv.
[257] Ibid, xiv.

History of Anime

even showed "aggression and nurturance" compared to classic *shōjo* characters.[258] Popular *shōjo* anime series with magical themes such as *Sailor Moon* and *New Cutie Honey* presented cute but powerful and even sexy young girls.[259] These two series not only became hugely popular but also introduced a new concept in that the protagonist must transform herself to acquire her power. This trend continued with other magical girl anime series and films which created a big media franchise. For example, the fact that the protagonist's power comes from her accessories (jewelry, makeup, magic prism) in *Sailor Moon* led to a boom in the demand for this merchandise.[260] This new trend in *shōjo* continued in the 2000s.[261] Other interesting television series also helped to energize the genre in this period, such as *The Vision of Escaflowne*, which is based on a girls' manga.[262]

Increase in International Popularity and Recognition

Sports anime in the *shōnen* genre grew in popularity in the 1990s. *Slam Dunk* and *One Piece* became worldwide hits.[263] Anime for the mature audience on social issues also continued to be produced. For example, Takahata directed *Only Yesterday* and then *Pom Poko*.[264] *Pom Poko* had the highest-earning domestic motion picture in Japan in 1995 and was nominated to compete for the Best Foreign Language Film Category at the American Academy Awards in the same year.[265]

Miyazaki's masterpiece *Princess Mononoke* broke all box office records in 1997 and became the highest-grossing film of all time in Japan until the

---

[258] Ibid, 150.
[259] *Sailor Moon*: Directed by Junichi Sato, Kunihiko Ikuhara and Takuya Igarashi with Screenplay by Sukehiro Tomita (Toei 1992-1997). The Japanese title is *Bishōjo Senshi Sērāmūn*. *New Cutie Honey:* Directed by Yasuchika Nagaoka (Discotek 1994-1995). The Japanese title is *Shin Kyūtī Hanī*.
[260] MacWilliams, "Introduction", 9.
[261] Napier, *Anime from Akira to Howl's Moving Castle*, xiv.
[262] *The Vision of Escaflowne*: Directed by Kazuki Akane with Screenplay by Hiroaki Kitajima et al. (TV Tokyo 1996). The Japanese title is *Tenkū no Esukafurōne*.
[263] *Slam Dunk:* Directed by Nobutaka Nishizawa with Screenplay by Nobutaka Nishizawa and Yoshiyuki Suga (Toei 1993-1996). *One Piece:* Directed by Kōnosuke Uda et al. with Screenplay by Junki Takegami and Hirohiko Kamisaka (Toei 1999-present).
[264] *Only Yesterday:* Directed by Isao Takahata with Screenplay by Isao Takahata based on the manga of the same name by Hotaru Okamoto and Yuko Tone (Toho 1991). The Japanese title is *Omohide Poro*. *Pom Poko:* Directed by Isao Takahata with Screenplay by Isao Takahata (Toho 1994). The Japanese title is *Heisei Tanuki Gassen Ponpoko*.
[265] Hu, *Frames of Anime*, 135.

release of *Titanic*.[266] It was also the most expensive anime film, and the first animated feature nominated for an Academy Award.[267] The film confirmed Ghibli and Miyazaki's social perspectives and styles with its discourses on environmental issues and questioning the effect of industrialization and human conflicts with nature.

In the same year, director Satoshi Kon released his first film and masterpiece *Perfect Blue*, a psychological thriller.[268] In the film, Kon took anime to new heights by blending the surreal with reality and fantasy.[269] As Mes describes, the film "finally convinced a lot of people that animation might be more than just a children's medium" in the West.[270]

Another important auteur Shinichiro Watanabe emerged with his first debut as co-director of *Macross Plus*, a sci-fiction *mecha* anime, in 1994.[271] He became more recognized with the release of *Cowboy Bebop* a *film-noir* (neo-noir) style sci-fi series with anti-heroes at with the center, with its music being a very integral part of the show.[272] The series had international acclaim and is seen as one of the greatest anime series.

Developments in the Industry in the 1990s

On the technological side, even though computer-generated imagery (CGI) was first used in some of the scenes of *Golgo 13: The Professional* in the 1980s, the first Japanese film to be fully computer-animated is widely regarded as *A.L.I.C.E* in 1999.[273] In the same year, Takahata's *My Neighbours the Yamadas*

---

[266] *Princess Mononoke*: Directed by Hayao Miyazaki with Screenplay by Hayao Miyazaki (Toho 1997). The Japanese title is *Mononokehime*. Napier, *Anime from Akira to Howl's Moving Castle*, 7 and 18. *Titanic*: Directed by James Cameron with Screenplay by James Cameron (Paramount Picture 1997).

[267] Odell and Le Blanc, *Studio Ghibli*, 109.

[268] *Perfect Blue*: Directed by Sotashi Kon with Screenplay by Sadayuki Murai based on *Perfect Blue: Complete Metamorphosis* by Yoshikazu Takeuchi (Madhouse 1998). The Japanese title is *Pāfekuto Burū*.

[269] Ortabaşı, "Otaku Fantasy", 275.

[270] Tom Mes, "Interview: Satoshi Kon", *Midnight Eye: Visions in Japanese Cinema* 02nd November 2001: http://www.midnighteye.com/interviews/satoshi-kon/.

[271] *Macross Plus*: Directed by Shōji Kawamori and Shinichiro Watanabe with Screenplay by Keiko Nobumoto (Crunchyroll 1994-1995). The Japanese title is *Makurosu Purasu*.

[272] *Cowboy Bebop*: Directed by Shinichirō Watanabe with Screenplay by Keiko Nobumoto (Sunrise 1997-1998). The Japanese title is *Kaubōi Bibappu*. Denison, *Anime*, "Analyzing Anime in Context", olb and Poitras, "Contemporary Anime", 58.

[273] *Golgo 13*: Directed by Osamu Dezaki with Screenplay by Shukei Nagasaka (Toho 1983). The Japanese title is *Gorugo Sātīn*. *A.L.I.C.E.*: Directed by Kenichi Maejima with Screenplay by Masahiro Yoshimoto (GAGA Communication 1999). "History of Anime", wp.

History of Anime   39

was Ghibli's first entirely computer-generated feature.[274] Miyazaki also used computer techniques for the first time for some images in *Princess Mononoke*. However, since he mainly continued to rely on traditional cel-animation mainly, "the difference from traditional cel-animation is virtually undetectable on the screen".[275] By the late 1990s, DVD sales began to dominate sales and allowed for multi-language subtitles and dubbed versions, which increased sales and exports.[276]

On the industrial side, Gonzo was founded in 1992 with the aim of expanding digital animation in Japan.[277] Bones was established in 1998 by some Sunrise staff members, and P.A. Works was set up in 2000. Funimation, an American entertainment company, was also founded at this time and dubbed anime for distribution overseas. With the advent of the internet in the 1990s, fans in the U.S.A found a new medium to connect and share knowledge with other fans around the country, and fan site forums proliferated.[278] However, this new technology also caused anime and manga to lose their central position within *otaku* culture, and a new type of computer game called "gal-games" or "beautiful girl games" rapidly took over.[279] Moreover, a decline in advertising revenue along with the rise of the internet and alternative entertainment like online streaming, impacted the anime industry in both positive and negative aspects at the beginning of the new millennium.[280]

Impact of Globalization, International Awards and *Isekai* in the 2000s and 2010s

In the 2000s, despite some struggles in the industry, the anime market evolved with more sophisticated works in genres and subgenres. One of the most viewed anime of the period was *Pokemon*, adapted from the video game series.[281] The success of the series turned "a global media-mix phenomenon from a TV series to video games, trading cards, endless merchandise".[282] *Pokemon* even became "something of a social issue in the US [and other parts

---

[274] *My Neighbours the Yamadas*: Directed by Isao Takahata with Screenplay by Isao Takahata (Shochiku 1999). The Japanese title is *Hōhokekyo Tonari no Yamada-kun*. Odell and Le Blanc, *Studio Ghibli*, 112.
[275] Bordwell and Thompson, *Film*, 386.
[276] Cubbison, "Anime Fans", 50 and Denison, *Anime*, "Chapter 6", olb.
[277] Poitras, "Contemporary Anime", 63.
[278] Mizuko, "Introduction", xxiv.
[279] Azuma, "The Animalization", 184.
[280] Yamaguchi, "The Evolution", wp.
[281] *Pokemon*: Directed by Kunihiko Yuyama with Screenplay by Takeshi Shudo (OLM Inc. 1997-present). The Japanese title is *Poketto Monsutā*.
[282] Condry, *The Soul of Anime*, 216.

of the world], as many preteens became addicted".²⁸³ Therefore, it is considered to be "the central event of anime's overseas popularity" at the beginning of the millennium.²⁸⁴

Miyazaki and International Acclamations

Prominent animators continued to receive international acclamations in this period. But the most important one is Miyazaki. Miyazaki and his *Spirited Away* became a turning point in terms of the anime's global acceptance and recognition.²⁸⁵ In the film, a young girl trapped in an otherworldly bathhouse has to find a way to save her parents, who turned into pigs, and during her journey, she learns how to connect with nature and to be selfless. With both its narrative and visual style, the film is seen as "the most quintessential Japanese film that Miyazaki has ever made".²⁸⁶ It won an Academy Award for Best Animated Feature in 2003 (the only non-English-language film to have won in this category).²⁸⁷ The film showed that anime can achieve both critical acclaim and mainstream acceptance.²⁸⁸ Miyazaki also created other masterpieces, such as *Howl's Moving Castle*, *Ponyo on the Cliff by the Sea* and *The Wind Rises*.²⁸⁹ *The Wind Rises* was nominated for Best Animated Feature at the Oscars, and Miyazaki was introduced by Ghibli aficionado John Lasseter at the Academy to receive an Honorary Award in 2014.²⁹⁰ Although he has announced his retirement many times, Miyazaki recently made a new movie based on Genzaburo Yoshino's 1937 book *How Do You Live?* slated to be released in 2023.²⁹¹

---

²⁸³ Kinko Ito, "Manga in Japanese History", *Japanese Visual Culture*, 46.
²⁸⁴ Clements, *Anime*, 397.
²⁸⁵ *Spirited Away*: Directed by Hayao Miyazaki with Screenplay by Hayao Miyazaki (Toho 2001). The Japanese title is *Sen to Chihiro no Kamikakushi*.
²⁸⁶ Robbins, "Bringing Anime", 9.
²⁸⁷ The film also won the Berlin Film Festival's Golden Bear Award in 2002.
²⁸⁸ Condry, *The Soul of Anime*, 87.
²⁸⁹ *Howl's Moving Castle*: Directed by Hayao Miyazaki with Screenplay by Hayao Miyazaki based on the novel of the same name by Diana Wynne Jones (Toho 2004). The Japanese title is *Houru no Ugoku Shiro*. *Ponyo on the Cliff by the Sea*: Directed by Hayao Miyazaki with Screenplay by Hayao Miyazaki based on *The Little Mermaid* by Hans Christian Andersen (Toho 2008). The Japanese title is *Gake no ue no Ponyo*. *The Wind Rises*: Directed by Hayao Miyazaki with Screenplay by Hayao Miyazaki based on the novel *The Wind Has Risen* by Tatsuo Hori and the Life of Jiro Horikoshi (Toho 2013). The Japanese title is *Kaze Tachinu*.
²⁹⁰ Odell and Le Blanc, *Studio* Ghibli, 147.
²⁹¹ Mishan, "Hayao Miyazaki", wp.

History of Anime 41

The other foremost director Takahata died in 2018, and his *The Tale of Princess Kaguya* was nominated for an Oscar for Best Animated Feature in 2015.[292] Oshii's *Ghost in the Shell 2 Innocence* was nominated for the Palme d'Or at the Cannes Film Festival in 2004.[293] Mamoru Hosoda's film *Mirai* was nominated for an Academy Award in 2018; which is the first non-Ghibli anime nominated for a Oscar.[294] Satoshi Kon made his sophisticated anime films *Millennium Actress* and *Tokyo Godfathers* during this period.[295] Both qualified for submission for Best Animated Feature category at the Oscars but were not approved by the committee for inclusion on the ballot.[296] Ōtomo's second major anime *Steamboy* won Best Animated Feature Film at the Catalonian International Film Festival.[297] Emerging director Makoto Shinkai's *Your Name* became the third highest-grossing anime film of all time as of 2022—380 million US dollars—after *Demon Slayer the Movie: Mugen Train* and *Spirited Away*.[298]

More of Everything in Anime

In the new millennium, anime about "more of everything" increased.[299] The real robot genre regained its popularity in 2002 after the release of *Mobile Suit Gundam SEED* and in 2007 *Gurren Lagann* which received widespread critical

---

[292] *The Tale of Princess Kaguya*: Directed by Isao Takahata with Screenplay by Isao Takahata and Riko Sakaguchi based on *The Tale of the Bamboo Cutter* by an unknown author (Studio Ghibli 2013). The Japanese title is *Kaguya-hime no Monogatari*.

[293] *Ghost in the Shell 2 Innocence*: Directed by Mamoru Oshii with Screenplay by Mamoru Oshii based on the manga by Masamune Shirow (Toho 2003). The Japanese title is *Inosensu*. Hu, *Frames of Anime*, 135.

[294] *Mirai*: Directed by Mamoru Hosoda with Screenplay by Mamoru Hosoda (Toho 2018). The Japanese title is *Mirai no Mirai*. The film was also nominated at the Golden Globe Awards in the same year.

[295] *Millennium Actress*: Directed by Satoshi Kon with Screenplay by Sadayuki Murai and Satoshi Kon (Madhouse 2001). The Japanese title is *Sennen Joyū*. *Tokyo Godfathers*: Directed by Satoshi Kon with Screenplay by Keiko Nobumoto and Satoshi Kon (Sony Pictures 2003). The Japanese title is *Tōkyō Goddofāzāzu*.

[296] Poitras, "Contemporary Anime", 58-59.

[297] *Steamboy*: Directed by Katsuhiro Otomo with Screenplay by Sadayuki Murai and Katsuhiro Otomo (Toho 2004). The Japanese title is *Suchīmubōi*.

[298] *Your Name*: Directed by Makoto Shinkai with Screenplay by Makoto Shinkai (Toho 2016). The Japanese title is *Kimi no Na wa*. *Demon Slayer: Mugen Train*: Directed by Haruo Sotozaki with Screenplay by Ufotable based on the manga of the same name by *Koyoharu Gotouge* (Toho 2020). The Japanese title is *Gekijō-ban "Kimetsu no Yaiba" Mugen Ressha-hen*. Mishan, "Hayao Miyazaki", wp.

[299] Naomi Starlight, "Best Anime of the 2010s: A Look at Anime From 2010 to 2019", *Reelrundown* 26th February 2020: https://reelrundown.com/animation/Best-Anime-Series-and-Films-of-the-2010s-Anime-from-2010-to-2019.

acclaim.[300] As anime related to martial arts was gaining popularity in this period, *Naruto* became one of the most popular anime in Japan and abroad.[301]

Apocalyptic, Dark Fantasy and Horror

Sophisticated and more apocalyptic themes, dark fantasy and horror (especially zombie themes) in *mecha* and other genres continued expanding. For example, in *Attack on Titan*, humans fight against humanoids who eat humans; in *Tokyo Ghoul*, ghouls and creatures eat humans; in *Demon Slayer*, the protagonist fights against demons by using martial arts; and in *Death Note*, a teen discovers a mysterious notebook that gives the user the supernatural ability to kill anyone whose name is written in its pages.[302] These anime became some of the top domestic anime works of all time. *Demon Slayer* was submitted for the Academy Awards 2021, and its related merchandise sales were a boost for the anime market.[303]

In this period, more experimental trends also emerged.[304] Considered "an experimental filmmaker who liked to upend the conventions of genres and franchises he worked on", director Oshii Mamoru directed *The Sky Crawlers*,

---

[300] *Mobile Suit Gundam SEED*: Directed by Mitsuo Fukuda with Screenplay by Chiaki Morosawa (JNN 2002-2003). The Japanese title is *Kidō Senshi Gandamu Shīdo*; *Gurren Lagann*: Directed by Hiroyuki Imaishi with Screenplay by Kazuki Nakashima (Gainax 2007). The Japanese title is *Tengen Toppa Gurren Lagann*. "History of Anime", wp.

[301] *Naruto*: Directed by Hayato Date with Screenplay by Katsuyuki Sumisawa, Junki Takegami based on the manga of the same name by *Masashi Kishimoto* (TXN TV Tokyo 2002-2007).

[302] *Attack on Titan*: Directed by Tetsurō Araki, Masashi Koizuka, Yuichiro Hayashi and Jun Shishido with Screenplay by Yasuko Kobayashi, Hiroshi Seko, Shintarō Kawakubo based on the manga of the same name by Hajime Isayama (Tokyo MX 2013-present). The Japanese title is *Shingeki no Kyojin*. *Tokyo Ghoul*: Directed by Shuhei Morita with Screenplay by Chūji Mikasano based on the manga of the same name by Sui Ishida (Tokyo MX 2014). The Japanese title is *Tōkyō Gūru*. *Demon Slayer*: Directed by Haruo Sotozaki with Screenplay by Ufotable based on the manga of the same name by Koyoharu Gotouge (Tokyo MX 2009-present). The Japanese title is *Kimetsu no Yaiba*. *Death Note*: Directed by Tetsurō Araki with Screenplay by Toshiki Inoue based on the manga of the same name by Tsugumi Ohba (Madhouse 2006-2007).

[303] Tadashi Sudo, "What Is Happening in the Anime Industry in 2020-2021? An Analysis of The Animation Industry Report 2021", trans. Kim Morrissy, *Anime News Network* 03rd November 2021: https://www.animenewsnetwork.com/feature/2021-11-03/what-is-happening-in-the-anime-industry-in-2020-2021-an-analysis-of-the-animation-industry-report-2021/.179153 and "History of Anime", wp.

[304] Film Hub Midlands, "Research Material Anime Japan 2020", 7 and "History of Anime", wp.

History of Anime   43

refused genre tropes by showing that "anime comes in such wide varieties of science fiction as to confound critical vocabulary".[305]

Shōjo

According to Napier, the *shōjo* was an even more important icon in the 2000s than in the 1980s, dominating a large part of the Japanese visual imagination.[306] While classic *shōjo* characters (*bishōjo*) continued, such as in *Naruto*, darker characters with complex traits (which emerged in the 1990s), also strengthened in line with more challenging narratives.[307] They sometimes even transformed from *shōjo* to more mature characters during their journey.[308]

Otaku Changes and Moe

Azuma says that while *otaku* culture was based on "narrative consumption" from 1980 to 1995, the trend changed to "database consumption" at the turn of the millennium, especially after 1995, with the help of the internet.[309] That meant "a shift from the supremacy of the narrative and characters—as well as from the myths of authorship to databases of affective elements (*moeyōso*)"—in the context of *otaku* culture.[310]

Picard describes this shift from "grand narratives" to "little narratives that are constructed to allow affective responses to characters".[311] Therefore, with the effect of this change in *otaku* culture, the popularity of *moe* style characters among *shōjo* characters emerged and popularized.[312]

Moe characters have various "affective (*moe*) elements", such as hair tied up like feelers, cat ears, tail, maid costume, etc.[313] They were even drawn with "slender legs or arms, bigger heads, thin waists, and sometimes even

---

[305] Bolton, *Interpreting Anime*, 61. *The Sky Crawlers*: Directed by Mamoru Oshii with Screenplay by Chihiro Ito based on the novel series of the same name by Hiroshi Mori (Production I.G. 2008). The Japanese title is *Sukai Kurora*. Denison, *Anime*, "From Cyberpunk to Steampunk Anime", olb.
[306] Napier, *Anime from Akira to Howl's Moving Castle*, 169.
[307] Ibid., 170.
[308] Ibid.
[309] Azuma, "The Animalization", 184.
[310] Ibid., 181.
[311] Martin Picard, "Gēmu Communities and Otaku Consumption. The (Sub) Culture(s) of Videogames in Japan", in *Japan's Contemporary Media Culture between Local and Global Content: Practice and Theory*, eds. Martin Roth, Hiroshi Yoshida and Martin Picard (Heidelberg: CrossAsia-eBooks, 2021), 28.
[312] "History of Anime", wp and Starlight, "Best Anime", wp.
[313] Azuma, "The Animalization", 183.

disproportionately big breasts".[314] For Azuma, "nothing symbolizes this transformation so perfectly as *Dejiko*", in which the protagonist princess is depicted as a catgirl with colored eyes and hair with a maid-style uniform and navy ribbons.[315]

Elegant "gothic Lolita" characters also presented "an ambivalent configuration of female strength/powerfulness and cuteness/fashionableness (that is, 'grotesque cuteness')"; though male *otaku* developed different relationships with these characters.[316] Such portrayals may be found in *Hell Girl, Death Note, Rozen Maiden* and *Princess Princess*.[317]

Okuno defines "feeling Moe" from the perspective of *otaku* as "a special, uncertain, love-like fondness towards the manga and anime heroines".[318] Moreover, Clements indicates that the advent of computer games increased the gamification and objectification of female characters. Female characters are presented as "prizes to be won or artifacts to be refined" in the games.[319]

Harem and Slice of Life

In this period, genres such as romance, *harem* and *slice of life* (*nichijō* or *mundane*) gained ground in anime. In the *harem* genre, an ordinary male protagonist is surrounded by multiple potential love interests, and the genre is mixed in with humor, romance and sexuality.[320] Examples are *Love Hina* and

---

[314] "History of Anime", wp.

[315] *Di Gi Charat:* Directed by Hiroaki Sakurai with Screenplay by Hiroaki Sakurai and Nobuharu Kamanaka based on the manga of the same name by Koge-Donbo (TBS 1998-1999). The Japanese title is *De Ji Kyaratto*. Azuma, "The Animalization", 183-84.

[316] Sugawa-Shimada, "Grotesque Cuteness", 209 and Starlight, "Best Anime", wp.

[317] *Hell Girl:* Directed by Takahiro Omori with Screenplay by Kenichi Kanemaki (Tokyo MX 2005-2006). The Japanese title is *Jigoku Shōjo*. *Rozen Maiden:* Directed by Kou Matsuo with Screenplay by Jukki Hanada based on the manga of the same name by Peach-Pit (TBS 2004). The Japanese title is *Rōzen Meiden*. *Princess:* Directed by Keitaro Motonaga based on the manga of the same name by Mikiyo Tsuda (Studio Deen 2006). The Japanese title is *Purinsesu Purinsesu*.

[318] Okuno, "Roots of Cool Japan", 5.

[319] Clements, *Anime*, 453.

[320] Cheeky Kid, "Top 10 Best Harem Anime", *ReelRundown* 29th March 2022: https://reelrundown.com/animation/Best-Harem-Anime; Brenner, *Understanding Manga and Anime*, 89; Jason S. Yadao, *The Rough Guide to Manga* (London: Rough Guides, 2009), 263.

Oh My Goddess!.[321] The harem anime in which a female protagonist is the lead is called *reverse harem*, and *Ouran High School Host Club* and *The Wallflower* are examples.[322]

Slice of life focuses on the everyday life of the characters and modern romances.[323] They sometimes feature *bishōnen* characters who are boys in middle or high school with feminine features. They are thin and have "stylish hair, clear skin, and distinctive feminine facial features despite retaining the physical body of a male".[324] At first glance, even difficult to recognize whether the character is a boy or a girl.

Isekai and Its Significance in Relation to Otaku and Community Production

Maybe the most intriguing anime genre that emerged in this period is *isekai* (literally strange world, another world, different world). *Isekai* is a subgenre of fantasy that appeared in the 2010s and has dominated manga and anime ever since.[325] In *isekai* stories, characters struggling with their ordinary lives suddenly transfer to another world or into their favorite games or are

---

[321] *Love Hina*: Directed by Yoshiaki Iwasaki with Screenplay by Kurō Hazuki based on the manga of the same name by Ken Akamatsu (TV Tokyo 2000). The Japanese title is *Rabu Hina*. There were additional special OVAs as well. *Oh My Goddess*: Directed by Hiroaki Gōda with Screenplay by Kunihiko Kondo and Nahoko Hasegawa based on the manga of the same name by Kōsuke Fujishima (AIC 1993-1994). The Japanese title is *Aa! Megami-sama*.

[322] *Ouran High School Host Club*: Directed by Takuya Igarashi with Screenplay by Yōji Enokido based on manga series by Bisco Hatori (Nippon TV 2006). The Japanese title is *Ōran Kōkō Hosuto Kurabu*. *The Wallflower*: Directed by Shinichi Watanabe from the manga of the same name by Tomoko Hayakawa (Nippon Animation 2006-2007). The Japanese title is *Yamato Nadeshiko Shichi Henge*. Brenner, *Understanding Manga and Anime*, 89.

[323] Clements, *Anime*, 452.

[324] "History of Anime", wp and Starlight, "Best Anime", wp.

[325] Amanda Pagan, "A Beginner's Guide to Isekai", *New York Public Library* 15th July 2019: https://www.nypl.org/blog/2019/07/15/beginners-guide-isekai-manga; Naomi Starlight, "Isekai Anime: Explaining the Genre's History, and How It's Changed", *ReelRundown* 25th March 2022: https://reelrundown.com/animation/Thoughts-on-the-History-of-the-Isekai-Genre; Naomi Starlight, "Admit It: You Enjoy the Wish Fulfillment in Isekai Anime", *ReelRundown* 23th March 2022: https://reelrundown.com/animation/Is-Wish-Fulfilment-in-the-Isekai-Genre-Always-Bad. Examples in the 1990s and 2000s in manga and anime, *Fushigi Yuugi*, *The Vision of Escaflowne*, and *Inuyasha*. The protagonists in these anime works are girls vis-à-vis boys who dominate current *isekai* anime. Also, in these previous series, there was usually one single love interest and a few different potential love rivals vis-à-vis current *isekai harem*.

reborn/reincarnated in a new world either by accident, suicide or murder.[326] They face new adventures, epic battles, and romance—even come across multiple love interests with the addition of full of magic—while searching for their way back home. Although these type of stories is not new and can be found in Western children's literature, Japanese folklore and even in earlier anime,[327] they became known as the *isekai* genre in the 2010s. *Isekai* especially rose to prominence after the 2012 release of *Sword Art Online*.[328] In this anime, the characters are trapped in a VR game.[329] *Isekai* has had a significant impact on increasing the popularity of light novels within the broader media-mix. Furthermore, it contributed to the rise of massively multiplayer online gaming and gaming communities.[330]

Lu categorizes the *isekai* genre into four subgenres.[331] One, the "standard *isekai*"—which focuses more on action, adventure and drama—and where the protagonists use their overpowering abilities to achieve their goals. Two, "romance *isekai*" (or *harem isekai*) shows a special skill that usually makes mainly male-centric protagonists more attractive. Three, "slow life *isekai*" (or *slice of life*) portrays characters with ordinary lives and no interest in becoming a hero. Finally, "outliner *isekai*" deals with revenge and having a second chance at life.[332] *Re: Zero Kara Hajimeru Isekai Seikatsu, KonoSuba: God's Blessing on this Wonderful World* and *Tensei Shitara Slime Datta Ken* are

---

[326] Tani Levy, "Entering Another World: A Cultural Genre Discourse of Japanese Isekai Texts and Their Origin in Online Participatory Culture", *Japan's Contemporary Media Culture*, 96. As the protagonists get transported to another world either physically or mentally, Levy categorizes this transportation into three categories: transfer (*tenii*), summoning (*shōkan*) and reincarnation (*tensei*).

[327] Examples of a hero going into a fantasy world in Western children's literature are *Alice in Wonderland* and *The Wizard of Oz* and in Japanese folklore *the Tale of Urashima Taro*.

[328] *Sword Art Online*: Directed by Tomohiko Itō with Screenplay by Yukie Sugawara et al. based on the novel series of the same name by Reki Kawahara (A-1 Pictures 2012). The Japanese title is *Sōdo Āto Onrain*.

[329] Pagan, "A Beginner's Guide to Isekai", wp.

[330] Kim Morrissy, "Mushoku Tensei Is Not the Pioneer of Isekai Web Novels, But..".., *Anime News Network* 19th March 2021: www.animenewsnetwork.com/feature/2021-03-19/mushoku-tensei-is-not-the-pioneer-of-isekai-web-novels-but/.170429; Levy, "Entering Another World", 93 and Starlight, "Isekai Anime", wp.

[331] Curtis Lu, "The Darker Sides of the Isekai Genre: An Examination of the Power of Anime and Manga" (MA Thesis: University of San Francisco 2020): https://repository.usfca.edu/capstone/1009.

[332] Ibid., 6-20.

some of the most successful *isekai* series. Reincarnation is popularized in *isekai* with *Mushoku Tensei: Jobless Reincarnation*.[333]

What makes *isekai* different and more appealing than other genres is that its stories usually originate from light novels (*raito noberu*)—posted online by amateur authors—which are developed with the help of *otaku*. Web novel sites, such as *Shōsetsuka ni Narō* (*Let's Become Novelists*), are the key platforms in this process.[334] Functioning as "platforms of participatory culture", they enable fans to write and read stories, as well as to participate in creating and developing the stories using feedback, ratings and reactions. The significance is that *isekai* stories are directly linked to the *otaku* community.[335] They are a "fan-based media production" which is a result of a communal creativity and production process since the 2010s.[336]

As Morrissy indicates, "from 2018 onward, the anime industry saw an explosion of titles originating from *Narō*".[337] Also, *isekai* usually features an apathetic, socially awkward, and lonely modern-day Japanese male protagonist, "a loser incel *otaku* type".[338] Those characters find a chance at a new life and become a hero in an *isekai* world, which is not possible for *otaku* in their own real life. Plus, by actively interacting with short stories and participating in a communal creativity and production process, fans also find a way to create or enter communal fantasy worlds in which they can change or reconstruct the course of stories (which they cannot do in real life). So, for all these reasons, *isekai* allows audiences struggling in life to feel their "wishes are fulfillment" through protagonists and their stories.[339] Because of that, the genre has constantly drawn the attention of young *otaku* men.[340]

Isekai mixes genres and provides interconnectedness and intertextuality by self-referencing tropes of different genres that draws fans into more these stories. For example, in *isekai* stories, the audience can re-encounter the characters, themes and places that they already know and adore from previous anime works.

---

[333] Kim Morrissy, "Mushoku Tensei", wp.
[334] Levy, "Entering Another World", 92.
[335] Ibid., 90.
[336] Ibid., 89.
[337] Kim Morrissy, "Mushoku Tensei", wp.
[338] Pagan, "A Beginner's Guide to Isekai", wp. and Starlight, "Admit It", wp.
[339] Starlight, "Isekai Anime", wp.
[340] Pagan, "A Beginner's Guide to Isekai", wp. However, *isekai* featuring female protagonists has recently been on the rise. Those *isekai* stories tend to lean more towards *slice of life* style.

Isekai is also connected to the advent of computer role-playing games (RPG). Some stories are set in worlds based on different types of role-playing games such as *shōnen* action games, *otome* (romance with a female protagonist) games, as well as dating sims and battle royales.[341]

In summary, as Levy indicates, it can be said that "in a simplified way, *isekai* stories can be understood as fictional works within different types of media about *otaku* that are created by *otaku* to be consumed by *otaku*".[342] This has led to *isekai* stories attracting new audiences for more than a decade. Nowadays, *isekai* is ruling the manga and anime industry. In fact, "the acquisition of fan-based source materials through big publishing corporations marks a shift from subcultural media creation merging into pop cultural media distribution".[343] However, the influx and abundance of *isekai* stories also threatens to throw the industry into a vicious circle whereby themes, stories and characters repeat themselves. That cycle reduces the quality of the work and harms creativity. The fact that *isekai* stories are seen as a safe option by authors and producers to get their works into anime adaptation can have the effect of flooding the market with too many cliché stories and kitsch products.[344] This environment also reinforces the already dire working conditions that animators continue to face. In this way, although it is very popular, the *isekai* trend in anime brings a risk of recession in creativity and prevents new genres from emerging.

Impact of Technology and Digitalization from 2000-2020

At the beginning of the millennium, the advent of technology and digitalization also brought the anime industry to a new level regarding anime and anime-related products. During this period, the anime industry gradually evolved—first through the development of the internet—and after that by developments of social media, smartphones and online streaming platforms.

During this period, tie-ins and overlaps between video games, film and animation also increased.[345] The industry shifted from cel-animation to computer-generated animation.[346] The studios have gradually favored "cel-shading (or toon shading), in which animation was made with 3D tools, but

---

[341] Paul S. Price, "A Survey of the Story Elements of Isekai Manga", *Journal of Anime and Manga Studies* 2 (2021): 64.
[342] Levy, "Entering Another World", 107.
[343] Ibid, 93.
[344] Lu, "The Darker Sides", 29.
[345] LaMarre, *The Anime Machine*, ix and Cavallaro, *Anime Intersections*, xi.
[346] Poitras, "Contemporary Anime", 589 and LaMarre, *The Anime Machine*, ix.

then processed to look as if it were 2D".³⁴⁷ As a result, "a mix of digitally painted two-dimensional images and three-dimensional computer effects has become an accepted technique for producing anime".³⁴⁸ As Condry indicates, today's anime includes claymation, puppet animation, digitally simulated paper-cut animation, full three-dimensional computer graphics, and more.³⁴⁹

In 2000, original net animation (ONA), meaning Web anime, appeared with the release of *Azumanga Daioh*.³⁵⁰ The first full-length ONA series was *Magical Play* in 2002.³⁵¹ At this time, streaming services began to emerge.

The Rise of Streaming Services and Changes to the Otaku Community

Crunchyroll, one of the major anime streaming services, was established in 2006. While alternative forms of entertainment like video games and cell phones led to a decline in anime production around 2006,³⁵² with the rise of the internet and file sharing, anime has found platforms to increase its global presence after 2010.

The covid pandemic from 2020-2022 created a situation whereby online streaming platforms like Netflix overtook TV anime. Streaming platforms also began producing their original animations. For instance, in 2019, Netflix partnered with Production I.G. and Anima to produce *Ghost in the Shell: SAC_2045* and *Altered Carbon: Resleeved*.³⁵³ These platforms are increasing in popularity and introducing anime to a new wide range of audiences from around the world. Therefore, they have transformed anime from a niche to a more mainstream genre.

As the online circulation of anime "exploded",³⁵⁴ the advent of the internet and new digital platforms have also changed the interaction of the *otaku*

---

³⁴⁷ Clements, *Anime*, 450.
³⁴⁸ Poitras, "Contemporary Anime", 58-59.
³⁴⁹ Condry, *The Soul of Anime*, 89.
³⁵⁰ *Azumanga Daioh*: Directed by Fumiaki Asano with Screenplay by Kiyohiko Azuma (Aija-do Animation Works 2000). The Japanese title is a combination of the author's name Azuma and manga with *daioh* meaning "great king".
³⁵¹ *Magical Play*: Directed by Hiroki Hayashi with Screenplay by Hiroshi Ōnogi (AIC 2001-2002). The Japanese title is *Maho Yugi*. Cf. "History of Anime", wp.
³⁵² Yamaguchi, "The Evolution", wp.
³⁵³ *Ghost in the Shell: SAC_2045*: Directed by Kenji Kamiyama and Shinji Aramaki with Screenplay by Kenji Kamiyama based on the 1980s Japanese manga series *Ghost in the Shell* by Masamune Shirow (Netflix 2020-2022). The Japanese title is *Kōkaku Kidōtai: SAC_2045*. *Altered Carbon: Resleeved*: Directed by Takeru Nakajima and Yoshiyuki Okada with Screenplay by Dai Satō, Tsukasa Kondo based on the novel *Altered Carbon* by Richard K. Morgan and TV series *Altered Carbon* by Laeta Kalogridis (Anima 2020).
³⁵⁴ Mizuko, "Introduction", xxiv.

community. The demand for printed *otaku* magazines declined. For example, *Animage* started its online edition in 2007. The English version of *Newtype*, *Newtype USA*, ended its publication in 2008, along with *Anime Insider* in 2009 and *Shonen Jump* in 2012.

While the *otaku* community depended on conventions, Akihabara and media markets to circulate their works and to connect with peers in the previous decades,[355] online platforms have brought a revolution by expanding anime culture further than ever before. The internet allows *otaku* to create, archive and recirculate media content,[356] introduce their works to the *otaku* community worldwide, and participate in and discuss anime content with others transnationally.

Mizuko explains the change in the communication style of *otaku* as "transforming one-to-many broadcast model of communication to many-to-many and peer-to-peer communication", and says that "arming with personal digital media and plugged into the end-to-end architecture of the internet, *otaku* have truly found their medium".[357]

As the internet and digital platforms have helped transform watching anime into a mainstream behavior for general audiences, "*otaku* culture transformed from a niche subculture to a ubiquitous and profitable market".[358]

The Internet, YouTube, AniTubers and VTubers

The internet has affected all sorts of *otaku* activities. For example, in the 1980s and 1990s, the main method of distributing *doujinshi* (a self-published work derived from existing anime or manga) among *otaku*s was *doujinshi* conventions such as Comiket. But nowadays, digital media, especially YouTube, have boosted *doujinshi* works and opened the way for the emergence of more *doujinshi* creators.

Fansubbing (fans providing subtitles for anime) also benefitted from the internet. The internet has allowed fansubbing and scanlation (fan translation of manga) to spread more than ever and increased collaboration for fansubbing worldwide. Even online fansubbing communities emerged, and digisubbers organize "highly disciplined volunteer work teams that translate, subtitle, and distribute anime episodes to millions of fans around the world".[359]

---

[355] Ibid., xviii.
[356] Levy, "Entering Another World", 91.
[357] Mizuko, "Introduction", xviii.
[358] Garner, "The Digital Otaku", 14 and 24.
[359] Mizuko, "Introduction", xxv.

History of Anime

Besides, anime music videos (AMVs), fan-made music videos by adding clips from anime, have also emerged with the help of the internet and online platforms such as AnimeMusicVideos.org and YouTube.

YouTube has played a particularly important role in these activities. For Garner, YouTube presents "an integral medium for the reinvention of *otaku* culture, providing a setting suited for the circulation of anime and the communal negotiation of cultural meanings through video invention".[360] With the help of YouTube, anime has reached a wider audience, generated "a community of inventors who create, share, and remix digital compositions", and permitted *otaku* "to invent meaning and fluid, cross-cultural identities".[361] YouTube has become one of the centers for fan critics to share their evaluations of anime works. AniTubers are YouTube creators who emerged to focus on anime, anime-related works, and review anime films and series.[362]

Virtual Youtubers (VTubers) arose with the advent of virtual reality. VTubers feature content similar to AniTubers. But they use animated 2D/3D virtual anime avatars with anime-character-style appearances, anime facial expressions and "anime-esque bodily gestures". The avatars make audience to feel that as if they are directly engaging and interacting with their favorite anime characters.[363] This "embodies" otaku for otaku in anime. VTubers have become popular not only in Japan but internationally as "an innovative cultural phenomenon" since 2016.[364] The first VTuber, Kizuna Ai, who has more than 3 million followers as of October 2022, was announced as the ambassador of the "Come to Japan" Campaign for U.S. citizens by the Japanese National Tourism Organization's New York Office in 2018. This honor shows the effect of VTubers on anime fans and *otaku* around the world.

---

[360] Garner, "The Digital Otaku", 17.
[361] Katelin Garner, "The Digital Otaku: Anime, Participatory Culture, And Desire" (Master Thesis: California State University, August 2019), 5 and 14.
[362] Cooper D. Barham, "9 Anime YouTubers Worth Watching", *Geeks UnderGrace* 16th October 2017: https://www.geeksundergrace.com/anime-cosplay/primer-anime-youtubers/" "Anituber" and *Urban Dictionary* 05th November 2018: https://www.urbandictionary.com/define.php?term=Anituber.
[363] Suan, "Virtual YouTubers", 187, 193 and Lu et al., "More Kawaii", 5.
[364] Zhicong Lu, Chenxinran Shen, Jiannan Li, Hong Shen and Daniel Wigdor, "More Kawaii than a Real-Person Live Streamer: Understanding How the Otaku Community Engages with and Perceives Virtual YouTubers", *Proceedings of the CHI Conference on Human Factors in Computing Systems* (CHI '21) in Yokohama Japan: https://dl.acm.org/doi/10.1145/3411764.3445660: 2 and 5; Stevie Suan, "Performing Virtual YouTubers: Acting Across Borders in the Platform Society", *Japan's Contemporary Media Culture*, 187.

Therefore, as Mizuko states, with the help of the internet, *otaku* culture has been "situated at a transnational confluence of social, cultural, and technological trends that are increasingly global in reach".[365]

Cool Japan as Global Soft Power

The Government of Japan's initiative "Cool Japan" was part of the larger background to the explosion of anime in the middle of this period. The Japanese government decided to become a global "soft power" by promoting itself through its cultural influence. "Cool Japan" was the unofficial slogan of the idea and the concept was developed in the "Cool Japan Proposal" in 2009.[366] Part of this included anime and manga, along with otaku. Of course, the project had financial interests at its heart. The initiative has attracted both acclaim and criticism.[367]

---

[365] Mizuko, "Introduction", xii.

[366] The concept was traced from 2002 by Douglas Gray, "Japan's Gross National Cool", *Foreign Policy* 11th November 2009: https://foreignpolicy.com/2009/11/11/japans-gross-national-cool/. According to the Cool Japan Proposal, and the Cool Japan Initiative Report, Cool Japan covers all aspects of contemporary Japanese culture from—subcultural products, such as manga, anime, characters and games—to traditional cultural heritage, such as Japanese traditional cuisines and commodities. In 2013 the Cool Japan Fund, a public-private fund, and in 2015 the Cool Japan Public-Private Partnership Platform was set up in order to commercialize the "Cool Japan" and increase overseas demand for Japanese products across a variety of areas, such as media and content, food and services, fashion and lifestyle, as well as tourism. In 2016, anime was included in the report entitled Content Industry Current Status and Direction of Future Development. The report said that overseas demand is to be captured under the government initiative in three stages: 1) creating a Japanese boom, 2) selling relevant products/services, and 3) encouraging foreign tourists to purchase products/services in Japan. See Cabinet Office Intellectual Property Headquarters, "Cool Japan Initiative": https://www.cao.go.jp/cool_japan/english/pdf/cooljapan_initiative.pdf; Cool Japan Movement Promotion Council, *Cool Japan Proposal*: https://www.cao.go.jp/cool_japan/english/pdf/published_document3.pdf; Cool Japan Fund, "What is Cool Japan Fund?": https://www.cj-fund.co.jp/en/about/cjfund.html and Ministry of Economy, Trade and Industry, "Content Industry Current Status and Direction of Future Development" (April 2016): https://www.meti.go.jp/english/policy/mono_info_service/content_industry/pdf/20160329001.pdf.

[367] Some initiatives of the Fund were seen as examples of the program's success such as investing in Sentai Filmworks and giving an emergency fund to keep businesses afloat during the COVID-19 pandemic. However, the Fund has also been criticized for "a lack of strategy, discipline which gives rise to unprofitable projects", and with that, "the policy fails to define what is meant by creative industry and is based on questionable data and anecdotal evidence". For example, Daisuki, a streaming service that the Cool Japan funded was taken over by Anime Consortium Japan and closed in August 2017.

The State of the Anime Industry in 2023

While anime products are diverse and change according to popular tastes and demands in all periods, anime's popularity has always grown despite ups and downs in the industry. Today, the main segments in the anime market are TV, film, online streaming, video (DVD/Blu-ray), as well as merchandising, music, amusement and live entertainment. According to the Anime Industry Report released by The Association of Japanese Animations (AJA), the industry continued growing in a straight between trajectory from 2010-2020, but the COVID-19 pandemic hit the industry like all others.[368] For AJA, the market size became 2.4 trillion yen (17.5 billion dollars) in 2020, 3.5% less than 2019, due to the effect of COVID-19.[369] Also, according to Grand View Research, the global market was valued at $23.56 billion US in 2020. At the beginning of the COVID-19 pandemic, productions in all segments, except for streaming platforms, were either suspended or postponed, but online streaming helped anime get through the pandemic, accounting for the majority of Japan's overseas sales.[370] It became "maybe the world's most COVID-resistant form of popular entertainment" in general.[371] The market size started to expand again

---

Asagaya Anime Street, a shopping strip supported by Cool Japan closed in 2019. The Fund is also criticized for not addressing the problems of anime production studios and the labor problems in the industry. See Eric Margolis, "Cool Japan Campaign at a Crossroads 10 Years After Setting Sights Abroad", *Japan Times* 31st May 2021: https://www.japantimes.co.jp/culture/2021/05/31/general/cool-japan-success/; Kim Morrissy, "In a Struggling Anime Workplace, 'Cool Japan' Feels Like a Joke", *Anime News Network* 04th September 2021: https://www.animenewsnetwork.com/feature/2021-09-04/in-a-struggling-anime-workplace-cool-japan-feels-like-a-joke/.176373; Saito Yuta, "Cool Japan Fund's Big Ambitions Mostly Fall Flat", *Nikkei* 06th November 2017: https://asia.nikkei.com/Business/Companies/Cool-Japan-Fund-s-big-ambitions-mostly-fall-flat?page=1; Christian Morgner, *Governance and Policy Development of Creative and Cultural Industries in Japan from* (Routledge Handbook of Cultural and Creative Industries in Asia Routledge: 2018), 48 and Morrissy, "In a Struggling Anime Workplace", wp.
[368] The Association of Japanese Animations, "Anime Industry Report 2021 Summary": https://aja.gr.jp/download/anime-industry-report-2021-summary, 2.
[369] Ibid.
[370] "Anime Market 2021-2028", *Grand View Research*, wp.; Sudo, "Anime Industry", wp. and Denison, *Anime*, "History, Industry and Anime Definition", olb.
[371] Patrick Brzeski, "How Japanese Anime Became the World's Most Bankable Genre", *Hollywood Reporter* 16th May 2022: https://www.hollywoodreporter.com/business/business-news/japanese-anime-worlds-most-bankable-genre-1235146810/.

in 2021 and was valued at $24.80 billion US that year.[372] When looking at global demand for anime, it grew 118% over between 2020-2022, making it one of the fastest-growing content genres by that metric during the pandemic.[373] During this period, increasing sales of anime content via application games and internet streaming platforms is likely to drive segment growth, and internet distribution is expected to register a higher compound annual growth rate (CAGR) of over 14.0% from 2021 to 2028.[374]

Merchandising also seems likely to continue dominating the market in the near future.[375] Since online streaming platforms both in Japan and abroad are demanding more anime projects than before, the sector is optimistic about the current and future state of the anime industry as major anime studios indicate that their production lines are fully booked for the next several years.[376]

Since the anime industry has significantly contributed to the economic growth of Japan, the anime market has always been highly competitive. Currently, there are approximately 622 studios engaged in developing anime content in Japan, with 542 located in Tokyo.[377] Key studios include Studio Ghibli, Toei Animation, Kyoto Animation, Madhouse, Sunrise, P.A. Works, Pierrot, Production I.G, Gonzo, and Bones. Although prominent studios dominate the industry, many anime firms sometimes cooperate on productions or are involved in single big projects.[378] This is because of the difficulty of creating full anime films, which Condry explains as a "collaborative creativity of anime".[379]

---

[372] "Anime Market Size, Share & Trends Analysis Report by Anime Type (T.V., Movie, Video, Internet Distribution, Merchandising, Music) by Region (MEA, Japan) and Segment Forecasts 2022-2030", *Grand View Research*: https://www.grandviewresearch.com/industry-analysis/anime-market#:~:text=b.-,The%20global%20anime%20market%20size%20was%20valued%20at%20USD%2024.80,USD%2026.89%20billion%20in%202022.

[373] "Demand for Anime Content Soars", *Parrot Analytics* 11th January 2022: https://wwwparrotanalytics.com/press/demand-for-anime-content-soars/.

[374] Ibid.

[375] "Anime Market 2021-2028", wp.

[376] Sudo, "Anime Industry", wp. The Association of Japanese Animations, "Anime Industry", 3.

[377] Ben Dooley and Hikari Hida, "Anime Is Booming. So Why Are Animators Living in Poverty?" *New York Times* 25th February 2021; "Anime Market 2021-2028", wp. and The Association of Japanese Animations, "Anime Industry", 8.

[378] Condry, *The Soul of Anime*, 7; Poitras, "Contemporary Anime", 64; "Anime Market 2021-2028", n.p. and Brenner, *Understanding Manga and Anime*, 17.

[379] Condry, *The Soul of Anime*, 7.

Although subcontracting anime production to other Asian countries, especially South Korea, dates back to the 1960s[380]—the anime wave in the 1900s and the 2008 global financial crisis—expanded this trend. Nowadays, the Japanese anime industry is increasingly outsourcing its production. The majority of frames are drawn in overseas studios, especially in South Korea, Thailand, India, China and the Philippines.[381] Even entire episodes are produced outside of Japan.[382] All these situations in the anime industry bring their own challenges and problems.

One of the most vital issues that has not been solved since the inception of the anime industry is labor conditions. The industry is famous for its hours-long low-wage abysmal working conditions. As animators, especially in-betweeners, stay at the bottom of the production process hierarchy, they are usually hired on piece-work contracts. Since drawing frames takes a considerable amount of time, piece-work contract works against them, resulting in more work and lower earnings. In fact, anime's problem with exploitative labor practices causes animators to struggle to survive on their salaries, inevitably leading to burnout and even suicide.[383] It is even more difficult for young animators to stay in the industry and have a steady career. According to The Animator Dormitory, about 90% of animators quit their jobs within three years due to being unable to cover even the minimum cost of

---

[380] According to Kim, subcontracted production in the Japanese anime industry "was encouraged by politico-economic factors that included location, diplomatic agreements, wage levels, and exchange rates, and then materialized by a Taylorist work organization that went along with technologies of celluloid animation". Joon Yang Kim, "South Korea and the Sub-Empire of Anime: Kinesthetics of Sub-Contracted Animation Production", in *Mechademia 9: Origins*, ed. Frenchy Lunning (Minneapolis: University of Minnesota Press, 2015), 91 and Suan, "Repeating Anime", 142.

[381] Laikwan Pang, *Creativity and Its Discontents: China's Creative Industries and Intellectual Property Rights Offenses* (Durham: Duke University Press, 2012), 170; Yoshitaka Mōri, "The Pitfall Facing the Cool Japan Project: The Transnational Development of the Anime Industry under the Condition of Post-Fordism", *International Journal of Japanese Sociology* 20.1 (2011): 30-42 and Hu, *Frames of Anime*, 138.

[382] For example, Toei established a subsidiary animation studio to handle in-between celluloids, backgrounds, and finishing in the Philippines since 1986. Today the company has done 70% of the animation, backgrounds and finishing projects for Toei. Toei Animation Co, "Toei Animation Phils" 26th December 2022: https://corp-toei--anim-co-jp.translate.goog/ja/company/affiliated_companies.html?_x_tr_sl=ja&_x_tr_tl=en&_x_tr_hl=en&_x_tr_pto=sc#a03; Suan, "Repeating Anime", 152, Hu, *Frames of Anime*, 5 and Kim, "South Korea", 93.

[383] Eric Margolis, "The Dark Side of Japan's Anime Industry", *Vox* 02nd July 2019: https://www.vox.com/culture/2019/7/2/20677237/anime-industry-japan-artists-pay-labor-abuse-neon-genesis-evangelion-netflix and Suan, "Repeating Anime", 151.

living, especially in Tokyo which is one of the most expensive cities to live in the world.[384] Another reason why the labor problems persist is "production committees". These are ad hoc coalitions of toy manufacturers, publishers and other companies that are created to finance each project.[385] They get a lot of the revenue but pay animation studios a set fee.[386] So even though anime productions and revenue have been increasing, the budget struggles remain the same. That means studios have to produce with low costs, including low wages for animators. Things have not improved with the advent of Netflix and Disney because they apply the Japanese industry practices in the production process.

The chronic labor problem and its effect on labor shortages are also causing companies to increasingly rely on outsourcing. Demands of online streaming platforms have even increased outsourcing since all episodes are usually finished before anime is released. All these bring three complications. First, labor costs offshore are even cheaper overseas than in Japan—which triggers, reinforces and strengthens Japanese animators' low-wage conditions—and increases the risk for the Japanese industry of losing its ability to cultivate new talent.[387] Second, while Japanese animators struggle, other Asian animators also struggle with low wages and a lack of recognition for their contribution to the anime business.[388] Third, since several animation companies have been merging and engaging in co-productions in other nations,[389] along with outsourcing, the production process has become "more and more decentralized and transforming the content of Japanese pop-culture products, slowly breaking the Japanese monopoly".[390] As MacWilliams says, "manga and anime

---

[384] "Low Wages in the Anime Industry", *YouTube*: https://www.youtube.com/watch?v=dZgQCAgRLC4&t=2s.

[385] "Japan's Animation Industry Failing to Cultivate Next Generation of Talent", *Nippon* 10th August 2017: https://www.nippon.com/en/currents/d00337/ and Dooley and Hida, "Anime Is Booming", wp.

[386] Dooley and Hida, "Anime Is Booming", wp.

[387] Morrissy, "In a Struggling Anime Workplace", wp. and Hu, *Frames of Anime*, 144.

[388] Kim indicates that "neighboring Asian animators and animation workers deserve to be recognized as having supported the animation boom in 1980s Japan and the 'anime' wave that started in the 1990s". Kim, "South Korea", 93.

[389] "Anime Market 2021-2028", wp.; Condry, *The Soul of Anime*, 7; Hu, *Frames of Anime*, 138; Cavallaro, *Anime Intersections*, 2; Brenner, *Understanding Manga and Anime*, 17 and Suan, "Repeating Anime", 142.

[390] İbrahim Akbaş, "A 'Cool' Approach to Japanese Foreign Policy: Linking Anime to International Relations", *Journal of International Affairs* 23.1 (2018): 112.

are no longer solely the provenance of Japanese artists", bringing into question the image of Japanese anime and the "purity of the art".[391]

Moreover, competition for anime has been increasing not just in Asia but globally. Seeing animation "as a key sector for the birth of a new national identity and for the cultural development", the Chinese government supported its own animation studios in 2006.[392] Lately, Chinese production companies have been paying Japanese studios large premiums to produce films for their domestic market.[393] Hong Kong has also been producing its own brand of anime, and South Korea has also developed its national animation industry.[394] The popularity rise of South Korean *manhwa* (a comic mainly influenced by Japanese manga) by way of online access has also threatened the Japanese anime business.[395] Webtoons (digitalized South Korean *manhwa*) quickly became mainstream with the 2020 partnership between Crunchyroll, an American anime streaming giant and Naver-Line Webtoon, a South Korean webtoon platform.[396] Even some Japanese studios such as Telecom Animation Film and MAPPA have started to produce anime adaptations of *manwa*, such as *Tower of God* and *God of High School*.[397]

---

[391] MacWilliams, "Introduction", 17.
[392] Vincenzo De Masi, "Discovering Miss Puff: A New Method of Communication in China", *KOME-An International Journal of Pure Communication Inquiry* 1.2 (2013): 44; Laikwan Pang, *Creativity and Its Discontents: China's Creative Industries and Intellectual Property Rights Offenses* (London: Duke University Press, 2012), 170; Pang, *Creativity*, 171. Pang says that major Chinese universities such as Beijing Film Academy, Communication University of China, and Renmin University of China established animation departments, following the government's agenda to improve animation industry in the country. However, since animation production is under the control of the Chinese government, it keeps affecting the creativity of animators which results in producing less competitive anime works.
[393] Dooley and Hida, "Anime is Booming", wp.
[394] Hu, *Frames of Anime*, 144 and Pang, *Creativity*, 170.
[395] Tomohiro Osaki, "South Korea's Booming 'Webtoons' Put Japan's Print Manga on Notice", *Japan Times* 05th May 2019: https://www.japantimes.co.jp/news/2019/05/05/business/tech/south-koreas-booming-webtoons-put-japans-print-manga-notice/.
According to Osaki, manhwa is even seen "emerging as a threat" for manga, and Japanese experts say that manhwa is "overshadowing the global presence of manga".
[396] D. J. Boyd, "Crunchyroll and the Webtoon-Image: Reterritorialising the Korean Digital Wave in Telecom Animation's Tower of God (2020) and MAPPA's The God of High School (2020)", in *Streaming and Screen Culture in Asia-Pacific*, eds. Michael Samuel and Louisa Mitchell (Palgrave Macmillan, Cham, 2022), 285.
[397] *Tower of God*: Directed by Takashi Sano with Screenplay by Erika Yoshida (Tokyo MX 2020-present). The Korean title is *Sin-ui Tap*. *God of High School*: Directed by Sunghoo Park with Screenplay by Kiyoko Yoshimura (Tokyo MX 2020).

In addition, Western animation and anime have fed each other for decades, so similar patterns can be found in both. The rise of anime-influenced Western animation in the 2000s led to disputes over the legitimacy of the "anime" designation. Besides, some referred to anime-influenced Western animation as "anime style". The success of *Avatar: The Last Air-Bender* led to an uptick in this discussion.[398] The rise of anime films and series produced by online streaming platforms, such as Disney and Netflix, also contributed to the dispute.[399] The main criterion, or sticking point, is that anime is considered a uniquely Japanese cultural art form.

As Suan indicates, all these developments show that anime is no longer dependent on Japan as a defining characteristic.[400] Increasing anime production in other Asian countries and similar products in the US will rival Japanese anime more and more in the near future. While the anime market continues to grow, intertwining the production process with the involvement of animators from different backgrounds and nationalities will both enrich and de-centralize anime. Therefore, the development of technology, globalization and the decentralization of anime will likely bring more challenges and debates in the near future. This brings us to our final point, which is the direction and future of anime both as products and industry wise.

Conclusion and the Future of Anime

Japanese animation has constantly been developing and transforming not only in terms of narratives and visuals, but also with regard to production, distribution and merchandising. Because of that, when looking at the history of anime, some questions arise about its future.

---

[398] *Avatar: The Last Air-Bender.* Directed by Michael Dante DiMartino and Bryan Konietzko (Nickelodeon 2005-2008). According to Bakonyi, what made *Avatar* different from previous animations that also had some anime effects is the storyline. More mature and complex narrative style and characters' traits of *Avatar* resemble anime, so it can attract not only children but also adults. It mixes both Western and anime style with its "Western-style character animation with a focus on squash and stretch, intense research, and use live-action footage for reference; and Japanese-style visual richness in color, background, camera movements and visual storytelling cues". It is produced by Nickelodeon, an American company, but since it was mostly done by Korean animation studios, the TV series helped Korean anime to be more recognized as well. Kat Bakonyi, "The Influence of Japanese Animation on Avatar: The Last Airbender", *the UCLA School of Film and TV.* https://www.academia.edu/16755745/The_Influence_of_Japanese_Animation_on_Avatar_The_Last_Airbender.
[399] Matt Schley, "The Push to Go Digital Opens New Doors for Anime", *Japan Times* 20th January 2020.
[400] Suan, "Repeating Anime", 147.

In the past, anime expanded and found a space for itself along alongside live-actions at a time when live-action provided limited visual spectacles about apocalyptic worlds, giant robots, etc. So, can anime still be appealing in an era in which every dream and an imaginative world can be created by special effects through CGI in live-action? Although no one can be certain, the answer may be "yes". Dreaming and drawing of dreams and endless imaginations is something that is quintessentially human. Also, as MacWilliams says, anime plays an increasingly important role in "shaping the collective imaginations, experiences, and feelings of people throughout the world".[401] Therefore, considering the increasing in video games and virtual reality nowadays, new developments and the advent of technology can only feed people's wondering about imaginary, virtual worlds, or other possible worlds. In that sense, anime can always appeal to people and it will continue doing so.

This is probably why *isekai* genre has dominated the industry over the last ten years. The problem is that it has increasingly employed repeated themes and characters, as well as cheap merchandising, has in turn raised questions of declining quality in the industry. It also has reinforced low-wage and pushing writers to produce easy-to-write *isekai* type stories that question creativity in anime. With the effect of digitalization and the *isekai* genre, the question becomes, has the creativity in anime reached its limits?

Since anime is not monolithic, Clements emphasizes that "new technologies, talents and tastes are less likely to destroy old structures than they are to create new ones alongside the former paradigms".[402] This may mean that anime is likely to continue to discover new approaches, new genres and expand and transform itself. However, it needs to be soon and the industry has to take more action toward new approaches and genres that bring a new boom in anime regarding themes, character styles and products. Otherwise, the industry appears to be increasingly destined to become a cycle of cliches that will harm the quality of anime and its appeal.

The current state of the anime industry raises other questions, too. Outsourcing, international cooperation and the rise of anime-style products raise the question of how Japanese is anime? Or has the product become diluted? Will anime still stay Japanese or become a "stateless" product, similar to its "stateless" themes and characters? Mizuko suggests that even though U.S. media producers have been implementing "anime-like styles and themes", Japan seems to be maintaining its role "as the central site of production for *otaku* cultural products".[403] However, whether we can claim

---

[401] MacWilliams, "Introduction", 5.
[402] Clements, *Anime*, 479.
[403] Mizuko, "Introduction", xix.

that anime is still fully Japanese when so much of it is mainly produced in other Asian countries—even though they are created by Japanese writers, directors and studios—is becoming increasingly challenging to say.

Suan asserts that since anime is created through repetition and the minor variation of anime-esque conventions, animators apply and reproduce these conventions regardless of their location and background.[404] Even "Chinese co-productions or anime made in China or South Korea (or elsewhere) are continuing this practice of citation".[405] Therefore, on one hand, these anime-esque performances "frees us from the bonds of national ownership" on the production side and make anime "stateless", on the other hand.[406] Anime is still, in a sense, Japanese because—"the anime-esque is so closely associated with Japan"—that it does not matter who makes it or where.[407] According to Tsugata and Pointon, although anime-esque brings standardization to anime by imposing certain drawings, production processes that include different anime workers from different backgrounds still constantly create "constant cross-pollination".[408] It is the same for different genres and types of work created in different countries, such as anime-style products. This means that while anime will continue to be associated with Japan, it will increasingly become more transnational, more decentralized, and therefore more "stateless". Even though its anime-esque conventions continue, themes and stories will be inspired by the imaginations of various animators from different backgrounds, regions and countries. There will be an increase in expanding cooperation and outsourcing between studios in the coming decades.

Another problem facing anime in the future is: How will the industry cultivate a new generation of young talents in Japan in the face of outsourcing, low wages and abysmal working conditions? Japan's continuing brain drain among the young and chronic labor shortages may cause a reduction in creativity, variety and quality anime.

While the number of women directors increased, such as Naoko Yamada and Sayo Yamamoto, the industry needs more voices and perspectives from women directors as well as animators to develop new anime genres and imagery.

In conclusion, the future of anime is bright. Despite challenges—including threats from internationalization— anime remains a distinctly Japanese cultural phenomenon supported by *otaku*.

---

[404] Suan, "Repeating Anime", 147.
[405] Ibid., 154.
[406] Ibid., 155.
[407] Ibid., 153.
[408] Susan Pointon, "Transcultural Orgasm as Apocalypse: Urotsukidoji: The Legend of the Overfiend", *WideAngle* 19.3 (1997): 44 and Tsugata, "A Bipolar Approach", 32.

Chapter 2

Spatial Trialectics and Indian Spiritual Philosophy in Tezuka's *Buddha* and Morishita's *Buddha: The Great Departure*

A. P. Anupama
VIT-AP University

Amar Ramesh Wayal
VIT-AP University

ABSTRACT: Contriving a built environment requires a complex trialectic relationship between the physical, social and hybrid spaces where humans interact at different scales. These assorted spaces configure a mind-body dualism synchronous with the associated symbols and images. This article aims to reformulate the thirdspace, propounded by Edward Soja, to form a Trialectic relationship between the first space (physical space), the second space (conceived space), and the third space (hybrid space). The third (hybrid space) is an amalgamation of mind and body, conscious and unconscious, the first and second spaces. In order to trace the development of the "thirdspace" of Edward Soja, it is pertinent to comprehend the three divisions of space put forth by Henri Lefebvre in his essay *The Production of Space*. From here, we will examine Osamu Tezuka's *Buddha*, a manga, and Kōzō Morishita's *Buddha: The Great Departure*, an animated historical spectacle based on Osamu Tezuka's *Buddha*, from the vantage point of "thirdspace". The purpose will be to elucidate an Indian spiritual philosophy that is demonstrably analogous with the hybrid space fabricated to transform the worlds we live in.

KEYWORDS: Anime, Buddhism, Physical Space, Social Space, Spiritualism, Thirdspace.

***

Introduction

When we think of religious epics, we tend to gravitate toward stories from the Bible, the Old Testament, the Ramayana and the Gospels. *Ramayana: The Legend of Prince Rama* (1992),[1] *My Last Day* (2011),[2] *Saint Young Men* (2006)[3] and *Manga Bible* (2006-2019)[4] are a few well-known Japanese animes that are similar to the Ramayana. They all deal with the stories of Rama and Jesus Christ.

Known as Japan's "god of manga"[5] or the "Walt Disney"[6] of Japan, Tezuka is a well-known Japanese manga writer and cartoonist who began writing Buddhist manga series in 1972. While his masterpiece, *Hi no Tori*,[7] is a multi-volume work focused on the human search for immortality blended with Japanese historical period dramas, Tezuka's *Buddha* is his own Japanese interpretation of the birth and travels of the Buddha.[8] Tezuka's cinematic visual style in animation, however, is what made his Buddha so popular among anime fans. He employed framing, juxtaposition, and even written sound effects to give print media a dynamic feel. He stated that "if manga was his bride, animation was his mistress". If so, this explains why he chose to divert such "massive energies into the affair".[9] Because of its cinematic visual appeal to the audience, Tezuka's *Buddha* was an experimental one that became a hit—not only in Japan—but also in India and the West.

Theory and Method for this Study

Even if research on Tezuka's *Buddha* has not been thoroughly examined, there are a few studies that should be singled out to demonstrate the applicability of the current study. Depending on the target audience, the surrounding situation, or the ideological goals, contemporary religious studies narratives have undergone numerous changes. Walker, in his article, "Buddha, Canonical

---

[1] *Ramayana: The Legend of Prince Rama*: Directed by Koichi Sasaki with Screenplay by Narendra Sharma et al. (Toei 1992).
[2] *My Last Day*: Directed and Screenplay by Barry Cook (Campus Crusade for Christ 2011).
[3] Hikaru Nakamura, *Saint Young Men* (Tokyo: Kodansha, 2006-present).
[4] Akin Akinsiku (text) and Ajinbayo "Siku" Akinsiku (art), *Manga Bible: From Genesis to Revelation* (New York: Penguin Random House, 2007).
[5] Benjamin Evan Whaley, "Drawing the Self: Race and Identity in the Manga of Tezuka Osamu" (Master's Thesis: Stanford University, 2007), 1.
[6] Paul L. Swanson, "Swanson Review of Tezuka Osamu Buddha", *Japanese Journal of Religious Studies* 31.1 (2004): 233-40.
[7] Osamu Tezuka, *Hi no Tori* (Various Publishers, 1958-1988). The Japanese title means "Bird of Fire" often translated into "phoenix".
[8] Tezuka Osamu Official, "Buddha", https://tezukaosamu.net/en/manga/434.html.
[9] Ada Palmer, "Film is Alive: The Manga Roots of Osamu Tezuka's Animation Obsession", *Academia.edu* (2009): https://www.academia.edu/5142140/Film_is_Alive_The_Manga_Roots_of_Osamu_Tezukas_Animation_Obsession.

Authority, and Remix Theory in the Study of Religion", used remix theory to show how it may be used to comprehend the ideas in religious traditions.[10] By rejecting Husserl's ego and emphasizing the significance of language, history and culture as mediators of meaning, Cruz investigated the idea of transcendence through Tezuka's manga series Buddha.[11]

In 2011, Kōzō Morishita made an anime of Tezuka's manga *Buddha*[12] called *Buddha: The Great Departure*.[13] This study intends to examine these works as a basis to explore how Indian spiritual philosophy has been rooted in the "thirdspace" of human beings. The transformation is mainly vested on the social space of both the works on the same subject. We argue that they distinctly draw the relationship among first, second and third spaces.

1) The First Space is the mythological representation of Buddha's birth and life;

2) The Second Space is the social space surrounding Buddha's growth and spiritual transformation and;

3) The Third (Lived) Space is the cognitive outcome of the anime.

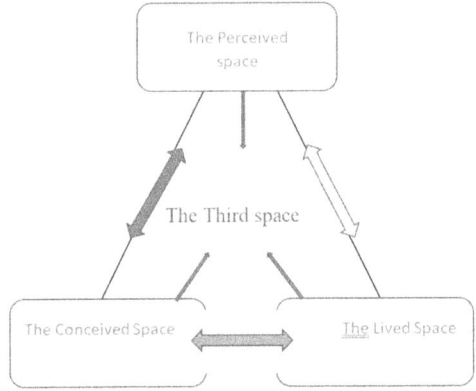

Figure 2.1. The Tripartite Relationship Between the Three Spaces. Source Domingues, et. al, 39.

---

[10] Seth M. Walker, "Osamu Tezuka's *Buddha*, Canonical Authority, and Remix Theory in the Study of Religion", *Journal of the American Academy of Religion* 90.2 (2022): 431-49.
[11] Noelle Leslie Dela Cruz, "Transcendence in Osamu Tezuka's Buddha: Reading Manga through Paul Ricoeur's Hermeneutic Phenomenology", *Academemia.edu*: https://www.academia.edu/16909125/Transcendence_in_Osamu_Tezuka_s_Buddha_Reading_Manga_through_Paul_Ricoeur_s_Hermeneutic_Phenomenology.
[12] Osamu Tezuka, *Buddha* (London: HarperCollins, 2006).
[13] *Buddha: The Great Departure*. Directed by Kozo Morishita with Screenplay by Reiko Yoshida (Toei Animation 2011).

Basic Plot and Storyline of the Manga-Anime

Tezuka's eight-volume manga series of *Buddha* ran from 1972-1983. He based his manga on the tradition of Buddha. Tezuka mixes a blend of adventure and spectacle that helps the audience to understand the journey from the historical circumstances of misery in the world to a spiritual transformation as Buddha. The story begins in ancient India. People are tormented by poverty, drought and caste oppression. But they have happily gathered for the birth of their young prince Siddhartha. Later in life, Siddhartha's frustration with life and circumstances caused him to embark on a spiritual journey. While on this journey, he becomes "enlightened", or the Buddha.

The anime version opens with the birth of Siddhartha, the prince of Shakya who, according to the declaration of an ascetic monk, is destined to become "the king of the world". The anime follows the transformations that have taken place in the life of Siddhartha in the due course of life. As he grows up, he begins to question his life and the teachings of Brahmins. After witnessing the death of a classmate, he questions the reason for his death and the life after death. During his journey of spiritual enlightenment, Siddhartha meets a lower caste girl Migaila, who encourages him to travel from inside of the palace to the outer world in order to see the disease, hunger, poverty and the harsh realities faced by the poor and low caste people. The film ends with a low caste figure, Chapra, who meets prince Siddhartha in war, and ends up changing their fates.

The Tripartite Relationship of Space in Manga and Anime: Unveiling Its Intersections

"Every society produces its own space according to its mode of production".[14] The idea of space in *Buddha* is essentially occupied by visual images and holds social space third which is animated by gestures and actions of those who inhabit it. Tezuka reminds us of the basic fact that the space occupied by Siddhartha has an interior as well as an exterior. This, in turn, goes hand in hand with the tripartite relationship of space propounded by Lefebvre. This means that there is "an architectural space defined by the inside-outside

---

[14] Silke Kapp and Anna Paula Baltazar, "Out of Conceived Space: For Another History of Architecture", Paper Presented at the *Proceedings of Spaces of History/Histories of Space: Emerging Approaches to the Study of the Built Environment, University of California, Berkeley, 30th April and 01st May 2010:* https://escholarship.org/uc/item/30d070b0 and Derek Gregory, et al., eds., The Dictionary of Human Geography (Wiley-Blackwell, 2009): 698.

relationship, a space which is a tool for the architect in his social action".[15] The "reading" of space is thus merely a secondary and practically irrelevant upshot, a rather superfluous reward to the individual for blind, spontaneous and lived obedience.[16] When we think about space, the three divisions that come to mind are the physical, the social and the mental.

So in *Buddha* and its adaptation *Buddha: The Great Departure*, the practices of space emerge from the birth of Siddhartha, which may be the perceived space arising out of the experiences of Tezuka. The different characters modify and appropriate these spaces—so that the spiritual transformation of Siddhartha into Buddha (which is the conceived space)—meets with the lived space in the audience watching the manga and anime. Thus, one can say that there is a construction of the spaces, re-signification of spaces, and finally there is a production of the experiences.[17]

Figure 2.1: exemplifies the tripartite relationship between the three spaces and the unfolding of the "third space". It is evident from the model that the spaces are in cyclic form. It begins with the perceived space, which includes the spatial practices of production and reproduction. The perceived space advances to the conceived space and ends in lived space, which is an amalgamation of both the perceived and conceived spaces. All the three spaces create a dialectical tension between them to arrive at the next stage of understanding. The perceived space of the anime narrates the epic story of Siddhartha, where the audience analyzes the story directed by the director.

The perceived space actually begins with a monk from the upper Brahmin prophesying that one-day, Siddhartha will become the enlightened one. The birth of Siddhartha can be theorized in the words of Lefebvre:

> Nature appears as the vast territory of births. "Things" are born, grow and ripen, wither and-die. The reality behind these words is infinite. As it deploys its forces, nature is violent, generous, niggardly, bountiful, and above all open. Nature's space is not staged. To ask why this is so is a strictly meaningless question: a flower does not know that it is a flower any more than death knows upon whom it is visited. If we are to believe the word "nature", with its ancient metaphysical and theological

---

[15] Henri Lefebvre, *The Production of Space*, trans. Donald Nicholson-Smith (Cambridge: Blackwell, 1991), 129.
[16] Ibid., 143.
[17] Fabiana Florio Domingues, Letícia Dias Fantinel and Marina Figueiredo, "Between the Conceived and the Lived, The Practice: The Crossing of Spaces at the Arts and Crafts Fair of Namorados Square in Vitoria/ES, Brazil", *Organizations & Society* 26, 88 (2019): 39.

credentials, what is essential occurs in the depths. To say "natural" is to say spontaneous.[18]

The spontaneous nature of earth has been exemplified through the prophesy of the Brahmin. But Siddhartha was born into an age when caste discrimination dwells upon the kingdom of Kapilavastu. Growing up like the first song of Suddhodana, he is quite apathetic about his life and the privileges he enjoys. However, he meets Tatta, a child thief. She comes from the lowest caste but changes Siddhartha's life. In keeping with Lefebvre, the significance of this perceived space is that it is the material understanding of the space and which requires a body to construct and produce the life to the story. He states that "spatial practice, as the process of producing the material form of social spatiality, is thus presented as both medium and outcome of human activity, behavior and experience".[19]

Along the way, the story also gets entangled with the previously mentioned Chapra, another young boy from the Shudra caste. He escapes from his fate by saving the life a Kosalan, who later adopted him as the son. He considers himself to be an orphan warrior and resides with the Kosalan general. Siddhartha's acquaintance with Tatta causes him to see the world beyond the palace walls. This leads him to a life-changing experience. The perceived space takes Siddhartha to the conceived world—where though he has already been unhappy with the caste system—he is confronted with the human realities of disease and death. These harsh realities compel him on a spiritual journey, leaving behind his wife, Yashodhara and young child. Hence at the age of twenty-nine, Siddhartha decides to become a monk, cuts his hair, wears saffron clothes and enters into the conceived space, which is an amalgamation of the social space. The society (social space) is the outcome of several aspects, such as

> signifying and non-signifying, perceived and directly experienced, practical and theoretical. In short, every social space has a history, one invariably grounded in nature, in natural conditions that are at once primordial and unique in the sense that they are always and everywhere endowed with specific characteristics.[20]

In other words, a conceived space is "a place for the practices of social and political power; in essence, it is these spaces that are designed to manipulate

---

[18] Lefebvre, *Production of Space*, 70.
[19] Ibid., 66.
[20] Ibid., 222.

those who exist within them".²¹ The characters Tatta and Chapra add feelings of caste into the mind of Siddhartha to reach the lived space. The socially conceived space incorporates the actions of both the individuals and the collective of all who are born and die, suffer and act. The socially constructed space makes reference to Buddhist concepts like Samsara, rebirth and death. Samsara literally translates to "wandering on". According to Buddha, people have been travelling in a space where birth, death and rebirth are intertwined. This constant movement between places is comparable to a process in which a soul is born into a body, lives there, dies there, and is then reincarnated into another body. Three attributes of existence—impermanence, suffering and self—are used by Buddhists to describe samsara, which makes it easier to understand how it works.

Nothing in life is permanent, and impermanence teaches us this. If we accept this, we can put an end to our suffering. Similar to this, in order to overcome pain, one must give up all self-attachments and adopt the concept of no-self.²² When we accept these ideas, samsara recurs until we achieve nirvana, at which point we are guided to be reincarnated. According to Buddhism, this rebirth entails a person's deeds (*karma*) that cause them to experience samsara, a new existence after death. In adhering to the Buddhist doctrine of life, the social space in the anime educates us that "one could live in one's life but not be controlled and suffer by one's attachment to the things of that life and, when one died, one was not reborn but attained the liberation of the spiritual state of nirvana".²³

Chapra and Tatta have been interwoven into the narrative and changed the fabric of the story. Chapra and his mother have been rescued from bondage by the little boy Tatta. Tatta has the ability to send his soul into another living entity—so that he can see things through the eyes of an eagle—and has the power to travel great distances in the body of a horse. This interjection of perceived space and conceived space creates a dialectical tension in the audience as they witness the history of Buddha through the narration of Tezuka. Moreover, the period is mysterious to the common man. But as the story progresses, the audience will come to know how the conceived space becomes a symbol of class struggle, violence and categorical rejection. In view of the fact that,

---

[21] Ibid.
[22] Irene Jue, "Ralph Waldo Emerson: From Buddhism to Transcendentalism, the Beginning of an American Literary Tradition" (Bachelor's Thesis: California Polytechnic State University, 2013), 3.
[23] Joshua J. Mark, "Buddhism", *World History Encyclopaedia*: https://www.worldhistory.org/buddhism/.

every space is already in place before the appearance in it of actors; these actors are collective as well as individual subjects inasmuch as the individuals are always members of groups or classes seeking to appropriate the space in question. This pre-existence of space conditions the subject's presence, action and discourse, at the same time as they presuppose this space, also negate it. The subject experiences space as an obstacle, as a resistant "objectality" at times as implacably hard as a concrete wall, being not only extremely difficult to modify in any way but also hedged about by Draconian rules prohibiting any attempt at such modification.[24]

The characters Tatta and Chapra are representatives of caste driven society—both as collective and individual subjects—and they have thrown the space into question. This space has been subject to class and caste conflicts. At one-point Chapra rescues General Budai of Kosala—whose army was destroyed in a battle—and rises up as the adopted son of Budai. Eventually, he takes charge of the Budai's army and confronts Siddhartha. Chapra strives to escape poverty. This gives the anime the touch of both adventure and historical representation. It was his hard work that has taken him to stature in the military.

A parallel is the amalgamation of perceived and conceived space when Siddhartha falls in love with a low-caste beggar. But when the three—Siddhartha, Tatta and Chapra meet face to face on the battlefield—"it comes with a sad note of resignation towards the tragic ways that mankind's nature draws us together and connects us, only to cut the ties apart just when we seem to be at the point of reconciliation".[25]

Though the conceived space of Tatta is slightly misrepresented in the story, it provides us with a good example of how the social space links between humans and all other forms of life end up using and misusing the other. Toward the end of the film, we see Tatta deciding to take revenge for his mother's death. Despite Siddhartha's attempts to convince him, he is unable to forgive the Kosalans for killing his mother. After seeing the tragedy of Tatta and the caste system, Siddhartha decides to become a monk at the age of twenty-nine, leaving behind his wife and child. The social space of Siddhartha interpenetrates and superimposes themselves upon one another—to attain the lived space, which is the space of mental experience—where Siddhartha

---

[24] Lefebvre, "Production of Space", 58.
[25] Bob Clark, "Every Saga Has a Beginning: Osamu Tezuka and Kozo Morishita's 'Buddha: The Great Departure'", *Wonders in the Dark* 09th July 2011: https://wondersinthe dark.wordpress.com/2011/07/09/every-saga-has-a-beginning-osamu-tezkua-and-kojo-morishits-buddha-the-great-departure/.

Spatial Trialectics and Indian Spiritual Philosophy 69

attains spiritual salvation. The real cause behind this is that "social spaces interpenetrate one another and/or superimpose themselves upon one another. They are not things which have mutually limiting boundaries and which collide because of their contours or as a result of inertia".[26]

Siddhartha's spiritual transformation starts from his meetings with Dhepa and Asaji. Dhepa is a non-Brahmin monk whose philosophy is that humans are meant to be always tolerated. He burns out one of his eyes in order to join Tatta. But Siddhartha befriends Dhepa—even though Dhepa finds Siddhartha's teachings absurd—and ridicules them. Asaji is a child whom Siddhartha met during his spiritual transformation. One day while meditating under a Papal tree, Siddhartha gained spiritual enlightenment and renamed Buddha ("Enlightened One"). Afterward, he started teaching others about his path to enlightenment. Thus, the major difference between conceived social space and lived space is the change in life experience.

> . . . . (social) space is not a thing among other things, nor a product among other products: rather it subsumes things produced, and encompasses their interrelationships in their coexistence and simultaneity—their (relative) order and/or (relative) disorder. It is the outcome of a sequence and set of operations, and thus cannot be reduced to the rank of a simple object.[27]

Lived space is the space of mental and spiritual awakening. It is produced when Siddhartha identifies the meaning of his life by finding out the interrelationships and co-existence of his birth and life, mind and body, conscious and unconscious, real and imagined on this earth. Living space, as in the words of Lefebvre, is Buddha's place of experimentation in human life which is "alive and it speaks".[28] Despite being constant, the subjects' engagement and enlightenment with world events, his or her spatial presence, ambiguities, inconsistencies and conflicts occur in his or her daily life. Such exchanges produce dynamics that are not neutral but instead expose the will, interests and perspectives of the persons in his immediate vicinity.

Thirdspace: Situating the Indian Spiritual Philosophy of Buddha

Edward Soja contests that the social space can be seen as "simultaneously real and imagined, concrete and abstract, material and metaphorical".[29] It is here

---

[26] Lefebvre, "Production of Space", 87.
[27] Ibid., 73.
[28] Ibid., 42.
[29] Edward Soja, *Thirdspace Journeys to Los Angeles and Other Real-and-Imagined Places* (Oxford: Blackwell Publishing, 1996), 65.

that the core notion of thirdspace arises. The thirdspace moves beyond the dialectics. The thirdspace is not, in fact, a dialectical rejection but more of an interpretation of space or more of acceptance and a way of seeing them as interconnected. In thirdspace, we can see how the spiritual teachings of Buddha have changed the characters and developed them into as true humans. Soja states that this space is seen by Lefebvre as "both as distinct from the other two spaces and encompassing them".[30] This space is referred to as that which is "directly lived" and inhabited by those who aim to decipher and "actively transform the worlds we live in".[31] The social practices in space develop as a result of the involvement of the subjects, that is "as the outcome of their sensations and of their corporality in relation to the experience of the environment".[32]

Indian spiritual philosophy is deeply rooted in the ancient philosophical and religious traditions of the land. It arises out of human inquiry into the mysterious existence of life and death. Indian sages called "rishis" or "seers" developed the practice of spiritual journeys which delve deep into finding truths about nature and the universe. Thus, while philosophy provided a correct view of reality and vision of life, religion brought about the fulfilment and correct way of life. In short, if philosophy is theory then religion is practice. Thus, in ancient India, philosophy and religion often complement each other.[33] The Indian spiritual practices which Buddha attained before reaching the thirdspace can be categorized as the following.

1) Meditation (perceived space) by which the mind could be calmed where there exists a conflict between the perceived and conceived space before attaining serenity

2) Asceticism (conceived space) means the testing of one's physical body by arduous tasks

3) Awakening, where he entered a state of mind in which he could recall his past lives and understand what kept him and others tied to the cycle of rebirth.

---

[30] Ibid., 67.
[31] Ibid.
[32] Timon Beyes and Chris Steyaert, "Spacing Organization: Non-Representational Theory and Performing Organizational Space", *Organization* 19.1 (2011): 51.
[33] National Institute of Open Schooling, "Religion and Philosophy in Ancient India" (Indian Culture and Heritage Secondary Course), https://www.nios.ac.in/media/documents/SecICHCour/English/CH.08.pdf, 111-26.

The "thirdspace" evolves out of these three, which is noted for the spiritual teachings of Buddha for the betterment of society. On a philosophical and existential level, the judicial abuse caste system felt by the people caused them to question the institution of Hinduism. It taught that there was only one supreme being and that is Brahmins. They claim to have created the Universe. They took complete hold of divine order and maintained it. But Buddha taught that human soul is immortal and the goal of life is to perform one's *karma* which should be in accordance with one's *dharma*. This had the purpose of breaking from the cycle of rebirth and death and attaining a complete reunion with the oversoul.

Japanese culture is renowned for incorporating Buddhist beliefs into conventional mythology, movies and anime. Karma, Buddhism's central concept, describes how deliberate actions bind us to reincarnation in Samsara and how we can escape Samsara by following the Buddhist Path. The concept of self is founded in Zen philosophy at the level of the unity of body and soul. Buddhists hold that the above-soul, or super-soul, is a part of the over-soul. The human soul still preserves its innate purity because the oversoul is the purest. Similar to the most pure or most complete thing, it may protect us from all the challenges, doubts, shams and flaws of the worldly life.

Soja's "Thirdspace" represents "a dynamic realm in which established binaries/dualisms that dominate our contemporary cultural understanding (such as subject/object, social/historical, center/margin, real/imagined, material/mental) are reworked in an effort to open up other possibilities for understanding".[34] He states that the thirdspace does not combine but it transforms into a new identity, which is the self of the individual. In *Buddha*, we could see the transformations of several characters under the spiritual teachings of Buddha. According to Soja,

> [T]hirding is much more than a dialectical synthesis; it introduces a critical "other-than" choice that speaks and critiques through its otherness.... It does not derive simply from an additive combination of its binary antecedents but rather from a disordering, deconstruction, and tentative reconstitution of their presumed totalization producing an open alternative that is both similar and strikingly different.[35]

This otherness is the journey of self-realization or *moksha*. *Buddha* ends with the spiritual reincarnation of many souls, including Dhepa, Asaji, Sujatha, Devadatta and Vishaka. Dhepa ridicules Buddha's teachings and even

---

[34] Soja, *Thirdspace Journeys*, 5.
[35] Ibid., 61.

attempts to kills Buddha at one point. But Buddha saves him on another occasion and finally, he becomes his disciple. Asaji, another discipline of Buddha, once catches a fever after pursuing a group of monks during the monsoon season. Buddha saves him by sucking the pus from his body. Buddha taught all his disciples that man's duty is to seek liberation from the spiritual world. He taught his followers "the realization of four noble truths".

1) Suffering in human life;
2) Cause of suffering;
3) Cessation of suffering, and
4) The path of liberation from these sufferings.

Point 4 has helped them to do justice to their own identity. The characters could construct a new relationship with their own self and with the world. The third space self is one in which the characters find comfortable with the change when they adapt, shape and see life beyond from the perspectives of the common man. These constructions of self-reveals that there occurs a gathering together of the various dichotomies of a person's identity and by juxtaposing those elements, one is better in understanding the relationships between them and how those relationships contribute to the person's "third space self".

Conclusion

Hear what enlightens our brains, perceive divinity, and experience God's presence inside us. When our entire being serves the Almighty, we will experience eternal tranquility within ourselves. This suggests that within the third space lies not only the reimagining of structures but also a more radical movement, and one has to find it out in the due course of life through the process of "thirding". The paper articulates that manga and anime's third space exemplifies Indian spiritual philosophy by urging righteous living, detachment from world illusions, and merging with the Divine, the ultimate reality.

Chapter 3

Metamodernity, American Transcendentalism and Transhumanism in Japanese Anime

Steven Foertsch
Baylor University

ABSTRACT: Recent theorists of cultural studies have noticed the emergence of metamodernity as an ideal type, categorized by an oscillation between postmodern deconstructivism and modern idealism, into a form of transcendentalism. I argue in this chapter that this type of transcendentalism, informed by the historical American Transcendentalist Movement, is the emerging ideal called "Transhumanism". I use a case study of five Japanese anime to demonstrate how transhumanist, metamodernist, and transcendental thinking often recur in key core plot points and narratives found within. I further suggest that meditation on the major themes in these anime, especially those of metamodernity and transhumanism, is necessary if we are to understand our place in the world today and into the future.[1]

KEYWORDS: American Transcendentalism, Anime, Ergo Proxy, Hegemony, Metamodernity, Meta-Subjectivity, Neon Genesis Evangelion, Psycho-Pass, Serial Experiments Lain, Sword Art Online, Transcendentalism, Transhumanism.

***

Introduction

Anime, or Japanese television and film animation, is rich with examples of transhumanist thinking. Mostly found in the science fiction genre, these

---

[1] My thanks to Harrison S. Jackson, Xin Wang, Shuhan Wang, Heewon Yang and the anonymous reviewers for reading and offering suggestions to improve this manuscript. Finally, I'm grateful to all my friends who watched anime with me over the years.

examples of metamodernist transcendental imagination often are pervaded by an undertone of dystopian reality, an enslavement of the subjective self in favor of the emerging collective individuation, and a rapture from the human condition.

While many may think of *The Matrix* as the seminal example of this major thrust in the popular imagination, it appears as though Japanese culture has been an early adopter of a critical stance towards utopian technocracy—which is largely headed by the technofascist social-engineering class universal—to the statist world hegemony (called by some algorithmic governmentality).[2]

While transcendental thinking has been explored at length through literature related to the American Transcendentalist Movement, and its logical predecessor in European Romanticism, there is a new emerging transcendental epistemology. This new type of extremely transcendental logic has developed in relation to syncretic East/West international culture and manifests metamodernist idealistic incarnations of the neoliberal world order. I argue that this unique type of transcendental thinking is found at the syncretic core of the metamodern popular culture and mass media (hegemony)—through pop culture (e.g. anime), the internet and virtual reality—as reflected in Japanese culture. I will use a case study of five anime to demonstrate this. Transhumanism is the best term to capture the essence of these ideas reflected in these anime.

Transhumanism

There is undoubtedly a rich historical background influencing the contemporary discourse surrounding the term "transhumanism". I define "transhumanism" as "the aspiration of a socio-ontological bodily human individual to a state of transcendence through technological advancement". This type of thinking is not new to human epistemology.[3] Indeed, it was quite prevalent in Renaissance humanist ideology, Pietist discourse in Early Modern Swabia (which influenced Hegel[4]), the pursuit of secular reason and human advancement in the Enlightenment, the early Industrial Revolution and the Luddite movement (negative example), early 2000s social engineering, otaku

---

[2] Antoinette Rouvroy, "La Gouvernementalité Algorithmique: Radicalisation et Stratégie Immunitaire du Capitalisme et du Néolibéralisme?", *La Deleuziana* 3 (2016), 30-36; Fatemeh Savaedi and Maryam Alva Nia, "<null> me <null>: Algorithmic Governmentality and the Notion of Subjectivity in Project Itoh's Harmony", *Journal of Science Fiction and Philosophy* 4 (2021): 1-19.
[3] David Noble, *The Religion of Technology* (New York: Alfred A Knopf, 1997).
[4] Glenn Alexander Magee, *Hegel and the Hermetic Tradition* (Ithaca: Cornell University Press, 2001).

culture (reality as a large database).[5] Nothing new here, only a *new application*. In this contemporary metamodernist epistemology, AI, alternate or virtual reality, internet culture and computer programming are emphasized as the vessel by which the human epistemology is taken into a "higher" plane of reality.

The first terminological innovations broaching the topic of transhumanism, such as "posthumanism", were explored in the Josiah Macy Foundation conferences on cybernetics held in New York City from 1946-1953.[6] The term "transhumanism" itself was coined in 1957 by Julian Huxley, who focused on "realizing the inherent potentialities in man".[7] This terminology was later taken up by philosophers such as Bostrom, More, Vita-More and Kurzweil, who sought to define an all-encompassing epistemology.[8] Operating under the framework of "Humanity Plus" (or H+) and "Extropy", they, among others, founded the World Transhumanist Association in 1998.[9] They then released the "Transhumanist Statement" in several iterations. They rewrote it twice after its initial release in 1998, once in 2008, and once more in 2020.[10] Emphases of these manifestos and their associated framework are the extensions of the human lifespan artificially, the eradication of disease, the elimination of suffering, the augmentation of human intellectual, physical and emotional capabilities, space colonization, and super intelligent machines, among others.[11]

There are certainly many critics of this perspective, including philosophers such as Francis Fukuyama and Hava Tirosh-Samuelson. Many cite the inherent threat transhumanism poses to egalitarianism, existential security

---

[5] Azuma Hiroki, *Otaku: Japan's Database Animals* (Minneapolis: University of Minnesota Press, 2009).
[6] Hava Tirosh-Samuelson, "Transhumanism as a Secular Faith", *Zygon* 47.4 (Hoboken: Wiley, 2012): 710-34.
[7] Julian Huxley, "Transhumanism", *Ethics in Progress* 6.1 (2015): 12-16.
[8] Nick Bostrom, "Transhumanist Values", in *Ethical Issues for the 21st Century*, ed. Frederick Adams. (Charlottesville: Philosophical Documentation Center Press, 2003), 1-12; Max More, "The Overman in the Transhuman", *Journal of Evolution and Technology* 21.1 (2010): 1-4 and Natasha Vita-More, "Transhumanist Art Statement", *Transhumanist Art* 01st January 1982: https://web.archive.org/web/19980523093459/http://www.extropic-art.com/transart.htm.
[9] Gregory R. Hansell and William Grassie, eds., *H± Transhumanism and Its Critics* (Philadelphia: Metanexus Institute, 2011).
[10] Natasha Vita-More, "The Transhumanist Manifesto", *Humanityplus.org*. (2020): https://www.humanityplus.org/the-transhumanist-manifesto . They renamed it from "statement" to "manifesto".
[11] Bostrom, "Transhumanist Values".

and democratic idealism.[12] They also criticize the project as one seeking to reproduce naïve Enlightenment values of universal rationalization, including utilitarianism. They also point out the contradictory nature of the epistemology itself, e.g., critical cultural transhumanists vs. technologic posthumanists.[13]

Transhumanism is undoubtedly an eschatological epistemology that sees itself as humanity's only hope. However, by unleashing the pandora's box of technological advancement, our species has little choice—but to try to get ahead of it and control the implicit chaos—before it inevitably destroys us (what Verdoux calls "rational capitulationism").[14] There is also little doubt that the ethical underpinnings of this epistemology are hinged on a distinctly utilitarian logic, which has been suggested to be deeply flawed by many thinkers, e.g., Nietzsche thought this was a "slave morality".[15] Finally, transhumanism seems to have a latent fatalism to it—for all its hope for humanity—it is largely an epistemology of fear. The moral urgency of saving lives seems to outweigh any cost—and this is the same type of rhetoric used to justify the War on Terror or the Patriot Act—as well as countless other human rights abuses across history.[16]

Regarding my own perspective, this chapter owes large inheritance to the poststructuralist thinkers of the last five decades, such as Foucault, Derrida, Habermas, Herman and Chomsky, Deleuze and Guattari, among others.[17] They inevitably have a negative view of any ideal, such as transhumanism.

---

[12] Cf. Francis Fukuyama, "Transhumanism", *Foreign Policy* 144 (2004): 42-43; Philippe Verdoux, "Transhumanism, Progress and the Future", *Journal of Evolution and Technology* 20.2 (2009): 49-69 and James Hughes, "Contradictions from the Enlightenment Roots of Transhumanism", *Journal of Medicine and Philosophy* 35.6 (2010): 622-40.

[13] Cf. Tirosh-Samuelson, "Transhumanism as a Secular Faith", 710-34 and Hughes, "Contradictions from the Enlightenment Roots of Transhumanism", 622-40.

[14] Verdoux, "Transhumanism, Progress and the Future", 49-69. Cf. the ethical and pragmatic dilemmas of this predicament in William H. U. Anderson, ed., *Technology and Theology* (Wilmington: Vernon Press, 2020).

[15] Stefan Lorenz Sorgner, "Nietzsche the Overman, and Transhumanism", *Journal of Evolution and Technology* 20.1 (2009): 29-42.

[16] Bostrom, "Transhumanist Values".

[17] Michel Foucault, *Discipline and Punish*, trans. Alan Sheridan (New York: Random House, 1991); Jacques Derrida, *Rogues* (Stanford: Stanford University Press, 2005); Jürgen Habermas, *The Structural Transformation of the Public Sphere: An Inquiry into a Category of Bourgeois Society* (Cambridge: Massachusetts Institute of Technology, 1991); Edward Herman and Noam Chomsky, *Manufacturing Consent* (New York: Pantheon Books, 1988) and Gilles Deleuze and Felix Guattari, *A Thousand Plateaus: Capitalism and Schizophrenia* (Minneapolis: University of Minnesota Press, 2005).

The importance of deconstruction as a method is clear when discussing emerging Weberian ideal types such as transhumanism or metamodernity.[18] As such, this section is largely derived from philosophically informed subjective deconstructivism and its interaction with perceived externality. This method *requires* deep communication only available through the use of personal voice and, at times, colloquial delivery. Thus, an epistemological analysis follows accordingly.

The nature of every socio-philosophical work is derived from the social conditions in which it originated, so subjective epistemology is undoubtedly at work within the formation of this chapter. As such, I am an enacted receptor—Cooley's "looking glass self" or Goffman's "dramaturgical actor"—of the socio-ontological consequences of the neoliberal discursive and linguistic hegemony.[19] Thus I reproduce it, albeit in a fragmentary and, perhaps, Gramscian subaltern way.[20]

To the reader, it is an internally processed stimulus from the external, and to the subjective, it is an externalizing measure. Regardless of the extreme consequences of the theory of mind, I must consider this contribution as one mutually shared by hypothetical parties of individuals that form a social constitution of reality. This idea is what I and others have co-developed into the term *meta-subjectivity*, or *the autopoietic production and structuration of social reality through intersubjective discourse and narrativity*.[21]

How can we determine the socio-ontological validity of a definitional coinage such as "transhumanism"? One could argue that it comes down to the *intersubjective agreement* (Hegel) of subjectivities to give recognition through cognitive processes the validity of the existence of an ideal type, or Jungian "archetype".[22] Socio-ontological frameworks are formed precisely through

---

[18] Max Weber, *The Protestant Work Ethic and the Spirit of Capitalism*, trans. Talcott Parsons (New York: Charles Scribner's Sons, 1958).

[19] Charles Horton Cooley, *Human Nature and the Social Order* (New York: Scribner's Sons, 1902) and Erving Goffman, *The Presentation of Self in Everyday Life* (New York: Anchor Publishing. 1959), respectively.

[20] Antonio Gramsci, *Selections from the Prison Notebooks of Antonio Gramsci*, edited and translated by Quentin Hoare and Geoffrey Nowell Smith (London: ElecBook, 1999).

[21] Harrison S. Jackson, "*Ex Machina*: Testing Machines for Consciousness and Socio-Relational Machine Ethics", *Journal of Science Fiction and Philosophy* 5 (2022): 1-17; Harrison S. Jackson, "The Carceral Appropriation of Communications Technology Through the Imaginal", *Philosophy and Social Criticism* (2023).

[22] Cf. Georg Wilhelm Friedrich Hegel, *The Phenomenology of Spirit*, trans. V. A. Miller. (Oxford: Oxford University Press, 1977); Weber, *Protestant Work Ethic and the Spirit of Capitalism* and Carl Jung, *The Archetypes and The Collective Unconscious, Collected Works* Vol. 9. (Princeton: Bollingen. 1981).

these discursive processes of the linguistic reproduction of ideal types—which, of course, often have little bearing on the actual objective nature of reality—or what is "truth" anyway?[23] It most often finds itself impacting the incarnation of human organization, specifically Schmitt's "the political fighting collectivity", meaning the way in which humans organize themselves into collective bodies such as "the community" or "the state".[24] These are higher-ordered socio-ontological beings that determine their own endogamous identities through discursive practices (see Skocpol's state autonomy theory).[25]

The question then becomes: "What is the contemporaneous metamodernist push to define transhumanism?". It is undoubtedly a response to the logical consequences of the neoliberal cultural hegemony and social engineering capital—which manufactures international consent and discursive conformity of all subjectivities—through control of the mode of linguistic domination.[26] Mainly, individual subjectivities have noticed the encroachment of the despotic signifier in especially the field of social surveillance and linguistic reproduction (auto-correct functions and natural language processing, or *algorithmic governmentality*), brought about by the advent of the omnipresent panopticon.[27] Transhumanist thinkers would do well to recognize the reproduction of the oppressive capitalistic mode within their own ideality.

This surveillance and linguistic domination system creates and reproduces a synaptic system that incorporates the whole of cyber society as *its own ontological individual,* much like Adam Smith's invisible hand, Deleuze and Guattari's despotic signifier, Marx's alienation, or Tocqueville's "bureaucracy that turns citizens into subjects".[28] Regardless of whether the subjective

---

[23] Foucault, *Discipline and Punish.*
[24] Carl Schmitt, *The Concept of the Political* (New Brunswick: Rutgers University Press, 1976).
[25] Theda Skocpol, *Bringing the State Back In* (Cambridge: Cambridge University Press, 1985).
[26] Cf. Herman and Chomsky, *Manufacturing Consent* and Foucault, *Discipline and Punish.*
[27] Cf. Deleuze and Guattari, *A Thousand Plateaus*; Rouvroy, "La Gouvernementalité Algorithmique"; Savaedi and Nia, "Algorithmic Governmentality and the Notion of Subjectivity in Project Itoh's Harmony" and Foucault, *Discipline and Punish.*
[28] Cf. Adam Smith, *An Inquiry into the Nature and Causes of the Wealth of Nations* (Amsterdam: Metalibri, 2007); Deleuze and Guattari, *A Thousand Plateaus*; Karl Marx, *Economic and Philosophic Manuscripts of 1844,* trans. Martin Milligan (Moscow: Progress Publishers, 1959) and Alexis de Tocqueville, *Democracy in America* (New York: HarperCollins Publishers, 1969).

bodily individual human objects to the existence of this process, it still exists and is present in the day-to-day reproduction of social ontology. This reproduction forms its own subjective collective individual, capable of its own self-awareness, self-determinism and agency. While many may be skeptical to this claim, sociologists such as Hannan and Freeman and their organizational ecology theory have been demonstrating for decades that organizations seek out self-interest and self-reproduction in much the same way that bodily individuals do.[29] So it may not be such a great leap to suggest that an AI could perform a similar function without "human input".[30]

Thus, to the claims of the transhumanist thinkers, I am a wary agnostic. Whether or not the abstract ideals of transhumanism are practically obtainable is not within the purview of this chapter. Although the authorial subject guesses that the same reality we are subject to will continually be reproduced—regardless of intentionality or medium—much like Nietzsche's eternal recurrence.[31] I ultimately respond that true enlightenment likely comes from our acceptance and comprehension of *samsara* (cycle of birth, death and rebirth).

Metamodernism

While largely relate aesthetic arts, the term "metamodernism" must be brought into discourse surrounding the humanities and social sciences if we are to understand just how and why postmodernism "died".[32] The rampant cynicism by which the postmodernists were known for has given way to a new form of epistemology, entirely focused on a bastardized hybridization (perhaps Hegelian/Fichtean synthesis) of modern optimism and postmodern cynicism.

Taking the postmodernists to their logical conclusions, metamodernists reject the implicit nihilism found within postmodern meta-analyses and instead embrace a culturally relativistic sense of optimism and self-affirmation. A core analysis of this is provided by Timotheus Vermeulen and Robin van den Akker.[33]

---

[29] Michael T. Hannan and John Freeman, "The Population Ecology of Organizations", *American Journal of Sociology* 83.5 (1977): 929-84.
[30] Thus, the need for ethical treatment of AI and transhumanist beings. The ethical questions are found in numerous anime, particularly in the Cyberpunk genre, e.g. *Ghost in the Shell* canon. See Jackson, "*Ex Machina*".
[31] More, "The Overman in the Transhuman", 1-4.
[32] This might be a bit of an overstatement since it is apparent that postmodernism is still very active in academia and reflected in all kinds of pop culture.
[33] Timotheus Vermeulen and Robin van den Akker, "Notes on Metamodernism", *Journal of Aesthetics and Culture* 2 (2010): 1-12. These two scholars have been at the forefront of the metamodernism discussion, especially in relation to Cultural Studies and the arts.

Ontologically, metamodernism oscillates between the modern and the postmodern. It oscillates between a modern enthusiasm and a postmodern notes on metamodernism irony, between hope and melancholy, between naivete and knowingness, empathy and apathy, unity and plurality, totality and fragmentation, purity and ambiguity. Indeed, by oscillating to and fro or back and forth, the metamodern negotiates between the modern and the postmodern. One should be careful not to think of this oscillation as a balance however; rather, it is a pendulum swinging between 2, 3, 5, 10, innumerable poles. Each time the metamodern enthusiasm swings toward fanaticism, gravity pulls it back toward irony; the moment its irony sways toward apathy, gravity pulls it back toward enthusiasm. Both the metamodern epistemology (as if) and its ontology (between) should thus be conceived of as a "both-neither" dynamic. They are each at once modern and postmodern and neither of them. This dynamic can perhaps most appropriately be described by the metaphor of metaxis. Literally, the term metataxis (motajy´) translates as "between".[34]

Thus, I regard metamodernism and its relative terminology as one deriving from this contemporary oscillation between comparative deconstructionism and transcendental idealism.

The work of Vermeulen and van den Acker is not the only contribution to this theoretic coinage. There have been many other theorists that have come at this new emergence in a systematic way, e.g., Gibbons, Vermeulen; Pruitt; Rowson; Severan; Josephson Storm.[35] Other theoreticians have breached the realms of specific topics like religion, politics or race.[36]

---

[34] Ibid., 6.
[35] Robin van den Akker, Alison Gibbons and Timotheus Vermeulen, ed, *Metamodernism: Historicity, Affect and Depth After Postmodernism* (New York: Rowman and Littlefield, 2017); Daniel Joseph Pruitt, "Popular Culture as Pharmakon: Metamodernism and the Deconstruction of Status Quo Consciousness" (MA Thesis: The Graduate School at the University of North Carolina at Greensboro, 2020); Jonathan Rowson, "Metamodernism and the Perception of Context: The Cultural Between, the Political After and the Mystic Beyond", *Perspectiva* 26th May 2021: https://systems-souls-society.com/metamodernism-and-the-perception-of-context-the-cultural-between-the-political-after-and-the-mystic-beyond/; A. Severan, *Metamodernism and the Return of Transcendence* (Windsor: Palimpsest Press, 2021); Josephson Storm and Jason Ānanda, *Metamodernism: The Future of Theory* (Chicago: The University of Chicago Press), 2021.
[36] Michel Clasquin-Johnson, "Towards a Metamodern Academic Study of Religion and a More Religiously Informed Metamodernism", *Theological Studies* 73.3 (2017): 1-11; Hanzi Freinacht, *The Listening Society: A Metamodern Guide to Politics, Book One*

Up until this point, though, an application of metamodernity has not been specifically written— within a context of social history and cultural hegemony, or on anime and its context —regardless of its origins in aesthetic and literary theory. This chapter is an attempt to correct this deficit so far. Metamodernism as an ideal form—undoubtedly has a large contribution to social theory—and anime is undeniably a paramount example of this metamodernist trend. Both are an attempt to find meaning within the aftermath of postmodern deconstruction and a goal of striking contemporary relevance.

There is an obvious connection between the idealistic "modernity" highlighted within metamodern discourse and the inheritance of American transcendentalism. My argument is that this synthesis is transhumanism—which takes aspects of the transcendental movement—and substitutes the natural "other" with the artificial or "technological".

Transcendentalism in a United States Context and Cultural Hegemony

The major contributions of the American literary "Transcendentalism" movement found in the nineteenth century will facilitate an understanding of the correlation between transhumanism and metamodernism. Transhumanism theory is largely derived from a rapturous intent found within the bodily subjective individual, and to ignore the intellectual inheritance of American transcendentalism is to invalidate its impact on generating this metamodern idealist movement.

While early American transcendentalists such as Emerson or Thoreau found themselves displacing their subjectivity into the generalized other of "nature", metamodernist individuals find themselves displacing their will into the generalized other of "technology".[37] Thus it is the heritage of American transcendentalism that gives a foundational bedrock to Silicon Valley's metamodern technologic aspiration of rapture (through algorithmic governmentality). I will now attempt to make those connections.

Emerson, one of the seminal intellectuals of the American transcendentalism movement, believed that nature was everything external to us, meaning not just the natural world but also art, other individuals, etc. In order to become

---

(Frederikssund: Metamoderna ApS, 2017) and James Brunton, "Whose (Meta)modernism?: Metamodernism, Race, and the Politics of Failure", *Journal of Modern Literature* 43.3 (2018): 60-76.

[37] Cf. Friedrich Nietzsche, "Second Treatise: 'Guilt,' 'Bad Conscious', and Related Matters", in *On the Genealogy of Morality*, trans. Maudemarie Clark and Alan Swensen (Indianapolis: Hackett Publishing Company, 1998). Nietzsche's definition of will largely derives from a subjective individual's ability to maintain a promise over the passage of time.

the highest self, each individual had to experience the mysteries of the universe on their own, through self-reflection immersed in the natural world, which offered a greater understanding of the divine order of reality that society could not provide on its own.[38] This externalization of the means by which enlightenment was achieved by the individual has a notable internal/external mechanism, in which the self seeks enlightenment through an interaction with the "other", with a strong requirement of self-reflection and reliance.[39] This is undoubtedly a reproduction of Cartesian, and thus Aristotelian dualism, imported through Enlightenment rationalism.[40] There are naturally striking similarities found in transhumanism today, where individuals view the dualistic ability to transcend through technology as the means to enlighten themselves.[41]

In Henry David Thoreau's influential work *Walden*, we also can pick up similar threads of this intellectual inheritance.[42] Reflecting on the dubious legacy of "civilized" life, he calls individuals to cast off the shackles of society and to embrace self-reflection in nature. While Thoreau is highly skeptical of technological advances bringing about the enlightenment of the individual, he still externalizes this enlightenment through the context of God and nature and a rejection of the present circumstance.

While there is not enough room to review other Transcendentalist writers such as Whitman, Hawthorne and Peabody, all focus on several common core tenets to the American Transcendentalist movement: a triumph of the individual over themselves, often through the natural "other", an enlightenment through self-determination, and a greater understanding of reality through mediated experience and reflection outside traditional means. These core ideas were passed down to and enshrined within American society, the logical consequences of which can be seen in the ideal type of "individualism",

---

[38] Ralph Waldo Emerson, *Nature* (1836), *American Transcendentalism Web*: https://archive.vcu.edu/english/engweb/transcendentalism/authors/emerson/nature.html.

[39] Ralph Waldo Emerson, "Self-Reliance" (1841), *American Transcendentalism Web*: https://archive.vcu.edu/english/engweb/transcendentalism/authors/emerson/essays/selfreliance.html.

[40] Cf. Rene Descartes, *Meditations on First Philosophy*, *Internet Encyclopedia of Philosophy* (1996): https://yale.learningu.org/download/041e9642-df02-4eed-a895-70e472df2ca4/H2665_Descartes%27%20Meditations.

[41] Some examples would be *Ghost in the Shell*: Directed by Mamoru Oshii with Screenplay by Kazunori Itō (Shochiku 1995); Tsutomu Nihei, *Blame!* (Tokyo: Kodansha, 1997-2003) and *kaiju* ("giant monster") anime like *Attack on Titan*: Directed by Tetsurō Araki et al. with Screenplay by Yasuko Kobayashi et al. (NHK 2013-present).

[42] Henry David Thoreau, *Walden; Or, Life in the Woods* (The Project Gutenberg eBook of Walden, 1995): https://www.gutenberg.org/files/205/205-h/205-h.htm.

touted by meritocracy, Manifest Destiny and contemporary identarian discourse, to name a few. Often considered one of the key ideological principles of American society, the impact of transcendentalism on contemporary cultural manifestations is too large to ignore.

The innovation of transhumanism to the intellectual inheritance of transcendentalism, though, is not the identification of the enlightening "other" with nature but with technological advance. Through a rejection of the contemporary circumstance and an embracement of the cultural other—both transcendentalism and transhumanism seek an illumination moderated, a mediated subjective transcendence—through self-reflection. After the deconstructive process of postmodernism, metamodernity has sought to reassert a pragmatic idealism by seeking meaning within the past as it applies to the present.[43] Since interaction with nature has largely been deprived of us through the relations (mode) surrounding late-stage capital, it is no longer a pragmatic retreat. Metamodernists have few other choices than to externalize transcendence (and the cultural inheritance of transcendentalism itself) into the technological process.

A note of key importance to the legacy of this train of thought is as follows. Contemporary U.S. "pop-culture" dominates neoliberal cultural and trade hegemony. So this would mean that transcendentalism has been transposed into transhumanism in nations outside of the United States. Much like Ritzer's "McDonaldization" thesis on globalization, this inherited American transcendentalism is given a unique character in each of the countries it is present.[44] It is my speculation that this common, transnational transcendental inheritance produces neoliberal transhumanism, which can be likened to the syncretic dialectic idealism latent within metamodern epistemology. See Figure 1 below for a visual depiction of this dialectic phenomenon.

This is an *international* movement encouraged by international capital, social engineering technocrats, and technofascists. Japan, then, is certainly no stranger to this process.

---

[43] Cf. Vermeulen and van den Acker, "Notes on Metamodernism", 1-12 and Severan, *metamodernism and the Return of Transcendence*, 56-57.
[44] George Ritzer, *The McDonaldization Thesis* (London: SAGE, 1999).

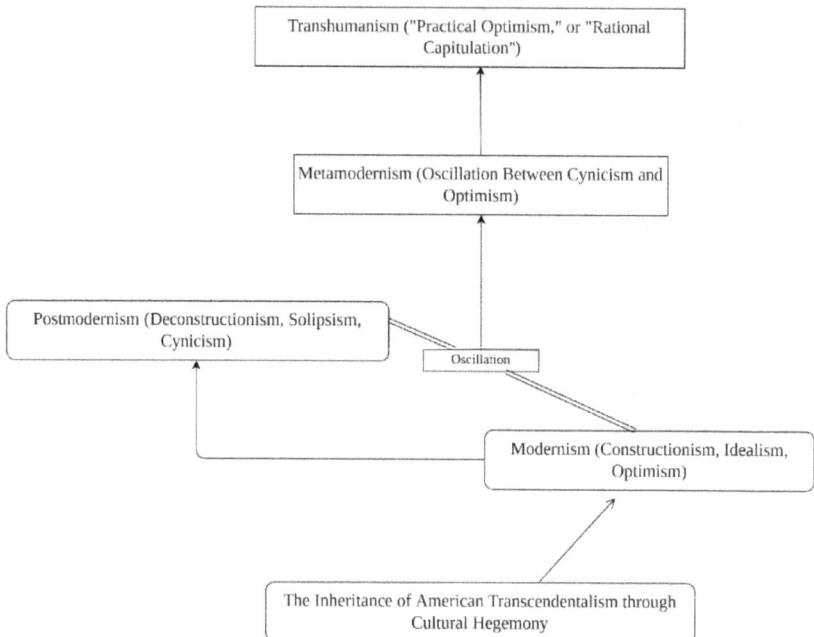

Figure 3.1. Dialectic Diagram of Transcendentalim, Metamodernity and Transhumanism. Source Steven Foertsch.

A Note on Japanese Hegemonic and Contextual Considerations

How far does the Western cultural hegemony go? It is undoubtedly under contestation at this very moment, given the recent Russian invasion of Ukraine and Russian attempts to form an "antifascist" block in union with China, India, Pakistan, Saudi Arabia and Ethiopia, etc.[45]

The state of Japan, where I center my historical and socio-cultural analysis, is currently under a semi-feudatory status to the United States. This is largely the historical byproduct of years of Western-inspired social reforms, such as the

---

[45] See the "First International Anti-Fascist Congress" held by Russia in 2022. These recent trends to form an Anti-Western influence block largely stem from the Russian response to the expansion of NATO by the United States. This is likely to keep the military alliance relevant after the collapse of the Soviet Union. See "1st Anti-Fascist Congress Attended by Military Attaches from 26 States—Defense Ministry", *TASS* 02nd September 2022: https://tass.com/defense/1501587.

Meiji Restoration and the U.S. occupation of Japan after World War II.[46] Here Japanese leaders willfully chose the United States as an occupier over the USSR (much to the contrary belief that Japan surrendered because of the atomic bomb).[47] Much of this legacy is entirely military and economic, e.g, the United States currently operates at least seven known military bases in Japan.[48]

Japan's number one trade partner, however, is not the United States but China.[49] Many of the United States' East Asian clients are in a similar circumstance—and it is difficult to gauge the level of *cultural* influence China may have on its trade partners—especially those from the same geographic location and cultural lineage. Japan is undoubtedly inclined to "free market capitalism", much like fellow US client South Korea is. But is Japanese culture equally as "submissive" to Western neoliberal hegemony? Is this Chinese trade influence assisting Japanese culture in articulating criticism of its "occupier"?[50] Or perhaps this critique is entirely native to the postmodern and metamodern Japanese condition?

The propagation of anime and its assessment of the neoliberal order must be considered in this context. Can Japan still be counted as a transmitter of neoliberal cultural hegemony?[51] Japanese anime symbology has had an especially large influence on the younger generations of the "West", indeed, even in Russia and China.[52] This influence is certainly evident in

---

[46] Christopher Bolton, Istvan Csicsery-Ronay and Takayuki Tatsumi, *Robot Ghosts and Wired Dreams: Japanese Science Fiction from Origins to Anime* (Minneapolis: University of Minnesota Press, 2007).

[47] Carnegie Council for Ethics in International Affairs, "Did Nuclear Weapons Cause Japan to Surrender?", *Carnegie Council* (2022): https://www.carnegiecouncil.org/education/008/expertclips/010.

[48] Between 1965-1990 and during the "East Asian Miracle", Japan as well as other East Asian economies experienced a rapid growth. Many Americans were concerned that Japan would overtake the United States as the first economy in the world. This was foiled by the "paper tiger" Asian financial crisis in 1997-98, which stymied Japanese economic growth. While it is speculative as to why this growth was reigned in, the new "economic threat" in American eyes is China, which is projected to overtake the United States as the world's largest economy by around 2030.

[49] Chosun Ilbo, "China's Economy Could Overtake U.S. Economy by 2030", 05th January 2022: http://english.chosun.com/site/data/html_dir/2022/01/05/2022010500491.html.

[50] Of course, it could just as easily be simply financial or "business".

[51] Steven Foertsch, "Children of the Mind and the Concept of Edge and Center Nations", *Journal of Science Fiction and Philosophy* 5 (2022): https://jsfphil.org/volume-5-2022/children-of-the-mind-and-the-concept-of-edge-and-center-nations/.

[52] Susan Napier, "Why Anime?", *Japan Spotlight* (March/April, 2004): https://www.jef.or.jp/journal/pdf/cover%20story%206_0403.pdf and Susan Napier, "The World of Anime Fandom in America", *Mechademia: Second Arc* 1.1 (2010): 47-63.

metamodernist internet discourse and can be easily seen in pro-gaming groups and individuals, streaming or content creation circles like Hololive Production or "virtual YouTubers" ("Vtubers"), and virtual reality chatrooms like VRChat. But the question then becomes, perhaps to echo Gramsci, "is this subaltern"?[53] Or is it simply a reproduction and reification of the Western neoliberal cultural hegemony?

Is dystopian transhumanism in Japanese culture, particularly found in science fiction anime, a sign of resistance or conformity to the neoliberal cultural hegemony? Resistance to technocracy is obviously not just a uniquely American or European phenomenon.[54] Also, social engineering algorithmic governmentality is pervasive in contemporary Japanese society—and this makes sense—since the majority of Japanese exports are focused on technology.[55] Perhaps this trend in Japanese animation is simply a reproduction of the cultural hegemony inherited through Westernization models and its feudatory status. Many historical accounts certainly seem to suggest as much.[56] In the end, it is inconclusive that the Japanese people reproduce these narratives, discourses, and symbols willingly or unconsciously. It could very well be the case that Japanese assertions against technofascism are tapping into the residual East/West divide, fueled by past and present cultural influence from China.

Anime Case Studies

I have traced out my argument above and now want to demonstrate its viability (or potentiality) through case studies of five well-known anime.[57] The lens through which these will be examined is metamodernity, transcendental thinking, and transhumanism. While informed by cultural studies, my analysis is developed largely in spirit with post-structural philosophers who reflect on mass media such as Foucault, Derrida, Habermas, Herman and

---

[53] Cf. Gramsci, *Prison Notebooks*.
[54] See television shows such as Black Mirror or online RPG video games such as Cyberpunk 2077.
[55] Rouvroy, "La Gouvernementalité Algorithmique"; Savaedi and Nia, "Algorithmic Governmentality and the Notion of Subjectivity in Project Itoh's Harmony".
[56] Bolton, Csicsery-Ronay, Tastsumi, *Robot Ghosts and Wired Dreams*.
[57] This analysis owes large inheritance to content analysis methodology derived from cultural studies, especially on work that has covered anime in the past. Cf. Bolton, Csicsery-Ronay, Tastsumi, *Robot Ghosts and Wired Dreams*; Susan J. Napier, *Anime from Akira to Princess Mononoke: Experiencing Contemporary Japanese Animation* (New York: Palgrave, 2001). See also Ian Condry, "Anime Creativity: Characters and Premises in the Quest for Cool Japan" *Theory, Culture, and Society* 26 (2009): 139-63.

Chomsky.[58] It does not focus on anime production like is found in Condry or otaku culture.[59] This analysis focuses directly on the philosophical content itself as reflected in narratological choices, plot progression and symbological usages. The goal is to demonstrate the transhumanist underpinnings implicit within these case studies of postmodern and metamodern Japanese content.

Neon Genesis Evangelion

Neon Genesis Evangelion (NGE or EVA) originally premiered on TV Tokyo in 1995.[60] It has garnered an incredible amount of influence in popular anime culture over the years, being one of the seminal examples of the "mech anime" revival of the 1990s. NGE's widespread appeal has led to twenty-six episodes, six movie adaptations, light novels, manga and video games. It set the standard for the future of the industry in so many ways—artistically, thematically, symbolically—and specifically for *mecha*. My primary focus will be on the anime series—with samples from movie adaptations—in order to explore the relevant themes.

Shinji Ikari is a fourteen-year-old boy who is thrust into life-and-death battles by his father, Gendo Ikari. Gendo is the director of a military research group named Nerv—whose objective is to combat the invading "Angels" on behalf of humanity—ever since the "Second Impact" (a global catastrophe). Angels are alien beings who came from space in order to wipe out humanity for their sins. These Angels are nearly indestructible due to their impenetrable force fields called "AT Fields".

Gendo, for a variety of reasons (including selfish metaphysical reunification with his deceased wife), enlists Shinji to fight these Angels in a machine called an "Evangelion Unit". These machines are the only hope for humanity—because they can create and penetrate the AT fields of the Angels—enabling humanity to destroy them.

Shinji is not alone, however. He has several peers fighting Angels alongside him. The enigmatic Rei Ayanami, a closed-off and quiet girl who pilots Unit 00, and Asuka Langley Soryu, a proud, fiery and abrasive prodigy who pilots Unit 02. Together they take down multiple Angels, occasionally getting injured along the way. Although outnumbered and often outgunned, defeating the

---

[58] Cf. Foucault, *Discipline and Punish*; Derrida, *Rogues*; Habermas, *Structural Transformation of the Public Sphere*; Herman and Chomsky, *Manufacturing Consent*.
[59] Cf. Condry, "Anime Creativity: Characters and Premises in the Quest for Cool Japan"; Napier, "Why Anime?", wp. and Napier, "The World of Anime Fandom in America", 47-63.
[60] *Neon Genesis Evangelion*: Directed by Hideaki Anno with Screenplay by Hideaki Anno (TV Tokyo 1995).

Angels would mean defending the world from the Third Impact and total destruction.

The background of the Evangelion Units (Evas) is then slowly revealed to the main characters and the viewer. The Evas are pilotable mechas (cybernetic robots). They were produced by the labs of NERV by combining Angel genetics and Particle-Wave Matter with human souls (pilots). Even more horrifying, the original vessels for the Angels are Shinji and Asuka's own mothers. It is this "soul connection" that enables them to pilot the Evas. It is also unveiled that Rei Ayanami is the exception. This is because she is actually a clone of Shinji's mother fused with a part of the body of the Angel Lilith (counterpart to Adam). Lilith is being kept in the basement of Nerv in a crucified state in order to be used as source material for evas.

Lilith is the progenitor of all of humanity, which is called the "Lilin". The Lilin are actually a single Angel themselves—who possess the Fruit of Knowledge diffused—throughout the entire species of individuals. They are doomed to an existence of loneliness and separation from their fellow Lilin. After Shinji defeats the last Angel, a mysterious organization called Seele, the funding agency of Nerv, commands Gendo to trigger the "Human Instrumentality Project", the final purpose of the Evangelion project.

By triggering the Third Impact willfully, Seele seeks to advance humanity to a stage where it no longer feels this separation: essentially, for all of humankind to be reunited within the Angel Lilith. This realignment would lead to a transcendence never before experienced by humanity: it would become an immortal god with a human soul. The tool to do this is Shinji Ikari and Evangelion Unit 01, who are thus crucified by Seele-controlled Evas.

Shinji is instrumentalized in this way to usher in the Third Impact, which is successful. Being at the center of the impact, however, gives Shinji incredible power to decide the ultimate fate of the Lilin. Shinji grapples with the meaning of being human, which is plagued by feelings of isolation. He soon makes a breakthrough, and reunites with the others, who congratulate him for his success in breaking down the barriers between human beings.

Depending on which episode or movie watched, the success of instrumentalization is unclear. In some cases, Shinji rejects instrumentalization in favor of a separate existence fueled by love and misunderstanding. This ambiguity is enough for our purposes, however, which are to analyze the transcendent themes underlining *Neon Genesis Evangelion*.

There are clearly overt Christian themes in *Evangelion*, which directly hint at the state of transcendence latent within the human species. This is not unlike the American transcendentalist thinkers who viewed the human condition as

Metamodernity, American Transcendentalism and Transhumanism 89

one to be honed through transcendental experience and natural interaction with the Christian God.

Even with the overt Christian symbology and narrative—such as crucifixion, Adam and Lilith, Angels, the Spear of Longinus or the Holy Lance that pierced the side of Christ, Fruit of Knowledge, etc.—the interest lies in *how* Shinji managed to achieve godhood. Note the term "Human Instrumentality", which may be based on the original Japanese "補完 (*hokan*). *Ho* translates literally to "supplement, supply, make good, offset, compensate, assistant, learner" and *kan* to "perfect, completion, end".[61] There is an indication within this term that humanity is not complete and needs to undergo a transformation in order to achieve perfection. The vessel to do this is a mechanized suit fused with Angel and human life, an Eva.

The direct connections to transhumanism, as previously defined in this essay, seem clear. Shinji, an awkward and insecure fourteen-year-old boy, with the help of a mechanized suit imbued with special transcendental properties (one of which is his immortal mother incarnated in the Eva unit), manages to overcome his shortcomings and attain godhood. The instrumentalization of all of humanity through this one mechanized vessel gives birth to a single immortal being—a combined humanity and an Angel with a human soul—which will advance humanity itself to the next stage of transcendence.

Serial Experiments Lain

Serial Experiments Lain is an anime television series that was released in 1998.[62] It appeared right before the true consequences of the internet were culturally realized. Given this context, this anime was startlingly ahead of its time and predicted many of the logical outcomes that a truly interconnected world would undergo.

Following the story of a junior high school girl named Lain Iwakura, Lain slowly descends into a technologic mystery that unravels the very fabric of her reality. Beginning with the suicide of a classmate Chisa Yomoda, Lain receives a message (email) from this classmate on "The Wired". The Wired is the name for the internet in this anime and is assumed to be omnipresent. Lain's friend Chisa, claims that she abandoned her physical body to integrate with The Wired. She also claimed to have met "God" there.

---

[61] "Human Instrumentality Project", *Evangelion Wiki*: https://evangelion.fandom.com/wiki/Human_Instrumentality_Project.
[62] *Serial Experiments Lain*: Directed by Ryutaro Nakamura with Screenplay by Chiaki J. Konaka (TV Tokyo 1998).

The line between what is reality and what is fiction quickly starts blurring together as Lain chases this mystery further into The Wired. She soon discovers that The Wired is actually the invention of a genius (Masami) whose control of it makes him god-like. He did this through experimentation with children and integration of the psychic capabilities of the mind into the functioning neural network of The Wired. It is then revealed to both Lain and the viewer that Lain herself is a byproduct of this experimentation—an autonomous sentient artificial intelligence—that can function both in The Wired and in the "real" world. The "god" of The Wired then attempts to (violently) convince Lain to return to The Wired exclusively to completely eliminate the demarcation between The Wired (Virtual Reality) and Reality.

After defeating the god of The Wired, Lain then comes into her own power in this process—essentially in complete control of The Wired as a god—and thus a complete influence on reality itself. Notable in this power is the ability to erase or create memories in individual minds linked to The Wired. Meditating on this newfound ability, Lain chooses to delete her presence from reality completely, save for an observational role. In the end, Lain flouts spacetime, achieves immortality and exercises near omnipotence through her integration with The Wired.

The connections to transhumanism found within the metamodern state are pronounced in *Serial Experiments Lain*. A socially awkward and isolated teen girl discovers her true self within the internet and through the avenue of technology, achieves enlightenment and ascendance to godhood. This is not unlike the transcendentalist search for the true self through the medium of nature. Themes of death and rebirth, self-discovery and transcendence flood its symbols and images. While the anime is quite often disturbing and dystopian, the final episode leaves the viewer with a feeling of resolution and sublimity. All the hardships experienced by Lain up until that point have been settled through technology—with the infinite power of a god now in her hands—to do with as she pleases.

Ergo Proxy

Released in 2006 with only twenty-three episodes, *Ergo Proxy* is by far one of the bleaker settings in which I explore transhumanism.[63] It is set in a post-apocalyptic wasteland, where the remnants of humanity are sheltered in, or reliant on, domes entirely run by "AutoReivs". The world outside the domes is irradiated and almost entirely uninhabitable for biological life.

---

[63] *Ergo Proxy*. Directed by Shuko Murase with Screenplay by Dai Satō (Wowow 2006).

AutoReivs are a type of android that mostly serve the needs of the human population and can no longer biologically reproduce without human assistance. Meanwhile, the government of one of these domed cities, called Romdeau, has been conducting experiments on "proxies", a human-like beings with near godlike power. They are said to contain the key to the survival of the human species. A virus starts spreading within the AutoReivs called the "cogito" virus, which gives them self-awareness. Revolts begin to spring up as a result.

The series follows two main characters in Romdeau. Re-l Mayer is an investigator searching for clues about murders related to the cogito virus. Vincent Law is an "immigrant" connected to the mystery of the proxies. As the two dive deeper into the origins of the cogito virus and the secret of the proxies, they realize the cogito virus is connected to the presence of the proxies. They meet humans living just outside the dome of Romdeau—and later travel outside Romdeau to other domed cities—which are in varying states of decay. There they meet other proxies with a variety of temperaments, most verging on insanity. Through battling them, Vincent Law discovers that he is actually a proxy himself. Indeed, he is the important "Ergo Proxy" created by the first proxy (Proxy One) as the "proxy of death".

Re-l and Vincent both learn that the proxies were immortal and near-omnipotent creations of the fragments of humanity after a nuclear exchange. In "Project Boomerang", the remaining humans created proxies for the expressed purpose of rehabilitating the Earth and creating habitable pockets so that humanity could return. In the meantime, these humans left the Earth for space, destined to return in the far future (thousands of years). Proxy One then reveals to Ergo Proxy the nature of this role and his hatred of it. Romdeau, with ongoing cognito riots and without the support of a proxy, begins to collapse.

After a confrontation between Proxy One and Ergo Proxy that ends in Proxy One's death, the sun reemerges from the blackened-out sky. Proxies are not meant to survive in the sunlight, and Vincent must flee. Vincent and Re-l escape with friends from the collapsing Romdeau. In the distance, there is a spacecraft, which could hint at the original humans' return to Earth.

Transhumanism in this context is the escape from a post-apocalyptic hellscape into the relative human paradise of the domes. Humanity outside the domes was depicted in episode seventeen as blind, gaunt and virtually unable to reproduce in large numbers. Humanity on Earth was entirely beholden to the whims of the proxies, godlike entities who determined every aspect of their lives. Immortal and immensely powerful, these beings were tasked with rehabilitating the Earth—but ended up having existential crises of their own—much like the AutoReivs and their cogito virus. Ultimately, it was unclear if the humans could exist on Earth once again (the return was speculative). But the cogito virus, and the self-reflection of the proxies themselves, begot a new type of humanity not beholden to the biological consequences of radiation poisoning. If humanity never returned, the AutoReivs and the proxies would have continued to recreate something like human existence on Earth.

It was impossible for humanity to solve the problems it created without relying on the "other". Additionally, the emotional suffering of the proxies also hints at their latent function. Much like the meaning of the name "proxy", proxies were created to be the *literal proxy* of humanity in case it ceased to exist. As such, it receives transhumanist understandings of rapture, transcendence, godhood and immortality. These proxies were far superior to the human race in every way—and operated as gods of the Earth for thousands of years—a surrogate, an elegy, a new incarnation of a long dead species.

Psycho-Pass

Later than many of our cases, *Psycho-Pass* came out in 2012 and was immediately popular.[64] Its success with both critics and audiences alike led to many spinoffs, including three movies, multiple video games and novel adaptations. In this case study, I will focus on the TV anime and movie content; but themes discussed in this context are most certainly applicable to other mediums.

Psycho-Pass follows the story of rookie inspector Akane Tsunemori. He works for Japan's Ministry of Welfare's Public Safety Bureau in the Criminal Investigations Department in the not-so-distant future. The setting is after a global hegemonic realignment (and possible nuclear exchange). In this world, Japan is one of the few states that emerged stable and relatively intact, albeit with a new form of governmental oversight.

This form of computerized governmental oversight is called the "Sibyl System". Pervasive in all of society, the Sibyl System measures all citizen criminal potentiality and reports it to law enforcement officers. This "crime coefficient" determines whether someone is a "latent criminal", a label which regulates individual freedoms accordingly. If your "crime coefficient" is over a certain threshold, for example, law enforcement officers could arrest and detain, institutionalize or kill you according to the Sibyl System's judgement.

Operating within this system are the officers of the Public Safety Bureau. This bureau is comprised of teams of "inspectors" (who are not latent criminals) and leading "enforcers" (who are). On the spot decisions are made

---

[64] *Psycho-Pass*: Directed by Naoyoshi Shiotani and Katsuyuki Motohiro with Screenplay by Gen Urobuchi et al. (Fuji TV 2012).

through gun-like weapons called "dominators". These weapons have trigger locks directly linked to and determined by the Sibyl System and its crime coefficient matrix.

While the setting of this dystopian case is incredibly rich and well fleshed out, I will only focus on the transhuman characteristics found within this anime. Much of what follows is an exposition of many key plot points revealed to the viewer after at least one season of viewing (or within the side movies).

The main adversary in the first season is a man named Shogo Makishima, a criminal mastermind who nevertheless maintains a low crime coefficient ("criminally asymptomatic"). This quirk was the major plot point of multiple seasons, where the investigative team has to wrestle with the blind spots of the Sibyl System. Only later is it revealed to the viewer why this criminally asymptomatic problem exists in the first place.

The Sibyl System is revealed to the viewer and Inspector Tsunemori to be entirely comprised of the brains of criminally asymptomatic individuals. These individuals form a collective consciousness that calculates crime coefficients which regulate society and enforcement. Makishima was actually propositioned to join Sibyl; which he reacted to with subversion and violence (as do others in later seasons and movies).

The Sibyl System claims that by giving administrative power to the criminally asymptomatic, ethics and individual morality are put aside in favor of order and social stability. Ultimately, the Sibyl System promises individual criminals and murderers a chance to do "good" and achieve a form of omnipotence and immortality over the Japanese population in exchange for their individual agency and bodily form.

The connections to transhumanism are quite clear. Here is an instance where the criminally asymptomatic are given an option to essentially determine all of social reality for the Japanese people. The Sibyl System actively decides who lives and who dies, who is jailed as a latent criminal, and who can serve as an inspector. Sibyl dynamically determines careers for individuals, and in later seasons is revealed to have complete control of politics, the economy and the military (foreign interventionism). It exerts a near omnipotent influence. Sibyl is everywhere, in every camera, dominator and robot helper found throughout Japan. In this sense, it suggests Sibyl is nearly omnipresent in Japan.

By donating their brains to Sibyl, these individuals achieve a sense of transcendence from their bodily state: a conceivably immortal existence through hivemind, a collective personhood, with each individual as a single vote (much like cells in a body). While morally dubious, and the contestation of many of the anime's ethical narratives, transhumanist thinking is alive and well within the extremely popular *Psycho-Pass* canon.

Sword Art Online

Sword Art Online, known by fans as SAO, has been remarkably successful in generating numerous iterations through various media. The original anime was released in 2012, and since then it has seen multiple seasons, spinoffs, light novels and films.[65] This canon is remarkably lengthy, so for practical purposes I will only focus on the core seasons of the anime SAO I-III (not including the spinoff *Alicization*).

The story of SAO follows an awkward young man named Kazuto "Kirito" Kirigaya, who is a player of *Sword Art Online*, a virtual reality video game that allows the user complete immersion through a helmet called "NerveGear". The first season focuses on Kirito's experience in Aincrad, a fictional world much like *World of Warcraft*, in which he and every other user is trapped. The game creator, Akihiko Kayaba, does this because of his ultimate beliefs and goals.

Kirito meets a fellow player in this world, named Asuna Yuuki, who he ends up marrying in game. Together they manage to find Kayaba's player character and defeat him, freeing almost all those trapped within the game. Asuna, however, is unveiled to be trapped in another version of the game called *Alfheim Online*. There she is held hostage by an obsessive villain, Nobuyuki Sugou, who wishes to marry Asuna against her will.

Kirito infiltrates and manages to foil Sugou's plans, and makes virtual world access available to all, restoring *Sword Art Online* and *Alfheim Online* to former players. A year later, a similar game called *Gun Gale Online* is experiencing murders related to the NerveGear, now called "AmuSpheres". Kirito is hired to solve these murders, and with the help of friend Shino "Sinon" Asada, they discover the three murderers; but one gets away.

Kazuto "found" himself within these virtual reality settings, and they quickly came to dominate his world and self-identity. In the outside world, Kazuto was just another normal person, but in SAO, he was "Kirito", a "beater" (a "beta" testing "cheater"), set apart by his unparalleled ability in game. This also applied to Asuna, who reached a high leadership level in multiple guilds with which she was involved. While often held against their wills, both found themselves and their self-identity through the medium of technology, where they distinguished themselves as beyond just a normal human.

---

[65] *Sword Art Online*: Directed by Tomohiko Itō with Screenplay by Yukie Sugawara et al. based on the novels by Reki Kawahara (Tokyo MX 2012).

Multiple villains in the series, such as the original creator of SAO Kayaba or Alfheim's Sugou, often viewed themselves as a sort of deity within the world, with control over the life and death of their players. This is especially true for Kayaba, who sought to create a world free from impurities within the virtual. This course of thinking is incredibly transhumanist. Both the individual players manifesting themselves and the creators' aspirations of godhood serve to reify the contemporary application of transcendentalist themes today: the individual self is made better through the medium of technology, even if sometimes used for ill purposes.

Discussion and Conclusion

All the cases above demonstrate a clear transhumanist undertone but vary in application. Just as a reminder, "transhumanism" was defined earlier in the work as "the aspiration of a socio-ontological bodily human individual to a state of transcendence through technological advancement". The above cases of Japanese anime all conform to this definition in spirit, making it synonymous with transhumanist art.[66] They therefore reproduce the logical consequences of American Transcendentalism, metamodernist oscillations, and the hegemonic Japanese cultural context.

Most instances of transcendental transhumanist thinking within our cases focused, interestingly, on bildungsroman transformation or "coming of age" stories.[67] Multiple instances of this can be seen—from *Neon Genesis Evangelion*, *Serial Experiments Lain*—to *Sword Art Online*. This may hint at the nature of the anime medium as a young adult experience (*Shōnen*) but may also refer to the growing pains many are feeling throughout the rapidly accelerating pace of technological advancement.[68] There may also be correlations with masculinity renegotiations.[69] While the world changes, two things are asserted in these stories as ever-present: the self-realization and determination of the individual (linked to American transcendentalism and meritocratic mastery), and the medium of constantly shifting technology to achieve it.

Oftentimes empowerment through the medium of technology is seen as a praxis—the telos being the triumph of humanity—over its own biological

---

[66] Vita-More, "Transhumanist Art Statement", wp.
[67] Napier, *Anime from Akira to Princess Mononoke*.
[68] Verdoux, "Transhumanism, Progress and the Future", 49-69.
[69] Ian Condry, "Love Revolution: Anime, Masculinity, and the Future", in *Recreating Japanese Men*, eds. Sabine Frūstück and Anne Walthall (Berkeley: University of California Press, 2011), 262-83.

limits.[70] The key focus on this idea is the unnatural extension of the human lifespan, either individual or species wide. Few anime within this case study have reflected on the necessity of the artificial extension of human life. Rather, they assert an implied form of immortality that is not debated on a moral level.[71] We can see this clearly pronounced in *Ergo Proxy, Serial Experiments Lain, Psycho Pass*.[72] It is quite remarkable that this trend is almost ubiquitous within our case study of anime, and it begets another conclusion.

Transhumanism and the immorality it promises contains a heavy implication of godhood—bringing together the traditional forms of omniscience, omnipotence and omnipresence (see particularly anime examples with internet components). Once the basic natural limitation on humanity (mortality) is overcome, it is only a brief step forward into the unknown to attain a supra-human or overman state of transcendence.[73] Whether or not this is attainable (or a slippery slope logical fallacy), the case studies demonstrate these very qualities in *Psycho Pass, Neon Genesis Evangelion, Sword Art Online, Serial Experiments Lain* and *Ergo Proxy*. The impact of the constant and continued presence of humanity's technological advance on its culture is evident within these anime.

All of these themes, the self-realization of the individual, the pursuit of immortality and the pursuit of godhood through technology, are directly related to our historical contexts of American Transcendentalism and metamodernist oscillation. American transcendentalism sought nature as the generalized other necessary for the realization of the self. Many of these themes are repeated in a clear way through transhumanism *simply by switching the medium from nature to technology.*

In metamodernity, we find an oscillation between modern idealism, associated with self-determination and practicality, and postmodern critical deconstructivism. I find these themes within the animes of the case study— where the transcendental pragmatism associated with metamodernity— conforms largely to the negotiation between these two paradigms. It manifests in transhumanist thinking—rapturous in intent—but seemingly

---

[70] Bostrom, "Transhumanist Values"; Huxley, "Transhumanism", 12-16 and Fukuyama, "Transhumanism", 42-43.
[71] See the ubiquitous ethical dilemmas and questions in Anderson, *Technology and Theology*.
[72] Bolton, Csicsery-Ronay, Tastsumi, *Robot Ghosts and Wired Dreams*.
[73] Sorgner, "Nietzsche the Overman, and Transhumanism", 29-42. For a response, see More, "The Overman in the Transhuman", 1-4.

pragmatic in means.[74] The focus on the dystopian nature of technological advances in many of the anime examined may be likened to the influence of postmodernity. I also see a retrieval of the self and individual assertion of being within this anime sample, synonymous with the idealistic period of modernity. It is only through metamodernal analysis that we see these themes converge together to form a transhumanist metamodern perspective.

Given our cultural understanding of Japan, I conclude that Japanese anime is part of the process of creating and reifying this new turn into transcendentalism. Japanese anime is a forerunner of international neoliberal popular culture, and it is difficult to ignore. How this will all play out remains an open question. It will be interesting to see, however, how future generations of thinkers understand the issues in an age where technology comes to dominate more and more. One might even factor in Habermas' penetration of the lifeworld idea into the discussion.[75]

Likewise, it is impossible to predict Japan's cultural resistance or conformity to this common hegemonic culture to which it has contributed so much. While the influence of China on Japanese culture may be growing, Chinese culture, in general, is not overly suspicious of the expansion of technology into everyday life. Perhaps this hints at Japan's affinity with Western culture, especially when we regard American transcendentalist thinking found within the case study.[76]

One should note that this chapter has only provided a sample of anime that illustrate my main points. Several other anime comes to mind as a potential follow-up on the themes in this chapter. *Akira* or the *Ghost in the Shell* canon has a large quantity of material regarding transhumanism.[77] The anime genre of *kaiju* (怪獣 "strange beast")—such as *Attack on Titan*—is another example with transhumanist thinking. The genre of *kaiju* often uses technology as the only way humans can fight against such godlike monsters. Likewise, other

---

[74] See "rational capitulationism" in Verdoux, "Transhumanism, Progress and the Future", 49-69.

[75] Habermas, *Structural Transformation of the Public Sphere*.

[76] An interesting comparative connection could be drawn from the South Korea—which is known for its capitalist-dystopian outlook within popular culture—particularly in film and television. Some examples could be found in *Squid Game*: Directed with Screenplay by Hwang Dong-hyuk (Netflix 2017-2021); *Parasite*: Directed with Screenplay by Bong Joon-ho (CJ Entertainment 2019); *Okja*: Directed with Screenplay by Bong Joon-ho (Netflix 2017) and *Oldboy*: Directed by Park Chan-wook with Screenplay by Hwang Jo-yun et al. (Show East 2003).

[77] *Akira*: Directed and Screenplay by Katsuhiro Otomo (Toho 1988).

mecha anime—such as *Mobile Suit Gundam* and *Code Geass*—demonstrate a clear connection to the ideas in this chapter.[78]

My conclusion is that the implications of Japanese anime go far beyond just mere entertainment. They exemplify complicated and holistic processes within the Japanese historical context, its inheritance of American transcendentalism and its production of metamodernity, and associated transhumanist thinking as cultural artifacts. As technological innovation continues to build upon itself in the future, social theorists and philosophers—must grapple with many difficult questions—just as the creators have in the artistic creation of their anime. What does it mean to be human? How can we overcome the limits of our human nature? How do we understand our reality in a constantly changing age? How do we become more than we are now? Ultimately, the response to these questions is crucial. The answers may determine the very construct of our social reality, now and into the future.

---

[78] *Mobile Suit Gundam*: Directed and Screenplay by Yoshiyuki Tomino (Nagoya TV 1979-1980) and *Code Geass*: Directed by Gorō Taniguchi with Screenplay by Ichirō Ōkouchi (JNN 2006-2007).

Chapter 4

(Re)Making the Monsters of Everyday Life: Minzokugaku and Yuki Urushibara's *Mushishi*

Drew Richardson
University of California Santa Cruz

ABSTRACT: Japanese native ethnographers, such as Yanagita Kunio and Minakata Kumagusu, were concerned with the loss of tradition in the face of rapid modernization and societal change. They studied the lives and customs of rural villages, the peculiarities of regional dialects, and tales of Japanese monsters. As markers of the old, the authentic, the nostalgic and reminders of childhood's belief in flights of fancy, monsters were indispensable for these folklorists. This chapter analyzes Urushibara Yuki's *Mushishi*, a manga (1998-2008) and animated series (2005-2006 and 2014), to uncover how monsters became key signifiers in imagining the Japanese countryside. Moreover, this chapter argues that Urushibara re-imagines folklore and its practitioners through the creation of *mushi*, a new kind of monster. Rather than relying on *yokai*[1] or other creatures of Japanese folklore, Urushibara has re-created the monsters of everyday life to remedy the alienating effects of Japanese folk studies as a discipline premised on loss.

---

[1] Matthew Meyer, "Introduction to Yōkai", *Yokai.com*: https://yokai.com/introduction/. Meyers says of Yōkai (妖怪) that they "are strange, supernatural creatures and phenomena from Japanese folklore. The word is a combination of the characters 妖 (*yō—attractive, bewitching, calamity*) and 怪 (*kai—mystery, wonder*). Over the years, many different English words have been used as translations. Yōkai can be translated as *monster, demon, spirit*, or *goblin*, but it encompasses all of that and more. The world of yōkai also includes ghosts, gods, transformed humans and animals, spirit possession, urban legends, and other strange phenomena. It is a broad and vague term, and nothing exists in the English language that quite describes it. Yōkai is one of those words—like samurai, geisha, ninja, and sushi—that is best left in its native tongue".

KEYWORDS: Folklore, Japanese Native Ethnography, Minakata Kumagusu, Monsters, Yanagita Kunio, Yokai Minzokugaku.

***

Introduction

Why would a folklore-inspired monster manga, deeply concerned with questions of authenticity and folklife, re-imagine monstrosity in its entirety? This question is at the center of most analyses of Urushibara Yuki's award-winning manga *Mushishi*.[2] Nature, nostalgia, and the supernatural are united in Urushibara's work, which includes *Bioluminescence* (1997), *Mushishi* (1999-2008), *Filament* (2004), *Waters* (2009-2010) and *When a Cat Faces West* (2018-2020). *Mushishi* has been faithfully twice serialized twice as an animated series in 2005 and 2014, and as a live-action film was also produced in 2006. *Mushishi* fits with several other animated series and films in what is now part of a new *yokai* boom in Japan, including *Mononoke* (2007), Natsume's *Book of Friends* (2008-2018), and the recent tremendously popular *Demon Slayer: Kimetsu no Yaiba* (2019-present). The critical difference between *Mushishi* and these other series, however, is that while they rely on traditional depictions of Japanese monsters such as *yokai* or demons, *Mushishi* has created an entirely new, radically alien, and ontologically different kind of life.

Viewers of the animated series are first introduced to the concept of *mushi* through the aged voice of an elderly woman, resembling the professional storytellers of folkloric tales in places such as Tono, Iwate. She warns: "They are kept at a distance. Course and mysterious. . . . . They seem to be completely different from the flora and fauna that are familiar to us. This group of strange-looking creatures has inflicted fear onto humans since long past, and have come to be called '*mushi*'".[3] While "*mushi*" is a Japanese word meaning insect or bug (虫), this opening monologue presents viewers with a scroll on which the term is rendered in an older, seldom used Chinese character (蟲) which defamiliarizes the word and suggests "multitude". *Mushi* are unseen by most humans—they are bizarre and sometimes microscopically small. They swarm and flutter in grotesque formations evocative of bacteria, viruses, slime molds, protozoa, fungi and other utterly alien life. Yet they are also steeped in the familiar language of Japanese monsters—of *yokai*—for their capacity to haunt, mesmerize, and transform. Moreover, like yokai, They are tightly bound to human sensory experience and folklife.

---

[2] Yuki Urushibara, *Mushi* (Tokyo: Kodansha 1999-2008).
[3] *Mushishi*: Directed and Screenplay by Hiroshi Naghama based on the manga by Yuki Urushibara (Fuji TV 2005-2006), Episode 1, "The Green Seat".

Scholarship on *Mushishi* has sought to explain the curious existence of *mushi* through primarily environmental, ecological and ontological perspectives that de-center humanity and re-situate the human body within a new lifeworld. John Branscum discusses how human/*mushi* co-dependencies and parasitism reframe both the "human body as ecosystem and microbiome"[4] and the "ecosystem as an entity",[5] which undermines the discrete separation of bodies and their ecosystem. Similarly, Steven R. Anderson discusses the relationship of *mushi* with "illness, disability, and bodily invasion"[6] in order to challenge ideas of disability where human bodies "are transformed through *mushi* interaction, becoming both abled and disabled".[7]

Mio Bryce and Jason Davis, on the other hand, move beyond the human body to raise broader ecological questions by contrasting the environmental visions of *Mushishi* with Miyazaki's *Nausicaa of the Valley of the Wind*[8] and they argue that Urushibara's series "invites us to reconsider what an ecosystem means".[9] Lastly, Kevin Cooley writes against anthropocentric notions of the animate in his analysis of the dyads of life/motion and death/stillness in the medium of animation. Through an examination of "animated stasis", where the anime "interrogat[es] motion and the claims it often seems to make over life in animation", *Mushishi* presents a novel wedding of life and stillness.[10]

Rather than addressing the implications of a *mushi*-oriented worldview, this chapter seeks to answer the question of why Urushibara has chosen to re-imagine monsters as *mushi* in the first place. I argue that Urushibara's careful integration of notions of the folk, folklore and its practitioners aligns with Michael Dylan Foster and Jeffrey A. Tolbert's concept of the folkloresque, where she utilizes "an emplacement of invented situations and characters into a nostalgically configured landscape and imagine folkloric habitus in a way that seems to 'blend Japanese mythology with modern psychological

---

[4] John Branscum, "Me, Myself, and Mushi: Reframing the Human and the Natural in Urushibara Yuki's *Mushishi*", *Works and Days* 32 (2014-2015): 319.
[5] Ibid., 324.
[6] Steven R. Anderson, "Powers of (Dis)Ability: Towards a Bodily Origin in Mushishi", *Mechademia* 9 (2014): 77.
[7] Ibid., 85.
[8] *Nausicaä of the Valley of the Wind*: Directed and Screenplay by Hayao Miyazaki (Toei Company 1984).
[9] Mio Bryce and Jason Davis, "Mushishi", *Resilience: A Journal of the Environmental Humanities* 2.3 (2015): 137.
[10] Kevin Cooley, "Past the End of the Catbus Line: Mushishi's Apparitional Actants", *Animation: an Interdisciplinary Journal* 14.3 (2019): 185.

realism'".[11] Furthermore, the careful blending of Yanagita's folklore studies and the works of Minakata Kumagusu have allowed for the re-imagining of a more vital representation of monsters and ethnographers, where the discipline of folklore can coincide with its object without relegating it to the distant past.

Mushishi in Context

Mushishi offers its audience very little continuity. Each episode is a self-contained tale, evocative of Japanese folklore though not comprised of it. They chart the protagonist, Ginko, as he unravels the mysterious interaction between humans and the indefinable *mushi*. Ginko is the eponymous *mushishi*, a *mushi*-master striving to create harmony between worlds. In his review of the manga, Paul Jackson notes that the interaction between the worlds of *mushi* and humans is characteristic of Shinto. He states that "Episode 1 also introduces the central tenets of Shinto, Japan's native religion. . . . In *Mushishi*, this other realm [non-human world] is visualized as an expansive, ever-moving river of green light".[12] The identification of *mushi* with *kami* ("sacred power") and, more broadly, Japanese folklore and its creatures is a defining element of the series. In fact, Urushibara carefully cultivates images of Japanese tradition: a *mushishi* from one episode appears to be a *yamabushi*,[13] or practitioner of *shugendo*.[14] He is identifiable by his peculiar manner of dress. The homes of villagers have the thatched roofs of *minka* dwellings, such as those preserved as heritage sites in the village of Shirakawa, Gifu. The prologue and epilogue to each chapter—or episode in the anime—often have passages strikingly similar to Japanese proverbs, invoking a sense of ageless wisdom. While these passages sound like proverbs, they are Urushibara's creation, like the relationship between *mushi* and *kami*; in the manga, they are distinct for their use of a different font, while in the anime, they are narrated by the voice of an aged woman.

---

[11] Michael Dylan Foster and Jeffrey A. Tolbert, *The Folkloresque: Reframing Folklore in a Popular Culture World* (Boulder: Colorado University Press, 2016), 44.

[12] Paul Jackson, "The Space Between Worlds: *Mushishi* and Japanese Folklore", *Mechademia* 5 (2010): 341.

[13] "*Yamabushi*", *Britannica*: https://www.britannica.com/topic/yamabushi. "The Shugen-dō practitioner, the *yamabushi* (literally, "one who bows down in the mountains"), engages in spiritual and physical disciplines in order to attain magical power effective against evil spirits. Mountains, considered in folk religions 'other worlds', were for the esoteric Buddhists training grounds for ascetics".

[14] "*Shugen-dō*", *Britannica*: https://www.britannica.com/topic/Shugen-do. "a Japanese religious tradition combining folk beliefs with indigenous Shintō and Buddhism, to which have been added elements of Chinese religious Taoism".

Jackson goes on to make comparisons between *Mushishi* and Hayao Miyazaki's celebrated film *Spirited Away*, which featured an array of spirits and monsters from Japanese folklore. Though *Mushishi* effectively evokes the spirits and monsters of Japanese folklore, it is critically important to note that *mushi* are neither *kami* nor *yokai*. The central question of investigation, then, is if *Mushishi* has carefully built its connection to Japanese tradition, why have *kami* and *yokai* been usurped by *mushi*?

In order to better understand *Mushishi*, it is useful to situate it in its literary tradition. The voluminous works of Mizuki Shigeru, especially *GeGeGe no Kitaro*, stand as the most obvious influence on *Mushishi* and its genre. Mizuki's manga utilized Japanese folklore—transforming its creatures into characters in his works—and revitalized public interest in ghastly tales. Perhaps a nod to Mizuki is the similarity between his character Kitaro, the *yokai* boy, and Urushibara's Ginko. Ginko, like Kitaro before him, is missing an eye. This is concealed by a sweep of silver hair obscuring one side of his face. Mizuki did more than merely create manga. He also created an encyclopedia of *yokai* and conducted extensive research. He "labels himself as a 'yokai researcher' and has made a project of seeking out and illustrating yokai from around Japan".[15] One of the objectives of this chapter is to demonstrate how Urushibara Yuki is, like Mizuki, more than merely the creator of manga and is more akin to a *yokai* researcher.

It is interesting to note that at the end of each *Mushishi* volume, Urushibara has contained an afterword describing her inspiration for each *Mushishi* tale. The inspiration for the stories tends to be rooted in folk stories she was told as a child, her biography, as well as her imagination. Additionally, she occasionally includes short depictions of real folk stories. These after-words plainly demonstrate her knowledge and research of folklore, albeit they allow for imagination and personal experience to serve a crucial role in the creation of *mushi*. Mizuki Shigeru is perhaps not so different, even if he did place a greater emphasis on the real content of Japanese folk stories. Michael Dylan Foster writes that Mizuki "creates a referential ecology for the past that is robust and encyclopedically complex; he transmits to his readers an image of a yokai-infested world that may be richer and more varied than ever existed in the cultural imaginary of prewar, or even pre-Meiji, Japan".[16] In other words, Mizuki not only retold his stories but invented them to be more vibrant than their original sources by instilling them with new life. It is in this light that I wish to begin an exploration of *Mushishi* as a re-invention of Japanese folklore.

---

[15] Michael Dylan Foster, *Pandemonium and Parade* (Berkeley: California University Press, 2009), 169.
[16] Ibid., 177.

The Role of Yanagita Kunio and Minakata Kumagusu in *Mushishi*

Mushishi is not only concerned with the object of folklore but the study of folklore itself—*minzokugaku*—variously translated as "native ethnography", "folkloristics" or "folklore studies".[17] The fundamental players whose dialogue give rise to the discipline are the bureaucrat and folklorist Yanagita Kunio, and the polymath naturalist Minakata Kumagusu. Yanagita was the leading figure in the discipline, a bureaucrat in the Ministry of Agriculture and Commerce who sought to categorize and preserve the folkways of an older Japan imperiled by the rapid forces of modernization. For Yanagita, the rural folk—first characterized as mountain villages and later as island communities—provided a vision of an ordinary Japan that could provide the keys to formulating a national identity. In contrast, Minakata's position was radical, eccentric and subversive. A transient naturalist with reading knowledge of seventeen languages and an expert in slime mold, Minakata was a free-thinking outsider and foil to Yanagita and his discipline. His methods were nearly anti-disciplinary, a transnational interweaving of biology, folklore studies and naturalism. Traditionally, histories of *minzokugaku* encapsulate the field in this Yanagita-Minakata dyad wherein Yanagita is the central, authoritative figure and Minakata is the radical, free-thinking outsider.

Reflection of Yanagita-Minakata Dyad in *Mushishi*

This is developed in *Mushishi* in several ways. One, the episodic nature of *Mushishi*, its mode of storytelling, and its similarity to the tales of Yanagita's *Tono Monogatari*, or Legends of Tono. Two, the nature of *mushi* themselves, beings with ties to the everyday lives of common people, which embody an unresolved tension between Yanagita and Minakata's views of the nature of *minzokugaku* and its object. Three, the importance of telling and cataloguing tales in *Mushishi* that re-imagines the work of *minzokugaku* scholars, albeit with some important distinctions; and four, the similarities between itinerant *mushishi* and the researchers of *minzokugaku* themselves.

This chapter will discuss how Urushibara has re-imagined not only folklore, but the discipline of *minzokugaku* and its practitioners. This reimagining is not simply an exercise, for its differences from historical content allow for the creation of a *minzokugaku* that does not banish its object, *yokai* or *mushi*, to a discourse bound and separated from human experience.

---

[17] *Minzokugaku* scholars were not in agreement in the naming of their emerging discipline. Even the word *minzokugaku* can be written in Japanese with two different sets of characters suggesting folklore studies and ethnology, respectively: 民俗学　民族学.

Yanagita Kunio and the *Tales of Tono*

Mushishi usually opens or closes episodes with mysterious passages of grave portent. These are diverse and range from proverbs and warnings to prayers for a good harvest. These remarks are thematically important to the episode and establish a sense of mystery through their brevity and vagueness. They are remarkably similar to Yanagita Kunio's *Tono Monogatari* (*Legends of Tono*), which is distinct from Yanagita's other work in its vitality because it does not relegate the supernatural to mere objects to folklore. Gerald Figal writes that "marvelous stories about *tengu* and his own writing about them were not idle amusements for Yanagita. They were, in fact, crucial in the textualization of an essential knowledge of the 'folk heart'".[18] Indeed, Yanagita believed that these tales were "true" because they revealed truths about societies. Yet, Yanagita's belief in the "truth" of these tales seems to occasionally elude this explanation and enter the realm of real belief, such as in his letters to Minakata Kumagusu where he insists that "mountain men" (*yamaotoko*) are real. This is perhaps why Yanagita so fervently insisted on the truth of these tales. Stylistically, the passages from *Mushishi* resemble the tales of Tono. For example, on the subject of mysterious disappearances, compare: "Lots of unusual things wash up on the seashore. Nuts from distant southern lands and seashells, giant deep-sea fish, and on rare occasions, people. And empty boats with no one in them as well"[19] with "In Tono, each year larger numbers of peasant children are kidnapped by *ijin*. Most are girls".[20] The unsettling quality and air of mystery in the texts is achieved through brevity, a matter-of-fact quality of the language, and an ending line that raises more questions than it answers. Moreover, the ties to Yanagita in the *Mushishi* passage are reinforced by the reference to sea-borne nuts, which he claimed were his inspiration for writing on southern Okinawa in *Kaijo no Michi*.[21]

Ginko's concluding monologue from the episode "The Sound of Rust" provides another example. He states: "the townspeople say that they still sometimes hear, though just faintly, a very hoarse, but strangely lovely and familiar singing voice echoing through the mountains".[22] Yanagita describes a similar phenomenon.

---

[18] Gerald Figal, *Civilization and Monsters: Spirits of Modernity in Meiji Japan* (Durham: Duke University Press, 1999), 115.
[19] *Mushishi*, Episode 8, "Where Sea Meets Man".
[20] Yanagita Kunio, *The Legends of Tono*, trans. Ronald A. Morse (Lanham: Rowman & Littlefield Publishers, Inc., 2008), 27.
[21] Yanagita Kunio, *Kaijo no Michi* (Tokyo: Daigaku Shuppankai, 1992).
[22] *Mushishi*, Episode 23, "The Sound of Rust".

Along the mountainous area of Shiromi there is a spot called Hanaremori (detached woods). One small area called the *choja's* house has no one living there. There is a man who sometimes goes there to make charcoal. One night, someone raised the straw mat that hung over the entrance to his hut and peeped in. Inside was a woman with long trailing hair divided down the middle. In this area it is not unusual to hear the screams of women late at night.[23]

The resemblance between these passages suggests that Urushibara was likely familiar with *Tono Monogatari*. Evanescent or vanishing women is a persistent motif in Japanese folklore. Like the tales of Tono, the stories of *Mushishi* do not form a linear narrative. Rather, they are separate episodes. With the exception of Ginko and a few others, Urushibara's characters—mostly villagers—appear to be very similar. They are plain, lack significant development, and are, frankly, difficult to tell apart. The plainness of the characters emphasizes the real focus of these stories: the mysteries of *mushi*. As in *Tono Monogatari*, the villagers are the nameless objects of the supernatural. The structures of these texts produce a sensation of timelessness, especially when combined with the wonderfully evocative short passages. The tensions of these stories are never fully resolved. Indeed, the women in the mountains may still be heard singing, even now.

Hashimoto Mitsuru writes that Yanagita believed "traditional folk beliefs flowed 'silently from family to family, and from mother to daughter'. . . . these beliefs were 'based on the natural demands of everyday life'".[24] Part of the sense of authenticity of *mushi* in the series is due to their ties to the everyday lives of common people and experiences. Every instance of *mushi* ties these mysterious beings to the lives of humans. Often, these ties are established through human sensory experience: sight and sound, primarily. In the episode "Tender Horns", Ginko discovers a village that has been afflicted by two kinds of *mushi*, Ah and Un, both of which are connected to sound.[25] Their names are derived from the Japanese phrase *a-un no kokyu* which signifies a harmonious relationship. The *mushi* Ah eats sound, infecting human ears and causing deafness; while Un eats silence, infecting human ears to create a cacophony. This phrase also connects these *mushi* to *komainu*—or *shiisa* in Okinawa—the guardian lion-dogs that sit on either side of shrine gates, one mouth open, one mouth shut. This is but one of many *mushi* that are related

---

[23] Kunio, *Legends of Tono*, 28.
[24] Hashimoto Mitsuru, "Chiho: Yanagita Kunio's 'Japan'", in *Mirror of Modernity: Invented Traditions of Modern Japan*, ed. Stephen Vlastos (Berkeley: California University Press, 1998), 136.
[25] *Mushishi*, Episode 3, "Tender Horns".

to human sensory experience. In "Eye of Fortune, Eye of Misfortune", a poor-sighted girl is granted an extraordinary vision by a *mushi* infecting her eye.[26] However, this becomes a curse, as the sight continually advances into preternatural vision: seeing through people, walls and villages, into vastness, and eventually into the future itself.

Mushi are also connected to cognitive human experience in dreaming and memory. In "The Pillow Pathway", *Mushi* make their home in a man's pillow, making his dreams come true and bringing miracles and ruin.[27] There is a fascinating exploration of human memory in the episode, "Those who Inhale the Dew", where a *mushi* changes human lifespan to match its own, resulting in death and rebirth each day, without memory of the previous days.[28] The lack of memory is disruptive yet there is a sweetness to the day-long lives—in experiencing the sensations of each day as if it were the first and the possible avoidance of the future's weight on human consciousness.

Finally, to complete the spectrum of human experience in a way that may have been pleasing to Yanagita, *mushi* are connected to local village traditions and lifeways. The "Heavy Seed" tells of a mysterious seed that, when planted, causes the death of the weakest person in the village in exchange for a bountiful harvest.[29] Here is a connection of *mushi* to agriculture and rice-cultivation, the pinnacle of folk life. The importance of community living is also the subject of "The Chirping Shell", wherein *mushi* come to shore, hiding in shells, to avoid a disaster at sea.[30] The *mushi's* cries warn their brethren to come to shore and avoid danger. A comparison is made between the warning cries of the *mushi* and the necessity for communal support in village life. A man who lost his wife at sea to tragedy blames the village, isolating himself and his daughter. When his daughter listens to the sea-song of a shell, she hears the cry of the *mushi* instead, which mutes her. Ginko advises the girl's father that she must listen to the voices of others to regain her speech, forcing them to re-integrate into the community. Ultimately, the father is able to warn the community of coming danger and avoid disaster, fostering a reconciliation that underscores the theme of warning and communal voices.

Mushishi's mysterious beings have a clearer relationship to human life than *yokai* in traditional folklore. Their influence is felt in human perception, cognition and every aspect of rural life. These connections serve to make the stories feel authentic and traditional, a remarkable feat for stories of imagined

---

[26] *Mushishi*, Episode 25, "Eye of Fortune, Eye of Misfortune".
[27] *Mushishi*, Episode 4, "The Pillow Pathway".
[28] *Mushishi*, Episode 6, "Those Who Inhale the Dew".
[29] *Mushishi*, Episode 9, "The Heavy Seed".
[30] *Mushishi*: Zoku-Sho, Episode 2, "The Chirping Shell".

beings. In both form and content, *Mushishi* emulates Yanagita's model of mysterious tales that encapsulate the daily lives of the folk.

Minakata Kumagusu and Mutating Life: Where Science Meets Folklore in Ontology

While *mushi* may very well be Yanagita's monsters of everyday life, the fact remains that the creatures are remarkably different from *kami* and *yokai*. If Urushibara wished it, she could, in the same manner as Mizuki Shigeru, have written these stories as re-imaginings of authentic Japanese monsters and still connected them robustly to rural life. What accounts for the other aspect of *mushi*, the similarities they bear to micro-organisms, bacteria, protozoa and plant life? In some respects, Ginko fulfills the role of a wandering physician, curing patients of supernatural ailments or parasitism caused by *mushi* that are, like microscopic bacteria, invisible to the human eye.[31] However, this medical treatment never simplifies *mushi* or strips them of their mystery. While Jackson may have remarked in his review that by the first chapter, *Mushishi* has established concepts of Shinto and *kami*, it is also true that *mushi* are defined as *midorimono*—literally "green things"—which suggests a relationship to plants, protozoa, fungi or even slime molds. The following section situates the *mushi* within discourse on the mysterious in the works of Minakata Kumagusu "whose theory of human culture had more in common with the cultures of slime mold. . . . [for] both were sites of ceaseless phantasmagoric change—not unilinear progress—that spurred the unfixing and mixing of sharply cut taxonomic boundaries".[32]

The sharp disagreement between Yanagita Kunio and Minakata Kumagusu over the existence of mountain men was a pivotal moment that established Minakata as a radical thinker, working outside of the confines of the emerging discipline of *minzokugaku*. Mark Driscoll articulates the difference in their perspectives.

> [Minakata Kumagusu] understood Yanagita's nativism project as translating into modern terms the older discourse of essential Japaneseness, what he referred to as *kokutai* (国体) Minakata implicitly opposed *kokutai*, rendered as the static "Japanese essence", with the standard biological concept of *hentai* (変体), or "mutating organic

---

[31] The wandering physician or medicine man is a common in Japanese folklore as a potential *ijin* or outsider. They often have connections to the miraculous or supernatural. See also the animated series *Mononoke*. Directed by Nakamura Kenji with Screenplay by Chiaki J. Konaka et al. (Fuji TV 2007).

[32] Gerald Figal, *Civilization and Monsters*, 53.

matter". His most important scientific work involved tracing the hybrid genealogies of slime molds and other forms of *hentai*.³³

If Yanagita's insistence on the connection of folk beliefs and everyday life can be understood as *kokutai* in its desire to locate the origins of Japaneseness, then perhaps Minakata's idea of *hentai* can explain the microbial element of *mushi*. Driscoll's definition of *hentai* as "mutating organic matter" is particularly useful for discussions of *mushi*, which undergo astonishing and sometimes horrific transformations in their interactions with their human hosts. Even slime molds, Minakata's primary object of study, is comparable to many forms of *mushi*.

Within the discipline of *minzokugaku*, Yanagita was a towering figure whose theories went mostly unchallenged by other scholars with the exception of Minakata who took him to task in a series of letters. It is fitting that the dual nature of *mushi* captures the two major theoretical perspectives in the study of Japanese ethnography. While the narrative structure and folkloresque elements of *Mushishi* are derived from Yanagita-inspired folklore studies, the re-invention of monsters as *mushi* is indebted to the work of Minakata.

This dual nature—the marriage of Yanagita's *kokutai* to Minakata's *hentai*—is not so much at odds with itself as it may seem. Minakata and Yanagita did agree on the nature of the mysterious. Yanagita insisted on the irreducibility of mystery. In his tirade against monsterologist Inoue Enryo (who sought to enlighten Japanese by dispelling beliefs in the supernatural), he states that "I think the reports of the inexplicable [*fushigisetsu*], on the other hand, will probably remain hundreds of years hereafter".³⁴ Likewise, Minakata suggests that science will never be able to penetrate some mysteries: "Rather than actually analyzing the reasons or causes behind *mono-fushigi*, [scientists] go only so far as to dissect mysteries [*fushigi*] and turn them into groups of phenomena".³⁵ While Yanagita's insistence on the irreducible mystery of the supernatural is straightforward, Minakata's view may seem to be counter-intuitive for a scientist. Minakata believed that while science was enormously successful at predicting how phenomena work, it is unable to answer the question of why. Thus, Minakata and Yanagita were each opposed to the work of Inoue Enryo encouraged modernization while debunking all supernatural claims.

---

³³ Mark Driscoll, *Absolute Erotic, Absolute Grotesque* (Durham: Duke University Press, 2010), 8.
³⁴ Gerald Figal, *Civilization and Monsters*, 117.
³⁵ Ibid., 56.

Mushishi never resolves the dual natures of *mushi*. Their *hentai* and *kokutai* aspects are essential for their capacity to both transmit ideas of rural Japanese life while remaining living elements of the present. *Mushi*, unlike *yokai*, resist the debunking of Inoue through their living and transforming bodies—which allows them to embody notions of Japanese rural life and tradition—in a form compatible with modernity.

Gerald Figal argues that the Minakata mandala's depiction of causality and coincidence correspond to scientific knowledge and "karmic transmigration".[36] Consequently, science is both limited by, and reliant upon, the web of contingency that governs human behavior and leads to scientific discovery. While scientific practice facilitates an understanding of cause and effect—in order to navigate a world of contingency—Minakata describes a set of strategies he calls "tact".[37] Tact includes attuning to dreams, or the unconscious completion of routine tasks. Attention to contingent relations through tact demands a re-orientation of oneself in the world.

Ontology has remained a major thread in scholarship on Minakata to the present day. In "Attuning to the webs of *en*: Ontology, Japanese Spirit World, and the 'tact' of Minakata Kumagusu",[38] Casper Brunn Jensen, Miho Ishii and Philip Swift argue that Minakata was a "maverick scientist" who offered a "proto-ontographic answer" to the challenge of anthropological participant-observer studies, particularly in the case of imperceptible spirit-worlds.[39] They argue that techniques of tact—attention to the relations of coincidence at the edge of human perceptibility—may allow the anthropologist to overcome disbelief and effectively study the ontological difference of spirit-worlds. Though the language of critics has evolved over time, scholarly engagement with Minakata's mandala characterizes his work as offering radically new avenues of thought, a re-thinking of ontological difference before ontology.

While Minakata's embrace of ontological difference and the role of the ethnographer provides a model for *mushi* outside the confines of Yanagita's *minzokugaku*, his fervent desire to protect local shrines and forests represents an early environmental sentiment that is reflected in the relationship of humans and *mushi*. Minakata's reputation for environmentalism has been elaborated on by Brij Tankha who labeled him a "pioneer environmentalist"

---

[36] Ibid., 56-57.
[37] Ibid., 71.
[38] Casper Brunn Jensen, Miho Ishii and Philip Swift, "Attuning to the Webs of *en*: Ontology, Japanese Spirit Worlds, and the 'Tact' of Minakata Kumagusu", *Hau: Journal of Ethnographic Theory* 6.2 (2016): 149-72.
[39] Ibid., 160.

and foregrounded Minakata's desire to protect shrine forests.[40] Tankha's assessment also draws parallels between Minakata's resistance and peoples' rights activism, which emphasizes the potential for radical action in addition to radical thought. Similarly, Tom Gill describes Minakata as "an activist for environmental protection about half a century before it became fashionable".[41]

Many of the environmental, ecological, and ontological themes that critics have identified in the aberrant lifeforms of *mushi* can be traced back to the work of Minakata Kumagusu. Likewise, the elements of the folkloresque and similarity to *Tono Monogatari* can be traced to the work of Yanagita Kunio. The dual nature of *mushi* demonstrates connections between the monsters of Urushibara's work and key figures in Japanese native ethnography, such as Yanagita and Minakata. I will now turn to ways that *Mushishi* re-imagines the discourse of folklore studies itself.

Disciplining *Mushi*

Connections between individual chapters of *Mushishi* are difficult to establish and the chronology of the series is uncertain. However, one thread that connects some of the tales is storytelling—both the oral telling of tales—as well as the transcription of them onto paper. The final aspect of *mushi* that remains unaddressed is the relationship between *mushi* and writing. Like other elements of *mushi*, the relationship of *mushi* and writing is briefly touched upon in the first chapter, "The Green Seat".[42] This chapter tells the story of a boy possessing "the hand of god", which causes his kanji and drawings to come to life through his calligraphy as *mushi*. His writing becomes literally monstrous in that each stroke of his brush writes *mushi* into existence.

"A Sea of Writings", demonstrates the connection of *mushi* and writing in much greater detail.[43] Following the defeat of a terrible *mushi* by her ancestors, a young girl is cursed by an ink-black mark covering most of her body. In order to maintain the binding of this *mushi*, she must continually transcribe stories of defeating *mushi*, as told to her by itinerant *Mushishi*. Her transcription of these tales of encounter, defeat and subsequent binding, mirror the practice of scholars such as Inoue Enryo. As she ages, the tattoo slowly shrinks as though it were the source of ink for her recordings. The writing of these stories is literally a means to contain monsters—a practice

---

[40] Brij Tankha, "Minakata Kumagusu: Fighting Shrine Unification in Meiji Japan", *China Report* 36.4 (2002): 556 and 558.
[41] Tom Gill, "Tsurumi Kazuko on Minakata Kumagusu", *Kazuko Tsurumi: The Adventure of Ideas* (Tokyo: Japanime, 2014), 154.
[42] *Mushishi*, Episode 1, "The Green Seat".
[43] *Mushishi*, Episode 20, "A Sea of Writings".

that is reflected in the discipline of *minzokugaku*—which, by writing of monsters as folklore, banishes them from the present. Finally, the difficulty of the task of transcription is addressed when it is revealed that the *mushi* eventually escape their written bindings and must be re-written into new texts. The continual re-writing of the old, combined with the recording of the new, is a Herculean task, and there is the suggestion that this may not be possible to continue forever. Eventually, some *mushi* will escape, and others will go unrecorded. While this may be a problem for the characters of *Mushishi*, it addresses one of the central problems of *minzokugaku*.

> Inoue Enryo, as Gerald Figal has shown . . . . approached folk culture as a terrain of superstition that had to be eradicated in order to achieve modernity. For both de Certeau and Figal, the surveillance and enlightenment origins of popular studies did not significantly alter when the scholars became more sympathetic to their objects. They may have shifted to a celebratory register, but the objects were still rendered powerless in their appropriation to a different discourse.[44]

In other words, the very existence of *minzokugaku* or folklore studies is premised on the disappearance of folklore and the folk. Even though writers such as Yanagita were dearly attached to these traditions, the writing of them as folklore identified them as being outside of modern Japan and banished them to a discourse detached from the workings of everyday life. *Mushishi* challenges this banishment through its depiction of the practice of *minzokugaku* in the oral telling of stories and their transcriptions. Though *mushi* may be bound in text, they are fantastically able to reassert themselves and it is a great labor to keep them constrained. Although the *mushi*-as-text is shown to be a problem in the series, it is also enormously vital. In this fantastic re-imagining of the writing of *minzokugaku*, the monsters are not so easily tamed, allowing for the simultaneous and vital co-existence of monsters and folklore. In other words, *Mushishi* is able to re-imagine folklore studies and folklorists without having to suffer the loss of its object.

Mushishi mirrors *minzokugaku* scholarship not only in the writing of texts, but also in the portrayal of Ginko and other *mushishi* as native ethnographers. Christy argues that popular imaginings of *minzokugaku* "appeal to a pastoral romance", in which the ethnographer traverses "a rural landscape with a rucksack on his back and a soft cap on his head, faded and beaten by the sun,

---

[44] Alan Christy, *A Discipline on Foot: Inventing Native Japanese Ethnography* (Lanham: Rowman & Littlefield Publishers, Inc., 2012), 151.

wind and rain. Above all else, he is walking".[45] Ginko and his fellow *mushishi* are, like native ethnographers, always on the move. It is an interesting contrast, however, that while the native ethnographer is always walking in search of the mysterious, Ginko is walking away from it, for it follows him. It is no coincidence that the opening theme song for the first season of the anime is Ally Kerr's "The Sore Feet Song".

Christy further connects *minzokugaku* to the idea of travel and experience: "By placing travel at the root, these claims sustain the field's key representation: namely, that *minzokugaku* is a science of experience".[46] Ginko is marked as a foreign traveler—or perhaps an *ijin* (outsider)—by his strange appearance and foreign clothes: a white button-up shirt, pants and overcoat. This science of experience fits neatly with Ginko's own mode of investigation and inquiry. While he has read numerous texts in the past, the *mushi* he encounters are almost always displaying a new phenomena that he must come to terms with individually. This is congruent with the idea that "texts are generally the objects that provide a gateway back to re-constructing the experience of fieldwork (the encounter)".[47]

In this sense, the writings on *mushi* are meant to recreate their stories, but are not overly prescriptive on how to understand a situation in the present, for, that is the role of the *mushishi* and his individual experience of fieldwork is primary. Like *mushi*, and the writing of *minzokugaku*, the presentation of *mushishi* as native ethnographers is a fantastic one, and differs starkly from the reality. Christy notes how Shibusawa Keizo, the founder of the Attic Museum and very wealthy financier of native ethnography, would frequently "foot the bill for group tours" and "Shibusawa's journeys rarely lacked for a company or a festive atmosphere".[48] The lonely wanderings in *Mushishi* are a representation not of how native ethnographers usually traveled but of the romanticized journeys envisioned by Yanagita—visions that often overtook reality in his depictions of his own journeys.[49] *Mushishi* are the native ethnographers of Yanagita's romantic vision. Just as Yanagita "clearly recognized the limitations to villagers understanding themselves", Ginko, too, takes up the task of explaining the villager's own traditions to the villagers. In the Yanagita mode, Ginko alone is the privileged outsider who finds meaning in the lives of the rural folk.[50]

---

[45] Ibid., 45.
[46] Ibid., 46.
[47] Ibid.
[48] Ibid., 50.
[49] Ibid., 49.
[50] Ibid., 57.

Finally, although the kinds of travel employed by Shibusawa Keizo are not featured in *Mushishi*, the desire to collect objects, such as in Shibusawa's Attic Museum, is represented in the figure of Adashino. Adashino is a wealthy doctor who provides Ginko with funds in exchange for the objects he comes across. However, this element—the collection and preservation of objects is also problematized—as Adashino's acquisitions are cursed or undisciplined and harm unsuspecting villagers.

A final similarity between Yanagita's model ethnographer and *mushishi* is their active role in curing various ailments. While in Urushibara's narrative, the curing of *mushi*-related illness grants the *mushishi* a purpose in the lives of the villagers and is a convenient plot device, some of Yanagita's model ethnographers were itinerant physicians, such as Tokugawa era travel writer Sugae Masumi (1754-1829). In *Mushishi*, native ethnographers are re-imagined as *mushishi*, lonely wanderers in the attractively romantic vision of Yanagita. Through their travels and encounter with *mushi*—fieldwork—they collect tales and occasionally objects that will form the basis of *minzokugaku* scholarship. Their ability to address and correct problems and imbalances demonstrates the activity of *mushi* in the present and the need for such wanderers. They are not merely recollecting what has been lost but using their talents to heal problems of the present.

Conclusion

Yuki Urushibara captures the essence of *yokai* and the discipline of *minzokugaku*, revitalizing and transforming each in the world of *Mushishi*. *Mushi* are, as Yanagita desired, intricately connected to human experience and the rhythms of life. They remain important for village life. Moreover, they are doubly mysterious for their dual nature that supports both Yanagita and Minakata's views of the folk object. This unresolved tension prevents *mushi* from being easily dispelled and preserves their mystery. *Mushi* have a strong relationship to writing and stories and can be contained by text—but are also able to escape from it—a living catalogue rather than a dead one. Lastly, *mushishi* are native ethnographers re-imagined. They are solitary travelers in the way that Yanagita envisioned that carry out fieldwork through travel on foot and individual experience. However, they also ameliorate the disorders of the present caused by *mushi*, making them more than collectors of a lost past.

Rather than relying on *yokai* or other creatures of Japanese folklore, Urushibara has re-created the monsters of everyday life. *Mushishi* has re-imagined not only monsters as *mushi* but *minzokugaku* scholars as *mushi*-masters. The combination of Yanagita's folklore studies and Minakata's mutating life has created space for a folkloresque re-enactment of monsters and an ethnography that neither defeats its object nor banishes it to a discourse outside of contemporary life. In this fashion, *mushishi* offers a correction to the alienating effects of Japanese folk studies as a discipline premised on loss.

Chapter 5

The Refashioned Tengu: Tradition and Contemporary Romance in *Black Bird*

Tara Etherington
University of Toronto

ABSTRACT: The *tengu* is recognized in Japan as a creature from folklore and historical texts who often leads pious and innocent humans astray through trickery and malice. This creature still features in both Shinto and Buddhist religious iconography at shrines and temples as a reminder of the evils and temptations leading toward deviation from more righteous paths. Despite its mountain folklore origins, the *tengu* has been adapted and refashioned in popular culture by manga artists such as Kanoko Sakurakouji, who fuses the traditional with the contemporary in her girls' manga (*shōjo*) series, *Black Bird* (2009-2014). The *Black Bird* series uses iconic *shōjo* manga tropes such as coming-of-age narratives and the *bishōnen* (beautiful boy) character to marry together and refashion the *tengu* as a love interest who speaks to the intersects of tradition, gender and ideals of romance that are able to transcend translation and resonate with global contemporary audiences.

KEYWORDS: Tengu, Buddhism, Shinto, Gender, Hybridity, Japan, Manga, Refashioning, Romance Fiction, Bishōnen.

***

Introduction

Supernatural creatures in literature and folklore serve many purposes. In some cases, these creatures are used to entertain and reinforce ideas and behaviours related to culture, society and religious beliefs. This chapter looks at how a Japanese supernatural creature, relatively unknown to Anglophone readers, has been adapted to appeal to contemporary readers. The "*tengu*" is refashioned by Kanoko Sakurakouji in her *Black Bird* manga series with references to both its historical origins and contemporary stylizations that appeal to *shōjo* ("girls") manga readers. When read in English translation and by a reader who has little or any knowledge of Japanese culture, religion or philosophy, the *Black Bird tengu* is an unfamiliar supernatural creature that may be mistaken with bearing some similarities with the more familiar Western vampire. However, the sales success of the series in the U.S., ranking fourth in the Top 10 *Shōjo* Manga in the 2013 Summer, Fall and Winter charts, suggests that the *tengu* can operate across transcultural narratives to speak to audiences reading the manga in English translation.[1]

To effectively decode this creature and its role in the series, the non-native reader requires additional contextual knowledge to appreciate the history of the *tengu*, the stylistic workings of manga, and its myriad of modern influences. Comparable genres to *shōjo* manga's demographic, such as Anglophone Young Adult (YA) fiction, are interested in exploring emotions related to human interactions and the location of the "female" in social discourses. This is principally true in instances where the female protagonist is subjected to masculine or patriarchal discourse. To address such topics and to differentiate from *shōnen* ("boys") manga that typically includes male characters who project traditional "male" behaviours and roles, such as "protector, provider, authoritative [and] pillar", several *shōjo* manga artists have "refashioned" these traditionalized gender roles and expectations in their works.[2]

The introduction of foreign ideas into Japan has been met historically with a desired philosophy to harmonize potential conflicts with traditional cultural beliefs and values, which often resulted in customized and hybridized adaptations. Roger J. Davies and Osamu Ikeno acknowledge in their collaborative work, *The Japanese Mind*, how "refashion[ing]" foreign ideas, such as multiple and conflicting religious faiths, is part of the Japanese mentality to embrace new ideas.

> [S]ince ancient times the Japanese people have demonstrated the ability to take in foreign ideas and cultural forms and refashion them according to the dictates of the Japanese character, thus creating something new and valuable of their own.[3]

---

[1] "Top 10 Shojo Properties—Summer 2013", *ICv2* 30th October 2013: https://icv2.com/articles/comics/view/28057/top-10-shojo-properties-fall-holidays-2013 and "Top 10 Shojo Properties—Fall/Holidays 2013", ICv2 07th March 2014: https://icv2.com/articles/comics/view/28057/top-10-shojo-properties-fall-holidays-2013.

[2] Megan Harrell, "Slightly Out of Character: Shōnen Epics, Doujinshi and Japanese Concepts of Masculinity", *The Virginia Review of Asian Studies* 5 (2007): 5.

[3] Roger J. Davies and Ikeno Osamu, eds., *The Japanese Mind. Understanding Contemporary Japanese Culture* (Clarendon: Tuttle Publishing, 2002), 38.

The Refashioned Tengu 119

While this idea of refashioning is rooted in philosophies born from Japanese Buddhism and Shinto practices, prominent recognition of this trait was most evident in the Meiji Period (1868-1912).[4] During this time, Japan willingly imported Western ideologies and material products into its culture and society alongside their own (occasionally contradictory) practices to transform conflicting traditions into hybrid forms.

This chapter will seek to illustrate how folkloric and religious affiliations of the *tengu* are merged with stylistic tropes found in *shōjo* manga to refashion it in Kanoko Sakurakouji's *Black Bird* manga series. This study will demonstrate through close readings how this hybrid and alluring creature resonates with contemporary readers to address topics of tradition, gender and romance.

What is a *Tengu*?

The first question for any reader attempting to engage with *Black Bird* is: what is a "*tengu*"? In its simplest form, a *tengu* is commonly translated to "demon" in English and stems from the Japanese collection of folkloric demons known as *yokai*. In the Glossary provided at the back of the first volume of the series, the following definitions are provided.

1) "Demons": In the Japanese version, they are called ayakashi and yokai. The terms essentially mean the same thing, although yokai adds the kanji for "suspicious". Both terms can be translated as monsters, goblins, or spirits.

2) Tengu: are a type of yokai and often appear as half human and half bird.

3) Karasu Tengu: a type of tengu literally meaning "crow tengu" because of their half-human, half-crow appearance.[5]

While the glossary does acknowledge the *tengu* as a type of *yokai* that is considered suspicious, it does not provide any further contextual background to determine what a *tengu* is. The added definition of "Karasu Tengu" highlights that the term *tengu* may be categorized into multiple types. *The Oxford Companion to World Mythology* describes *tengu* as "depicted with

---

[4] Shinto and Buddhism overlapped and intersected considerably during the Edo (1603-1868) and Meiji eras across a diverse range of branches, interpretations and practices. This chapter will refer to these belief systems collectively, recognizing that native scholars such as Haruko Wakabayashi, Hirata Atsutane and others engaged and employed them differently in seeking to define *tengu*.

[5] Kanoko Sakurakouji, *Black Bird* Vol. 1 (San Francisco: Viz Media, 2009), 190.

wings, bird-like beaks or long noses, and sometimes red faces and the clothing of monks, especially those of the *yamabushi*", highlighting another variation compared to the *Karasu Tengu*.[6]

Historically, there are many interpretations of what constitutes a *tengu* in Japanese literature, art and accounts by Japanese scholars of religion and belief, such as Haruko Wakabayashi and Hirata Atsutane. In *The Seven Tengu Scrolls*, Haruko Wakabayashi states that

> The earliest known reference to *tengu* in Japan is found in the eighth-century *Nihon shoki* (The Chronicles of Japan). The word "*tengu*" originated in China, where *tian gou*, as its literal meaning "celestial dog" suggests, refers to a comet or an animal. The *tengu* popularly known in Japan today have beaks or long noses, wings, and human bodies, and are often disguised as *yamabushi* (mountain ascetics). . . . .
>
> In traditional Japanese folktales, *tengu* are usually depicted as forest spirits or deities. They can be mischievous (kidnapping children from villages) or comical (playing tricks on people who wander into the mountains).[7]

From Wakabayashi's observation, there is a difference between the commonly associated image of the *tengu* in contemporary Japan and its complex folkloric origin. While Marinus Wilhelm de Visser agrees that the etymology of *tengu* stems from the Chinese legendary creature, *tian gou*, he interprets another understanding of the creature that developed within Japan as resembling a black dog that eats the sun during an eclipse.[8] Similar to Wakabayashi's account, he acknowledges that the Japanese counterpart is often depicted as possessing avian or anthropomorphic characteristics that evolved from these Chinese roots.

Some of the earliest accounts of *tengu* are ascribed to the *Konjaku Monogatarishū* (*Anthology of Tales from the Past*), written during the late Heian Period (A.D. 794-1185), where they are presented as the antithesis of Buddhism.[9] The *Konjaku* characterises *tengu* as troublesome opponents to

---

[6] David Lenner, ed., *The Oxford Companion to World Mythology* (Oxford: Oxford University Press, 2005), 376.

[7] Haruko Wakabayashi, *The Seven Tengu Scrolls* (Honolulu: Hawai'i University Press, 2012), xiii-xiv.

[8] M. W. de Visser, "The Tengu", *Transactions of the Asiatic Society of Japan* 34.2 (1908): 25-99.

[9] Wakabayashi, *Seven Tengu Scrolls*, 30.

Buddhism, capable of possessing people (especially women), and shape-shifting into humans from their original form of a kite-like creature.[10] Another literary account, the *Tengu zōshi*, are a set of narrative scrolls dating to A.D. 1296 which consist primarily of short tales about the *tengu* and are the earliest surviving scrolls in which many *tengu* are illustrated. Haruko Wakabayashi identifies five physical types that characterise *tengu* in these scrolls.

> The first, and most numerous, appear largely human but have beaks. They occur, wearing clerical robes. . . . The second. . . . dress as monks and *yamabushi* but have beaks and short hair. The third have beaks, hair, and wings, and sometimes claws. . . . . The fourth are depicted as kites [birds]. . . . . Finally, there are *tengu* who appear completely human, which makes them hard to identify.[11]

The versatility of the *tengu* image, marked as having some human or grotesque features, has lent itself to wide interpretations of this supernatural creature and its adaptability to suit contemporary audiences.

In contrast, Wilhelm Hansen's study of Hirata Atsutane, a renowned Japanese scholar and one of the most significant theologians of Shinto in the later Edo period (A.D. 1603-1868), reveals a theory of *tengu* that falls into two categories: "the *tengu* that is a bird or beast transformed over time. . . . [or] a human who had been transformed due to some evil influence".[12] In Atsutane's *Thoughts on Supernatural Beings of Past and Present* (*kokon yomikō*), he acknowledges how his accounts of the first category of *tengu* are formed from the passing down of stories from the *sanjin* [mountain people] to explain supernatural creatures where "the birds grow hands from their wings" and for beasts "their front legs grow wings, and after a while, they stand upright and change form to look like people".[13] For the second category, Atsutane frames his understanding of the relationship between *tengu* and Buddhism from *The August Pillar of the Soul* (*Tama no mihashira*) by Hayashi Razan, a Japanese neo-Confucian philosopher and writer in the Edo period.

> [M]any [tengu] are Buddhist priests or *yamabushi* who have undergone demonic transformations. It is thought that the reason people began to call them *tengu* is that, with their big noses and their

---

[10] Visser, "The Tengu", 61.
[11] Wakabayashi, *Seven Tengu Scrolls*, 144.
[12] Wilburn Hansen, *When Tengu Talk: Hirata Atsutane's Ethnography of the Other World* (Honolulu: Hawaii University Press, 2008), 80.
[13] Ibid., 80.

protruding lips, their heads look like *tengu* [the other kind of *tengu*, the animal transformation *tengu*].[14]

Like Wakabayashi, Atsutane associated *tengu* with a kind of Buddhist evil. He interpreted Edo period folkloric understandings of them in his *Senkyō ibun* [*Strange Tidings from the Realm of Immortals*], which records his interaction with a so-called "Tengu Boy" who described supernatural experiences in his youth after living in the mountains.[15] Building upon these accounts from Japanese folklore and religious characterizations, artists have also sought to capture the many images of the *tengu*, with depictions based on the *Tengu zōshi* resembling a kite-like bird and later depictions in the fourteenth century showing a red-faced humanoid demon with a long nose.[16]

A wood-block painting from Sekien Toriyama's collection *The Illustrated Night Parade of a Hundred Demons* is one of the closest illustrations to the physical shaping of the kite-like *tengu* that was re-imagined in light of previous accounts and illustrations.[17] Additionally, an interpretation of a "Mountain" or (*Yamabushi Tengu*) with its long nose and monstrous appearance has been found in a shrine in the Oita Prefecture of Japan.[18] These creatures, as Wakabayashi explored, are more mischievous in character as they are seen to challenge the purity and relevance of Buddhist priests' faith and practices.[19]

Popular understandings of the ancient *tengu*, along with their associations with Buddhism and their adaptations into Shinto beliefs, have resulted in a clearer distinction between the "Crow" (or *Karasu Tengu*) and the Mountain (*Yamabushi Tengu*) measured by their mischievous interference with humans. According to Mark Schumacher, the Mountain *Tengu* is now considered to be

---

[14] Ibid.

[15] Hansen, *When Tengu Talk*, 2.

[16] While the latter interpretation is commonly associated with the wide-ranging definition of *yamabushi* or "mountain" *tengu*, other names such as *Hanataka tengu* (long-nosed *tengu*) specifically depict a more human entity often with a red face and long nose. In Japan, this form of *tengu* is popularly characterized in traditional masks used in *Noh* theatre. Thanks to the reviewer for specifying this point.

[17] Sekien Toriyama, "Konjaku Zoku Hyakki [Night Procession of One Hundred Demons]", *The British Museum*: https://www.britishmuseum.org/collection/object/A_1915-0823-0-63.

[18] "Tengu Japan's Large Nosed Mountain Goblin", *Japan Experience* 18th February 2013: https://www.japanallover.com/2013/02/tengu/.

[19] Carmen Blacker, *The Catalpa Bow: A Study of Shamanistic Practices in Japan* (London: George Allen & Unwin, 1975), 139; Keller R. Kimbrough, "Battling 'Tengu', Battling Conceit: Visualizing Abstraction in *The Tale of the Handcart Priest*", *Japanese Journal of Religious Studies* 39.2 (2012): 275-305 and Wakabayashi, *Seven Tengu Scrolls*, xiv-xv.

a mainstream version of the *tengu* species. It serves both as founder and king of all *tengu* species with a more protective attitude toward humanity compared to its ancient crow ancestor, who has been demoted to its "messenger".[20] However, given Wakabayashi's previous assessment that the "crow/avian" *tengu* is more popular in today's Japan, it seems that due to the multiple interpretations and variations of the *tengu* species in Japanese folklore, it is likely that there is truth in both of their observations. What is consistent in these accounts is the idea that *tengu* were monstrous, dangerous creatures capable of shapeshifting into figures that could allure unsuspecting victims and evoke fears for one's safety.

Shōjo Manga: Gender, Romance and *Bishōnen*

Compared to the images of its past, the *Black Bird tengu* is a fusion of the traditional avian image and qualities that currently appeal to *shōjo* manga readers. During the pre-war period, *shōjo* manga was associated with a state of being, primarily among young urban middle and upper-class girls who attended all-female secondary schools and read girls' magazines. The term in this period "implied a certain refinement, marked by chastity, sentimentality, and the use of polite language", which still lingers in the meaning of the term today through its marketing to readers.[21] Today, the complexity of the term "*shōjo*" sees a mixed address of preadolescent and adolescent topics, with some scholars observing the suggested translation of "*shōjo*" to "girl/young women" as implying an age before sexual awareness and/or development.[22] However, Jennifer Prough argues that while *shōjo* manga may be associated with virginity, innocence and sexual inexperience, the expansion of the genre may stretch beyond preadolescence.[23]

Intellectual and sensitive *shōjo* manga, focusing on the transition of childhood into adulthood, gained popularity through the experimental creativity of a group of *shōjo* female manga artists known as the "Magnificent 24" (24 *nen gumi*) born around 1949, and generally thought to include Keiko

---

[20] Mark Schumacher, "Tengu: The Slayer of Vanity", *Buddhism and Shintoism in Japan*: https://www.onmarkproductions.com/html/tengu.shtml.
[21] Deborah Shamoon, *Passionate Friendship: The Aesthetics of Girls' Culture in Japan* (Honolulu: Hawai'i University Press, 2012), 2-3.
[22] John Whittier Treat, "Yoshimoto Banana Writes Home: *Shōjo* Culture and the Nostalgic Subject", *Journal of Japanese Studies* 19.2 (1993): 353-87 and Jennifer Robertson, *Takarazuka: Sexual Politics and Popular Culture in Modern Japan* (Berkeley: California University Press, 2008), 364.
[23] Jennifer Prough, *Straight from the Heart: Gender, Intimacy, and the Cultural Production of Shojo Manga* (Honolulu: Hawaii University Press, 2011), 8.

Takemiya, Moto Hagio, Ryōko Yamagishi and Yumiko Ōshima.[24] This group of artists embraced wide-ranging concerns in their stories, including human relations that delved deep into the psyche of their characters.[25] Although addressing "human relations" has not been identified in comparable YA fiction scholarship in the same way, the increased interest in the role of emotions in YA fiction parallels that of *shōjo* manga. Compared to its historical roots, contemporary *shōjo* manga also features human relations that have been stylised to differentiate it from other (gendered) genres.

> *Shōjo manga* also underwent a process of transformation, resulting in a new style of visualization. Rather than more action/dialogue based plot construction of the standard *shōnen* manga, these artists began to experiment with how to express emotion, inner thoughts and feelings, memories and musings—the stuff of *ningen kankei* (human relations).[26]

Prough borrows her definition of *ningen kankei* from Shinmura Izuru's account, stating that "*ningen kankei* is defined as (1) person-to-person association or interaction within society; (2) relations between individuals including a correspondence of emotions; and (3) the number one workplace complaint".[27] The expansion of thematic interests, such as the core value of human relations in *shōjo* manga, particularly shown through narratives of female development, is an aspect of the genre that has continued into the present. Themes such as innocence, romance and complex emotions encouraged experimentation with several visual stylistic traits, including large eyes and gender ambiguity.[28] Both of these traits are now associated with the *shōjo* genre's canonical texts.

What is clear from the above scholarship is that distinctions have yet to be made between the concept of *shōjo* manga as a genre of innocence and young adolescence versus the sexually active (or sexually aware) adolescent. In a similar vein to Anglophone Young Adult fiction, the boundaries between sexual content in *shōjo* manga and other more graphic genres, such as ladies' comics and *ero*-manga, appear to be categorized based on the explicitness of the sexual

---

[24] Masami Toku, "Shojo Manga! Girls' Comics! A Mirror of Girls' Dreams", *Mechademia* 2 (2007). 18-32 and Prough, *Straight from the Heart*, 47-49.
[25] Prough, *Straight from the Heart*, 48.
[26] Ibid.
[27] Izuru Shinmura, *Kōjien* [Dictionary] (Tokyo: Asahi Sonorama, 1998), n.p..
[28] Shamoon, *Passionate Friendship*, 114; Prough, *Straight from the Heart*, 49; Deborah Shamoon, "Revolutionary Romance: *The Rose of Versailles* and the Transformation of Shojo Manga", *Mechademia* 2 (2007): 3-17 and Toku, "Shojo Manga!", 27.

content.[29] However, the genre of *shōjo* manga continues to engage its anticipated female readership with female coming-of-age and human relationships that are vocalized through the protagonist's emotive responses. *Sailor Moon*, arguably one of the pioneering manga of its time in re-formulating the magical girl sub-genre, is a typical example of the cute, early exploration of girl power, female friendship and adolescent romance that is still classified as a *shōjo* manga.[30]

Another component of the *shōjo* genre that commonly features is the *bishōnen* character. *Bishōnen* originated in *shōjo* manga as characters to explore aspects of female sexuality as well as to challenge binary gender and sexuality discourses.[31] In the twenty-first century, there are arguably two major uses of *bishōnen*—to serve as a desirable love interest for the female protagonist to explore avenues of her sexuality typically circumscribed by social expectations, and in boys' love (*yaoi*) manga, which was originally written for a similar female audience. Jennifer Prough writes

> The bishōnen (beautiful boy) can best be described as beautifully androgynous . . . . their hair is typically long and flowing, their waists narrow, their legs long, and their eyes big . . . . because shōjo manga is about human relations and romance, there are almost always love interests for the protagonist, her friends, or both.[32]

The importance of including a love interest for the female protagonist has become a staple of contemporary *shōjo* manga, where regardless of his mortality or supernatural qualities, he is a *bishōnen* that is both desirable (and marketable). In female coming-of-age manga, the appeal of the desirable hybrid capable of expressing anxieties, curiosities and defiance of socially accepted norms has merged with the *bishōnen* identity to meet contemporary interests. Titles such as Kanoko Sakurakouji's *Black Bird* take this concept one step further and use the supernatural in a female coming-of-age narrative while also addressing more mature topics such as adulthood and sexual relations.

---

[29] Kinko Ito, "The World of Japanese Ladies' Comics: From Romantic Fantasy to Lustful Perversion", *Journal of Popular Culture* 36.1 (2002): 68-85.
[30] Naoko Takeuchi, *Pretty Guardian Sailor Moon* Vol. 1 (New York: Kodansha Comics, 2011).
[31] Mark McLelland and Dasgupta Romit, eds., *Genders, Transgenders and Sexualities in Japan* (London: Routledge, 2005), 7.
[32] Prough, *Straight from the Heart*, 53.

Black Bird and the Refashioned *Tengu*

Black Bird follows the story of Misao Harada, a human with the ability to see supernatural creatures. On her sixteenth birthday, she is attacked by demons who desire her blood and flesh. She is saved by her former childhood friend, Kyo Usui, whom she discovers is a form of demon, a *tengu*. In addition to her powers, she learns from Kyo and his *tengu* clan that she is the legendary "Senka Maiden", a prophesied female whose blood and flesh are prized by demons because of their extraordinary powers. According to the ancient text, *Senka Roku* (the only existing account of a Senka Maiden's fate), her prized qualities will also determine the most powerful demon in the supernatural world.

> If a demon drinks [her] blood, he is granted a long life.
> If he eats [her] flesh, he gains eternal youth.
> If he makes [her] his bride, his entire clan will prosper.[33]

The plot of *Black Bird* demonstrates a victimized female operating within the realms of patriarchal discourse to construct its romantic narrative. In *shōjo* manga, this romantic "damsel-in-distress" storyline is common, yet the darker, supernatural realms of the *tengu* provide a space for mature topics such as death and sex to be explored. To appeal to her contemporary audience, Sakurakouji has refashioned her *tengu* and demon creatures into dangerous yet alluring specimens that support the young adult undertones of the narrative.

Sakurakouji experiments with the idea of a supernatural creature with a desirable human form, who also possesses some of the traditional avian qualities such as an extended beak and large wings.[34] Her *tengu* are substantially different from their folkloric models and are portrayed as having strong sexual appetites. Sakurakouji's interpretation of *tengu* is based on fusing the traditional with the contemporary to create an appealing entity that reflects historical Japanese customs, beliefs and attire. In Kyo's "true form", his beak represents the characteristic beak of the Crow *Tengu* that is almost elongated in a way reminiscent of the Mountain *Tengu*. While the nose of the Mountain *Tengu* has been described by some scholars such as Elizabeth Moriarty as phallic and sexually suggestive, Kyo's clothing and long hairstyle pay tribute to traditional Japanese clothing that in modern Japan is reserved for special occasions.[35] A notable use of traditional Japanese clothing that is fitting for this series is for *seijin shiki*, Shinto coming-of-age ceremonies,

---

[33] Sakurakouji, Kanoko. *Black Bird* Vol. 5 (San Francisco: Viz Media, 2010).
[34] Sakurakouji, *Black Bird*, Vol. 1.
[35] Elizabeth Moriarty, "The Communitarian Aspect of Shinto Matsuri", *Asian Folklore Studies* 31.2 (1972): 91-140.

which highlights the series' hybrid approach to traditional and contemporary views on female sexuality. Kyo's artistic depiction also possesses several of the classic *bishōnen* characteristics that Prough describes, including long hair, slender limbs, a narrow waist and large eyes.[36] In Kyo's "true form", his beak confirms his physical origins from the Crow *Tengu* but is elongated in a way reminiscent of the Mountain *Tengu*. Although categorized in the series as male, his appearance as both a human and a *tengu* are relatively androgynous. While Sakurakouji's *tengu* represents anxieties surrounding coming-of-age and sexual relations, their clothing suggests a secondary purpose to illustrate tensions between tradition and its incorporation (or lack of incorporation) in contemporary society.

Marrying Traditional with Contemporary Coming-of-Age Narratives

In the *Black Bird* series, Misao undergoes several emotive transitions as part of her romance-based coming-of-age narrative. Notably, she is not supported by any strong female characters and is forced to make decisions within a patriarchal discourse inspired by traditional codes of *bushidō* drawn from Confucianism, which prioritized qualities such as loyalty, duty and valour during the Edo period.[37]

As Misao's childhood idolization of Kyo begins to waver in the series, she is further devastated at the destiny she now faces to either be eaten by demons or unceremoniously lose her virginity to Kyo. In Chapter 1, Kyo explains that, from the day of her sixteenth birthday, she will be considered mature enough to become a physical target of demons to extract the powers which her blood and flesh hold.[38] Unless she accepts Kyo's marriage proposal and thus his protection, she is fated to meet a brutal end at the hands of the other demons. The conditions that Kyo sets are "be eaten" or "sleep with [him] and become [his] bride" and leaves no room for Misao to make an independent choice to preserve her life. This scene relates to a young girl's transition from childhood into adulthood. Sixteen is a significant age in many cultures, both Western and Japanese, including as a recognized legal age for marriage for women, sexual consent and as a transitional period where many physical and psychological changes take place.[39] The prized qualities of Misao's blood represent a clear link to ideas of menstruation and fertility throughout Misao's

---

[36] Prough *Straight from the Heart*, 53.
[37] Thomas Cleary, *Code of the Samurai: A Modern Translation of the* Bushido Shoshinsu (Boston: Tuttle, 1999), 22.
[38] Sakurakouji, *Black Bird*, Vol. 1.
[39] "Marriage in Japan", *U.S. Embassy and Consulates in Japan*, https://jp.usembassy.gov/services/marriage/marriage-in-japan/.

development. It is declared that if a demon and the Senka Maiden foster an heir to the demon's clan, "the tengu clan will have attained prosperity", reiterating that at sixteen, she is both sexually active and able to conceive to fulfil the prophecy.[40] This also corresponds with the intended North American age bracket indicated on the back of the volumes ("T+ for Older Teens"). The Young Adult Library Services Association (YALSA) in North America set the guidelines for a "young adult" between twelve and eighteen years old, whereas in Britain, "young adult" often means no older than fourteen or sixteen.[41]

Black Bird establishes the transition from girlhood to adulthood, much like Linda Christian-Smith's observations of the female adolescent's transition through romance in YA fiction.[42] Misao's hesitation to engage in sexual relations with Kyo in ways that contradict her idealized views of love and romance prohibits her progression into adulthood, similar to criticisms found in YA fiction narratives.[43] Misao's questioning of Kyo's intentions and trustworthiness is a small glimpse into the multitude of thoughts, emotions and anxieties that are common in female coming-of-age stories as well as contemporary *shōjo* manga. Masami Toku has argued against interpretations that the *shōjo* female protagonist's objective is to ultimately overcome all obstacles in the name of love. Instead, she believes that popular trends have shifted to depict the female protagonist's journey as defying and challenging patriarchal discourse.[44] For Misao to achieve maturity, she must overcome her feelings of isolation and her frustration that she must marry Kyo in order to be protected from other demon threats.[45] However, by Volume 3, Misao has accepted these roles as her destiny and acknowledges what she must do in order to reach a new stage of socially recognized maturity. First, she recognizes that her conduct must be accepted by the social institution of the *tengu* community, which correlates with Trites's observation of similar tropes found in Anglophone YA fiction.[46] In order to survive in the demon world, Misao must suppress her emotions, particularly in instances where acts are committed in her honour. In Chapter 13 she is required

---

[40] Sakurakouji, Kanoko. *Black Bird* Vol. 15 (San Francisco: Viz Media, 2012).
[41] Alison Waller, *Constructing Adolescence in Fantastic Realism* (London: Routledge, 2009), 9.
[42] Linda K. Christian-Smith, "Romancing the Girl: Adolescent Romance Novels and the Construction of Femininity", in *Becoming Feminine: The Politics of Popular Culture*, eds. Leslie G. Roman and Linda K. Christian-Smith (London: Falmer Press, 1988), 76-101.
[43] Shiri Reznik and Lemish Dafna, "Falling in Love with High School Musical: Girls' Talk about Romantic Perceptions", in *Mediated Girlhoods: New Explorations of Girls' Media Culture*, ed. Mary Celeste Kearney (Oxford: Peter Lang, 2011), 151-70.
[44] Toku, "Shojo Manga!", 19.
[45] Sakurakouji, *Black Bird*, Vol. 1.
[46] Roberta Seelinger Trites, *Disturbing the Universe: Power and Repression in Adolescent Literature* (Iowa City: Iowa University Press, 2000), 3.

to respect the *tengu* code of honour that contradicts her own values and correlates with the *bushidō* codes of loyalty, duty and valour. When Kyo is about to kill a *kitsune* (fox spirit) in revenge for kidnapping Misao, she looks away in fear of the violent act that he is about to commit.[47] Like the *tengu*, the *kitsune* has been modified from its appearance in folklore and presented as a desirable yet dangerous creature in human form. In Japanese mythology, foxes were intelligent and portrayed as both loyal and untrustworthy in different interpretations. Amongst their many magical powers they were thought to be capable of possession, transformation into human form, flight and creating illusions.[48]

Kyo orders her to watch. She complies and cries while watching him slaughter the *kitsune*. Misao's excuse for obeying him is that Kyo has committed this act "for her sake" and out of respect for his loyalty she combats her fears in front of the assembled company. Misao's sense of obligation to comply with these social pressures, which are linked to the *tengu* code of decorum, emphasizes her growing awareness of the steps required to achieve maturity and respect within this world. Contrary to her previous acts of resistance to Kyo's wishes, which were often followed by infantile behaviour, Misao's acceptance of the *tengu* institutional values position her as an individual now operating within a community.

Misao's hesitancy to decide whether to become a part of the demon world by marrying Kyo is fuelled by her sense of incompatibility with the "other". However, the narrative suggests that once this anxiety is removed, the ability to progress returns. The detailed attention to Misao's emotions is intended to generate interest and empathy for its readership. To support this further, Shamoon observes that *shōjo* manga has evolved to "express and read about the emotional experience of adolescence",[49] and Maria Nikolajeva notes that

> Since male and female rites of passage . . . . follow different patterns, it should be anticipated that fictional representations of masculinity and femininity reflect the actual situation, yet at the same time is affected by other power hierarchies.[50]

---

[47] Kanoko Sakurakouji, *Black Bird* Vol. 3 (San Francisco: Viz Media, 2010).
[48] Kiyoshi Nozaki, *Kitsuné — Japan's Fox of Mystery, Romance, and Humor* (Tokyo: The Hokuseidô Press, 1961).
[49] Shamoon, *Passionate Friendship*, 13.
[50] Maria Nikolajeva, *Power, Voice and Subjectivity in Literature for Young Readers* (London: Routledge, 2010), 105.

The adolescent journey into adulthood in *Black Bird* is therefore characterized by its portrayal of an emotive and occasionally distressing experience. In this case, Misao's feelings of isolation are created by her divided status between two worlds and her reluctance to choose one over the other.

This coming-of-age journey, filled with horrors, fears and anxieties, highlights Misao's transition from a subject of innocence into a maturing individual through gendered and culturally constructed pressures. Although she is often left feeling without agency and subjected to a pre-determined fate, she is in fact always left in a position in which she must make choices in relation to her own desires. This also extends to her choice to engage sexually with the man she loves by coaxing a verbal confession of his true feelings for her. The reader's empathy toward Kyo starts to shift when anecdotes are provided by other characters, which convinces Misao that Kyo does have a caring and sympathetic character despite the sexually charged and stoic persona he portrays. Examples include his devotion to checking in on Misao through magical whirlpools during their time apart and Misao's growing trust in his concern for her well-being.[51] Once she has established that Kyo is sincere in his feelings towards her, she begins to accept her gendered role within the demon world.

The juxtaposition of modern and traditional attitudes toward sexuality are also addressed in the second volume through the display of material objects. In Chapter 8, after fending off the threat posed by Kyo's brother who attempted to kidnap and rape Misao, Kyo summons Misao to talk with him in his bedroom. The top left-hand panel features contrasting traditional and contemporary iconography that indicates the meaning behind Kyo's concept of "celebrating" the success of recent events and illustrates the panel's capacity to speak to the reader's contextual knowledge beyond the words of the text. While it is indicated that Misao comprehends Kyo's sexual intentions and responds aggressively toward his suggestions, the Anglophone reader can deduce the suggestive nature of the scene though perhaps is not aware of the detailed visual and subtle semiotics occurring within this panel. While the top panel shares more symbolism with Edo Japan, there are several contemporary references that emphasize the merging of traditional and modern values regarding sex and sexuality in a closed setting.

First, the futon (bed) and the screen behind the futon are both reminiscent of typical traditional Japanese house pieces. Placed on the cover of the futon is a spiral bound book labelled "48 Ways" which, although modern in its appearance, is analogous with ancient Japanese sex manuals known as

---

[51] Kanoko Sakurakouji, *Black Bird* Vols. 4 & 5 (San Francisco: Viz Media, 2010).

koshokubon. According to Timothy Clark in his edited collection, *Shunga: Sex and Pleasure in Japanese Art*, these books, while erotic in nature, were in fact informative and often illustrated guides popular amongst all sectors of society. They were often exchanged between copy holders and book lenders to inform both men and women of the secrets of receiving pleasure from one another.[52] The screen behind the futon features a highly suggestive piece of *shunga* art and bears a strong resemblance to one of the well-known colour-painted erotic illustrations by Kitagawa Utamaro depicting lovers in the upstairs room of a teahouse.[53] Finally, the most modern item in the panel, and one that the Anglophone reader is perhaps the most familiar with, is the boxed Western-style lingerie. The only item that Misao is expected to wear is also the only materially obvious item connected to her contemporary status compared to the historic representations associated with the image of the *tengu*. The contrast of past and present objects further highlights the role of the *tengu* as a challenger of contemporary values, the refashioning together of the old and the new, as well as ever-recurring anxieties surrounding female sexual development. By also presenting Misao's anxieties in a humorous format in this scene, the sincerity of the sequence's tone is relaxed to make light of the situation and to establish the engagement of sex as a human function that is not altered by Kyo's *tengu* status when they eventually consummate their relationship in Chapter 32.

Conclusion

The *tengu* in Sakurakouji's *Black Bird* manga series is evidently a hybrid. A creature who represents many polarities including the past, present and future; Japanese and Western thought; love and lust; fear and comfort; and modern versus traditional. By crossing boundaries and fusing oppositions, *Black Bird* is capable of challenging contemporary notions of female adolescence to appeal to the Anglophone reader. The series draws upon historical, religious and folkloric references to understand Kyo's and Misao's dominant and submissive behaviours. Although such characteristics are present in Anglophone Young Adult literature, there are some cultural boundaries that prevent a fluent understanding of this series and therefore require additional contextual understanding. For Sakurakouji's series, the *tengu* poses as an external vessel of the young protagonist's conflicting thoughts and desires as she leaves the security of childhood to tackle new,

---

[52] Timothy Clark et al., eds., *Shunga: Sex and Pleasure in Japanese Art* (London: The British Museum Press, 2014), 28-29.
[53] Kitagawa Utamaro, "Utamakura (Poem of the Pillow)", *The British Museum*: https://www.britishmuseum.org/collection/object/A_OA-0-133-6.

adult obstacles and responsibilities as a young woman while navigating the constraints and limits of societal expectations. The versatility of the *tengu*, much like the Western vampire, places the focus on Misao's sexual development as opposed to the monstrous or immediate threat the *tengu* may pose to her. Consequently, Kyo's image as a *tengu* really does very little to the narrative except to remind the reader that he is from another era representing traditionalist views and in turn displaces contemporary topics in an alternative fantastical setting. *Black Bird* uses the supernatural as a secondary function that runs parallel to the romance story to bypass contemporary social barriers that dissuade the discussion of sexual relations and responses to gendered power relations.

In *Black Bird*, Sakurakouji's modernized *tengu* are versatile, traditional and hybrid creatures. As refashioned entities, they are designed to personify concerns, topics and allegories of female sexuality and patriarchal discourse in a relatable fashion to a contemporary audience.

Chapter 6

Where is the Real Me? Encountering Transhumanism and Cybernetic Divinity in *Serial Experiments Lain*

Anik Sarkar
Salesian College Siliguri

ABSTRACT: Aired in 1998, *Serial Experiments Lain* (SEL) was ahead of its time. While the internet had been launched in cyberspace, the implications and impact were hardly known. Although there were many other anime (*Akira, Princess Mononoke* and *Ghost in the Shell*) that captured the techno-social anxieties to come, SEL was radical and avant-garde. It used an experimental episodic form (or layers) to enmesh events that bordered real and dreamlike states. The eponymous 14-year old Lain, confronted with cryptic experiences of otherworldly contact in cyberspace, explored questions of existence (ontology). There Lain comes to realize that consciousness and lived experience is not just associated with the physical and transient states of matter, but also belongs in the technological realm known as The Wired. Even the promise of immortality can be found there. Foreshadowing Neuralink, transhumanist discourses and the mainstreaming of Virtual Reality (VR), the anime throws significant light on volatile identities and encountering cybernetic divinity—on spaces that resemble paradise-like states—where nothing expires or decays.[1] In this chapter, I progressively work through the 13 layers of the series in order to build an overall conceptual picture. I will explore how SEL anticipates certain tendencies in the twenty-first century and how the anime also embodies a religious subtext that becomes prominent towards the end.

---

[1] As such, SEL provides a medium with which to address recent debates on transhumanism, posthumanism and mind uploading.

KEYWORDS: Divinity, Identity, Integration, Posthuman, Singularity, Transhumanism.

***

Setting the Stage

Wires extend across poles and residential colonies; they stretch alongside the busy streets of a city. A humming sound accompanies us, as we follow these wires that move past houses and buildings, stations and shops, schools and alleyways, encompassing the entire geographical locale. They are as occupied as the people who inhabit the streets and the metros, buzzing with energy, transmitting signals. *Serial Experiments Lain* (henceforth SEL) begins with the wires and their signals, because the eponymous protagonist in the title is entangled in these wires and complex world(s), within and amongst them.

Iwakura Lain, a middle-school girl learns of her classmate Chisa's suicide early in the first episode. Shortly afterwards, she receives a message from Chisa: "I have given up the body, but in writing an email, I can communicate with you to show you I am alive".[2] When Lain asks for the second time, "Why did you die?", the reply from Chisa comes to her in a plain, straightforward response: "God is here".[3]

With an opening as elusive as the inspired "Godardian" typography that abruptly appear and disappear, we get a glimpse of a complex philosophical premise that is about to unfold.[4] What is real? A question that SEL probes into, time and again in its 13 "layers" (episodes). The narrative unfolding of SEL is somewhat subversive, disjointed and proceeds in a spirit of enigma, which is why it is also linked to "experimental" and "avant-garde" genres.[5] SEL's peculiar medium then becomes representative of the very idea it wants to communicate: that reality is illusive, unpredictable and erratic. In other words, reality is a complex phenomenon that is progressively more enigmatic as it unfolds during our investigation. What is implicit in SEL is a question posed against transcendence: If total transcendence is achievable, could it be undertaken in physical reality or is it executable only inside cyberspace (The Wired)?

---

[2] *Serial Experiments Lain*: Directed by Ryutaro Nakamura with Screenplay by Chiaki J. Konaka (TV Tokyo 1998), Layer 1, "Weird".

[3] SEL, Layer 1.

[4] Shin-suke Nakajima, "Interview with Chiaki Konaka", *HK*: www.konaka.com/alice6/lain/hkint_e.html.

[5] Yasemin Kilinçarslan, "Siberpunk Animasyon Sinemasinda Katoptikon İzlekler Anime Film Serial Experiments Lain". *Journal of International Social Research* 9.43 (2016): 1947 and Timothy Perper and Martha Cornog, *Psychoanalytic Cyberpunk Midsummer-Night's Dreamtime: Kon Satoshi's 'Paprika'*, *Mechademia* 4 (2009): 326-29.

What Is The Wired?

The Wired is an ever developing, evolving virtual world similar to the real world's current internet of the early 2000s. It can be accessed through a Navi [small computer device or "navigator"]. It is an interconnected network, similar to the Internet/World Wide Web. It is an advanced form of communication at the center of the story of *Serial Experiments in Lain* . . . . The Wired is seen as a world where users can share their thoughts, have conversations, play games and socialize. There is a strong presence of Virtual Reality as a more advanced method of access to The Wired (with the help of physical devices comparable to, and even beyond, today's VR devices), allowing the user to project themselves into it and have physical interactions within The Wired and with other users.[6]

Both the real world and The Wired are in deep synchronization. At one point, The Wired's control and exertion over the real reaches to such potentials that people could be killed, or reality could be tampered with, as a direct consequence of actions undertaken in The Wired.

Lain's body and mind become sites of representation as it is believed that Lain's body is a material manifestation of The Wired and her consciousness is The Wired's collective (un)conscious. Connecting the speculative philosophies of transhumanism with the idea of attaining divinity in cyberspace, SEL sets the stage for daunting questions regarding technoculture and virtual reality (much before the emergence of the social media networks).

Daunting Questions in SEL

Questions on transhumanism (the technological and mechanistic preservation of human beings) is ubiquitous in pop culture and film as a part of our techno-centric world but is also the subject of much serious academic discussion.[7]

Is immortality attainable through technology? Could we in any manner map and upload our transient, immaterial states of consciousness into a machine that could continue to sustain us? Or is it possible to transmute our fragile, dying selves into something concrete that preserves us as we are? Is it a far-fetched dream, a fleeting possibility, to be able to exist freely, fluidly and forever (without aging, slackening or encountering limits of any sorts)?

---

[6] "The Wired", *Serial Experiments in Lain Wiki*: https://sel.fandom.com/wiki/The_Wired.
[7] William H. U. Anderson, ed., *Technology and Theology* (Wilmington: Vernon Press, 2019).

Historically, humans have spent a considerable amount of time investigating ways that could improve how we live in a world with both its stupendous beauty and terrifying hostility.[8] Death and dying have haunted us more than anything else. So much so that "haunting" itself may be found in the popular imagination of the zombie phenomenon. Here we are confronted by our own mortality.[9] But how to precisely make our vulnerable bodies and minds "transcend" our corporal materialism has been the fantasy and of both science fiction and science fact.

We want to live "fully" and prolong our living with bodies that are agile, remediable, adaptive and durable. We have come to put our faith in state-of-the-art technology. We rely on what we have come to believe as the chief architect of our path towards salvation and what seems to forge seamless progression for the betterment of our species. This does not mean we cast a blind eye on its darker implications at a time when its entanglement with the environment and society in general is under suspicion. Technology has the potential for soul-destroying negatives as much as for life affirming positives.[10] Both these views on technology underlie and co-exist in SEL.

Layers of Lain: Transhumanist Discourse in SEL

SEL has a cult following for its ambiguous characters, its disjointed narrative, and its use of experimental devices like "typographics" (which includes hiding a reading list).[11] For this purpose, this chapter intends to examine the 13 "layers" (episodes) in their order of appearance. I will examine the puzzling statements offered in accordance to how they can be read as Lain's transition from a naïve transhumanist to her development into a posthuman deity-like figure (cybernetic divinity). In this exploration of SEL's layers, the focus is on philosophically exploring the events that exhibit transhumanist ideas.

Nick Bostrom says that transhumanism "affirms the possibility and desirability of fundamentally improving the human condition through applied

---

[8] The Cradle of Civilization pairs technology precisely with that activity. Charles Keith Maisels, *Archaeology in the Cradle of Civilization* (London: Routledge, 1998), 1-4.
[9] Timothy Madigan, "Problems with Zombies", *Philosophy Now* 96 (2013), 4.
[10] For an exploration of these very problematics, see Robb Torseth, "Who Am I? Personhood and the Self-Defeating Epistemology of Transhumanism", in *Technology and Theology*, 20-36.
[11] "Typographics" is a compound word—combining "type" and "graphic"—mainly used to describe montage of text and graphics in the anime and used for stylistic effects. For a detailed discussion, see *Serial Experiments Lain Wiki*, https://lain.wiki/wiki/Typographics. For details on the "Reading List" see *Lain Official Reading List* http://www.cjas.org/~leng/readlist.htm.

reason, especially by developing and making widely available technologies to eliminate aging and to greatly enhance human intellectual, physical, and psychological capacities".[12] Bostrom views transhumanism as a natural recourse of human progress in the modern world. Humans have always looked at death as "dragon-tyrant" and they previously had no arsenal to battle this monster. But now there is a possibility![13]

Doede states that transhumanism aims "to transform human nature through technological interventions so radical that Homo sapiens will transition in the relatively near future into a superior successor post-human species, one that transcends the fragilities and failures of our fleshly finitude".[14] Transhumanists understand the mind in a physical body as a site for enhancement—where there is the possibility of a flight progressing past limitations—to a state of transcendence. In the hyper-augmentation of the body, there is a strong focus on individualism. Here the human body's limitations have to be won over—"in line with modernity's celebration of the subject"—as "radicalization of the promises of modernity".[15]

Body and Existence in SEL

Similarly, SEL in many ways poses the question of existence, both for the individual "body" and "bodies" collectively. For Lain, existence can happen in multiple spaces, irrespective of whether the space is in the real world or The Wired. The real world offers a limited physical space which requires the subject (here Lain) to have a human body in order to navigate the world. As the anime progresses, Lain's real body is a hindrance to movement (progression). The more she gets immersed in The Wired, the more she gradually and subconsciously tries to overcome her physicality.

Lain's classmates find her absorbed in virtual reality. She begins to use her Navi to check emails but progressively becomes absorbed with interfacing between the real and The Wired. The question of physicality and existence (consciousness) for Lain is explored through her naïve presence in the first few layers, and then as the anime proceeds, it is revealed that she can be in multiple places at the same time.

---

[12] Nick Bostrom, "Introduction—The Transhumanist FAQ: A General Introduction", in *Transhumanism and the Body*, eds. C. Merce and D. F. Maher (New York: Palgrave Macmillan, 2014), 1.
[13] Sascha Dickel and Andreas Frewer, "Life Extension Eternal Debates on Immortality", in *Post-and Transhumanism*, ed. Ranisch, Robert (Bern: Peter Lang, 2014), 124.
[14] Bob Doede, "Transhumanism, Technology, and the Future", *The Appraisal Journal* 7.3 (2009), 39-54. The quotations come from page 40.
[15] Dickel and Frewer, "Life Extension Eternal Debates on Immortality", 125.

In the article "Topologies of Identity in Serial Experiments Lain", Craig Jackson believes that a topological analysis can assist in understanding and interpreting Lain's plurality of identities in a number of different ways. The cases of self-intersection can be understood by conceiving of Lain as an expanding identity in a limited, closed universe—with the presence of many "geodesics" connecting two sites in such universes—that produces distorted spectral pictures and singularities of seeming uncertainty.[16] Lain's existence is a highly complicated phenomenon.

The questions about her physical/material existence arise out of a few distinct problems. First, the nature of her identity: Who or what is Lain? Can she be understood as a signification of "transhuman"? Has Lain surpassed the limits of physicality to be able to coexist in both realms? Is she supposed to be an embodiment of The Wired? The second problem arises from an ontologically governed position: Does "physical reality" or the real world that comprises Lain's home, her school and the streets exist at all? Or is it just another virtual space, derived from The Wired? Is, what seems like the physical reality in Lain's world, a mere simulation of concrete space, like an open-world videogame? For instance, a videogame running within another.[17] This argument can be supported by considering few examples.

1) Eiri Masami's appearance and absurd metamorphosis in the real world;
2) The unreality of Lain's parents;
3) The dead communicating with the living through emails;
4) Lain managing to erase herself from collective memory;
5) Lain's multiple and simultaneous presence across the physical world.

These considerations may lead us to believe that Lain and the components of the physical world are fictional—running as a simulation which makes the

---

[16] Craig Jackson, "Topologies of Identity in Serial Experiments Lain", *Mechademia 7* (2012): 191-202.

[17] See examples listed in the article "Game within a Game", *TV Tropes*: https://tvtropes.org/pmwiki/pmwiki.php/Main/GameWithinAGame.

anime "metatextual" as it points to its own unreality—its fabricated presence just like many postmodern, magical realism novels.[18]

Susan Napier mentions that in the free spaces of science fiction and fantasy—genres that have historically coexisted alongside depictions of the actual—are best portrayed in the free space of animation. This is because this medium is never constrained by a supposed commitment to reflect the real.[19] The overt technology of the animation medium itself draws attention to the artificiality of fantasy and the technical underpinnings of the science fiction genre.[20]

SEL as a Sci-Fi anime and an experimental medium not only becomes self-reflexive, but also hints at the simulation hypothesis propounded by Nick Bostrom.[21] If we are to abandon this idea, and take SEL's two worlds as separate spaces—one with the physical world and the second the immaterial and mystical world of The Wired—then we can proceed to "unlayer" SEL to reveal how the anime is a *bildungsroman* of sorts. SEL focuses on Lain's psycho-spiritual development. But in other sense, it can be read as an allegory of transformation or a movement from transhumanism to becoming a posthuman. As Luca Valera states:

> [if] the transhuman being is a being of passage, which still in some ways conserves the characteristics of the human being—although enhanced and amplified via technologies—the posthuman one is characterized as something radically new, which clearly exceeds the human frontier.[22]

The basic goal of posthumanism is not merely to enhance humanity through hyper-technology, but to progressively eliminate differences, making a "fluidity"

---

[18] Examples of metatextual novels that point to their own unreality are Mark Z. Danielewski, *House of Leaves* (New York: Pantheon Books, 2000) and Kurt Vonnegut, *Slaughterhouse-Five* (New York: Delacorte Press, 1969). For a relevant discussion of these works, see Elizabeth A. Wall, "Textual Persuasion: Trauma Representation in Mark Z. Danielewski's *House of Leaves*" (MA Thesis: State University of New York, 2022), 4-8 and Ralph Clare, "Worlds of Wordcraft: The Metafiction of Kurt Vonnegut", in *Critical Insights on Kurt Vonnegut*, ed. Robert T. Tally (Ipswich: Salem Press, 2013).

[19] Susan J. Napier, "When the Machines Stop: Fantasy, Reality, and Terminal Identity in 'Neon Genesis Evangelion' and 'Serial Experiments Lain'", *Science Fiction Studies* 29.3 (2002): 418-35.

[20] Ibid.

[21] Nick Bostrom, "Are You Living in a Computer Simulation?", *Philosophical Quarterly* 53.211 (2003): 243-55.

[22] Luca Valera, "Posthumanism: Beyond Humanism?", *Cuadernos de Bioética* 25.3 (2014): 483.

possible.[23] This is primarily the case for Eiri, while for Lain, the 'transhuman to posthuman' journey begins after she is born in flesh, as a human.

Layer 1

In Layer 1, Lain is introduced as a schoolgirl who "struggles with her status as a 'shōjo' in the realm of cyberspace".[24]

Regarding how the actual world and The Wired interact in the universe of SEL, there are primarily two schools of thought. On the one hand, The Wired is just a tool for interpersonal contact and an extension of the actual world. On the other hand, The Wired may be considered a different universe since it is made up of a complex web of computers, power and information that is global.[25]

Napier states that, as a situation that can no longer be relied upon to endure due to technological advancements and their rising capacity for both material and spiritual devastation, reality itself enters into the "apocalyptic discourse". Napier thus raises the question on personal identity. In an analysis of the *Neon Genesis Evangelion* and SEL, she asks a number of questions.

> What happens to a person's identity in a virtual environment? Does it transition into what Scott Bukatman refers to as "terminal identity", a new condition in which we discover "both the end of the subject and a new subjectivity constructed at the computer screen or television screen"? Does it therefore continue to contribute to what Bukatman calls "terminal culture", a setting where science fiction and realism converge into techno-surrealism and nothing is truly "knowable"?[26]

This problematic discourse on identity is especially true in the last episode of SEL, where the reality of Lain's existence is left open-ended. Jackson raises two questions on the ending of Lain in relation to her identity: "The final topology of Lain's identity remains unclear. Has she retreated deep into The Wired, or to some other universe beyond The Wired? Is her final identity confined to a kernel of memory in Arisu's mind?"[27] One way to reach an understanding

---

[23] Ibid.
[24] Steven T. Brown, *Tokyo Cyberpunk Posthumanism in Japanese Visual Culture* (New York: Palgrave Macmillan, 2015), 161.
[25] Elmo Gonzaga, "Anomie and Isolation: The Wind-up Bird Chronicle, Ghost in the Shell, Serial Experiments Lain, and Japanese Consensus Society", *Humanities Diliman* 3.1 (2002): 3.
[26] Napier, "When the Machines Stop", 419.
[27] Jackson, "Topologies of Identity in Serial Experiments Lain", 199.

would be to consider that Lain's final identity is an instance of becoming posthuman. This is made possible through an integration. Lain becomes clear about what her abilities are and their consequences as she decides to wipe out her memories from the world. Initially, she is unaware of her past, her existence as a software. Her incarnation as a human allows her to progress towards becoming a fully integrated being, as a person in flesh and having a digital presence. She has the ability to metamorphose, being able to fully access her body according to her will, after the "other" Lain vanishes in the final layer.

Layer 2

In Layer 2, entitled "Girls", Lain visits a pub called Cyberia with her school friends. Cyberia is in reference to Douglas Rushkoff's 1994 book of the same name. The book is described as a "dizzying" and a "dangerous guided tour" where he explores a confluence of cybernetic ideas, counterculture and the emergence of a radical digital milieu.[28] *Cyberia*'s influence on SEL is made clear with the naming of the pub where smart supplements like "Accela" are traded, and young cyber-enthusiasts meet to discuss developing technologies around The Wired. Accela's function in the anime is described as

> the hormone secreted after Accela triggers it affects the time-sense making it seem as if one's awareness is accelerated. Not only consciousness but the workings of the brain itself are altered, multiplying the brain's operational capacity by 2 to 12 times.[29]

Accela then, is our earliest encounter with the "nanomedicine" in accordance with transhumanistic potentials in the anime, where an external supplement is supposed to eliminate the need for a device to connect to The Wired. The mind itself, as a repository of thoughts and signals could connect univocally with the digital space, as it begins to parapsychologically attune to the Schumann resonance.[30] "Everyone is connected"—flashes the typography— which alongside the splash of red, and hallucinatory projections hijack visual representation in SEL, subverting the discourses of history, memory, truth, and reality.

---

[28] "Cyberia: Life in the Trenches of Hyperspace by Douglas Rushkoff", *Publishers Weekly*. https://www.publishersweekly.com/9780062510105.
[29] SEL, Layer 2.
[30] Natalie Colosimo, "The Schumann Resonances and Psychic Phenomena", *The Psychic School* [blog]: https://psychicschool.com/the-schumann-resonances-and-psychic-phenomena/.

At Cyberia, the person who ingested Accela breaks down into a frenzy, and in confrontation with Lain, he is anxious and baffled. He confuses Lain for a god-like figure whom he is familiar with in The Wired. Lain's cryptic reply, "No matter where you go, everyone's connected", is a testament to the fact that there are two versions of Lain: one which is awakened and powerful and the other naïve and lost.[31]

Layer 3

In Layer 3, entitled "Psyche", we encounter the Navi, a multi-purpose information terminal and "psyche", a chip that can dramatically boost the performance of a Navi. Activity within The Wired is limited by the machine, while "psyche" acts as a modular enhancement. We are also confronted with what is known as "Lain of The Wired", an almost mythical figure in the real world and yet a living goddess in the virtual. Lain of The Wired is the "other" version of Lain—demonstrated by a confident, robust and assertive persona—a reversal of the physical embodiment of Lain that predominantly features in the anime.

Layer 3 also introduces us to Lain's bear costume, a form of soft shell that Lain cocoons in. Napier says that "Lain's bear suit, which she dons throughout the series, attests to her own desire to escape reality, in this case by wearing a costume suggestive of a stuffed animal, an omnipresent signifier of cute shōjo (young girl) culture in contemporary Japan".[32] Lain suffers from an existential crisis and is on a quest to establish who she really is (herself). Her bear costume acts as a cover and a signification of innocence. She embraces this state of child-like innocence at the end of the anime. Here, her dad reminds her that she need not wear the costume anymore: she has found out who she is.

Lain constantly hears voices that call her over to The Wired. Since humanity's collective aspiration is understood to be the enhancement of connectivity and extension of life, the voices that Lain hears belong to that calling. In The Wired, the mind moves without hindrance, it lives without the fear of an earthly, physical death. It exists in the freest of states, in a hub where other minds congregate. Through the abandoning of the body, it has also transcended bodily pain and psychological anguish. But does this mind exert an identity of its own or does it dissolve into a collective consciousness as embodied through the character of Lain? Through Chisa's email, we get a hint of its individualistic identity. Eiri's (re)appearance also we are informed its ability to metamorphose into a physical body. This is later by Lain's (re)appearance.

---

[31] SEL, Layer 2.
[32] Napier, "When the Machines Stop", 432.

Layer 4

In Layer 4, entitled "Religion", a game called "Phantoma" immerses players in a dungeon-style fighting game. A "hole" has been identified in the program, a loophole or an opening that lets it connect with other programs. It also provides an opportunity for dangerous organizations to take advantage of the loophole and breach The Wired in order to control it.

Another point of interest in Layer 4 is when Lain's father warns her that The Wired and the real world aren't connected well. Therefore, she must not confuse one for the other. Lain replies that the border between the two worlds isn't clear and she plans to enter it and "translate"/transmute herself into it. As Lain's personality gets more and more involved or enmeshed with The Wired, her navigator too physically expands as a machine across her room. This signals the transhumanist integration of Lain, as devices add up like an assemblage, enhancing her capacities and expanding her domains to connect more prominently with an evolved access to The Wired.

Layer 5

In Layer 5, entitled "Distortion", more is revealed about the nature of The Wired, existence, collective consciousness (memory) and transcendence. A revelatory voice that says "I am God". This voice speaks of how humans are a "neoteny", i.e., they are no longer able to evolve and only crave to satisfy their desires of flesh. The Wired then becomes their exit, i.e., a mode of transcendence to a higher spiritual level, a place where people may continue to live on after their physical selves are abandoned.

In a flashback, Lain is having conversations with a doll which persuades her to tell a story. The doll replies that Lain is omniscient and there are no stories that she doesn't know. This infers the short, fragmented clips of voices that Lain is able to hear, demonstrate her full "connectedness" to The Wired. Lain is an embodiment of the human collective (un)conscious, and as such, she is a repository of all human stories.

The concept of the interconnectedness of plains of existence are also expanded on in Layer 5. Lain's otherwise passive mother, cryptically fills out the picture by saying that "Physical reality is nothing but a hologram of the information that flows through The Wired".[33] Her father suggests that The Wired may not just be an exchange of information but something more. The evolutionary processes from inception, resulting from the tangible connections, suggest that a "god-like" entity could have formed inside The Wired. Because everything is connected to a transcendental signified (a

---

[33] SEL, Layer 5.

central repository), this being could potentially oversee the globalized cybernetic network.

According to Doede, in a future event, our cognitive limitations will no longer be a barrier to the creation of the next generation of sentient artifacts, signifying the point at which computers will be better at self-designing than humanity. This will signal the self-creation of new intelligent objects with the AI's intellect (greater than that of humans), and the term "singularity" refers to the passing of this threshold.[34] Pointing to a future geared towards singularity, SEL depicts the "humanely" worlds and alternate futuristic societies with human presences that will be lost in this transaction. This is demonstrated by the joyful schoolgirls and Arisu's kindness towards Lain—the signifier of empathy and human experience—and the fleshly, momentous and spontaneous participation with which Lain is invited. By abandoning the "embrace of singularity", whose philosophy Eiri had been propagating, Lain acknowledges the significance and continuity of human livelihood in a physical plane. In a way, Lain also handles the precarious calling of singularity, opposing the annihilation of physical existence.

Layer 6

Layer 6, entitled "KIDS", the anime proceeds to unveil the discourse on connection. To be able to enhance and modify oneself, one needs to be able to establish a network with others in order to aid co-dependency and sharing of knowledge. Signifying this idea, a narrator speaks on the merits of establishing connections between people: how small voices could grow louder and lifespans could increase. Lain's father watches her sitting by the Navi, which now has occupied a major portion of her room, surrounded with coolants and heat-detectors. Lain is seen thanking others on The Wired for being kind to her.

A parallel could be drawn here, on the addictive use of social networking sites—specifically by youth—where their online personalities are highly revered and given social validation by strangers. Lain's friend Reika warns her about this condition: "A net-pal isn't the same as a real friend".[35] Passers-by on the road pray to a deity-like figure of Lain, appearing on the sky as the clouds part.

The project called "KIDS" is also revealed in this layer. KIDS is the namesake for a conductor and convertor of brain's electromagnetic waves into a powerful storehouse of energy. KIDS schematics made its way into The Wired. It can be deduced that The Wired is a repository of knowledge like the internet, where information can be retrieved through navigation. Unlike the

---

[34] Doede, "Transhumanism, Technology, and the Future", 43.
[35] SEL, Layer 6.

internet, The Wired that Lain uses is hyper-immersive. The Wired is both a place to access knowledge as well as a place where actions can be taken.

Layer 7

In Layer 7, entitled "Society", a man dressed up in an advanced VR suit walks in the city streets stating that no matter where his body is, he can send consciousness anywhere. "The real world isn't real at all", reads the Godardian frame.[36] The distinctions between virtuality and reality, analogue and digital have all been eroded.

As a small boy wants to go to a friend's place to play a game, the mother says: "Can't you play over the internet?"[37] The boy replies that his friend is going to teach him. The mother says that The Wired and the real world are one and the same. It can also be inferred at this point that the virtual Lain is a "self-conscious" entity navigating in cyberspace. Exploring the notion of mind uploading and transhumanism, O. Häggström, in "Aspects of Mind Uploading", poses a paradoxical question on identity:

> Even if it turns out uploads are conscious, I might still hesitate to undergo destructive uploading, because if the upload is not me, but merely a very precise copy of me (my personality traits, my memories and so on), then destructive uploading implies that I die. So will the upload be me? This is the problem of personal identity.[38]

What keeps Lain's identity intact in the physical realm if she is a material embodiment of The Wired? If it is to be thought that Lain is a part of a gigantic culmination of minds interacting in The Wired—her semi-aware nature in the first half of the anime—points to the fact that her identity and consciousness in the physical realm have minute and fragmentary recollections of her past. In fact, the physical Lain navigating in the real world doesn't have a solid memory of who she is. When Lain is asked about her birthday, and about her parents' birthdays, she doesn't seem to have an answer. Her identity in the real world is deformed and underdeveloped. Yet it appears to be fully conscious. Considering Häggström's take on mind uploading, a mind uploaded in cyberspace may not be the real person. It will merely be another version of us, as in the case with Lain.

---

[36] SEL, Layer 7.
[37] Ibid.
[38] O. Häggström, "Aspects of Mind Uploading", in *Transhumanism the Proper Guide to a Posthuman Condition or a Dangerous Idea?*, eds. Wolfgang Hofkirchner and Kreowski Hans-Jörg (New York: Springer, 2021), 11.

Layer 8

In Layer 8, entitled "Rumors", Lain of The Wired is said to be a god-like entity. Here she can create and erase memories. She knows everything and what everyone is doing. Her omniscient nature earns her the tag "peeping tom". The layer signifies the demerits of surveillance, centralization of data, and breach of privacy in a total network society. Layer 8 also foreshadows the rise of the social media and problematic algorithms that govern our choices. Steven T. Brown, in the introduction to *Cinema Anime*, writes:

> How does the increasing accessibility of the Internet to users all over the world contribute to the disciplinary programming of gendered subjectivities and bodies circulating in the analog world? How do techniques of online user-profiling and information-gathering figure in the emergence of new disciplinary technologies and the constitution of the Internet as a power knowledge grid? How does the ideology of the Internet as "digital democracy" conduct readers into a rarefied and regulated field of possibilities—manipulating and controlling individual bodies, turning them into normalized, serviceable subjects directed toward strategic ends and goals? These are just a few of the questions evoked by Serial Experiments Lain.[39]

Being in the era of surveillance capitalism, we come under the radar of many interconnected agencies which probe on our activities, monitor our habits, and study our patterns to gather our data in order to direct advertising towards us. In Lain's "other", we see the internet's global surveilling potential, its capacity to generate individual data profiles, and its unprecedented and almost unconscious algorithmic reach.[40]

Layer 9

In Layer 9, entitled "Protocol", the history and mechanics behind The Wired is partially revealed. We are taken to the past where Tachibana's chief researcher Eiri Masami develops a hypothesis of a worldwide neural network, a wireless

---

[39] Steven T. Brown, *Cinema Anime: Critical Engagements with Japanese Animation* (New York: Palgrave Macmillan, 2008), 4.

[40] Giorgi Vachnadze, "The Algorithmic Unconscious: Psychoanalyzing Artificial Intelligence", *The Shadow* 06th February 2021: https://medium.com/the-shadow/the-algorithmic-unconscious-psychoanalyzing-artificial-intelligence-323c52232c61. Here, referring to Possati's article "Algorithmic Unconscious: Why Psychoanalysis Helps in Understanding AI", Vachnadze says that "The algorithmic unconscious, very much like a human unconscious is articulate in its entropic features".

connectivity where humanity is plugged in at an unconscious level in the 7th protocol. The project of Xanadu is also disclosed as a reference to the "Mongolian utopia where written cultures would never be lost" and a "Hypertext that would make it real" in the world. Xanadu project was about a library in space that could be accessed by a telephone receiver. Later, an overview of Schumann Resonance is explicated, which is said to be the "brain wave" of the earth.[41] Krüger in the book *Virtual Immortality: God, Evolution and the Singularity in Post- and Transhumanism,* observes that

> Hans Moravec believes that the entire Earth will eventually be simulated by a gigantic computer as some kind of digital reserve: All possible pasts would then be reconstructed as permanent simulations to house the last humans and all those who were resurrected. According to Moravec, these unembodied, posthuman individuals would then even be able to dive into the mind of a virtual dolphin or an elephant.[42]

For transhumanists, a merging of identities and a collective consciousness is very likely in computer memories. The voice of the announcer reveals that there will ultimately be as many individuals on Earth as there are neurons in the human brain. The upshot will be the fusion of the entire globe into a single electromagnetic synaptic network. This is because it has expanded so quickly that it is similar to the neural network of the brain.[43] The channeling of collective thought into a single repository and its subsequent comparison with neurons in the brain hints at an ambitious project. But it also points to monism.

Layer 10

In Layer 10, entitled "Love", it is revealed that Lain was born in The Wired. She existed as a hologram, "A homunculus of artificial ribosomes". At the beginning of the episode, Lain asks Eiri, if he is God. The dialogues between them become unsettling as Lain speaks for Eiri, stating that to die is to abandon the flesh and has nothing to do with "death". Continuing to speak for Eiri, Lain states that The Wired's protocols were developed with a higher code, mixed with thoughts, information, emotions and memories that belonged to Eiri. He could stay forever as an anonymous entity in The Wired and rule the world by controlling information. This was his definition of being a god. As he believes all people are already connected on a collective unconscious level,

---

[41] Serial Experiments Lain, *Wiki*: https://sel.fandom.com/wiki/Layer_09.
[42] Oliver Krüger, *Virtual Immortality: God, Evolution and the Singularity in Post- and Transhumanism* (Bielefeld: Transcript Publishing, 2021), 276.
[43] Serial Experiments Lain, *Wiki*: https://sel.fandom.com/wiki/Layer_09.

Eiri's ultimate purpose is to bring all people together on a conscious level. Eiri thinks that the ultimate objective of human progress is the renunciation of bodies—the physical obstacles that prevent absolute communication—and the creation of the entire net of connections between people's thoughts. But for Wasylak, drawing from Baudrillard, it is comparable to putting a halt to evolution.[44]

Layer 11

Layer 11, entitled "Infornography", is where Lain implants the Navi emulator chip inside her head. This makes a tremendous flow of information possible. Here Lain requests not to be treated like a machine. But Eiri responds by saying that she is not hardware but software. Is Lain an AI, as in "An executable program within a body"?

Doede exposes, what he perceives to be, the real agenda of the transhumanist project. That project hopes to gradually replace our flesh with technologies of enhancement as the only path to human liberation by attaining immortal orders of posthuman being. But Doede suggests that it is the most cunning yet alluring path to sub-humanization that can exist since it is nothing less than an invitation to remodel and reconceptualize humanity in the image of our lower-selves.[45] This is because robots and AI are created in our image and made to act like us while their bodies are made of metal and their minds are code.

The project of transhumanism, especially as Eiri explains her identity to Lain, is a reduction to the levels of software code in a body and about being-in-the-wire. This then is sub-humanism rather than being posthuman (although as we find later in the anime, Lain is able to transgress her limitations).

Layer 12

In Layer 12, entitled "Landscape", the body is recognized as a machine, while Lain as the collective unconscious. In what underlies a Jungian framework, it is revealed that the information that humans have inside is not what they have acquired through their lived experiences of the world but is something that they have been carrying from their ancestors. This is revealed in the

---

[44] Katarzyna Wasylak, "Lain—The Cyber-ghost Versus Hyperreality", *academia.edu*: file:///C:/Users/banderson/Desktop/Lain_The_Cyber_ghost_Versus_Hyperreality.pdf.
[45] Doede, "Transhumanism, Technology, and the Future", 51. Again, cf. Torseth, "Who Am I? Personhood and the Self-Defeating Epistemology of Transhumanism", in *Technology and Theology*, 20-36.

Where is the Real Me? 149

statement: "The species called man is connected to his predecessors and information has accumulated within him".[46]

Layer 13

In Layer 13, entitled "Ego", we encounter Lain sacrificing her identity to erase collective memory. In this act, she manages to delete Alice's secrets and thereby save her from public humiliation. In this manner, Lain is also a forgotten entity, one whom the world doesn't remember.

Lain's self-actualization as a powerful posthuman happens in the final episode. Here she realizes the cause of her bodily existence and is able to wipe out memories while appearing again in the lives of people like Alice. According to Krüger, technological posthumanism tackles two important issues related to immortality.[47]

1) How can people recreate a flawless reproduction of themselves in a computer's memory?

2) How do we get to this bright future?

To understand the focus of technological posthumanism, we can take a hypothetical understanding of SEL. Lain signifies the birth of an individual from a collective resource of energy. This individual is gradually—as we see in the case of Lain moving towards an awakening—responding to a calling of becoming immortal, i.e., returning to the eternal state of collective resource and repository of energy. The individual embraces technological enhancement to do so. But as we see Lain's dependency on technology becoming visibly excessive, her room is a station of hi-tech computational machinery and her body is entangled in wires. Technological enhancement not only connects the individual to others with the same ideal, but also helps them transcend their bodily limitations and reach their ideal, becoming more-than-humans. This is the instance of becoming posthuman: "a reality that surpasses man in terms of completeness and accomplishment, since they are more connected and in tune with the energies that vivify the cosmos".[48]

No Longer Human(?): Cybernetic Divinity in SEL

The Wired can be looked at as deterritorialized, continually expanding, and an all-connecting hyperspace. There, contingent histories, repressed desires and

---

[46] SEL, Layer 12.
[47] Krüger, *Virtual Immortality*, 117.
[48] Valera, "Posthumanism: Beyond Humanism?", 487.

the collective unconscious exist. The Wired is where everything connects with everything else. It is a crossing of physical space that exceeds to become a transcendental realm.

Living in The Wired doesn't require a body, and so everything else that is characteristic of physical limitations are overcome in this process towards becoming cybernetically divine. Limitations in the physical world include the growth and aging of the body, the limited movement of the body, the mind unconnected with other minds and the mind that acquires information through sense-experiences (as in the earlier version of Lain's mind in a naïve state). All of these limitations have been overcome in The Wired: Lain is omniscient, omnipresent and immortalized. She is the culmination of connections and can control the collective memories.

Although everyone can connect to The Wired, Lain is someone special. She connects like none other: the physical Lain transgresses as an entity that no longer requires an external device to connect to The Wired. For Lain, The Wired is a paradise-like state where nothing can be diminished.

In "Secret to Becoming God in Serial Experiments Lain", Max Derrat states that the Knights and Eiri Masami had conspired to collapse the divide between the real and the virtual world by forcing human society to "download" the collective unconscious (or all information from The Wired) into their brains to achieve the ideal Jungian self.[49] This would then lead to total human connectivity forming a "global hive mind". Here all humans could connect wirelessly—by acclimatizing to the Schumann resonance—as a part of Eiri Masami's project called Protocol 7.[50] Derrat also states that Lain, The Wired and the collective unconscious are all the same. In fact, it was Lain's idea to experience a body and to forget her past experience as a god-like entity. This explains her naïve nature and frequent discordant sounds and visions from the other world. The collective unconscious as a seat of desires represents humanity's ultimate proclivity to unify knowledge and transcend all limitations.

In SEL, the postulation of total unification and connectivity through means of technology is intricately linked with the conception of divinity. Krüger, drawing from theologian Jennifer Cobb, argues that the divine potential in the progress of computer technology must be recognized.

---

[49] Max Derrat, "The Secret to Becoming God in Serial Experiments Lain", *YouTube*: https://www.youtube.com/watch?v=Zc6MsSmJJzU&t=61s.
[50] Ibid.

Like many other Protestant theologians in the United States, Cobb seeks an alliance between the sciences and Christian theology and legitimates her religious interpretation of cyberspace as the evolution of divine creativity in the universe.[51]

According to Teilhard, the stages of cosmogenesis, biogenesis and noogenesis (emergence and evolution of intelligence) represent a constant unfolding of the mind during the evolutionary process.[52] Krüger also argues that Russian cyberneticist Valentin Turchin adopted Teilhard's idea of the noosphere wherein he formulated the idea of a future synthetic consciousness in which human individuals would merge and achieve immortality.[53] A new and intelligent entity, supported by powerful synchronization, is supposed to be born out of the alliance and communication of collective consciousness shaped by cyberspace.

For Teilhard, at the "end of the world" the noosphere will finally reach a point of convergence when every individual awareness will combine to create a new, super-personal consciousness. Only the power of all-pervading love has the capacity to bring about the Omega Point and Jesus' presence is the reason mankind has been chosen to perform this function.[54]

Likewise, in the anime, a connection of Lain with the figure of Jesus has also been posited in many cases. Eiri Masami had tempted Lain to join him and take control of The Wired. This temptation came with a promise of immortality and power.[55] In the final episode Lain is shown talking to her father, elevated on a floating kitchen-table. After Lain sacrificed her physical body and erased the memory of her presence in the real world, her father suggests that the act represents her love for everyone. She begins crying. This was indeed an act of saving multiple individuals—including Arisu, Eiri and Chisa—who had given up their physical bodies for an immortal presence in The Wired.

Although Jesus' life and presence is integral in Christian thought, Lain is not supposed to be remembered. Lain could be understood as "cybernetically divine", if not a *Kami* or God. Eiri and Chisa couldn't return using their bodies, and according to them, the body wasn't important. Lain defied this by demonstrating a complete integration. Like Calvin Mercer posits: "With

---

[51] Krüger, *Virtual Immortality*, 280.
[52] Ibid.
[53] Ibid.
[54] Ibid.
[55] This parallels Satan's temptation of Christ by offering "all the kingdoms of the world" in Matthew 4:8.

resuscitation, life continues as before in the same body; with resurrection, life continues in a transformed body with new possibilities".[56] Lain's sacrifice and successful resurrection as a posthuman figure signals the birth of new prospects, both for humanity and herself.

Conclusion

Lain's understanding of existence transcends physical borders, including both the real world and The Wired. While the real world has limitations due to its finite and tangible nature, Lain's journey throughout the anime demonstrates her gradual movement towards transcending the limitations imposed by her physical body as she becomes increasingly engrossed in the limitless realm of The Wired. Lain's eventual transition into a posthuman is the culmination of her quest. Lain is released from the limits of a physical body by dwelling in the ethereal world of The Wired, allowing her to transcend the basic limitations of human life and attain a state of cybernetic divinity. The concept of a collective unconscious, which serves as a reservoir for human desires, represents humanity's intrinsic urge to seek the unification of knowledge and overcome all borders. Hence, technical interconnectedness, unity of knowledge and total transcendence are deeply linked with the concept of divinity in the anime *Serial Experiments Lain*.

---

[56] Calvin Mercer, "Protestant Christianity—Sorting Out Soma in the Debate about Transhumanism: One Protestant's Perspective", in *Transhumanism and the Body: The World Religions Speak*, eds. Calvin Mercer, Derek F. Maher (New York: Palgrave Macmillan, 2016), 138.

Chapter 7

Philosophy, Soul, Politics and Power in *Dragon Ball Z**

Issei Takehara
Independent Researcher

ABSTRACT: The Dragon Ball series is a deeply philosophical work. It illustrates the interrelations among the individuals whose actions are dictated by the lust for power. This desire for power manifests itself in the quest for the Dragon Balls, which are said to grant the wishes of anyone who has collected all seven of them. The Dragon Ball series, then, is a process of a power struggle narrated from the viewpoint of Son Goku and his journey involving the actors trying to achieve absolute power. In this sense, everyone fends for himself and everyone collects the Dragon Balls for one's own gain. *Dragon Ball Z* is loved timelessly for reasons we do not often realize. I argue in this chapter that *Dragon Ball Z* keeps captivating our minds because the anime is grounded in the serious philosophical argument about human nature. I will also attempt to explain the philosophy, the nature of the soul, politics and intrigue involved in *Dragon Ball Z*.

KEYWORDS: Compatibilism, Determinism, *Dragon Ball Z*, Ethics, History, International Affairs, Philosophy, Politics.

***

Introduction

Can the *Dragon Ball* anime teach us about real-world history, the philosophies that led to World War II, and the devastating effects of totalitarianism? I explore these themes, the worldviews behind them, and the way they manifest in *Dragon Ball*, perhaps the world's most-recognized Japanese manga and anime.

---

* Thanks to Derek Padula for his editorial assistance on this chapter.

Dragon Ball Z is the most popular series in the multi-billion dollar *Dragon Ball* franchise. Why is it so successful? Is it because of its incredible action, the beautiful animation and emotional soundtrack? These factors contribute to its success, but I argue that the most important factor is the culture and real-world philosophies that are imbued in the content by *Dragon Ball's* author and illustrator, Akira Toriyama.[1] The concepts inherent in this work appeal to our humanity, similar to a great film, sophisticated novel or painting.

You will see that the characters from *Dragon Ball Z* behave like real people with emotions and that their actions are analogous to the behaviors of real-world people and the nations they lived in during the global geopolitical conflicts of the early-to-mid twentieth century.

In addition, the events these characters experience, and their subsequent actions, unfold ad hoc, but given each character's personality, each moment was inclined to happen, yet not necessitated to happen.

The Vegeta and Frieza Arcs of *Dragon Ball Z* showcase mankind's bare desire for power, and our history affirms it. *Dragon Ball Z* is a story that reveals who we are as humans, urging us to reflect on ourselves.

Dragon Ball Z is a story about Son Goku, a super-powerful martial artist with a secret history. There are four main series in the Dragon Ball franchise, starting with the titular series, continuing into *Dragon Ball Z*, the anime-exclusive *Dragon Ball GT*, and the canonical continuation of the series in *Dragon Ball Super*.[2] The franchise as a whole is regarded as a comedic martial arts epic inspired by the ancient Chinese legend of *Journey to the West* (1592), about the Buddhist monk and his monkey guardian Sun Wukong, who is the inspiration for Son Goku (or Goku for short).

The original Dragon Ball story explores Goku's childhood adventures in his search for the seven mystical dragon balls that can grant any wish. Along the way, he meets several enemies who oppose him on his journey, but Goku's light-hearted nature and ability to enlighten to advanced martial arts techniques enables him to convert his enemies into friends and reach higher levels of spiritual attainment. Underlying the surface-level action and adventure are deep-seated philosophies that I will explore here.

Dragon Ball Z begins with the introduction of Goku's son, Gohan. The entire *Dragon Ball Z* story that follows derives from this one incident in the first

---

[1] Akira Toriyama, *Dragon Ball* (Tokyo: Shueisha, 1984-1995), Vols. 1-42.
[2] *Dragon Ball*: Directed by Minoru Okazaki and Daisuke Nishio with Screenplay by Toshiki Inoue and Takao Koyama (Fuji TV 1986-1989); *Dragon Ball Z*: Directed by Daisuke Nishio and Shigeyasu Yamauchi with Screenplay by Takao Koyama (Fuji TV 1989-1996) and *Dragon Ball Super*: Directed by Kimitoshi Chioka et al. with Screenplay by Akira Toriyama et al. (Fuji TV 2015-2018).

episode, when Gohan gets kidnapped by Raditz—a powerful warrior of the Saiyan race of aliens. Raditz is one of only four Saiyans left in the universe, and it turns out that Raditz is Goku's older brother. He has come from outer space to Earth to demand that Goku help him conquer the universe by force.[3] Such a plan would involve cleansing all life on Earth and eliminating Goku's friends along the way. When Goku refuses to cooperate, Raditz defeats Goku in combat, kidnaps Gohan, and leaves Goku no choice but to comply with his demand. But in a twist of fate, Goku teams up with his prior nemesis, Piccolo, to defeat Raditz and save his friends, family and the Earth. However, this victory comes at the cost of Goku's life. What follows is a grand epic through Heaven, Hell, the Earth, other planets, divine realms and multiple universes.

Here we are introduced to our first philosophical point. It is important to recognize that the seed has already been planted, and everything that happens afterward is naturally contained in the initial offense done by Raditz. Goku only intended to bring Gohan to meet his father's friends at a reunion, and it was not his intent to get involved with any of the events that ensued. Nonetheless, Goku has an innate desire to fight strong opponents and he becomes excited by the prospect of challenging himself, as well as reaching higher levels of skill in his martial arts and mind-body awareness. Therefore, I argue that Goku's involvement with a deadly foe was inevitable, although not necessitated, for he, too, is a power-hungry Saiyan. Thus, Goku's successive journey is best understood in relation to Compatibilism.

Compatibilism

Compatibilism, sometimes known pejoratively as "Soft Determinism",[4] reconciles the differences between the proponents of free will and those of

---

[3] Raditz feels that conquering the universe by force is justified. The political realism of Thrasymachus and Machiavelli demonstrate a similar political philosophy in *Dragon Ball Z*. Plato conveys the political realism of Thrasymachus in *The Republic*, ed. G. R. E. Ferrari and trans. Tom Griffith (Cambridge University Press, 2007). Thrasymachus argues that justice is the advantage of the stronger (338e4-339a3) and that in "all cities the same thing is just, namely what is good for the ruling authority. . . . the same thing is just everywhere—what is good for the stronger (339a2-5). See also Machiavelli for the advancement of the similar argument for political realism, *The Prince*, trans., and ed. Harvey C. Mansfield (Chicago: The University of Chicago Press, 1985), 34-38.

[4] NB there are various terms used for the same ideas in this discussion. I will stick to compatibilism and determinism for the purposes of this chapter. For if everything is fated, whatever one does will or will not happen whether or not one wills it. Leibniz thinks this is not only absurd but also immoral, for the will of an individual matters. Douglas Burnham, "Gottfried Leibniz: Metaphysics", *Internet Encyclopedia of Philosophy*. https://iep.utm.edu/leib-met/#H6.

determinism.⁵ Hard Determinism, sometimes known as Hard Incompatibilism, can be either physical (natural as in subject to physics) or metaphysical (as in beyond the physical).⁶ Metaphysical Determinism argues that every moment of existence was, is, and will be pre-ordained by a higher, or metaphysical, causal power. The main ethical problem with determinism is that if everything we do is determined from the beginning, then there is no way for us to take responsibility for what we do. Without freewill, our actions are pre-determined and hence the consequences of our actions are not our fault. Compatibilism allows this higher power, such as God, to be omniscient as well as omnipotent while also being benevolent—even if humans cause evil deeds. For if God is all-good and yet there is evil in the world, then God, too, would be responsible for the evil in the world.

Hence, a theory is needed that allows God to be good while explaining why God allows there to be evil in the world. One such theory is posited by the German philosopher Gottfried Wilhelm Leibniz. His theory of pre-established harmony propounds that the journey we take in life is *inclined* to happen yet is not *necessitated* to occur.⁷

Thus, what seemed like a simple catalyst in the *Dragon Ball Z* story was in fact dictated by the necessary conditions embedded in the characters themselves. In this way, it was inevitable and natural for Goku and Piccolo to team up against Raditz. Likewise, when the other two remaining Saiyans, Vegeta and Nappa, hear of Raditz's death and that the seven mystical dragon balls can grant any wish, they are naturally *inclined* to come to Earth in order to defeat Goku, get the dragon balls, and wish for immortality. The same

---

⁵ Michael McKenna, and D. Justin Coates, "Compatibilism", *The Stanford Dictionary of Philosophy.* https://plato.stanford.edu/entries/compatibilism/. The problem of freewill vs. determinism is a long standing one in philosophy. For an introductory discussion, see Tim O'Keefe, "Ancient Theories of Freedom and Determinism", *The Stanford Dictionary of Philosophy. The Stanford Dictionary of Philosophy.* https://plato.stanford.edu/entries/freedom-ancient/.
⁶ Carl Hoefer, "Casual Determinism", *The Stanford Dictionary of Philosophy.* https://plato.stanford.edu/entries/determinism-causal/.
⁷ Leibniz argues that there are two ways in which we can speak of necessity. "The one whose contrary implies a contradiction is absolutely necessary; this deduction occurs in the external truths, for example, the truth of geometry. The other is necessary only *ex hypothesi* and, so to speak, accidentally, but it is contingent in itself, since its contrary does not imply a contradiction. . . . . [so that] if one were to do the contrary, he would not be doing something impossible in itself". G. W. Leibniz, "Discourse on Metaphysics", in *Discourse on Metaphysics and Other Chapters*, trans. Daniel Garber and Roger Ariew (Cambridge: Hackett Publishing Company, Inc., 1991), 13. See footnote 9 for more on this below.

applies to Goku's eventual triumph over Vegeta by teaming up with his friends, leaving Vegeta in a bitter defeat.

Precondition, Cause and Effect in the Saiyan and Frieza Arcs

Everything that happened in this Saiyan Arc is a precondition for what happens in the ensuing Frieza Arc. I will now use historical examples to illustrate how the story development of *Dragon Ball Z* happens naturally, without any structural jamming.

Gohan's initial kidnapping instigated successive events that would last for years afterward. Here, the first episode contains everything that was to happen, just as Leibniz's dictum that the "predicate is contained in the subject", so the succeeding events are merely unfolding of the events that have occurred previously.[8] The flow must naturally follow what the preconditions establish without impinging on the characters and their freedom—i.e. compatibilism—in order to have a cogent effect.[9] So what seemed an innocuous kidnapping of Gohan had the effect of causing Goku's revenge against Raditz. This had the knock-on effect of how Raditz treated Gohan and everyone else but naturally increased Goku's anger against Raditz.

Of course, the Saiyans *qua* Saiyans do not care about the feelings of others. This is also seen when Vegeta killed his companion, Nappa after Goku broke his spine during their battle and was thus rendered useless as a warrior. It is ingrained in the philosophy of the Saiyans that they only care about satisfying their own curiosities for fighting and replenishing their hunger for power. Indeed, the Saiyan philosophy is the philosophy of political realism, and it is only concerned with itself and of its survival. It is self-interested and revolves around self-preservation and nothing more. I call this the Primitive Saiyan Philosophy. Goku's philosophy is fundamentally different. While the Primitive Saiyan Philosophy is individualistic and singularistic in its view (i.e., it does not accept any other idea but its own and there is only one truth), Goku's philosophy is pluralistic. Herein is the seed for empathy which leaves room

---

[8] "Predicate is contained in the subject", in this case, can be thought of as "Goku defeated Frieza". Defeating Frieza is the predicate, and the subject is Goku. In this way, it was inevitable that the story developed subsequently as it did.

[9] While Hard-Determinism does not care about what qualities each character may have, compatibilism allows for the natural qualities of the characters to retain their efficacy in relation to conditions or preconditions. It is in this sense Leibniz argued that, in compatibilism, you would not be doing anything contradictory to your character had you done something that you did not in fact do. This is because what you did at a particular moment in life is always a dictation of the natural phenomena occurring not just in you but also around you.

for ethics. Despite them sharing the same Saiyan roots, Vegeta and Goku's worldviews can be contrasted as representing political realism and liberalism respectively.[10]

A Historical Parallel

It is Raditz's independent action that led to Goku's anger, which then led to his death and the arrival of Vegeta and Nappa, and in turn the bitter defeat of Vegeta. To provide a historical parallel, I turn to the sequence of the Great Wars in the twentieth century, as the similarity is rather striking.

The event that triggered World War I was the assassination of the Austrian Archduke Franz Ferdinand. This was an individual and politically-motivated event which elicited the allied countries to jump into the quarrel. Similarly, Gohan's kidnapping triggered Piccolo's reluctant cooperation with Goku in fighting the common enemy. It was a personal event that happened at Goku's friend's house that stirred up the subsequent events. Furthermore, a parallel to the World Wars, Vegeta's bitter defeat is likened to Germany's bitter defeat at the end of World War I. Vegeta, then, is the embodiment of the philosophy of Adolf Hitler *at this point* of the story. That is, the abstract ideology that Hitler adhered to, i.e., a reign of terror, or a totalitarian movement.[11]

For example, Vegeta believes and professes numerous times the idea that Saiyans are the true warriors of the universe, which is similar to Hitler's idea of the true Aryan race. For Vegeta, it should not be possible to be defeated by a lower-class Saiyan (that is, Goku), but also such a defeat is a disgrace for the entire elite class of Saiyans. Vegeta's defeat caused a personal grudge against Goku. This took on wider implications and the political justification to destroy the weaker class of the Saiyan—all because they held the wrong view about the universe—and tried to disobey the chain of superiority. Like Hitler and

---

[10] Alexander Moseley, "Political Realism", *Internet Encyclopedia of Philosophy*: https://iep.utm.edu/polreal/#:~:text=Political%20realism%20is%20a%20theory,the%20domestic%20or%20international%20arena. Moseley summarizes Political Realism as "a theory of political philosophy that attempts to explain, model, and prescribe political relations. It takes as its assumption that power is (or ought to be) the primary end of political action". Cf. Shane D. Courtland, Gerald Gaus and David Schmidtz, "Liberalism", *The Stanford Encyclopedia of Philosophy: https://plato.stanford.edu/archives/spr2022/entries/liberalism/*.

[11] This abstract ideology Hitler adhered to is attributed to Vegeta in the Saiyan Arc. But the same ideology becomes more appropriate to attribute to Frieza in the Frieza Arc, which is why it is important to emphasize that I am not talking about the particular person as such but only the ideology by which a certain individual has acted. It is also, of course, consistent with Moseley's assertion that political realism is based on the "assumption that power is (or ought to be) the primary end of political action".

many German soldiers at the end of the First Great War, the defeat became personal as well as political.[12]

Back to the unfolding of the scenario, it makes sense that Vegeta and Nappa came to Earth. The Primitive Saiyan Philosophy is self-interested, and its sole interest is the acquisition of power and exercising destruction. This power-thirsty desire for annihilation explains why Nappa's first act upon their arrival to Earth was the destruction of everything he saw in the city upon which their space pods landed.[13] His behavior would have been the normal procedure, but (as Vegeta was quick to point out), it was the acquisition of power and not the destruction of the planet for which they came to Earth, i.e. getting the dragon balls to gain their power and immortality. The desire for the dragon balls moved them away from where they were, not only to survive but also to acquire absolute power through the dragon balls.

Power Struggles

As soon as the Saiyans arrive on Earth, Vegeta tries to find the warriors who have the highest combat powers since he believes they are the ones who killed Raditz. To do this, Vegeta uses an alien device called a Scouter, which is attached to the side of his head and around his ear. The Scouter is able to scan a planet for frequencies of energy being emanated from living beings, quantify their energy (combat power), and then display this number on their visor. A higher number determines a greater threat. In Saiyan society, all warriors are judged by this number at birth in order to determine their potential as warriors. They are then classified, such as elite or low-class, and their fate in society is decided. Raditz performed the same action upon his arrival to Earth. Here we see Vegeta judge Goku's fellow Earthling warriors who prepared for the impending battle. He is surprised at their rise in power compared to Raditz's time, yet still dismisses them as weaklings.

---

[12] For parallel issues in relation to the Holocaust, see Debórah Dword and Robert Jan van Pelt, *Holocaust: A History* (New York: W.W. Norton & Company, 2003), 51-53. The entire book discusses the issue delicately. In this book the authors discuss how millions of Germans did not want to accept the Versailles Treaty—and the Germans viewed it as the fault of the far-too-many Jews in the new government, the Weimar Republic—that the armistice had been signed. The book explains how Adolf Hitler expressed "hatred" growing in him, citing *Mein Kampf* that there was "hatred for those responsible" for the betrayal of the nation, and that there "is no making pacts with the Jews; there can only be the hard: either—or". Therefore, Hitler continued, "I, for my part, decided to go into politics".

[13] *Dragon Ball Z*, Episode 22.

Meanwhile, Goku had been killed by Raditz and was training in the afterlife with a deity of martial arts in the Other World. This realm is inspired by Buddhist, Daoist and Shinto mythology and contains all manner of deities. In this case, Goku trains with Kaiō-*sama* (The Lord of Worlds), a deity who watches over the planets.

Thus, flying towards the warriors with the strongest power level led them to Piccolo and Gohan. Vegeta soon recognizes Piccolo as the one who killed Raditz because he recognized the voice from Raditz's final Scouter transmission.[14] Nappa then realizes that Piccolo is a Namekian, an alien race of humanoid slug people. As a result, Vegeta is reminded of the legend that the Namekians have strange powers that are likened to magic and that some Namekians even have strong combat powers. However, the Saiyans had some doubts as to whether or not the dragon balls actually existed and whether they actually had the power to grant them any wish. But after meeting some of Goku's companions and their clear expectation of Goku's return from death via a wish on the dragon balls, their doubts were somewhat alleviated. The presence of a Namekian also made some affirmation as to the possibility of the existence of such things.

Vegeta and Nappa wanted to see how strong the Earthlings were, which prompted them to entertain themselves by letting their pet-monsters fight with Goku's companions. These Saibai-man, were eventually defeated while, with Nappa, killing many of Goku's friends along the way.[15] Nappa was then to fight with the now 5-year-old Gohan, Piccolo and Krillin. But even Gohan and Piccolo were no match against Nappa, despite becoming stronger than the time when they had fought against Raditz.

Goku sacrificed himself during the fight against Raditz and died. But his body was preserved like a glorified body by the Earth's god, *Kami* (Japanese for "deity" or "god").[16] Moreover, it was sent to Kaiō-*sama* (The Lord of

---

[14] This is also why Vegeta and Nappa found out about the dragon balls on Earth—since Raditz could not imagine Goku would sacrifice himself to save his son—to which Piccolo responded Goku can be resurrected with the dragon balls. Frieza found out about the existence of the dragon balls, in a similar way, on Planet Namek. Vegeta had mentioned about going to Planet Namek to get the dragon balls after seeing Piccolo on Earth.

[15] Saibai-man means "cultivation rangers". They were grown out of seeds in the soil.

[16] In *Dragon Ball Z*, a body is said to be preserved materially *without* quantity by God so that the individual soul can find its *own* corpse un-decomposed. Thus, when revived, the soul can get back its original body. This is what happened to Christ, whose body had suffered the absence of the soul for three days, until he was resurrected. Ordinarily, the body unoccupied by a soul would decay and rot. But God can preserve a body in such a way that the corpse would remain fresh, i.e. as a glorified body. I discuss these matters in detail in my blog. Issei Takehara, "History and Philosophy of Transubstantiation",

Worlds) along with his soul so that he could be trained to be stronger and skilled. Informed that Goku's resurrection was imminent, the Saiyans decided to wait for Goku's return. They were half incredulous and half curious. But they really wanted to show the traitor, Goku, the deaths of his own friends and his son in front of Goku's own eyes. However, when Goku was resurrected and approached to meet his allies, Vegeta sensed that Goku's combat power was so much higher than the Saiyans had expected. Thus it would be better to kill—Piccolo, Gohan and Krillin—before Goku arrives. Vegeta reasoned it would be cumbersome if the four of them teamed up against himself and Nappa. As a result, in the battle against Nappa, before Goku could arrive, Piccolo was killed protecting Gohan (the son of his nemesis). This decision by Piccolo signified a change of Piccolo's heart. He went from the resurrected spawn of a demon king—dedicated solely to killing Goku, enacting revenge on the part of his father (and self) and conquering the world—to a man who felt empathy for a child and sacrificed his life to protect him.

When Nappa then gets ready for an attack, Krillin says to himself something particularly interesting, "I feel like a *kamikaze* attacker".[17] This is an explicit reference to Japanese World War II fighter pilots who felt it was their duty to sacrifice their lives in suicide attacks in order to weaken their foes, so that the greater Japanese Empire could triumph. Also, earlier in the episode, Chaiotzu self-destructed himself to combat Nappa, and Piccolo then told Gohan, "Don't look away; this is what a battle looks like".[18]

Choosing Life or Death

At this point, the resurrected Goku came back to the scene to save his son and his best friend, Krillin, who were barely alive. Piccolo and Kami used to be the same person; hence, one's death entailed the other's death, and as Piccolo died, Kami also died. This fact had a deeper implication for the Saiyans who came to the Earth for the dragon balls. Since the dragon balls were made by Kami, when Kami died, the dragon balls also turned to stone. However, on seeing the connection of the dragon balls with Piccolo, Vegeta had earlier surmised that the dragon balls were probably the artifacts created by Namekians, which turned out to be the root (i.e., race) of Piccolo, hence of

---

Isseicreekphilosophyblog 24th February 2012: https://isseicreekphilosophy.wordpress.com/2012/02/24/history-and-philosophy-of-transubstantiation/.

[17] *Dragon Ball Z*, Episode 26. In Japanese, Krillin said "*Tokkōtai* (特攻隊)" and the English translation is "Japanese Special Attack Units". But it is often used to mean *kamikaze* ("divine wind"), the Japanese suicide fighter pilots during World War II.

[18] *Dragon Ball Z*, Episode 24. Again the lesson is that one should not pretend that what is terrible is not happening, i.e., be in a state of "denial".

Kami. This is the reasoning behind Vegeta's decision that it would become a little laborious if Piccolo and the others teamed up with Goku. Hence Vegeta decided that Piccolo was dispensable. The priority thus shifted from collecting the dragon balls to terminating the "traitorous" Goku, for the dragon balls could be found anyway if they went to Planet Namek, the home planet of Piccolo.

This shift in priorities will become important as the plot thickens since that is how real actors in the power struggle act out. The information Vegeta could gather about the dragon balls was enough to have them come to Earth, he concluded, and all he needed to do now was to exterminate the vermin that had disgraced the Saiyan race along with the planet Earth. But as soon as Goku arrived, Nappa was made useless in a single blow from Goku.[19]

Seeing this, Vegeta realized two things. One was that Nappa no longer had existential value. Vegeta said in response to Nappa's plea for help: "a Saiyan who cannot fight is of no use".[20] Vegeta kills Nappa without hesitation. The other thing he noticed was Goku's countenance, realizing something had completely changed from the time Goku had fought against Raditz. This quick wit and ability to discern and judge in an instance is what makes Vegeta a genius warrior.

Vegeta is, contrary to Nappa, equipped with cold-blooded intelligence that does not allow him to act on impulse. What defeated Nappa was his lack of calculation and inability to judge the circumstance at a moment's notice. Furthermore, while Vegeta shares with Goku some genuine talents, such as calculative combat styles and over-confidence in his own strength, he and Goku have crucial differences in the sources of their confidence. While Vegeta is confident in his own superiority, Goku is confident in his own potential. One sees power as absolute and complete while the other sees it as developing and with room for improvement. While Vegeta believes only in his own power, Goku believes in cooperation. This is nowhere more obvious than when Vegeta killed Nappa. While he could have still used and relied on what little strength Nappa had, Goku relied and believed in his companions until the very end of the battle, no matter how damaged they were. This unique confidence is why Goku was able to give the last *senzu* bean to dying Krillin

---

[19] See "Lesson Number One", *Dragon Ball Z*, Episode 29. Nappa did receive several blows from Goku, but it is obvious from the episode that all it took Goku was one blow with the *Kaiō-ken* technique. Goku, in this episode, explains to Krillin that this technique is like a "massive upsurge of energy. Everything is heightened: power, speed, even hearing and vision improve dramatically". In other words, you become many times stronger.
[20] Ibid.

and Gohan.[21] He did this as soon as he had arrived at the battle scene in order to revive their broken bodies. He did not hesitate, even though he fully knew it would be to his advantage to keep it for himself during the battle. In this way, Goku demonstrated the combination of power as strength. But this would require the willful participation of the parties involved. In other words, the parties involved must all work together for the common goal.

In contrast, Vegeta referred to Gohan and Krillin as "useless" toward the end of their fight. He also eliminated a potential rival force—he deemed unnecessary or which could be detrimental in the future to his maintaining absolute power—while he was still innocuous to him. This is a good strategy that is often used in political realism, yet it also isolated him in the end.[22] In this way, Vegeta suffered a bitter defeat, facing the team effort of the "inferior" lower-class Saiyan and Earthlings.

In the end, Goku did have the chance to kill Vegeta before the latter could escape, but he chose not to kill him. This ability to choose and having autonomy would play a large part in Goku's philosophy. There is a clear philosophical strategy embedded in this action. First, having the kind of character that Goku does, it was not possible to end his new nemesis' life, however contradictory it may seem. Second, Goku was a Saiyan, and despite putting his own friends, family and all of Earth at risk, Goku desired to fight strong opponents. Vegeta was the strongest opponent he had ever faced, and Goku wished to fight him again one day. Furthermore, Vegeta was the only Saiyan left besides Goku himself. In this respect, Goku felt a kinship affinity towards Vegeta, for he too can be an extended family member for him. It was this innate personality trait in Goku that allowed him to let Vegeta go.

This was the moment when for the first time a clear thesis was presented against the antithesis: Goku as the liberal warrior was met with Vegeta as the political realist warrior. Both belonged to the same race, but their philosophy of fighting was a contrast of opposites.

How would these two theses play out in the future? It is in the following episodes that the answer unfolds. And just as the First Great War ended prematurely, leaving many unsatisfied, the main players of the power struggle in *Dragon Ball Z* are also headed for the great collision. These actions were

---

[21] *Senzu* (仙豆, "sage bean") is a miraculous bean that heals the wounded and restores mental and physical power to the one who eats it.

[22] This is later discussed in more detail with Frieza's handling of his subordinates. But in particular, Frieza exterminated almost the entire race of Saiyans when they became stronger and disobedient to him.

inclined, but by this time, they were starting to seem necessitated by the previous perceptions, i.e., the "will" of each character.

Transformations in the Power Struggle with Historical Parallels

Transformations are a fundamental theme in *Dragon Ball* and history alike. In this section, I will explore the cyclical relationship between power struggles and transformations.

Transformations and Stages

In *Dragon Ball*, the characters undergo physical transformations in order to reach a higher level of power in their martial arts. These often occur in response to a need to survive a dangerous battle with a strong opponent.

Political thought has also had transformations occur throughout its history. This idea is illustrated by Hannah Arendt, a prominent political philosopher. She did extensive research on the cruelty conducted under a totalitarian regime. This led her to reveal some of the important distinctions between a totalitarian government and a tyrannical and despotic government ruled by a dictator. She argues in her book, *The Origins of Totalitarianism*, that there can be four phases when the dictatorial government is on the rise.[23]

In the beginning, before ascending to power, such a government—whether it be totalitarian or despotic—must appeal to the public to gain support from the ignorant masses and organize a mob-like mentality. In this first stage of power, they make distinctions between the state and their movement. Then by repeatedly calling the government the enemy of the people and by insisting that the masses will be safer and will be well taken care of under this ruler rather than any other one, the masses come to believe that their claim must be true. This is done through consistent repetition of messaging, which imparts confidence in the party leader on the masses over time.[24]

For example, in Germany, the Nazis combined their rhetorical consistency with the use of what is known as "power propaganda", which was nothing but a demonstration by means of violent intimidation. It thus became clear that the power of the Nazis was greater than that of the state. In *Dragon Ball*, we can presume that Frieza employed such a method to gather his underlings and convince them that they would be better off siding with the "almighty

---

[23] Hannah Arendt, *The Origins of Totalitarianism* (San Diego: Harcourt, Inc., 1966).
[24] See the "Totalitarian Movement" in Arendt, *The Origins of Totalitarianism*, 351-52.

Lord Frieza, the sovereign who reigns over the universe".[25] As evidence, we see Frieza never neglects using this type of propaganda when he tries to convince the Namekians to give him the dragon balls. He instills fear and intimidation by killing some of the strongest Namekian warriors, as well as children in the village, as a demonstration of power.

According to Arendt, the second phase occurs when such a regime is in power. The regime moves on to destroy the previously occupied offices and fill them with its own party members. An incoming dictator ruler does this to have the complete amalgamation of the state and the party. A totalitarian ruler goes beyond this, for he wants to concentrate the elite powers on the center of the movement and not waste their efforts on administrative issues of running the state. Totalitarianism is a movement and distinct from a state (which is stationary). As such, it uses the state as an outward façade and escapes the total amalgamation with the state by placing the second-rate officers in the hierarchy. Arendt explains by stating that "[o]ne should never forget that only a building can have a structure, but that a movement . . . . can have only a direction". She further argues that any form of governmental structure "can be only a handicap to a movement which is being propelled with increasing speed in a certain direction", for any structures would necessarily limit the space of activity.[26] This is why Frieza is never depicted at Planet Frieza giving orders, but is instead always at the center of the movement as if he were a magnet moving across the universe and extracting the strong warriors from the inhabitants of the planets.[27]

The secret police are also instilled in this phase of the totalitarian regime. The task of the secret police is to ferret out secret enemies, hunt down former opponents, and liquidate both open and secret resistance in any organized

---

[25] *Dragon Ball Z*, Episode 96. When Frieza's henchmen on Planet Frieza were informed that Frieza might have been killed, someone (presumably a Tsufurian) exclaimed with joy that "Frieza is now dead, who has killed our race, and we now have a new age coming!". Another Tsufurian responded with rage, claiming that "Frieza-*sama* has promised us prosperity to our race!" For more information on what happened between Frieza and Tsufurians, see my blog. Issei Takehara, "Categories and Races and the Meanings of the Names in Dragon Ball Z", *Isseicreekphilosophyblog* 07th February 2017: https://isseicreekphilosophy.wordpress.com/2017/07/07/appendix-i-categories-of-races-and-the-meanings-of-the-names-in-dragon-ball-z/.

[26] Arendt, *The Origins of Totalitarianism*, 398.

[27] Ibid., 360-61, fn. 52. This is a paraphrase of an excerpt from Hitler's declaration during the war that read: "I am nothing but a magnet constantly moving across the German nation and extracting the steel from this people. And I have often stated that the time will come when all worth-while men in Germany are going to be in my camp. And those who will not be in my camp are worthless anyway".

form.[28] This can again be likened with the scene where King Vegeta both openly and secretly rebels against Frieza, leading to the destruction of Planet Vegeta. Although technically, Planet Vegeta was not the previous government to which Frieza took over, and the Saiyans are best described as an auxiliary force employed by Frieza.[29]

The third phase in the totalitarian regime is to identify the "objective enemy" whose existence is contrary to the movement.[30] It is here where the form of the totalitarian regime is manifested, and terror in the name of total domination is carried out—the purpose of which is to destroy a moral human being and rid him of *spontaneity*. Arendt describes it well when she says that "to destroy individuality is to destroy spontaneity, man's power to begin something new out of his own resources, something that cannot be explained in the basis of reactions to environment and events".[31] This is why Planet Namek was in the process of recovery after a prior environmental tragedy (where all the beautiful plants and flowers as well as a large portion of the population were wiped out). It was the spontaneity of the Namekians who acted on their own accord to plant and to cultivate the planet into the beautiful place it once was. It is also the same reason why Frieza took that spontaneity away from them by destroying the people as well as the plantations when attacking a village. For Frieza, this spontaneity is that which could threaten his universal reign and therefore that which must be dominated as well as liquidated.

The fourth phase is the radicalization of the third, triggered by events that make the action hasten. In the case of the Nazis, the outbreak of war hastened the process, and in the case of Frieza, the stronger enemy hastened the transformation and the degree to which he became destructive.

Types of Transformations

I observe that there are at least three types of transformations that can be seen in various forms of government. Each of these types of transformations can be seen in *Dragon Ball Z*.

---

[28] Arendt, *The Origins of Totalitarianism*, 422. Arendt discusses two types of enemies of the state. Resistance from within is conceived of as a "real enemy" who is represented by a political party or individual who could destroy you. An "objective enemy" is anyone who is contrary to ideology of the party and needed to be "liquidated" to insure the "purity" of their ideology. In Nazi Germany the latter were represented by the Jews, homosexuals, the mentally ill and the physically weak, etc.
[29] *Dragon Ball Z*, Episode 78.
[30] Arendt, *The Origins of Totalitarianism*, 422.
[31] Ibid., 455.

First, by means of phases within the boundary of the limit. This is seen in totalitarian governments. Second, by means of transcending the boundary of the limit. This occurs in revolutions, i.e., overthrowing the current government from within the state, as if to rise from below. Third, by means of merging with the other powers. This occurs in the unification of countries, which happens through coercion or cooperation.

The Nazis used coercion by means of imperialism to occupy Austria and invade Poland. Unification always brings with it a problem of identity. Unification through cooperation is the only successful method since both parties are willing to be united and come to an agreement willingly. Thus they preserve some identity of each nation, as opposed to eliminating one or the other, as in the case of coercive unification. It is obvious that such a peaceful unification can only occur among liberal democratic nations since they tend to allow pluralism by nature.[32]

In *Dragon Ball Z*, transformation by phases occurs when it is within one's ability to transform into something else, as it is no longer useful to stay in the current form. Saiyans have the ability to transform into a monstrous Great Ape form which increases their strength ten-fold, but it often comes at the cost of conscious control of their bodies. Thus, Vegeta only transforms into the Great Ape when he judges it as necessary. Frieza's leading subordinate, Zarbon, transforms in the same way in that the situation of fighting Vegeta requires him to transform in order to survive, or else he would not have transformed.[33] Frieza is able to transform multiple times, and each transformation is also rendered in similar steps taken by totalitarian regimes, in that each transformation was ready as well as necessary to move to the next phase.

There is something curious about this transformation pattern, for in all cases, the transformer hides their ability to transform and does not reveal it

---

[32] Liberals do not have a single view of what counts as a good life for all. This may be because they have mostly been empiricists who, in principle, learn from experience regarding what is conducive to individual flourishing. Moreover, "liberals have often been pluralists and have thought that autonomous individuals might choose a great variety of very different, but equally good lives". They also believe that a truly autonomous being is made possible by exercising their power of choice. Thus liberals appear to be freer to act spontaneously yet this sometimes renders them "indecisive". So "a person incapable of making a choice and sticking to it will have a little chance of leading a happy life". Alan Ryan, "Liberalism" in *A Companion to Contemporary Political Philosophy*, ed. Robert E. Gooding, Philip Pettit and Thomas Pogge (New Jersey: Blackwell Publishing, 2007), 374.
[33] *Dragon Ball Z*, Episode 53.

until it is ready and necessary to do so.³⁴ This is also, however, how the international actors perform in power struggles, for no nation would send in every force they possess all at once, especially when the opponent appears to be weaker. Every state wants to conserve energy as much as possible for as long as possible, and to hide their true power until is necessary to reveal it.

Transformation and Revolution

I argue here that the transformation of transcendence, which is likened to political revolution, is analogous to the transformation into Super Saiyan. For to become a Super Saiyan, one needs to overthrow the present self and go beyond the limit set by oneself. It is a qualitative change since the substance, i.e., the self, remains the same, as is also the case in the political revolution when its own citizens revolt against the autonomous government, angered by the latter's treatment.

It is also noteworthy that the transformation into Super Saiyans requires anger as the motivational force. If we then compare this type of transformation to political revolutions, where a citizen body is so helplessly oppressed that they cannot take it any longer, it becomes obvious how such a transformation must occur and why it is always triggered by anger incited by the realization of its own powerlessness.

Transformation via Merging

Transformation via merging with other powers is either through coercion or through cooperation. The transformation by merging, as well as the dissolution of it, can be seen throughout *Dragon Ball Z*. For example, Piccolo merges with a fellow Namekian named Nail for the battle against Frieza in order to increase his power. Later examples include Cell's coercive merging with the Androids, Piccolo's re-merging with Kami, Goten and Trunks' fusion, and Goku and Vegeta's fusion via *potara* earrings.³⁵

The dissolution often happens by defeat or disagreement with the host body among the enemies, for they tend to attempt to dominate the objects of their merger by force, which results in an inharmonious relationship with the host body. This is why neither Cell nor Boo was able to achieve a homogeneous union with the merged bodies and ended up spewing out the bodies once

---

³⁴ See examples of Totalitarianism rhetoric in Arendt, *The Origins of Totalitarianism*, 419-23.

³⁵ "Fusion" in *Dragon Ball Z* is a technical term. I will only use the term "fusion" as is used in the storyline. Otherwise, I will use the term "merging" or "union" to make a distinction.

taken in. This was because their bodily constituents were both foreign and powerful enough to refuse to be fully integrated into the new host. In other words, their identity remained separate and heterogeneous from the host. This meant that the merger always assumed a hierarchical relationship, one dominant and the others subordinate. For example, this is demonstrated when Cell talks to Android 18 through the voice of Android 17.[36] The discourse shows that there is no respect for the identity of the merged individual, nor is there any will of the mutual governance of the main body, which has been proven time and again through history that it only results in disharmony within the state body, leading to the eventual dissolution of the union.

Although there are many transformations of this kind, I will focus on the one and only example of transformation by merging that appears in the Frieza Arc. Merging can be achieved by coercion or cooperation, and each of these can be subdivided into genuine or artificial. In the case of genuine merging, dissolution is difficult or impossible because the merged body is homogenously merged both in mind and in body, such as with Piccolo's mergers. Whereas in the case of artificial merging, the merged identities are somewhat preserved as distinct from one another, although the body is one. Examples of this latter case are fusions of Goten and Trunks as well as of Goku and Vegeta, which can be described as "artificial fusion by means of cooperation". This explains why both their voices are heard even in the fused body. In contrast, the merger of Cell with the androids or Boo with the main characters can be termed as "artificial mergers by means of coercion".

In contradistinction, a genuine merger can be achieved only through cooperation, for there cannot be any resistance in a genuine merger where both mind and body are united and the identity is integrated fully into the main host body. The instances in which this type of merger occurs are only with regard to Piccolo. This merger can also expect a greater increase in power. Conversely, an artificial merger by means of coercion can expect the least increase in power. Here, power is meant not only as a battle power in the quantitative aspect (i.e., measurable combat power with Scouters) but also as compatibility in the qualitative aspect (i.e., adaptability with the new body). This is why sometimes the host body can expect a better result in combat power by separating out the heterogeneous body that disobeys the host, as is the case of Cell and Boo. Such dissolution, however rare, can also actually happen in the genuine merge, when the heterogeneous quality begins to grow in the body. This is the reason why Kami forced out the evil from himself, which then emerged as the Demon King Piccolo.

---

[36] *Dragon Ball Z*, Episode 152.

Piccolo thus has a unique status in the *Dragon Ball* series, as this type of union has two peculiar features that the other types of mergers or transformations do not have. First is the incredible boost in power. Piccolo has merged twice in the *Dragon Ball* series, yet he has come to possess powers that could equal Saiyans, who have powered up several times. His strength indeed surpassed that of the Super Saiyans in the later seasons. Second, this merger is so complete that it does not dissolve by defeat, whereas all the other types of transformations do. This is analogous to real-world political mergers that are maintained or dissolved accordingly.

On the Conception of the Soul and Personal Identity in Dragon Ball

In this section, I will return to the philosophy of compatibilism and a discussion of how events unfold in real life and in *Dragon Ball Z*. To do so, I must discuss the soul.

Dragon Ball and the Soul

What is a soul in *Dragon Ball*? In lieu of the "common" notion of what a soul may be, in *Dragon Ball* a soul is treated as an immaterial yet corporeal substance.[37] It is immaterial because it is not tangible stuff that occupies a certain space and shape, but extends to all of the body parts and does not diminish in quantity even if a part of the body is cut off. It is corporeal because it can be in motion through space (for whatever moves in space needs some corporeity), yet it is usually invisible to the eye. It may be best likened to be some sort of energy or life force much like *qi* energy, an

---

[37] By the "common notion" of a "soul", I mean a notion loosely shared among commoners in the Western philosophy and Enryō Inoue, as well as Shintoism and some schools of Buddhism. However, one should carefully note that in Buddhism, the existence of a soul is highly contested. Some strict conventional Buddhists in Eastern philosophy, for the most part, believe that Buddha taught that there is no soul. A direct translation of the Japanese word *tamashii* (魂, or たましい) is "soul"—which is how it is used in *Dragon Ball Z*—and how I understand and use the term. Interestingly enough, the English translations in the subtitles of *Dragon Ball Z* use the term "spirit". Thus, one could only assume (evading the religious connotation of the term "soul") that it does not address the unique dichotomy of a memory embedded soul. For the description of the soul in Enryō Inoue (the most prominent scholar and a Buddhist priest) on the matter in early twentieth century in Japan, see Enryō Inoue, Yōkaigaku Zenshū [妖怪学講義全集], Vol. 3 (Kyoto: Kashiragi Shobō Press, 2004), 32-41. I have translated the relevant part from his book in my blog. Issei Takehara, "Enryō Inoue on the Soul", *Isseicreekphilosophyblog* 25th January 2017: https://isseicreekphilosophy.wordpress.com/2017/01/25/enryo-inoue-%e4%ba%95%e4%b8%8a%e5%86%86%e4%ba%86-on-the-soul-an-excerpt-from-his-yokaigaku-kougi-or-lectures-on-yokai-studies/.

aggregate of atoms or corpuscles or ethereal photons. A soul, then, is what has both of these traits: immateriality and corporeity.

The viewer's first experience with the soul in *Dragon Ball* occurs after Goku's death in the battle against Raditz. Goku's soul ascended into heaven, and he was given a spiritual body that Kami had arranged for him, identical to his original body in form.[38] In this scene, we saw numerous souls were present nearby Goku, but without their mortal bodies, as they waited in line to be judged by King Enma, a Buddho-Daoist-inspired deity of the afterlife, on whether or not they would go to Heaven or to Hell.[39] These other souls are called "death-candles".[40] These souls appear to move like flames, much like will-o'-the-wisps.

This concept of the soul is strengthened by an example at the end of the Frieza Arc. A wish is being made to revive Goku and Krillin after their battle with Frieza, but their souls can only be resurrected at the *locus* of their death. However, only death awaits them immediately afterward because Planet Namek had exploded during Goku's battle as a Super Saiyan, and they would thus be resurrected into the vacuum of space and die yet again. Vegeta then suggests that the souls as substances of Goku and Krillin be transported to Earth before resurrecting their bodies.[41] This transportability of the souls suggests its corporeity. When Krillin's soul was resurrected by this wish, his soul was transported to Earth first without a restored physical body, and his soul was nowhere to be seen. This demonstrates the soul's invisible immateriality and its mobile corporeity and ability to be in a specific location.[42]

Just before Porunga is summoned, and they are told by Kaiō-*sama* of this stipulation over souls, we see Vegeta have two different sets of reactions for one specific event. At the end of one episode, in the sequence immediately

---

[38] That the body Goku possessed when he was dead is a different type of body from what he had had when he was alive is obvious. This can be discerned from what Kaio⁻ said to Tenshinhan during the training on Kaio⁻'s planet. When Tenshinhan was worried about Chaotzu being beaten by Piccolo, Kaio⁻ said not to worry about him, because "the pain is just a reminiscence of the time when they were alive; it will disappear soon". This at least suggests that while their body was spiritual, it still possessed a weak and fading sense-perception of a corporeal body. See *Dragon Ball Z*, Episode 55.
[39] *Dragon Ball Z*, Episode 6.
[40] They are called 人魂, or *Hitodama*, which literally means "human soul" and they are traditionally depicted in the form of flames, hence the similarity with "will-o'-the-wisps" ("misleading or elusive goal or hope").
[41] *Dragon Ball Z*, Episode 106.
[42] *Dragon Ball Z*, Episode 107. Porunga is a Namekian version of Shenron, which is a dragon that appears when all seven Dragon Balls are collected to grant the ones who collected them the wish(es).

following the discovery that the dead would be resurrected only in the place where they died, Vegeta bursts into laughing with triumph. This is because he realizes that he has attained the highest power in the universe, since Goku and Frieza are both presumed dead, and Goku's resurrection to Namek would kill him again.[43] However, the following episode begins from the moment at which Bulma is informed by Kaiō-*sama* of the impossibility of Goku's resurrection, thus retelling the same scene but with a different response from Vegeta. In this version, Vegeta offers a solution to the problem posed by the apparent paradox—the souls of Goku and Krillin should be transferred to Earth before they get resurrected.[44] We can thus infer that *Dragon Ball* relies on a mind-body dualism.

Vegeta's Contrary States

Vegeta's two reactions to the same issue are distinct and contrary. It is conceivable that Vegeta could take either of these actions, but it is not possible for him to take both of these actions. How can we understand this?

As was inferred from above, *Dragon Ball* series takes a mind-body dualism as a given. As such, since souls are individual substances, Vegeta could reason that the souls be transported to Earth first and then resurrect Goku and Krillin. In this way, it illustrates the contrary emotions in Vegeta. The prior episode ended with Vegeta laughing, while the subsequent episode began with Vegeta using reason, imprinting on the audience Vegeta's two contrary emotional states. We know that Vegeta wants to reign over the universe, as evident from the history of the Saiyan race, and how proud Vegeta feels about his pedigree. Yet he would also be consistent with the Primitive Saiyan Philosophy, e.g., had he chosen to want to see how a stronger enemy than himself would fight. Indeed, Vegeta explains his rationale for the latter argument, in that he wanted to see what a legendary Super Saiyan is like, perhaps to find out how to become one himself. Following Vegeta's suggestion, everyone regains hope.

What is of an interest to us is how both viewpoints made sense to us as viewers. How can it be argued with consistency that Vegeta could have acted in two completely different ways? For have I not argued that all actions are contained in the subject being pre-established? Just as it would be impossible to imagine a square circle, it would also be impossible to imagine Vegeta claiming a victory on the one hand and offering a solution to bring Goku back to life on the other hand. The answer is quite simple. Because these two

---

[43] *Dragon Ball Z*, Episode 106.
[44] *Dragon Ball Z*, Episode 107.

versions are *not* contradictory actions of the agent, here Vegeta.[45] The argument for compatibilism makes it so that an action is the outcome of freewill, while at the same time, such an action is pre-established and is contained in the subject, making the action nothing but an inevitable consequence of unfolding events dictated by the previous states and the perceptions of the said agent.

These two episodes in *Dragon Ball Z* show us that compatibilism is possible, for both versions reflect and are rooted in the preceding status of Vegeta's psychological states, i.e., manifold perceptions. It is conceivable that Vegeta could act in the way he did in the first version, whose consequence is that Gohan gets angry at Vegeta and they begin to fight against one another, as such an activity is consistent with Vegeta's personal character. Yet it is also consistent with Vegeta's personal character to ridicule the intelligence of the Earthlings by suggesting that the problem is not that difficult to solve if one thinks about it rationally. Hence, it follows that both of those actions might as well have followed from the immediate states of Vegeta's essence. Since neither of the actions undertaken by Vegeta in two different versions is inconsistent or contradictory with his essence, they both may well have actually taken place.

This is a thought experiment carried out skillfully to see if an agent can act differently from how he has actually acted without changing his being. Even though the story settled with Vegeta taking the second version of the response, it shows that he could have acted differently without contradicting his own essence, which supports the claim that the choices can be made at our own freewill without being necessarily determined at the same time.

Changing Bodies and Souls

Another example of what a soul is for *Dragon Ball* is found in an episode when Captain Ginyū, the leader of a group of Frieza's henchmen, uses his technique called "Body Change". This technique allows Ginyū to transfer his soul into another person's body, while their soul enters his. Prior to using this technique, Ginyū injured his current body on purpose in order to steal Goku's body and trap Goku inside his previous and now-injured body. When the technique is used, we see a soul-like stream of visuals leaving each body and

---

[45] They are contrary but not contradictory. This is a standard argument in philosophy. "Contraries may both be false but cannot both be true. Contradictories are such that one of them is true if and only if the other is false". "Contradictories and Contraries", *Encyclopedia Brittanica*: https://www.britannica.com/topic/contradictories-and-contraries.

entering into the other.⁴⁶ After the technique is complete, their souls have changed places.

This in turn makes us think that it is not the souls in the Cartesian sense that were exchanged, but rather it is consciousness with souls, or simply "personal identity", that was exchanged. This is because the bodies that go through the soul-exchange remember what has happened to the respective souls, and are conscious that they are no longer in their original body. Goku thus struggles to comprehend what happened, and how to use his new and injured body. In contrast, Ginyū has performed this exchange many times prior and is not alarmed by what occurred.

This episode supports the overarching view in *Dragon Ball* that the souls are rather like consciousness in the Lockian sense. Namely, the soul in *Dragon Ball* is better understood as the view proposed and argued for by the seventeenth century British philosopher, John Locke, for he says "*self* is that conscious thinking thing . . . which is sensible, or conscious of Pleasure and Pain, capable of Happiness or Misery, and so is concern'd for it self, as far as that consciousness extends".⁴⁷ Simply put, what constitutes a personhood and the personal identity is none other than the consciousness of the actions past and the present, i.e. the memory of it.⁴⁸ So Goku's soul in Ginyū's body, being conscious of everything that has happened as Goku and, insofar as that consciousness extends back to Goku as a child and Goku a week before, it is indeed Goku himself.

---

⁴⁶ *Dragon Ball Z*, Episode 71.

⁴⁷ John Locke, ed. Peter H. Nidditch (Oxford: Oxford University Press, 1991), 341.

⁴⁸ Whether for Locke consciousness means memory, or even slightly implies it, is an ongoing philosophical debate among the Lockean scholars. See Shelley Weinberg, "Locke on Personal Identity", *Philosophy Compass* 6 (2011): 1-5 where she says: "May have interpreted Locke to mean by 'consciousness' either having the same memories. . . . . it is identical to what we can know about our own continuity through time . . . . which led some to argue that the criterion for personal identity is simply memory". There are adherents to the idea that memory should not be included in the concept of consciousness. See, in particular, Locke's contemporary Thomas Reid, *Essays on the Intellectual Powers of Man A Critical Edition*, ed. Derek R. Brookes (Pennsylvania: Pennsylvania University Press, 2002), 277 where he argues that Locke confounds consciousness with memory. See also Galen Strawson, *Locke on Personal Identity* (Princeton: Princeton University Press, 2011), 72-74 in which quite frankly on the chapter audaciously titled "Consciousness is not Memory", where he says, "It's clear consciousness—Lockean consciousness—isn't the same as memory". But I am convinced that memory does play a role in consciousness and in the identity of the personhood.

This also helps us shed light on the Piccolo or Nail identity problem after they merge. Who is this person? They both seem to share the memory of each's past and consciousness of past actions and feelings of pain and pleasure in one body. Does this mean that two persons are in one body? According to Locke, yes. But he summarizes such a case as follows: "Any Substance vitally united to the present thinking Being, is a part of that very *same self* which now is: Anything united to it by a consciousness of former Action makes also a part of the *same self*, which is the same both then and now".[49] This means that Nail's presence in Piccolo's body, in so far as they both share and retain consciousnesses of each self as distinct yet vitally united, supports the view that Piccolo and Nail are one and the same person. This is why their union is substantially bound and cannot be separated even in defeat.

However, Locke when writing on memory, states that the retention of memory is weak, although the attention and repetitions of events or ideas help to store these ideas in the mind, such as routine activity. Following Locke's line of reasoning, then, if not enough contact with the Namekians is there,

> Ideas in the Mind quickly fade, and often vanish quite out of the Understanding, leaving no more footsteps or remaining Characters of themselves, than Shadows do flying over the Fields of Corn; and the Mind is as void of them, as if they never had been there.[50]

This explains why Nail only appears audibly to Frieza while Piccolo is fighting against him. Even though Piccolo had never met Dende prior, when he talks to Dende, he calls Dende by his name (through Piccolo's voice), as if Piccolo had known him for a long time.[51] But Nail's presence via consciousness in Piccolo's body seems to disappear and gets replaced by Piccolo's own memory of Dende whenever he talks to him. It is as though the memory of Dende from Nail is assimilated into Piccolo's self as the years progress. This may be due to the fact that these ideas or memories, "if in the future Course of their Lives, they are not repeated again, are quite lost, without the least glimpse

---

[49] Locke, *An Essay Concerning Human Understanding*, 346.
[50] Ibid., 151.
[51] In *Dragon Ball Z*, Episode 80, Piccolo tells Dende to hide to avoid an impending battle. Further in the following Episode 81, when Piccolo tells Frieza that "*we* know your moves", he is speaking in the 2nd person plural, referring back to the fight against Frieza that Nail had had earlier. This part is spoken with Nail's voice to mock Frieza by saying: "you've become a giant, and you're using both hands, yet this is the best you've got?" Here, Nail's identity in Piccolo is reminiscing the battle he had had before he merged with Piccolo, where Frieza promised Nail that he would use only one hand to defeat him.

remaining of them".[52] This is also due to the fact that memories are oftentimes passive as Piccolo only remembers and is conscious of Dende's history or Kami's history when situations present to himself.

A Philosophy of *Dragon Ball Z*

I have proposed here three arguments, all of which are supported by how the story unfolds. One is that all events are contained in, and naturally follow from, a single event. Second is an elaboration of this theory in likening it to the historical events and geo-politics that *Dragon Ball Z* accurately depicts, namely, how self-interested individuals behave toward one another. Third, although each event is contained in the previous states, just as a predicate is contained in the subject, these events are at the same time the reflection of freewill exercised by the characters according to their own disposition.

Two Events with Many Choices

Specifically, I have picked two events to defend the thesis put forward at the beginning. One is exemplified by the story itself, with Goku's reaction to the events in his life, while the other is how Vegeta reacts with regard to the concept of the soul.

The conclusion is contained in the initial event in such a way that everything that occurs subsequently is pre-established, i.e., inclined, without being necessitated. Each individual acts out of his own freewill insofar as such action does not involve a contradiction. This in turn inclines an agent to act in a certain way in accordance with their dispositions to respond to the environment and or circumstances, though such action is not determined in the sense that it is necessitated. For instance, Vegeta's different actions are posited in that it could go either way, given that he is the kind of person that he is. This is how there can be two aspects of Vegeta without interrupting the plot or raising the "Suspension of Disbelief" regarding his character. Both aspects of Vegeta are thoroughly consistent with his being—while eventually ascribing Vegeta one version over the other—as if that had always been the case.

A similar device is used in the 1993 TV special, *Dragon Ball Z: The History of Trunks*, which tells the story of an alternative plotline in which Goku dies of a heart disease and the world is destroyed by androids.[53] This too is possible because dying of a disease is not contradictory to Goku's being, but is a

---

[52] Locke, *An Essay Concerning Human Understanding*, 151.
[53] *Dragon Ball Z: The History of Trunks*. Directed by Yoshihiro Ueda with Screenplay by Hiroshi Toda (Fuji TV 1993).

scenario that could be conceived of without changing Goku's being substantially and essentially.

Freewill and Ethics

The question the *Dragon Ball* series asks is: "What kind of options do we have, given the kind of beings that we are?" The series is more concerned about the freewill predicated by qualities possessed and displayed by each actor. In doing so, it advances the argument for freewill amid our biological constitutions. Otherwise, there would be no choice-making, and where there is no choice-making, there can be no room for ethics. In this way, Goku embodies the epitome of a moral agent *in potentiality*, and we experience the unfolding of his moral being *in actuality*.

The fundamental principle latent in the series is that every event is a logical result of the previous states such that what succeeds is an event that flows from them. *Dragon Ball Z* outlines its principal view that things could not have been different from how they are. This is why the future in which Goku has died of heart disease and the androids reign over the world makes sense and co-exists with the other timeline that actually occurred. The moment when this exercise of freewill is overtly manifest and advanced is undoubtedly the time when Vegeta reacts with an insult upon hearing Goku's death at the end of the Frieza Arc in one episode, and then redoes the same scene with a different response in the following episode.

Yet even without this obvious attempt to display the existence of freewill in the series, we see the characters ask themselves whether to fight or flee, for example, at any point in the story. Those options entertained by the characters are not forced upon them, but rather flow out of their being and circumstances. Perhaps the best illustration of this is in the sequence where everyone is still in search for the dragon balls on Planet Namek while trying to deceive and outdo the others.

This logical possibility to have a variety of choices relative to the circumstances is what makes the story exciting and attention-grabbing. We see the options that the characters face, and this certain unpredictability in their choice-making is what thrills us and keeps us guessing, even if we feel that we know that the main characters will win somehow. In storytelling, it is when this "somehow" is explained supernaturally or extraordinarily that a story appears no longer believable or interesting. However, when the ways in which the projected outcome takes place is explained logically, we find the story to be powerful, compelling, and authentic.

Pre-Established Harmony

The pre-established harmony (compatibilism) inherent in *Dragon Ball Z* is what holds the story together. The logical consistency in the story helps us reflect on the historical and social events in our own society, reinforcing the idea that we cannot have acted in any other way than we actually have. Often it is debated whether or not the end result may have differed had either of the Allies or the Axis Powers acted differently during the second world war. The atrocities and millions of deaths in World War II cannot be attributed to a singular cause (Hitler) when there were so many others.[54] Indeed, to let ourselves be lost in the endless conjectures of what the past could have been is nothing but a meaningless retrospection.[55] Even if we could change the past, we likely wouldn't. This is because our choices are inclined to have occurred out of our own volition, however dependent on the constant bond with the others they may seem. We have expressed ourselves in each decision we have consciously made and for our own reasons. Just as each international state acted for its own gain and preservation, so did the actors in *Dragon Ball Z* act in order to secure their own interests. Sometimes it is selfishness, while other times it is out of love for others. These interplays, imbued with intentions for situating ourselves in the world at large, converge into and form the present, at every moment.[56]

Conclusion

In conclusion, these Arcs in *Dragon Ball Z*, seen from Goku's standpoint, may be likened to the embodiment of a political liberalism, i.e., what a powerful caring individual would do to protect the others when surrounded by the

---

[54] For historical parallels and analysis, see Leo Tolstoy, *War and Peace*, trans. Louise and Aylmer Maude (New York: Oxford University Press, 2010). Here in the Appendix "Some Words about War and Peace", Tolstoy argues exactly this point when he says: "To say (which seems to everyone very simple) that the causes of the events of 1812 lay in Napoleon's dominating disposition and the patriotic firmness of the Emperor Alexander I, is as meaningless as to say that the causes of the fall of the Roman Empire were that a certain barbarian led his people westwards and a certain Roman emperor ruled his State badly, or that an immense hill that was being levelled toppled over because the last labourer struck it with his spade". Tolstoy advances this argument using historical events of the War of 1812 in his entire book in *War and Peace*, 1314-1315.

[55] Ibid.

[56] For those who are interested more in detail how exactly my argument is consistent with the story in *Dragon Ball Z*, please see my story analysis Issei Takehara, "Episode Analysis in Dragon Ball Z" *Isseicreekphilosophyblog* 16th April 2021: https://isseicreekphilosophy.wordpress.com/2021/04/16/appendix-ii-episode-analysis/.

selfish individuals. It is also a story of ethics in power politics of everyday life, taken in the larger scheme of things.

The *Dragon Ball* series, through metaphorical means, teaches us how to maintain the good in us when confronted with the evil. In a way, the conclusion is contained in the beginning: once you have learned how to use the power for someone else, you have achieved the absolute power that no one can take away from you. Goku, in this way, may be said to have possessed from the beginning "the seed of this enlightenment" when he refused, without hesitation, Raditz' offer to kill people for their own gain, but rather decided to use his power to help people instead. When the characters' personalities being so considered, the story unfolds seamlessly as the pre-established harmony maintains.

Goku formed a coalition with his nemesis, Piccolo, for it was mutually beneficial for them to defeat their common enemy, Raditz. Goku needed Piccolo's power to save Goku's son, Gohan, while Piccolo needed Goku's help to defeat Raditz to achieve his own ambition to eventually defeat Goku with his own hands. What is unique to Goku, however, is that he wants power not for its/his own sake but for saving the others. This may seem rather surprising and inaccurate, since all Goku cares about seems to be about getting stronger, simply because he lusts for power as a warrior race (Saiyan). But if we look at how he fights and how he gets stronger each time, we can see that he is always fighting for someone else. In the battle against Raditz, he chose to sacrifice himself over defeating his nemesis, Piccolo. The reason why he was able to become a Super Saiyan too was out of anger regarding Krillin's death. This is strikingly different from any other character when they become stronger, as is most obvious from the battle against Frieza. In Frieza Arc, each fended for himself, and everyone else gained power for his own sake, while Goku and his friends wished for power to save the others. Frieza's strength comes from the humiliation he suffers, while Goku's strength comes from the love for his friends. This is the reason why Goku is essentially stronger than Vegeta. Something Vegeta realizes at the very end of the battle against Buu at the end of the series.

For Vegeta reflects that he has fought "to have [his] own way, for enjoyment and for killing enemies, but above all, for [his] own pride". Goku is different, as Vegeta recollects, for Goku has fought "in order to be certain not to lose and to keep reaching his limits" while protecting his friends, which is why for Goku, killing the enemies is not as important as much as it is to better himself in battles.[57] We finally find out here that this is the inclination at play Goku had

---

[57] *Dragon Ball*, Episode 280. According to Vegeta, Goku fights for two reasons. One is to protect those whom he loves. The other is *so that he would not lose*, that is to say, "winning" is not important *just so long as he does not lose* because he has always fought

had when he did not kill Vegeta when he could have done so at the end of the Vegeta Arc. In short, *Dragon Ball Z* keeps captivating us not because the battles are exciting, but because we want to know how each actor chooses and acts in any given catalytic situations. Here we can get a glimpse of, and learn about how, we make conscious ethical decisions ourselves in everyday life when we are faced with making a choice, much like the characters from *Dragon Ball Z*.

---

to reach his limits with a stronger enemy, almost as if it is better that the strong enemies would not be dead as long as they have a slightest chance of not being evil at heart. It is as a result of this selfishness that Goku let Vegeta escape during his battle against Vegeta, as if Goku had known that Vegeta would come to have the slightest bit of a heart from the beginning and someday fight with Goku again to strengthen himself. Thus Goku's intuition, too, stems from him being the kind of person he is. That way, Goku can keep fighting them to reach his limits and become stronger. Vegeta on the contrary has always fought for his own pride, that is, he fights *to win*. While it is true that Goku enjoys fighting for his own interest, he knows he cannot lose because he would lose what is more important than his own life if he loses. In short, as Vegeta admits that, 1) Goku loves fighting simply *and,* 2) *because* he cares about others *at the same time*, while Vegeta fights primarily *for* his pedigree.

Chapter 8

The *Avatar* Aminated Series: A Queer Reading of Embodied Power

Martin Lepage
Independent Researcher

ABSTRACT: In 2005, the animated series *Avatar: The Last Airbender* (*ATLA*) attracted the attention of a very wide audience. In 2012, its sequel, *The Legend of Korra* (*TLOK*) invited growing audiences to follow an increasingly complex story, from Aang to Korra, two consecutive incarnations of the Avatar, a spiritual leader who can "bend" all four elements. Whereas Aang's quest is quite clear, Korra's journey is much more taxing. In fact, a major part of Korra's struggles is concerned with matters of identity, freedom, social justice and power. But how exactly does representation of these issues evolve from one show to another? Through a queer analytical lens, this chapter explores the many ways in which *TLOK's* narrative delves deeper than *ATLA's* into matters of life changes, healing, power and negotiation with cultural norms and traditions. More precisely, it looks at the many loci of normativity around each incarnation of the Avatar, and shows how the central characters of *ATLA* and *TLOK* depict transformations in terms of growth and struggle towards notions of power, healing and negotiating with trauma.

KEYWORDS: Airbender, Anime, Avatar, Cartoons, Gender, Normativity, Power, Queer, Television, Tradition.

***

Introduction

Ever since Nickelodeon's *Avatar: The Last Airbender* first aired in 2005, the animated series has attracted the attention of a very wide audience in North

America.¹ Doing so, *ATLA* has been implanting or cultivating teenagers' and (more or less) young adults' interests for topics such as spirituality, Eastern religions and rituals, with practices like yoga, martial arts and meditation, for instance, as well as broader themes like supernatural phenomena, magic, folklore, elemental iconology in video games and role-playing games, among many others. Four years after the last episode of *ATLA*, its 2012 sequel, *Avatar: Legend of Korra* invited growing audiences to follow an increasingly complex story, from Aang to Korra, two consecutive incarnations of the Avatar, a spiritual leader who can "bend" all four elements.² Whereas 11-year-old Aang embarks on a very clear quest with somewhat specific and attainable goals, Korra's journey as young woman is much more circumvoluted and taxing. Such a contrast in tone and content from *ATLA* to *TLOK* undeniably brings into question the legitimacy of the Avatar's place in the world. In fact, a major part of Korra's struggles is concerned with matters of identity, recognition, social change and power.

But how exactly does representation of these issues evolve from one show to the other? What can similarities and discrepancies between the two reveal, as the Avatar spiritual trajectory embodies a boy's perspective and experience over one short year, to a young woman's exploration of her own power through the course of several years? Following cartoon shows like *Adventure Time* (2010-2018) and *Steven Universe* (2013-2019), among others, it is more and more common to see queer or non-binary representation in kids' TV programming.³ As such, these shows also touch on broader intersectional issues of power, involving race, class, age, disability, neurodivergence, mental illness and trauma.⁴ Before these shows, even though they did not directly

---

[1] *Avatar: The Last Airbender*. Created by Michael Dante DiMartino and Bryan Konietzko (Nickelodeon 2005-2008). Hereafter *ATLA*.
[2] *Avatar: Legend of Korra*. Created by Michael Dante DiMartino and Bryan Konietzko (Nickelodeon 2012-2014). Hereafter *TLOK*.
[3] *Adventure Time*. Directed by Larry Leichliter and Created by Pendleton Ward (Cartoon Network 2012-2018) and *Steven Universe*. Created by Rebecca Sugar (Cartoon Network 2013-2019).
[4] Sirma Bilge, "Théorisations Féministes de l'Intersectionnalité", *Diogène* 225.1 (2009): 70-88; Richard C. King, et al., "'Look Out New World, Here We Come?' Racial and Sexual Pedagogies", in *Animating Difference: Race, Gender, and Sexuality in Contemporary Films for Children* (Lanham: Rowman & Littlefield Publishers, 2011), 33-52; Lori Kido Lopez, "Fan Activists and the Politics or Face in The Last Airbender", *International Journal of Cultural Studies* 15.5 (2011): 431-45 and Tim Gruenewald, "From Fan Activism to Graphic Narrative Culture and Race in Gene Luen Yang's Avatar: The Last Airbender—The Promise", in *Drawing New Color Lines: Transnational Asian American Graphic Narratives*, ed. Monica Chiu (Hong Kong: Hong Kong University Press, 2015): 165-87.

touch on notion of gender and sexual identity,[5] *ATLA* and *TLOK* portrayed considerable queer patterns in terms of power that can be scrutinized.[6] Following bell hooks' definition, this chapter approaches

> queer not as being about who you're having sex with (that can be a dimension of it); but queer as being about the self that is at odds with everything around it and has to invent and create and find a place to speak and to thrive and to live.[7]

In accordance with this definition, this chapter more specifically examines the influence and impact of certain characters on the Avatar's life trajectory. As models to follow, and/or counterexamples to challenge, they can be useful in outlining power relations and dynamics within and between dieges.[8] Rather than focusing on queer elements in the text, this chapter aims to uncover underlying structural and normative narratives about the embodiment of power performed by element bending.

The program of this chapter is as follows. First, it will contextualize the stories of *ATLA* and *TLOK* while outlining patterns that arise in terms of power, domination and resistance. After a short introduction to queer theory, it will explore the many ways in which *TLOK's* narrative delves deeper than *ATLA's* into matters of life changes, healing, power and negotiation with cultural norms and traditions. A queer analysis will highlight how, from one incarnation to another, Aang's and Korra's struggles reflect conditions of embodiment in negotiating with normativity and discipline within a specific time and cultural context. It will look at the many loci of normativity around each incarnation of the Avatar, especially those related to the four types of

---

[5] Jake Pitre, "Rated Q for Queer: The Legend of Korra and the Evolution of Queer Reading", *Red Feather Journal: An International Journal of Children in Popular Culture* 8.2 (2017): 23-33; Joanna Robinson, "How a Nickelodeon Cartoon Became One of the Most Powerful, Subversive Shows of 2014", *Vanity Fair* (2014): https://www.vanityfair.com/hollywood/2014/12/korra-series-finale-recap-gay-asami and Heather Wright, "'The Childish, the Transformative, and the Queer': Queer Interventions as Praxis in Children's Cartoons" (MA Thesis: City University of New York, 2018).
[6] Gayatri Viswanath, "Power and Resistance: Silence and Secrecy in Avatar: The Last Airbender", *SubVersions: A Journal of Emerging Research in Media and Cultural Studies* 2.1 (2014): 26-47 and Hillary Chute, *Graphic Women: Life Narrative & Contemporary Comics* (New York: Columbia University Press, 2010).
[7] bell hooks, "Are You Still a Slave? Liberating The Black Female Body", *The New School* (2014): https://livestream.com/thenewschool/slave. NB the spelling of the name all in lower case is correct as her *nom de plume* (pen name).
[8] Cf. Gérard Genette, *Figure III* (Paris: Le Seuil, 1972) and Samuel Archibald and Bertrand Gervais, "Le Récit en Jeu. Narrativité et Interactivité", *Protée* 34 (2006): 27-39.

element-bending. More precisely, it will examine Aang's quest and legacy as a maker of peace, Katara's role as a healer, Zuko's reconciliation with his political predispositions, Toph's achievements around the performance of bending powers, and finally, Korra's embodied journey through all four books of *TLOK*, serving as a point of reference for vectors of power.

The Avatar Universe: Fiction, Bending and Body Matters

To get a better sense of the Avatarverse, one can start with the opening to the first episode of *TLOK* as spoken by Aang's son Tenzin.

> Earth. Fire. Air. Water. When I was a boy, my father Avatar Aang, told me the story of how he and his friends heroically ended the 100-year war. Avatar Aang and Firelord Zuko transformed the Fire Nation colonies into the United Republic of Nations, a society where benders and non-benders from all over the world would live and thrive together in peace and harmony. They named the capital of this great land Republic city. Avatar Aang accomplished many remarkable things in his life. But sadly, his time in this world came to an end. And like the cycle of the seasons the cycle of the Avatar began anew.[9]

Compare this with the opening of *ATLA*, as spoken by Aang's friend come wife and waterbender, Katara.

> Water. Earth. Fire. Air. Long ago, the four nations lived together in harmony. Then, everything changed when the Fire Nation attacked. Only the Avatar, master of all four elements, could stop them, but when the world needed him most, he vanished. A hundred years passed, and my brother and I discovered the new Avatar, an airbender named Aang. And although his airbending skills are great, he has a lot to learn before he's ready to save anyone. But I believe Aang can save the world.[10]

From the very beginning of each series, we can hear by the tone of each opening sequence, how the two shows differ. Katara's silky voice introduces *ATLA* and the quest at hand. She delivers it, as she would, in a very inspirational, quirky and hopeful manner. This effectively starts the story on a soft note of mystery and good fun. In *TLOK*, Tenzin's deep baritone voice, in all his seriousness, precedes every episode with a call for duty towards balance.

---

[9] *TLOK*.
[10] *ATLA*.

In the same way, the story of Korra is very much about the consequences of the many changes made by Aang, her past life, to the world during his lifetime. *ATLA* takes us on a quest to defeat Firelord Ozai, a cruel tyrant whose forefathers have created a war-torn world and colonized a great portion of the Earth Kingdom. Having gained a great deal of land in the Earth Kingdom, the Fire Nation's raging war still struggles to invade the secluded Southern Water Tribe. The fourth nation, the Air nomads, were not so lucky as they, a pacifist people, were swiftly eradicated at the beginning of the war. Aang is the last of his kind, the last airbender, a target on whose shoulders rest the lives of millions, and his quest is very much straight forward. After having spent a hundred years frozen in an iceberg with his flying sky bison Appa, he still has three types of bending to learn before he can put an end to the war that decimated his people and plunged the world into chaos.

Three Seasons of *ATLA* and the Cycle of the Avatar

The three seasons or "books" of *ATLA* follow the cycle of the Avatar. Aang learns waterbending, earthbending, and finally, firebending. In *Book 1: Water*, Sokka and Katara, who found Aang in his iceberg, travel with the Avatar from the South Pole to the North pole, so that he and Katara can find a master waterbender to teach them. *Book 2: Earth* takes the audience through the vastness and diversity of the Earth Kingdom, and brings Toph to the party, a powerful young blind earthbender who teaches Aang earthbending. From the start, the Avatar's quest inevitably alerts the banished son of the Firelord, Prince Zuko, who hopes to get under the good graces of his father again, by capturing the Avatar. Against all odds, Aang will master firebending, with the help of Zuko, and face the Firelord in *Book 3: Fire*.

Korra' Journey in *TLOK*

Korra's journey seems much less linear than Aang's. Each book of *TLOK* centers around a particular villain troubling the peace in Republic City and around the world. Korra's challenges are much more complex than Aang's. *Book 1: Air* is very much concerned with issues around learning airbending, but also the spiritual aspect of being the Avatar. Korra, somewhat of a natural at each bending techniques, except airbending, travels from her native Southern Water Tribe to learn airbending with Tenzin, Aang and Katara's only airbender son, on Air Temple Island in Republic City.

This season also introduces Korra's inner circle, as well as a new context into which bending is integrated. Pro-bending, a competitive sport between two teams each composed of three types of benders, has become a very popular way of practicing bending. Korra's interest for pro-bending leads her to meet brothers Bolin and Mako, respectively an earthbender and a firebender, and later Asami Sato, a non-bender heiress to massive business conglomerate Future Industries. Korra's training is troubled as she must face Amon and his "Equalists", whose ultimate goal is to breach and break for good the boundaries between benders and non-benders and, more importantly, the privilege the former have over the latter. With the aid of her friends and others like Lin Beifong, Toph's eldest daughter, Korra neutralizes the Equalists' chaotic rebellious coup, but not without being temporarily stripped of her ability to bend the elements she already masters (earth, fire and water).

Book 2: Spirit goes back to the genesis of the Avatar as a still weak and wild Avatar Korra battles against her own power-hungry uncle Unalaq. Succeeding in breaking Korra's connection to the Avatar spirit, Unalaq momentarily seizes power and becomes the Dark Avatar. After a final fight during a cosmic event called "Harmonic Convergence", portals between the worlds are left opened, causing a weakened Korra to enter contentious waters.

Following this major reconfiguration of the world, the third season, *Book 3: Change* brings about the return of airbenders. As Republic City and the Earth Kingdom are drowning in dismay over the newly arrived spirits now cohabiting with humans, a new airbender Zaheer, escapes from his prison and reunites with the Red Lotus. This secret society aims to put an end to Avatar Korra's life, and in doing so, to cause the definitive end of the Avatar cycle. Korra almost takes her last breath, but the new airbenders and Korra's friends defeat Zaheer and the Red Lotus, leaving the Avatar poisoned with metal and severely hurt both physically and mentally.

Book 4: Balance, set three years after the events of *Book 3: Change*, finds Korra and her friends, scattered around the world, reunited amid an authoritarian political coup orchestrated by Kuvira, a powerful metalbender close to the Beifongs. Using the spirit vines that have invaded the world since Harmonic Convergence, Kuvira builds a superweapon that can cause incredible destruction against which Korra can do very little. In the end, a new portal to the spirit world is created and the possibility of Korra finally enjoying life with her friends opens up.

Power Dynamics in *TLOK* and *ATLA*

In short, *TLOK* portrays a series of power struggles reflecting changes in the very order of the world, whereas ALTA brings back an order that was once well established and furthers reconciliation between nations without really questioning the power dynamics that separate them in the first place. This chapter will delve deeper into the sociocultural and political structures portrayed in the Avatar universe in a later section. I will start now with observing some of the ways in which each Avatar deals with normativity around the four types of bending, as well as the ways in which certain characters redefine qualities inherent to the type of bending they practice, and culture associated with it.

In other words, before outlining and comparing the power dynamics as they are conveyed through and by the Avatar themselves, the interplay of these forces, at a microsocial level and in the life of an individual must be scrutinized. There is little use in comparing the inner monologue and emotional tapestry of two different human beings, as the entirety of their experience is valid and unquestionable. But the conditions under which they come to be who they are, the environment that watches them grow and become persons with agency, very much can be interrogated. Power relations in society predict, to a certain extent, the reach of one's potential. For that reason, Aang's and Korra's relation to their struggles are therefore somatically different. To better illustrate this phenomenon, this analysis of the power dynamics in *ATLA* and *TLOK* will primarily consider the notion of embodiment.

Ontology, Elements, Bending and the Spiritual World

The fundamental ontological difference between our world and the Avatar's is the human capacity to bend the elements, as well as to interact with the spirit world. For reasons of practicality, this chapter mainly focuses on the role of bending, as the ways in which power is portrayed in a fictional universe can certainly inform about our own realities and experiences. Airbending, earthbending, firebending and waterbending, the most normative loci of power under examination, can be interpreted as an exercise of one's authentic self. In the Avatarverse, everyone can fully realize themselves as benders or non-benders. Bending is a fighting technique that is conceived in very nuanced ways from one series to the other. *ATLA* portrays bending in somewhat rigids terms, whereas *TLOK* readily promotes its ever-evolving practice.

The Elements and Power

Each element is traditionally associated with a specific culture, a set of codes, rituals, qualities and traits which prescribe, as ideal types, the correct manner to interact with it and enact it. The best example of this impact is found in the ways each Avatar learns with great difficulty one element that opposes their native predispositions. Aang, as a master airbender and a natural at waterbending, found earthbending to be the most challenging. Air is associated with flux, movement and lightness, while earth is associated with solidity, stability and heft. Korra, born a natural waterbender, earthbender and firebender, found airbending the most difficult. The intangible and spiritual qualities of air proved hard to grasp for a pragmatic young woman.

Instead of turning to Aristotle to provide a succinct definition of element correspondences, or even to the Chinese *wuxing* (fire, wood, metal, water and earth), let us consider the one proposed by Iroh, a great firebending master, to his nephew Zuko, which seems more comprehensive.

> Iroh: Fire is the element of power. The people of the Fire Nation have desire and will and the energy and drive to achieve what they want . . . . Earth is the element of substance. The people of the Earth Kingdom are diverse and strong. They are persistent and enduring . . . . Air is the element of freedom. The Air Nomads detached themselves from worldly concerns and found peace and freedom. Also, they apparently had pretty good senses of humor . . . . Water is the element of change. The people of the Water Tribes are capable of adapting to many things. They have a sense of community and love that holds them together through anything . . . .
>
> Zuko: Why are you telling me these things?
>
> Iroh: It is important to draw wisdom from many different places. If you take it from only one place, it become rigid and stale. Understanding others, the other elements, and the other nations, will help you become whole.
>
> Zuko: All this four elements talk is sounding like Avatar stuff.
>
> Iroh: It is the combination of the four elements in one person that makes the Avatar so powerful. But it can make you more powerful, too.[11]

Iroh's description is very useful. It points to the fact that elemental qualities are mutable for individuals, but also for cultures at large. The following analysis will be more likely to profit from this interpretation as it refrains from blatantly categorizing everything under "masculine" or "feminine".[12] Rather, it

---

[11] *ATLA*: Directed by Ethan Spaulding with Screenplay by Michael Dante DiMartino, Bryan Konietzko and Aaron Ehasz (Nickelodeon 2008), Season 2 and Episode 9, entitled "Bitter Work".

[12] For instance, New Age and Pagan religions, as well as Chinese medicine traditionally would have water associated with the feminine, and fire with the masculine. Cf. Martin Lepage, "Queerness and Transgender Identity : Negotiations in the Pagan Community of Montreal", *Studies in Religion/Sciences religieuses* 46.4 (2017): 601-19. This chapter aims to steer away from this type of associations.

takes for granted that elements are not gendered and that qualities associated with them are not exclusive to one gender identity or another. For instance, earth could be associated with strength. Strength, in Western culture, is widely and stereotypically associated with manhood, masculinity and virility. With that said, no one would never accuse Avatar Kyoshi, a native earthbender, of not being strong. Being the tallest Avatar to ever live, her strength is never used to imply her to be less of a woman, or to be taking on specific masculine characteristics. It is just assumed that being strong is a part of who she is.

The Spiritual and Bending

The Avatar is a spiritual leader figure. Life after life, one incarnation after the other, following the same elemental cycle, the Avatar reprises the same role: to keep balance in the world and between worlds. Master of all four elements, the Avatar is a vector of power, a model for the best ways to use bending and/or enact one's own power.

When Aang finally faces the Firelord and defeats him, he does so in a non-traditional manner. He learns that "In the era before the Avatar, we bent not the elements, but the energy within ourselves. To bend another's energy, your own spirit must be unbendable, or you will be corrupted and destroyed".[13] This ancient wisdom, as time will pass, will be applied at many levels. It will also lead to several innovations, blends and mixes of techniques, allowing transformations to happen within themselves and through the multilayered power dynamics that shape people's lives.[14]

Such a phenomenon is not unknown to the Avatarverse. Toph's pushing the boundaries of earthbending to metalbending in her early years is a testament to it. This kind of creativity, which can only happen once a bender has been thoroughly challenged is particular to times of crisis and change. Research suggests that bending is a channel through which one realizes and enacts discipline or domination. In broad terms, bending can be used to elevate or realize oneself, to build someone up or to bring them down, to put oneself above others, or to forcefully impose your will on the outside world. For Aang, bending is rooted in martial arts and philosophy, a sacred exercise in ancestral

---

[13] *ATLA*: Directed by Joaquim Dos Santos with Screenplay by Michael Dante DiMartino, Bryan Konietzko and Aaron Ehasz (Nickelodeon 2008), Season 3 and Episode 21, entitled "Sozin's Comet, Part 4: Avatar Aang".

[14] Thomas Van Hoey, "The Blending of Bending: World-Building in Avatar: The Last Airbender and Legend of Korra", *Linguistics in Comics and Animation* (2016): 1-28 and Thomas Van Hoey, "The Blending of Bending: World-Building in Avatar: The Last Airbender and Legend of Korra (2018)", *figshare* (2020): https://doi.org/10.6084/m9.figshare.12652460.v1.

wisdom. But in Korra's world, bending is subject to controversy, to shortcuts, to hybridations, to popularization and democratization, rendering it more problematic.

Religious Studies, Gender Studies and Television

From a religious studies and gender studies perspective, *ATLA* and *TLOK* are interesting objects of study because of the intricate ways they integrate notions of spirituality, identity and power into an animated series for children. Gender representations and matters such as alterity, racism, class warfare, among others, are widely brought up, dealt with, and inevitably coloured by the media. It is undeniable that television thoroughly affects audience's perceptions and preconceived notions of self, for example. As such, how exactly do shows carrying spiritual messages portray power in relations to someone's life, their achievements and shortcomings, or the realization of their authentic self?

Following Charles Taylor's notion of ethics of authenticity,[15] religion is mediated today through individual experience mostly, and has largely become a matter of identity.[16] Instead of coming from a transcendent source of power and authority, religious experience occurs through a horizontal immanent sacrality which has different value for everyone and comes from no specific areas of culture and society.[17] The one area of culture and society which concerns this chapter is obviously televisual productions.

Television, as a medium, is a vector of a certain degree of normativity. While it gives its audience what it demands, it prescribes inadvertently numerous ways of being, acting and thinking.[18] Cusack specifies:

> Activities and sources that are primarily aesthetic (visual and performing arts, reading and watching films of fictions, immersive online games and anime) act as alternative meaning guides that some

---

[15] Charles Taylor, *The Ethics of Authenticity* (Cambridge: Harvard University, 1991).
[16] Jacques Beauchemin, *La Société des Identités: Éthique et Politique dans le Monde Contemporain* (Montreal: Athéna Éditions, 2005).
[17] Carol Cusack, John M. Morehead and Venitia L. D. Robertson, *The Sacred in Fantastic Fandom: Essays on the Intersection of Religion and Pop Culture* (Jefferson: McFarland, 2019).
[18] John Pungente and Martin O'Malley, *More Than Meets The Eye. Watching Television Watching Us* (Toronto: McClelland & Stewart, 1999) and Carol Cusack, "Fiction into Religion: Imagination, Other Worlds, and Play in the Formation of Community", *Religion* 46.4 (2016): 575-90.

people believe meet requirements that were previously unique to religion.[19]

Since the 1980s the vast majority of homes in North America house a television and, to some extent, rely on it for different reasons: news, entertainment, intimacy, and more importantly, as a supplement, if not an alternative, to parenting. As such, people have come to expect a certain level of quality as, it has been widely shown, TV representations of family values, socio-cultural relations, gender roles, politico-economical dynamics, among others, convey immense normativity. Like Garfield the cat satirically said in the 90s: "If they say it on television, it must be true!".

When it comes to the body, a major locus of power and domination in society, what can cultural productions such as *ATLA* and *TLOK* reveal about the interplay between TV and actual social behaviors? What do these spiritually complex shows have to say about the ways in which gender identity, or more specifically the power dynamics it entails, can be enacted, performed, internalized?

To answer these questions, the following sections proceed with a queer reading of the texts by unveiling power dynamics around gender in the Avatar's story. Through the analysis of what we would call "bending acts", i.e. queer representations and expressions of power, those dynamics put into contrast two different types of embodiment revolving around distinct sociocultural, within a network of influential characters.[20] The next section provides a key for understanding changes in power dynamics by focusing specifically on embodiment and on the Avatar's body as the channel for different sources of power.

Queer Theory, Power and Bending Acts

Since Simone de Beauvoir's statement "One is not born, but rather becomes, a woman", feminist studies and its offspring gender studies, gay and lesbian studies, and LGBT studies have kept showing the socially constructed nature of gendered identities and sexes.[21] Queer theory is a constructivist theory that questions the normative association of sex, gender and sexual orientation within someone's identity. It posits against the essentialist claim of the existence of a static, unchanging, biological and natural essence to the sexes. In this perspective, society forcefully compels people to take on gender roles

---

[19] Carole Cusack, "Are Fandoms a Modern Kind of Religion?", *SLAMmag* 1 (2021): 22-23.
[20] Judith Butler, *Bodies that Matter: On the Discursive Limits of "Sex"* (New York: Routledge, 1993).
[21] Simone de Beauvoir, *Le Deuxième Sexe* (Paris: Gallimard, 1949), 285.

that tie them to certain types of regulatory behaviors. Rather the association between gender and the biological category of "sex" is basically a fiction that establishes hierarchy though an endless array of repetitions and categorizations, forcing heterosexuality as the norm.[22] More precisely, gender is performative, in the sense that it has the potential to perform an identity. This notion, borrowed from Austin's linguistics, supposes that every utterance in discourse, which force people to identify with one gender or the other can be understood as a type of normative ritual where the body becomes the instrument—already gendered—through which the gender binary will manifest itself.[23] The body reproduces these norms through multiple acquired stylizations (with clothing, in the way the body moves and occupies space, with linguistic codes, aesthetics and visual narratives) that often go unnoticed to the person's awareness.[24] In the Avatarverse, bending is a performative act that partakes in that phenomenon.

Like gender, bending acts are always supported by a subject who gives them efficacy, as well as subverts them, by using them in alternative ways. This is what scholars in queer theory have come to know as agency, someone's power to act upon their own lives. This concept refers to the idea that a subject is inevitably at the heart of power relations that are constructed or transformed even though they are fought against.[25] This brief definition of agency can also be applied to every form of power relations and resistance tactics. In this respect, performance and ritual studies support queer theory as they suggest that every ritual enacts an identity validated by the community after it has been internalized through the force of experience.[26] This can be applied, to

---

[22] Judith Butler, *Trouble dans le Genre: Le Féminisme et la Subversion de L'Identité*. (Paris: La Découverte, 1990).
[23] John L. Austin, *How to Do Things with Words* (Oxford: Clarendon Press, 1962).
[24] Butler, *Bodies that Matter*; Teresa De Lauretis, *Théorie Queer et Cultures Populaires. De Foucault à Cronenberg*, trans. by M. H. Bourcier (Paris: La Dispute, 2007) and Marilyn Strathern, *Before and After Gender. Sexual Mythologies of Everyday Life* (Chicago: Hau Books, 2016).
[25] Elsa Dorlin, *Sexe, Genre et Sexualités. Introduction à la Théorie Féministe* (Paris: Presses Universitaires de France, 2008); Elsa Dorlin, ed., *Sexe, Race, Classe: Pour une Épistémologie de la Domination* (Paris: Presses Universitaires de France, 2009) and Jacques Guilhaumou, "Autour du Concept D'Agentivité", *Rives Méditeranéennes* 41 (2013): 25-34.
[26] Arnold Van Gennep, *Les Rites de Passage* (Paris: Émile Nourry, 1909); Victor Turner, *Le Phénomène Rituel. Structure et Contre-Structure* (Paris: Presses Universitaires de France, 1969); Victor Turner, *The Anthropology of Performance* (New York: PAJ Publications, 1986); Ronald Grimes, "Defining Nascent Ritual", *Journal of the American Academy of Religion* 5.4 (1982): 539-55; Richard Schechner, *Performance Studies: An Introduction* (New York: Routledge, 2006) and Michel Houseman, *Le Rouge est le Noir. Essais sur le Rituel* (Toulouse: Presses Universitaires du Mirail, 2012).

different degrees, to other aspects of identities like gender, social status, class and, in this study, privilege related to bending acts.

Bending acts are performative because their physical performance resonates beyond the scope of physical and material normativity. Bending acts performed by the Avatar involve not only the individual and their bending techniques, but also their opponents and allies. As such, they rather bend bending itself, from within and outwards, as a feat of power bringing the world and everyone in it under new lights. This notion relates to the social construct of reality itself, as a network of perceptions and perspectives that contradict, conflate or convolute to create meaning for the most people at once.[27]

To summarize, when a performance is successful, it stops being a performance in the eye on the beholder. Instead, it becomes truthful, authentic, gets recognized by the group to which one now belongs. If one can perform themselves in such a masterful, convincing and steady way, it *must* be because they are showing their true self. Doing so, an individual identifies as something on which the rest of the community agrees and, in turn, that they can use to identify this individual accordingly thereafter.

Objective reality, when it comes to one's own story, is quite elusive. It becomes thus much wiser to opt for a renewable self, reiterated a little bit differently with every act and utterance, to allow growth to manifest, to allow changes to take effect. This phenomenon certainly does not happen at the same pace and with the same ease in the distinct lives of an 11-year-old boy and a 17-year-old young woman, like the Avatars. Both make sense of their trajectory with different tools and dispositions ultimately culminating in somewhat predetermined displays of power. The following interpretation of this phenomenon reveals and compares its embodied impact on each Avatar.

Queer Character Interplay: The Avatar Within and Between Worlds

This final section closely examines and compares the ways in which each Avatar enacts their own power within a frame of specific, preestablished and/or interlocking social influences. It aims to scrutinize every type of bending, as it is conveyed by specific characters in the life of the Avatar. This will reveal manifestations of agency that are represented through the body of the Avatar, as a vector and nexus of multiple power dynamics within the Avatar's life and world.

Operating such a queer analysis first requires a thorough understanding of the many forces around the Avatar which prescribe particular bending acts.

---

[27] Peter L. Berger and Thomas Luckmann, *The Social Construction of Reality: A Treatise in the Sociology of Knowledge* (Garden City: Anchor Books, 1966).

This chapter already has provided a detailed account of the many discrepancies between the two eras of the Avatar. But before going through each of the characters that have the most impact on the Avatar's journey, let me contextualize how they integrate for themselves their own bending as a mode of agency.

Succinctly, this occurs on three fronts: bending as body techniques, cultural codes which prescribes them, and politics which dictates the rules around their enactment. The macrosocial contexts in which evolves either Aang or Korra are quite different. The world of the Avatar in Republic City is much more progress-oriented than it was before the 100-year war.[28] What was once a world with four very separate nations in pre-industrial somewhat medieval times, suffering from the dictatorship of a power-crazed tyrant, is now a political battleground for cultural blends, fast-advancing technologies, and marketable innovations. In this microcosm, bending techniques themselves are not conveyed in the same way and do not contain the same power.

Let me explore each bending technique through the lives of Aang, Katara, Toph and Zuko, as well as in relation to non-benders Sokka and Asami. Each type of bending, mediated through the specific experience of each character, will be put in contrast with the embodied experience of Avatar Korra. These specific characters were chosen, at the exception of Aang, whose shadow still looms large over Korra's life, because they appear in both *ATLA* and *TLOK*.

Avatar Aang: Airbender and Maker of Peace

Aang, 111 years old, counting the 100 years he spent frozen in the deep cover of an iceberg, is a master airbender. The arrow tattoos that run along in arms, legs and head are a physical marker of his mastery. At his young age, Aang can perform great displays of airbending. In *Book 1: Water*, the complexity of his airbending skills is not showcased, the main focus being on learning waterbending and evading Prince Zuko and the Fire Nation. As a fighting style, airbending deals mostly in avoiding hits, acting in quick and clever ways to minimize energy waste, and turning an opponent's power against them. As Aang comes into his own power, the way in which his airbending is portrayed changes. First, the audience sees him throw blows of air and wind with his arms, legs and mouth, hover, or climb at rapid rates and, as struggles arise, tries his hand at using airbending in more destructive ways. When Aang learns about the extermination of his people and finds the body of his old mentor

---

[28] Not much attention is paid to this either in *ATLA* or *TLOK*, as wars most often stop all social change for the better until they end.

Monk Gyatso, or when his sky bison Appa gets stolen in the Earth Kingdom's desert, he enters states of complete disregard for his peaceful dispositions.

The Air Nomads were a people involved in a Buddhist-like monastic life, travelling around the world or habiting four Air Temples. When Firelord Sozin started the war, the Air Nomads were the first under attack. For this reason, *ATLA* reveals a limited amount of information about them. What is known comes from Aang's memories, abandoned material culture and empty spaces. For this reason, there are very few consequences to Aang's life when it comes to any misuse of airbending. No one can really tell him what to do. As a very gentle soul, Aang only ever hurts anyone by mistake, e.g., burning Katara while learning firebending. The extent to which he uses airbending in ways that go against Air Nomad standard is negligible. In fact, whenever the Avatar enters a state of rage or great physical danger, they also tend to enter the Avatar state, which somewhat trumps most display of element bending in terms of force.

Aang's performance as a peacekeeper, as it is portrayed to be the function of the Avatar during war times, as well as the general contribution of the Air Nomads, is very much fulfilled. Once the war over, Aang was able to pass the teachings of the Air Nomads on to his son Tenzin who, in turn, passes it on to his three airbender children. However, when Harmonic Convergence triggers the rise of new airbenders among the non-bender population, Tenzin is unable to recreate the culture of the Air Nomads as his father taught him. Something else happens instead. The pacifist teachings of the Air Nomads inspired the new airbenders to insure peace in more active ways. Living in a world of great political conflict, especially with the threat of the Earth Empire and Kuvira, the Air Nation is dedicated to the protection of the vulnerable. Consequently, most new airbenders wear flying suits like uniforms, instead of using the traditional air gliders of their predecessors. Taking an active role in the defense of those in need, they also leave to non-airbender acolytes the exclusively pacifist ways of Air Nomads.

Avatar Aang's achievements set the bar very high for Korra. In terms of learning the four types of bending, Korra struggles the most with airbending. The elusiveness, the poise and the attentiveness of Air Nomads are more or less lost on her. Korra finally gains a handle on airbending when she encounters the simplified bending of pro-bending, after which Tenzin adapted his teachings to incorporate the practicality and the pragmatism of the popular sport. Airbending and its spiritual side never represented such a challenge in Avatar Aang's life.

Unfortunately, shortly after her first flutters in airbending, Korra suffers a major set back when Amon blocks her capacity to bend. Although temporary, this traumatic experience leaves Korra in great distress. It is only through the posthumous help of Aang's spirit that Korra gains back her bending as well as the ability to restore bending to those Amon attacked.

For all the above reasons, one would assume that Aang was a superior Avatar, being more helpful to the world as a boy than Korra was in her late teens and early twenties. This is a thought that occurs even to Korra. We rather posit that Aang had a leg up on Korra, and that his immense success was mostly the result of great collaboration, whereas Korra's achievements were somewhat imposed on her. While Avatar Aang and his team dealt swiftly with a clear quest to reverse the political order, Korra negotiated at every turn, very much by herself, the very conditions of her existence, and redefined at their core fundamental elements of the world.

Katara: Waterbender, Healer and Mother

Katara, 12 years old, is the only waterbender from the Southern Water Tribe, settled in the arid snowy and stormy conditions in the South Pole. Katara starts out as a young waterbender apprentice, having unleashed her ability, but not honed her skills. Her and her brother live with their grandmother, as their widowed father fights in the war against the Fire Nation. Sokka, an untrained guardian and goofy non-bender, has nothing on his sister who can hold her own, bending or no bending, against multiple opponents. After proving herself against sexist traditions in the Northern Water Tribe, Katara masters waterbending, and at a much faster pace than Aang. Even if the course of her life is very much marked by loss, she becomes a very powerful waterbender. Nevertheless, as Katara steps out of her icy sanctuary, she faces strife, mostly through the destructive use of firebending. In fact, when Aang unreadily tries to firebend, Katara ends up getting severely burned, which leads her to discover her healing powers.

Katara's role in the Avatar's life is to nurture, heal and provide the love of a mother to those around her. Stereotypically associated with healing and care, waterbending in Katara's life allow her to take an active role in her loved ones' safety and success. In that sense, Katara is very good at using waterbending in the corresponding way. Her contribution often proves to be pivotal to the Avatar's quest. For instance, without Katara's healing power, combined with the enhanced healing properties of the spirit water from an oasis in the North Pole, Aang would not have survived Princess Azula's lightning strike. Katara also defeats Azula before she could become Firelord in stead of Ozai or Zuko, tricking her onto a stream to freeze and contain her. She certainly is a creative and imaginative waterbender, but Katara's bending acts do not challenge the ways the Avatar interacts with any type of bending.

When hiding in the Fire Nation, Katara encounters an exiled elder waterbender from the Southern Water Tribe who, obsessed with revenge against her firebenders jailers, passes onto Katara the grim technique of bloodbending. Bloodbending is used to physically control people's bodies. Whether practiced during the power apex that brings the full moon every month, or through great mastery of waterbending, its use is very much prohibited and ill-advised. Katara is not known to use bloodbending other than one time, which does not lead to real harm.[29] Moreover, she is one of the only characters in both *ATLA* and *TLOK* who can resist bloodbending. Finally, a careful mother figure, she does not teach bloodbending to Avatar Korra, but instead teaches her to be a very apt healer. Korra is in fact presented as having a strong handle of waterbending from a very young age, and because of Katara, she enacts a very well-rounded waterbending, navigating floods and streams, snow, ice and seas.

Zuko: Firebender and Conflicted Rebellious Son

Prince Zuko of the Fire Nation is a very conflicted teenager, physically scarred by the fiery hand of his father, Firelord Ozai. Zuko is the picture of teen angst, blinded by anger and shame, all very powerful emotions from which derives his powerful firebending. Accompanied by his uncle Iroh, defrocked general, grieving, yet masterful firebender, Zuko spends most of books 1 and 2 trying to capture Aang in order to honorably find his way back into the Fire Nation. Confused, hurt, still mourning the early disappearance of his mother, and ever suffering from the cruelty of his sister Azula, Zuko only starts to question himself when his uncle is taken prisoner after the alleged death of Avatar Aang. No longer exiled, Zuko faces is own guilt. Having spent time in the Earth Kingdom, living with commoners, he mostly saw the immense damages caused by the incendiary conquests of the Fire Nation. Zuko defies his father during the Day of Black Sun, redirects lightning against him, a veritable physical bending feat, and goes on to reform and join the Avatar.

After this, Zuko becomes unable to muster his inner fire, required to firebend. To teach Aang, who is still very much on the fence about using any amount of firebending, they must find a non-destructive inner source of firebending. They find it in ancient Sun Warrior wisdom passed on by the last two dragons in the world: Fire is life, a sun within the self. After this realization, firebending, in the eyes of Aang and Zuko, but also to their friends, shifts from being the cause for all the pain stemming from the war to a possible solution to all of it.

---

[29] Her temporary quest to avenge the death of her mother rather led her to a state of forgiveness, which she channeled towards Zuko's former violent allegiance.

In the end, one cannot fight fire with fire. One always overpowers, destroying everything along the way. During the final battle, Azula almost shoots Zuko to death, while Aang is weak against the boost that Sozin's comet provides Firelord Ozai. Avatar Aang rather resorts to the Avatar state, before applying ancient giant lion turtle wisdom to bend energies and neutralize Ozai.

In Korra's days, Zuko is an elderly man, advisor to Korra who provides her with all the teachings he previously shared with Aang. Firebending is no longer associated with domination and with destructive power, and is practiced in more gentle peaceful ways. The ability to spark lightning has been turned into opportunity for firebenders at the Electric Company. Moreover, the more destructive kind of firebending, like the explosive power of only two known enemy firebenders, remain rare, just as is lavabending, a blend between earthbending and firebending. Bolin, for instance, possesses this ability as he is the son of both types of benders. Unlike Aang, for whom firebending represented a real ethical challenge, Korra does not gain very much from firebending acts. For her, it remains an efficient and fierce instrument which won't bring her much luck in her time.

Toph: Earthbender and Pioneer Rulebreaker

Toph Beifong might be the most interesting character to look at when it comes to power play in a character's life. Toph is an 11-year-old blind earthbender who, unknowingly to her parents, has learned and mastered original earthbending, primal ways that are not taught in mainstream Earth Kingdom culture.[30] When Toph and Aang meet, she has already overcome her so-called physical disability and possesses the skill to defeat multiple intimidating opponents. She explains that her blindness does not pose an obstacle to her, as it allowed her to explore a different way of interacting with the world through earthbending. Even though earthbending is most difficult for Aang to learn, the teachings around passive enactment of power turns out to be a revelation that will continue to help the Avatar prevail.

From the start, Toph does not correspond to the typical earthbender image. When Aang struggles to find a master earthbender to teach him, he sees in Toph an aspect of earthbending that speaks to him. Through Toph, Aang succeeds at learning earthbending by enacting its power in a non-traditional way. Instead of the blunt force that earthbending usually evokes, he integrates it as a technique to "wait and listen". Toph, in this manner, introduces Aang and his friends to a more comprehensive approach to bending, one that

---

[30] Toph rather learned earthbending from giant badger-moles, traditionally viewed as the original earthbenders. Her bending, instead of being based on force, rather stems from her ability to sense vibrations in the earth, which also allows her to "see".

encompasses more than fighting techniques, and allows for an expanding and mutable practice of bending.

When Toph leaves the rich comfort of her parents' estate, she partakes in a more nomadic life. It isn't exactly surprising to see her shortly thereafter push the limits of earthbending itself and develop metalbending. Applying her determination to the advancement of earthbending happened out of necessity. Nevertheless, Toph Beifong later becomes one of the most prominent figures in Republic City, as the former Chief of Police, revered as the inventor of metalbending and an inspiration to the Metal Clan.

Despite being of great influence in Aang's life, Toph's earthbending acts don't contribute to Korra's journey very significantly until the Avatar needs to fully recover from the Red Lotus' attempt on her life. The poison that they forced into her body left trace amounts of metal resisting to extraction via bending. In the swamp where she finds secluded elderly Toph, Korra would have to listen to her inner self, listen to hear fears, her trauma and wait with them, sit with them, so she can finally release her enemies, no longer weighing her down. Without such a release, it is doubtful that she would have been strong or willing enough to finally fight and beat Kuvira.

Non-benders and Spirits in the Mix

A final perspective on bending acts in the Avatarverse stands between two opposites: non-benders and spirits. Non-benders, like Sokka and Asami, have major roles to play in the success of each Avatar's endeavours. In a way, the fact that they are not benders allows them to take the lead in more mundane areas of their adventures. They are more attuned to the necessities of the physical world and their impact of the Avatar's well-being.

At the opposite end of the spectrum, spirits, with whom only Aang and Korra interact on a regular basis, adopt a different relationship to humans as Korra, with each defeat, reconfigures the world. For Aang, they are adjuvants, that help his quest. But with Korra, their role is plural: friends, companions, invaders, dark monsters and more. She brought down walls between worlds and, consequently, further loses herself in the storm. When she finally relinquishes control over her place in the world, she finds herself whole, free and ready to discover, along with Asami, what other changes await in the Spirit World. In the end, Korra truly redefines bending acts.

A Balanced Conclusion of Inclusion

The first book of *TLOK* starts with Air, but the second one could not just cycle back to Water. The cycle of the Avatar having literally began anew, Avatar Korra turned her world into an organism, a more tightly interwoven tapestry, allowing it to include a great deal of spiritual realities less limited to embodied perceptions. Yet it is through the body of the Avatar that all these changes in the world initially took place. In the end, Balance certainly prevails.

A good way to illustrate this is the analogy that Guru Pathik uses in *ATLA* to explain to Aang the flow of energy between chakras. As water flows, as life goes on, pools in a cascade, like chakras in the body, get messy, clogged. But cleaning the pools, unclogging the whole being, opens the chakras and lets the energy flow. Aang understands this analogy instantly, as he is like the air surrounding the pools, above the cascade. But Korra is the cascade itself, caught between the motions and the blockages, toiling and troubling the water even more.

In the Avatarverse, Balance is not the correct, weightless manipulation of seized forces. It is the release that allows rebirth and lets changes take their course, the freedom that comes with shedding deathly parts of life, and the beauty of essence and substance clashing and crashing in chaos. Avatar Korra's struggles do not make a martyr out of her. She didn't sacrifice herself for the greater good. Avatar Korra took the most of what was allotted to her in life and found middle ground between individual healing and growth, and her duties to the world as the Avatar. Very much like Aang who redefined what it meant to bend energies by taking away the Firelord's firebending, Korra took her power further, and impacted the very structure of the world available to her perception.

We can see the aftermath of Aang's transformative bending acts as the story of Korra unfolds. One can only hope that what would follow Korra does indeed keep transforming the world, any world, into a more inclusive place to live.

Chapter 9

The Pokédex, Knowledge Production and the Technocratic Colonial Project in Pokémon

Devon P. Levesque and D. Y. Turner
Queen's University

ABSTRACT: Focusing on the Pokédex, this chapter discusses the technocratic colonial imperative of the Pokémon anime. Following Edward Said's application of Michel Foucault's technique of discourse analysis to the production of knowledge, this chapter explores the intersection of encyclopedic knowledge and colonialism. The Pokédex was represented as an objective eye that contained and disseminated empirical knowledge and images. Underlying this was a faith in the progressive, scientific nature of encyclopedic knowledge to collate and preserve objective facts from which modernity and progress flowed automatically. By suggesting a link between science and religion, we argue that the encyclopedic power of the Pokédex informed the ethics of the anime. The concept of "friendship" was integral to the anime and video game series, but obfuscated the objectification and construction of the Pokémon as Other.

KEYWORDS: Colonialism, Friendship, Knowledge Production, Pokédex, Pokémon, Technology.

***

Introduction

Pokémon ranks among the most successful, both monetarily and acclamatory, media franchises in the world. The franchise's perpetual staying power demonstrates the underlying significance and appeal of its collectible objective and exploratory narrative to its generations of adherents. As such, it is useful to interrogate how an anime derived from a collection-focused game influences audience participation and understanding within the fictional and real worlds. The conjunction of game mechanics with its episodically presented story provides a unique blueprint through which to examine the Pokémon franchise's central narratives. This examination of the franchise, fundamentally, has the capacity to open up questions about the epistemology and ontology of truth and reality within historical discourse and representation.

Given the breadth of the Pokémon universe, since its inception in 1996, this chapter will focus on the original anime as derived from the game and manga. In several short years, from 1996 to 2001, Pokémon went from its initial Japanese release to become an international breakthrough hit within global popular culture.[1] This chapter examines the North American adaptations of the anime and associated materials during this period of peak popularity. This chapter will begin with a brief overview of the Pokémon game to help orient the reader to the overarching mechanics and story of the media. We then turn to a discussion about the conceptualization of colonial knowledge and its expression in the anime through its interaction with religion and the supernatural. Lastly, we outline the anime's representation of the exploitation and objectification of the Pokémon Other.

The anime, *Pokémon: Indigo League,* is about a fantastical sports league, where competitors battle each other with the franchise's eponymous Pokémon. Pokémon are creatures or "monsters" that populate the world with the uncanny ability to "evolve" into stronger forms. We argue that, in its journey from a Japanese video game to a North American anime adaptation, *Pokémon: Indigo League* and its associated source material presents the audience with a Saidian colonial logic that underlies its story mechanics, plot devices, narrative structures, and ultimately, the audience's reception and interpretation. The anime's presence in a circulating global context contributed to its complicated ideological structure, which influenced its themes and the North American localization. The focus on the encyclopedic Pokédex and the protagonist's journey to capture all known Pokémon stemmed from colonial practices of exploration and empirical knowledge production. The emphasis on objective, scientific thought mediated through technology reflected historical European colonial projects beginning in the seventeenth century. As a representation of historically based colonial logics, the anime works to normalize and rationalize the practices of capture, categorization and exploitation. This was made possible through the Pokémon anime's genesis from a video game because it brought to the media a unique participatory and tangible experience for the audience. By centering the audience's participation, the anime makes the viewer complicit within the

---

[1] Joseph Tobin, "Introduction", in *Pikachu's Global Adventure: The Rise and Fall of Pokémon,* ed. Joseph Tobin (Durham: Duke University Press, 2004), 3.

colonial practices and logic first developed in the game and demonstrated in the anime.

Pokémon Origins: The Game

The well-established narrative for the origins of the *Pocket Monsters*, or Pokémon, franchise is attributed to the favorite childhood activities of its creator, Satoshi Tajiri: collecting bugs and playing video games. Born in 1965 and growing up on the still-rural outskirts of Tokyo, Tajiri claims his inspiration for the franchise came from his time spent exploring the natural environment surrounding his hometown where he discovered, collected and exchanged insects and crayfish with other local children.[2] His childhood story both inspired and neatly maps over the gameplay mechanics of the first Pokémon games released in Japan, *Red* and *Green*, on the Nintendo Game Boy in February 1996. In the games, the player takes control of a young, new Pokémon trainer from rural Pallet Town that is soon instructed to set out and explore the world. In their travels across the Kanto region, the player is taught how to capture, battle and trade its 151 unique Pokémon with in-game non-playable characters or with other players via peripheral devices. The player's accomplishments are certified with badges presented after increasingly difficult battles with specially sanctioned Pokémon League affiliated trainers at a city's Pokémon Gym. This core gameplay loop developed in the *Red*, *Green*, and *Blue* 1996 releases has remained the cornerstone of the entire multimedia franchise to this day.

The Pokédex and Role in the Game

The presence of the encyclopedic Pokédex in these titles and the series' overall emphasis on Pokémon discovery and collecting has informed the narrative structure of every subsequent Pokémon property released. The Pokédex, as presented in the North American *Red* and *Blue* releases from 1998 is, fundamentally, the raison d'être for the player's adventures in the game. The term itself, a portmanteau of "Pokémon" and "Index", aligns closely with the original *"Pocket Monster Zukan"* (ポケットモンスター図鑑), with *zukan* indicating an illustrated reference book or guide. Introduced in its beginning segment, it is described as a "hi-tech encyclopedia" filled with incomplete, numbered entries. One of its compiler's, Professor Oak, hopes that the player

---

[2] Anne Allison, "Cuteness as Japan's Millennial Product", in *Pikachu's Global Adventure: The Rise and Fall of Pokémon*, ed. Joseph Tobin (Durham: Duke University Press, 2004), 41.

will fulfill the historic undertaking of composing "a complete guide on all the Pokémon in the world".[3]

From this moment onwards, the Pokédex remains eminently visible to the player throughout their time with the game. It is the first option in the pause menu, newly filled entries are presented to the player upon capturing or evolving undiscovered Pokémon, and certain characters within the game refer to it with envy or boast about their superior capabilities in filling it out. Each new Pokédex entry provides the name, entry number, image, height, weight, cry, description and a fantastical "fact" about the captured Pokémon. For those Pokémon that the player has seen in their journey but has yet to obtain, when possible, the Pokédex even provides the approximate habitat where the player can search so that they might capture it and complete its entry. Therefore, the Pokédex, as a technological marvel, facilitates its own knowledge production venture. Even after surpassing the strongest Pokémon trainers that *Red* and *Blue* have to offer, the game lacks a concrete end state except in the form of a diploma given by Professor Oak once the player has possessed at least one of every Pokémon and presents their completed Pokédex back to the professor.

The in-universe origin of the Pokédex is typically presented ambivalently, with such malleability assisting in its omnipresence within the franchise yet still alluding to the colonial sciences of the nineteenth century. Supplementary materials published only two months after the video game's February 1996 release in Japan present a historicized version of the Pokédex's creation. As the lore explains, systematic research on Pokémon began in France in the late eighteenth century with the work of Baron Tajirin before exploding in popularity across Europe, then finding its way to Japan by the end of the nineteenth century where the groundbreaking work of Professor Nishinomori, localized as Professor Westwood for the US, inaugurated a new era of Pokémon research with Japan at its center.[4]

In the anime, Professor Westwood V is introduced as one of the foremost Pokémon researchers that collaborated with Professor Oak to create the Pokédex.[5] Crucially, this timeline aligns with the Bakumatsu and Meiji eras of Japanese history, where Western modes of science were translated into the Japanese intellectual tradition and put into service of the new, modern

---

[3] Game Freak, *Pokémon Red Version* & *Blue Version* (Kyoto: Nintendo, 1998).
[4] Creatures Inc., *An Illustrated Book of Pocket Monsters* (Tokyo: Famitsu, 1996), 8.
[5] *Pokémon: Indigo League*. Directed by Yūji Asada and Masaaki Iwane with Screenplay by Yukiyoshi Ōhashi and Yūji Asada (TV Tokyo 1998), Episode 66, entitled "The Evolution Solution".

Japanese nation-state ruled by the emperor from 1868 onwards.[6] The industrialization and modernization program of the Meiji government viewed the production of encyclopedic knowledge as a marker of national progress and "civilization" vis-à-vis European empires and their accomplishments.[7] The Pokédex is thus narratively presented as a part of this tradition, with these historical parallels contextualizing how the creators of the Pokémon universe first deployed the Pokédex and how the audience is meant to interpret it.

The localization process, wherein Nintendo of America, Warner Brothers, and 4Kids Entertainment sifted through the original Pokémon media releases, included muting or outright dropping these more overt connections to construct a palatable and merchandisable product for a children's audience. However, the Pokédex's centrality and its implications as an encyclopedic venture could not be wholly excised.

Timeline and Localization

It is important to note the distinctions between the Japanese and North American iterations of the Pokémon franchise. The dissemination of Pokémon into different mediums in Japan over a nearly two-year span stood in stark contrast to the localization and simultaneous launch of several of these properties in September 1998 for the North American market.[8]

Pokémon in Japan

The success of the Pokémon video games in Japan quickly led to the development of derivative works in the form of manga releases, the anime series and consumer goods. The first Pokémon manga, *Pocket Monsters*, published in the magazine *CoroCoro Comic* in April 1996, never received a North American English language release. Instead, 1997 saw the release of two major properties that would be translated, localized and sold for an American audience. The *Pokémon Adventures* (*Pocket Monsters Special*) manga began its serialized run in Japan in March 1997 and was closely followed by the first episode of the *Pokémon: Indigo League* (*Pocket Monsters*) anime that aired on

---

[6] See Federico Marcon, *The Knowledge of Nature and the Nature of Knowledge in Early Modern Japan* (Chicago: The University of Chicago Press, 2015).
[7] Miriam Kingsberg Kadia, "Epistemological Exercises: Encyclopedias of World Cultural History in Twentieth-Century Japan", *Modern Asian Studies* 55.3 (2021): 836-37.
[8] Hirofumi Katsuno and Jeffrey Maret, "Localizing the Pokémon TV Series for the American Market", in *Pikachu's Global Adventure: The Rise and Fall of Pokémon*, ed. Joseph Tobin (Durham: Duke University Press, 2004), 80.

April 1, 1997.[9] Both of these entries to the Pokémon franchise closely followed the conventions established by the original video game releases. Their narratives centered around the journey of a young Pokémon trainer exploring the world, capturing Pokémon and earning badges to become certified by the official body recognizing top trainers, the Pokémon League.

The *Pokémon Adventures* manga is closely tied to its source material in the video games, effectively replicating the narrative of *Red*, *Green* and *Blue* in printed form, down to borrowing art and user interface assets from the Game Boy releases' Pokédex.[10] The anime series, on the other hand, though maintaining a similar narrative structure to the video games, deviated from its origins by introducing deeper characterization and stories more suited to its episodic televised context. It was paired with another manga, *The Electric Tale of Pikachu* (*Pocket Monsters: Dengeki Pikachu*), released simultaneously and loosely based on the scripts of those television episodes.[11] And, by July 1998, the first feature-length film *Pokémon: The First Movie - Mewtwo Strikes Back*, was released in Japanese theaters.[12]

Pokémon in North America

The North American experience of Pokémon was distinct from Japan's because it was first marketed in the North American context as a television show. Nintendo of America and Warner Brothers collaborated to bring the animated series to the public to help prime and facilitate the market for the video game, trading cards and other branded merchandise. This was part of a larger effort to localize the series for the foreign market of North America.[13] Whereas in Japan Pokémon first appeared as a video game, the creators of Pokémon were cognizant of the necessity to adapt both the anime series and the film to the local market to ensure success. Localization was pursued to the extent that the US localization staff had complete freedom to remake the film for a North American audience so long as the theme of "respect for life" was maintained.[14] Much of this localization work for the franchise was done by

---

[9] Hidenori Kusaka, *Pokémon Adventures: Desperado Pikachu* (San Francisco: Viz Media, 2000). *Pokémon: Indigo League*. Directed by Toshiaki Suzuki with Screenplay by Takeshi Shudo (TV Tokyo 1998), Episode 1, entitled "Pokémon, I Choose You!".

[10] Kusaka, *Pokémon Adventures: Desperado Pikachu*, 36, 53, 85 and 169.

[11] Toshihiro Ono, *The Electric Tale of Pikachu* (Tokyo: Shogakukan, 1997-1999).

[12] *Pokémon: The First Movie - Mewtwo Strikes Back*. Directed by Kunihiko Yuyama with Screenplay by Satoshi Tajiri et al. (Tokyo OLM Inc. 1998). NB The original theatrical version did not have the subtitle "Mewtwo Strikes Back" and the latter added a prologue, new animation, and CGI.

[13] Katsuno and Maret, "Localizing the Pokémon TV Series for the American Market", 80.

[14] Masakazu Kubo, "Why Pokémon Was Successful in America", *Japan Echo* 27.2 (2000): 59.

4Kids Entertainment, an American licensing company that was contracted by Nintendo of America.[15]

The Importance of the Localization Process to Pokémon

The importance of the localization process to Pokémon's success in and adaptation to North America cannot be overstated. The differences and changes between the two versions were, at times, stark and altered the message of the show. For example, the protagonist Ash Ketchum (*Satoshi*) was made more prominent in the North American rendition, which depicted and accentuated him as the sole hero of the series. The protagonist Ash, accompanied by Pikachu and flanked by his companions Brock and Misty, juxtapose the main antagonists of Team Rocket's Jesse and James who, in the North American context, were presented as more disagreeable, exploitative and incompetent. The emphasis on the moral dichotomy between these characters ran contrary to Japanese anime traditions that typically did not compartmentalize protagonists and antagonists as purely good or evil.[16]

The localization process brings into view the central importance of the dialectic tension of colonialism embedded in and fundamental to understanding the larger themes of the anime series and game. The meaningful distinctions between the Japanese and North American versions are important because the subsequent analysis is based on the North American iterations. Considering the historically different experiences with colonialism and encyclopedic knowledge is essential to understanding and interrogating Pokémon's specific North American depiction. A colonial logic operated as a foundation for the narrative of the anime and its character depictions. Colonial logics rationalize and normalize colonial practices and structures that support and operate through exogenous domination and oppression.[17] It is important to understand how colonialism, as an innate rationale within North America, structures realities and influences perceptions.

Colonial Logic

To understand how colonial logic develops, circulates and comes to dominate thinking we can turn to Edward Said's Orientalism, which refers to the

---

[15] Katsuno and Maret, "Localizing the Pokémon TV Series for the American Market", 81-84.
[16] Allison, "Cuteness as Japan's Millennial Product", 38-39.
[17] Patrick Wolfe, "Settler Colonialism and the Elimination of the Native", *Journal of Genocide Research* 8.4 (2006): 387-409; Lorenzo Veracini, *The Settler Colonial Present* (New York: Palgrave Macmillan, 2015) and Eve Tuck and Ruben Gaztambide-Fernandez, "Curriculum, Replacement, and Settler Futurity", *Journal of Curriculum Theorizing* 29.1 (2013): 72-89.

construction of the Orient by European colonial powers from the late eighteenth century onwards. Coining the term, Said asserted that as a Western means of dominating and gaining authority over the Orient, Orientalism is a style of "thought" based on an ontological and epistemological distinction between the Orient and the Occident. Said described how this style of thought, in literature, media, the arts and academic studies, produced the image of the Orient as a threatening, inferior and underdeveloped "Other".[18]

Foucault, Said and Cohn

Inspired by Michel Foucault's analysis of knowledge and power, Said used the insight that language makes the world rather than simply reflect it and reality. Said argued that while the Orient is an integral part of "European material civilization", Orientalism expressed materiality as a cultural and ideological mode of discourse. Drawing further inspiration from Foucault's notion of how the articulation of words, speech and images produce discourse, Said emphasized that the Orient was not a free subject of action and thought, but rather, a created and imaginary geographical entity constructed in the context of colonialism and Western dominance.[19] As defined by Foucault, discourses are not groups of signs, but "practices that systematically form the objects of which they speak".[20] An example of this can be witnessed in *Pokémon: The First Movie - Mewtwo Strikes Back* with the creation and birth of the first viable Pokémon clone: Mewtwo. The successful cloning of the first Pokémon demonstrated, in literal fashion, how humans were able to create and construct the Pokémon Other. It was not a figurative act, but a material process as argued by Said and Foucault.

Said argued that the Western discursive system of dominance and authority in the unequal relationship between the Orient and the Occident can be understood through the concept of "power/knowledge".[21] This is where a regime of knowledge not only describes, teaches and rules, but also "produces" the Orient. Orientalism to Said was not a false knowledge construction, but a power relationship with political and cultural implications. Therefore, Orientalism as discourse was not coincidentally tied to colonialism, but was useful and productive for colonial powers. Summarily, Said's argument was

---

[18] Edward Said, *Orientalism* (New York: Penguin Books, 2003), 2-3.
[19] Ibid., 2-3 and 22-23.
[20] Michel Foucault, *Archaeology of Knowledge*, trans. A.M. Sheridan Smith (London: Routledge, 2002), 156.
[21] Michel Foucault, *Discipline and Punish: The Birth of the Prison*, trans. Alan Sheridan (New York: Vintage Books, 1995), 27-28.

that Orientalism is a system of knowledge and a configuration of power that actively made colonization possible by legitimizing colonial rule.[22]

Orientalism's knowledge production was bolstered with the ascendency of European science, which imbued it with authority in the nineteenth and twentieth centuries. The appeal of science stemmed from its perceived objectivity based in empiricism; science was supposedly neither speculative nor idealistic, therefore, the knowledge flowing from science was seen as fact and not fabrication.[23] Alongside Said's observations, a wide range of other scholars have also studied the inextricable relationship between knowledge and power throughout colonial history, including anthropologist Bernard Cohn.

Cohn has argued that the modern British state, from the eighteenth century onward, depended upon the determination, codifying, controlling and representation of knowledge to govern and control itself and its colonies. To accomplish this, British colonial experts consciously devised "investigative modalities" to ascertain knowledge and facts that would assist in colonial governance. By making their colonies intelligible through historiographic, observational/travel, survey, enumerative and surveillance modalities colonial powers produced ontological and epistemological understandings of the colonial Other.[24] The centrality of empiricism to colonial rule and knowledge demonstrated how its underlying logic and technological innovations were deployed to reinforce its power.

The adoption and use of photography extended the reach and dissemination of colonial science and knowledge because it represented "the perfect marriage between science and art" as it was "a mechanical means of allowing nature to copy herself with total accuracy and intricate exactitude" through truthful delineations. Representation is a complex cultural process and therefore photographs must be understood as moments in broader discourses because photographic images derive evidential force from their "existential connection to a prior reality and the technical and cultural processes and discursive frameworks through which it is made meaningful". As the "eye of history", photography was granted inordinate power and weight in the mediation of knowledge. However, photographs are not innocent

---

[22] Said, *Orientalism*, 7-8.
[23] Ibid., 232 and Zaheer Baber, *The Science of Empire: Scientific Knowledge, and Colonial Rule in India* (Albany: State University of New York Press, 1996), 2-10.
[24] Bernard S. Cohn, *Colonialism and Its Forms of Knowledge: The British in India* (Princeton: Princeton University Press, 1996), 3-11; Fredrick Cooper and Ann Laura Stoler, eds., *Tensions of Empire: Colonial Cultures in a Bourgeois World* (Berkeley: University of California Press, 1997).

figurations of reality and truth, rather they are invested with meanings that reveal as much about its subject as it does about its producers.[25]

History, Photography and Encyclopedia

Historian James Ryan demonstrates how photography became integrated into colonial practices of hunting and surveying, which supported scientific pursuits to identify, capture and catalogue the colony and colonized. Photography, because it captured the real image, was viewed as innately objective.[26] Flowing from this, the encyclopedia became the ultimate representation of catalogued, objective colonial knowledge. Discursive entries accompanied with images marked the pinnacle of the totalizing colonial project.[27] As such, encyclopedias have been described as "a total body of vision, a continuous, unified form summing up the knowledge of a culture at a particular point in history".[28] The inordinate power ascribed to encyclopedias provides a way to understand the importance of the Pokédex in the original anime and its first film.

The Pokédex's capability of rendering its subject through a photographic lens to present real-time factual data holistically combines these practices. In the Pokémon universe, as in reality, the Pokédex-as-encyclopedia offers a scheme and model through which the world can be neatly ordered and understood. Furthermore, encyclopedic discourse provides the justification and rationale to know and control the Other through its creation in text and representation. By structuring epistemology and ontology through representations in the Pokédex, a socio-cultural understanding about the world and those who inhabit it as colonial logic is established. The resultant power afforded by this combination of modern photography and encyclopedic knowledge embodied by the Pokédex can be demonstrated through the interactions between the franchise's protagonists and the supernatural ghost-type Pokémon typically associated with the universe's pre-modern past.

Ghost-Type in the Pokédex and Pokémon

The Pokédex's all-encompassing knowledge, often employed alongside other technological implements intended for Pokémon capture, is portrayed in the

---

[25] James R. Ryan, *Picturing Empire: Photography and the Visualization of the British Empire* (London: Reaktion Books, 1997), 17 and 19-20.
[26] Ibid., 99-139.
[27] Alasdair MacIntyre, *Three Rival Versions of Moral Enquiry: Encyclopaedia, Genealogy, and Tradition* (Notre Dame: University of Notre Dame Press, 1990).
[28] Northrop Frye, *The Anatomy of Criticism* (Princeton: Princeton University Press, 1957), 55-56. Cf. Hilary Clark, "Encyclopedic Discourse", *SubStance* 21.1 (1992): 95.

anime and manga as providing the power to dispel the illusions and venerable stature of the series' ghost-type Pokémon. Ghost-type Pokémon make up the smallest of the fifteen standard categories of Pokémon present within the original release's Pokédex, where, of the 151 Pokémon extant in 1996, there were only three ghost-types: Gastly, Haunter and Gengar. Encounters with these ghosts were relatively rare compared to those of more mundane Pokémon, particularly those with designs inspired by everyday flora and fauna. As a result, ghost-type Pokémon mostly feature in uncommon sites like graveyards and ruins or associated with alternative temporalities like the ancient, pre-modern past or its memorialization in the present.[29] One such location was Lavender Town's Pokémon memorial tower, a large Pokémon gravesite, first presented in the original Game Boy releases that has since become a paranormal focal point for the fan community.[30] The player's exploration of the memorial tower is initially blocked by humanoid-looking ghosts until they have acquired a "Silph Scope" device, which deciphers these ghosts as Gastlys and Haunters. Thus unveiled, these spirits can be identified by the Pokédex and caught like any other Pokémon.[31] This encounter with ghost-type Pokémon serves as a prototypical model for the rest of the franchise, where narrative limitations are initially imposed upon the series' knowledge of the natural (and supernatural) world but are subsequently surpassed through the employment of technological marvels that make these Pokémon subjectable to the protagonists.

The mystery posed by the player's first encounter with ghost-type Pokémon within the original video game is carried forward into their portrayal in other mediums, such as the anime and manga. The episode "The Ghost of Maiden's Peak" depicts Ash's first encounter with a Gastly.[32] Blurring the lines between humans and Pokémon, this English-speaking Gastly utilizes illusions to adopt the form of the eponymous ancient maiden who lived over 2,000 years ago as well as that of an old mystic woman. Posing as the maiden's ghost during the annual Obon-like summer festival, this Gastly lures young men towards the

---

[29] Martyn Hudson, *Ghosts, Landscapes and Social Memory* (New York: Routledge, 2017); Sarah Surface-Evans, Amanda Garrison and Kisha Supernant, eds., *Blurring Timescapes, Subverting Erasure: Remembering Ghosts on the Margins of History* (New York: Berghahn, 2020).
[30] *Pokémon Red Version* & *Blue Version* and *Pokémon: Indigo League*. Directed by Toshiaki Suzuki and Izumi Shimura with Screenplay by Hideki Sonoda (TV Tokyo 1997), Episode 23, entitled "The Tower of Terror".
[31] *Pokémon Red Version* & *Blue Version*.
[32] *Pokémon: Indigo League*. Directed by Kiyotaka Itani and Takayuki Shimura with Screenplay by Takeshi Shudō (TV Tokyo 1997), Episode 20, entitled "The Ghost of Maiden's Peak".

maiden's shrine atop a seaside peak to revitalize her memory within the community. At first the supernatural encounter appears genuine. However, the Pokédex demystifies the maiden's ghost by revealing it to merely be just another Pokémon that can be battled and captured. The Ghastly only retreats with the threat of morning light signaled by distant ringing church bells, and not because of Ash, his companions and Team Rocket's confrontation with their own Pokémon, ofuda talismans, a cross and even vampire hunting implements. The episode's final scene depicts Gastly departing from the festival in conversation with the true ghost of the maiden, revealing to the viewer that human ghosts are present within the narrative universe as well.

There is a notable absence in the encyclopedic knowledge of the Pokédex when confronting Gastly within this episode contrary to the stream of facts it easily dispenses for non-ghost Pokémon. The Pokédex's knowledge of ghost-type Pokémon is seen to be imperfect, having only a passing familiarity with Gastly. That knowledge alone, however, proves to be enough to propel the group's investigation of the maiden's ghost forward in a manner unmatched by the religious symbols and charms employed throughout the episode.

The Pokédex's ability to discern a Pokémon with its lens, similar to the video game's Silph Scope, is the turning point in the episode that allows the human characters to fight back against the supernatural. The ofuda used to ward against the ghost's attempt to charm the cast's adult men were harmlessly blown away and the presentation of a cross is shrugged off with bewilderment. Instead, the terror of this supernatural encounter is rendered inert through its transformation into one more step on Ash's journey to document and capture all the world's Pokémon by way of the Pokédex's scientific objectivity.

The Electric Tale of Pikachu

The Electric Tale of Pikachu manga represents a different kind of encounter with ghost-type Pokémon in a form that evokes the series' inhabitants' spirituality within the chapter "Haunting My Dreams".[33] The antagonist in this chapter is an oversized Haunter known as "The Black Fog", a notorious terror within the region portrayed as regularly stealing the souls of people and Pokémon alike for decades. Where most are said to have given up on combating it, the manga's protagonists utilize their ingenuity to construct a super-charged Poké Ball with which to capture the rogue Pokémon.

---

[33] Toshihiro Ono, "Haunting My Dreams", in *The Electric Tale of Pikachu* 4 (San Francisco: Viz Media, 1999).

The primary confrontation occurs at the monumental tower in Lavender Town, described as an ancient and prehistoric settlement this time, where the effort to make use of the novel Poké Ball fails after the Haunter explodes within the device, grievously injuring itself. The Haunter is driven deep into the confines of the ruins where a second attempt to capture it is thwarted by the Pokémon's preference for self-annihilation, choosing to explode itself totally rather than be subservient to a human. With the destruction of the Haunter, the reader is presented with a gigantic ornate statue in its image, split in half. This leads Brock to remark that the original inhabitants of the site "worshiped Pokémon as gods", theorizing that this Haunter perhaps "grew accustomed to being treated like a god, until they abandoned it".[34] Once equated to a force of (super)nature, Ash and his companions' actions in this issue demystify the Black Fog such that they can defeat it, reducing it to yet another Pokémon to be captured.

The site of confrontation with the Black Fog in "Haunting my Dreams" presents a strong juxtaposition between a hypothetical shared past between humans and Pokémon and the violent, technologically fueled subjugation of Pokémon in the media's present. The allusions in this rendition of an ancient and monumental Lavender Town suggest a pre-modern era within the universe when human spirituality and reverence was invested within the Pokémon with which they shared their world.

Seemingly left behind in the present by a human society replicating a fantastic version of secularized modernity, this Haunter had chosen to lash out against humankind. Ash's suggestion that the Black Fog was just another Pokémon that could be captured is representative of both attitudinal and technological change within their society.[35]

Advanced technology, in this case a prototype Poké Ball, plays a role in the transformation of the supernatural identities of the ghost-type Pokémon into the mundane and their relationship with humans from respect and sacralization to one of imposition and subjugation. Seeing as the aim of the franchise is to capture and catalogue all the world's known Pokémon, even its portrayal of those forces located at the fringes of our senses inevitably subsumes them into one more category of empirical fact, either within the Pokédex or as a potential subject within a trainer's Poké Ball.

---

[34] Ibid., 36.
[35] Ibid., 14.

Colonial Representations in the Anime: Manipulation Through a Subtle Choice for the Audience

The opening sequence to *Pokémon: The First Movie - Mewtwo Strikes Back* offers a clear portrayal of colonial activity within the Pokémon universe based on historical colonialism. Pan flutes and the sounds of tropical fauna and Pokémon are mixed with visuals of scientists in pith helmets and khaki uniforms trekking through a dense jungle. The expedition is shown to pass by marsh-swallowed stones bearing pre-Colombian American inspired designs on their way to the ruins of a so-called "ancient civilization", where the film's extended prologue depicts the science team setting up survey equipment.[36] While not depicted visually, the introductory voiceover provided by the film's leading scientific figure, Dr. Fuji, exclaims that the expedition recovered fossilized remains of the legendary Pokémon Mew. Although the archaeological site is unnamed within the film, *Red* and *Blue* offers a Guyanese origin for the fossilized Mew that aligns with the tropical and colonial visual design of the scene.[37] In referencing South America by name in the video game and adopting a visual design inspired by it within the film, Pokémon locates one of its extraordinary so-called legendary Pokémon in a colonized milieu far away from the franchise's creators in Japan and the recipients of its English localizations in North America.

The overt colonial reference made here involving Dr. Fuji highlights the distinctions in motivation and practices between the anime's protagonists and the villainous Team Rocket, yet the similarities in their goals. Dr. Fuji's narration at the start of *The First Movie* informs the viewer that his work in creating the Pokémon Mewtwo was funded by Giovanni, the mysterious leader of Team Rocket. With Team Rocket's funding, Dr. Fuji agreed to clone the Pokémon Mew from its fossilized remains, thus giving life to Mewtwo. Through these experiments he presents himself at the forefront of a technological revolution in seeking to enact dominion over life itself through science, whether it be human or Pokémon.[38] Giovanni's ambitions are more straightforward, simply intending to keep and control a replica of what was then considered to be the most powerful Pokémon in existence.

In stark contrast, lacking endless funds or scientific know-how, Ash's effort to catch all the world's Pokémon and complete the Pokédex is presented as both exceptional and pure hearted. Ash stands out as the series' protagonist because of his intent to capture all the world's known Pokémon and become

---

[36] *Pokémon: The First Movie - Mewtwo Strikes Back.*
[37] *Pokémon Red Version & Blue Version.*
[38] *Pokémon: The First Movie - Mewtwo Strikes Back.*

the greatest trainer of all time. His all-encompassing ambition is reinforced within the anime's English opening and ending themes, the former announcing his destiny to "catch 'em all" and the latter naming every Pokémon that then existed.[39] Both the video games and the anime present other trainers as tending to specialize in Pokémon of a single typing or style of appearance, such as a preference for pink Pokémon. The Pokémon League itself is similarly structured, with its sanctioned gyms and the badges they bestow being themed around singular types. Ash's companions Brock and Misty, both former gym leaders, fall under this rubric as they specialize in rock-type and water-type Pokémon respectively despite their narrative alignment with him. Ash's need to capture every type and fill his Pokédex reflects his all-encompassing colonial need to know and control the Pokémon world. However, Ash's colonial outlook is softened by the friendships he establishes with his captured Pokémon.

Ash and Friendship

Ash's friendship with his Pokémon, notably with Pikachu, is emphasized from the beginning of the series and draws the audience into empathizing with him and rooting for his ambitions against those of his rivals. In the first episode of the anime, Ash originally clashes vigorously with his newly obtained Pikachu, eventually earning Pikachu's trust by risking his own life to protect Pikachu from a violent Spearow attack.[40] Their resultant deep friendship is demonstrated through Pikachu's special privilege to walk around outside of its Poké Ball, a Pokémon's primary enclosure, as well as Ash's unwillingness to evolve Pikachu as that would fundamentally change the Pokémon and sever Ash's specific and unique friendship. While Pikachu stands as an exception, the friendships Ash cultivates with his captured Pokémon assists in developing their innate abilities, eventually leading to their evolution into stronger forms.

Ash and Rivals

Despite this framing, these evolved forms represent additional entries to his Pokédex and thus serve to advance his goals to obtain all the Pokémon. Throughout the series, Ash is juxtaposed by his main rivals Jessie and James of Team Rocket. Team Rocket, as an organization, is dedicated to the capture, theft, exploitation and sale of rare or powerful Pokémon. Like Ash, they also seek to obtain all the Pokémon, but frequently demonstrate adversarial relationships towards them. Their oft-cited motto presents their organization's

---

[39] "Pokémon, I Choose You!".
[40] Ibid.

totalizing mission, its central tenets being "to unite all peoples within our nation, to denounce the evils of truth and love, to extend our reach to the stars above".[41] Their philosophy directly opposes Ash's, positioning them as the primary antagonists in the original series.

Ash and his rivals offer two versions of the colonialist, one friendly and the other villainous. The anime invites the audience to choose between these contrasting representations of the colonialist by seeing Ash's brand as noble, good and as a form of self/social betterment, whereas Team Rocket's is exploitative and evil. The North American anime succeeds in gaining the audience's compliance with its form of colonial understanding by forcing the audience to recognize and choose between two colonial alternatives. Ash's purpose is depicted as understandable and emphasizes the benefits of the colonial system as practiced by the protagonist. The anime also rationalizes his colonial practices of locking his Pokémon within a system of dependent service and compliance through portrayals of friendship. In this way, both Ash and the Pokémon work together to reproduce a colonial system as the best, if not only, alternative in the Pokémon world.

Effect on the Audience

Ash's virtuous colonialism is continuously reinforced throughout the anime by Team Rocket's persistent attempts to steal and capture Ash's Pikachu. As such, Ash's protection and seemingly better treatment of Pikachu (and all Pokémon by extension), epitomizes his representation as a heroic model of colonialism within the Pokémon universe. Ash's successful differentiation from the villainous Team Rocket earns Pikachu's unwavering friendship, the audiences' trust and his companion's admiration. Other examples of Ash's noble colonialism seek to demonstrate how he is a benevolent captor, deserving of appreciation and sympathy. This representation is strenuously reiterated again when the audience witnesses Ash setting one of his captured Pokémon free. In the episode "Bye, Bye, Butterfree" Ash proves his seemingly humane treatment of Pokémon when he releases his Butterfree allowing it to complete its life cycle.[42] The episode presents Ash's actions as selfless altruism. As the hero, Ash upstages the Pokémon which the anime is titled after by possessing enormous power to move within the world and to affect the lives of the Pokémon around him. The effect is to tacitly win the audience

---

[41] *Pokémon: Indigo League*: Directed by Shigeru Ōmachi and Yūsaku Takeda with Screenplay by Atsuhiro Tomioka (TV Tokyo 1997), Episode 19, entitled "Tentacool & Tentacruel".

[42] *Pokémon: Indigo League*: Directed by Yūji Asada and Akihiro Tamagawa with Screenplay by Yukiyoshi Ōhashi (TV Tokyo 1997), Episode 21, entitled "Bye Butterfree".

over to Ash, and by implication colonialism, as a positive phenomenon. Thus, making the audience complicit with colonialism.

The Pokémon Other

The narrative fixation on Ash's ambition of Pokémon mastery helps to normalize the use and exploitation of his Pokémon. The interiority and subject-position of Ash is reiterated by the narrator, featured at the beginning and end of every episode, who focuses on the protagonist to the exclusion of Pokémon. The inner thinking and feelings of Pokémon are hardly considered directly in the anime, instead their representations and motives are often mediated through human perceptions or technology, such as their Pokédex entries. This reinforces the binary of the Pokémon Other against the human. However, this binary is vulnerable.

True Feelings about Colonialism in Tentacool & Tentacruel

There exists in the Pokémon anime and film a handful of instances when Pokémon reveal their feelings about this colonial system. One of the clearest examples comes from the episode "Tentacool & Tentacruel". During their trip back to the mainland from Porta Vista, Ash and his companions are waylaid by a boat disaster. After rescuing the crew, the crew's employer Nastina, asks Ash and his companions to destroy the Tentacools that are negatively impacting her hotel island development. She emphasizes that the Tentacools are "despicable", "disgusting" and inedible. Misty quickly declines Nastina's offer and is angered by the "Tentacool extermination project". As she explains, the Tentacools surely have a reason for disrupting Nastina's development plans. Unable to convince Ash and his companions, Nastina resorts to enlisting the island's residents by offering a one-million-dollar reward to anyone willing to exterminate the Tentacools. Team Rocket agrees to Nastina's term and begins to attack. As the water-type specialist, Misty is especially aggrieved at Nastina's plan and the resident's willingness to disrespect the ocean.[43]

Immediately after Team Rocket implements their plans, a gigantic Tentacruel emerges from the water and wreaks havoc on the surrounding islands. The Tentacruel later speaks to the humans:

> We are Tentacool and Tentacruel. Hear us now. Humans have destroyed our ocean home, and now we will have our revenge. Now we will begin

---

[43] "Tentacool & Tentacruel", *Pokémon: Indigo League*.

to destroy your world, your home, as you have so cruelly tried to destroy ours. And not one of you has the right to complain about it.[44]

The audience only then learns that Nastina's island is built upon the coral reef that is home to the Pokémon. The Tentacruel explains that Pokémon "cannot turn away" but "must teach the humans the pain of having homes destroyed" because to do nothing would "only allow humans to be more cruel and inconsiderate in the future".[45]

Sceptical of Tentacruel's speech, Ash and his team decide to act and to "send the Pokémon back to the sea" with the help of their own captured Pokémon. Tentacruel, however, is unable to understand why Pokémon would willingly defend and fight for humans. Rather, Tentacruel is convinced that any Pokémon siding with humans are its enemies. This instance is one of the clearest articulations of a Pokémon's feelings towards humans and a perspective on the unequal relationship they share with humans within the colonial world created around them. Tentacruel is not alone, and its sentiments are echoed by the far more powerful, titular Pokémon in *Pokémon: The First Movie - Mewtwo Strikes Back*.

Exposé of Mewtwo in The First Movie

Mewtwo in *The First Movie* is another instance where a subservient Pokémon voices its thoughts on its relationship with humanity. Mewtwo's violent actions in the film represent an extreme rebellion against the empirical sciences of the Pokémon universe, with the normative capture, catalogue and control of its intelligent creatures.

Mewtwo, as a clone of Mew, epitomizes the "originariness" paradox which leads to originary-violence, as discussed by Jacques Derrida.[46] Furthermore, Mewtwo is the culmination of human technology and the colonial sciences that permeates the Pokémon anime. Mewtwo's presence within the anime exemplifies the structural process of how pure representation is not possible and leads to the potentiality of violence, as elaborated by Derrida. Echoing the sentiments of Tentacruel, Mewtwo in *The First Movie* also quickly recognizes the unequal binary invented by its human creators. While coming to consciousness in the lab, Mewtwo questions who and what it is. Eventually, Mewtwo comes to the realization that it is not a human person, but an artificial construct developed to serve and obey humans—its will, desires and

---

[44] Ibid.
[45] Ibid.
[46] Jacques Derrida, *Of Grammatology*, trans. Gayatri Spivak (Baltimore: Johns Hopkins University Press, 1974), 110.

preferences secondary to human intentions. When Mewtwo confronts Giovanni, the Team Rocket leader readily admits that Mewtwo's only purpose is to serve and fight for its master. He explains that Mewtwo is neither a partner nor an equal, but rather was "created by humans to obey humans".[47]

Giovanni's colonial perspective greatly upsets Mewtwo, who is unable to come to terms with his limited destiny as a tool for humans. As such, he declares that

> humans may have created me, but they will never enslave me . . . . I was not born a Pokémon, I was created. And my creators have used and betrayed me. So, I stand alone . . . . I will find my own purpose and purge this planet of all who oppose me. Humans and Pokémon alike. The world will heed my warning. The reign of Mewtwo will soon begin.[48]

In seeking his revenge, Mewtwo intends to take charge of the world, certain in his knowledge that "humans are a dangerous species" unfit to rule. However, Ash's benevolent colonialism and friendships once again obscure the objectification and construction of Pokémon as Other. This is represented in the anime with Pikachu willingly sacrificing itself to protect Ash from Mewtwo's attacks. Moved by this act of sacrifice, Mewtwo succumbs to Ash's efforts and, at the last second, backs down. By the end of the film, Mewtwo does not change the system but rather flees from it. In this way, Ash and his benevolent colonialism are recognized once again by the audience as the only working possibility.

Derrida and the Recognition of Exploitative Colonialism

In both foregoing examples, the violence perpetrated against Pokémon develops their recognition about their unequal position in an exploitative relationship. Moreover, the centrality of the Pokédex and the way its objective, colonial knowledge is wielded to inform relationships and construct the ontological Pokémon-human binary reveals how the violence stems from what Derrida called originary-writing (arche-writing), which leads to originary-violence (arche-violence).[49] Following Ferdinand de Saussure, Derrida conceived of meaning as conditioned by difference, and therefore, meaning and signification require difference to make the intelligible distinction between a thing and its representation. As such, within the

---

[47] *Pokemon: The First Movie - Mewtwo Strikes Back.*
[48] *Pokemon: The First Movie - Mewtwo Strikes Back.*
[49] Derrida, *Of Grammatology*, 9.

structure of writing exists the paradox that there must be, in every act of signification, something that remains unrepresented or excluded. Derrida termed this paradox as "oblitération" and explained that given the impossibility of true or complete representations, the entire system and logic of signification is corrupt and questionable. To describe this structural uncertainty, Derrida used the term originary-violence to define the irreducible possibility of corruption and misrepresentation.[50] Originary-violence is anterior, structural and necessary to all subsequent violence. Ash and the audience's fetishization of the Pokédex, as the objective and real representation of Pokémon, sparks the moment for the possibility for all consequential violence in the colonial system. By believing that the Pokédex can fully and truly capture the Pokémon is originary-violence realized and fundamentally corrupts any relationship between them.

In the Pokémon universe, Pokémon-human interactions are mediated through the Pokédex and objective, colonial knowledge rises to the level of totalizing project, which authenticates and corroborates the paradox of the system of representation. Taking this further, the anime's origins as a video game helps to carry the logic of its gameplay throughout its narrative, characters and world building. In so doing, the audience becomes a spectatorial accomplice to the colonial practices and system through their identification with the protagonist Ash.

Conclusion

The Pokédex and the historical colonialism presented in the anime and manga harkens back to the disciplinary reliance and failure in historical text and practice of the copy theory of historical representation. Stemming from modern, scientific Rankean historiography, historians up to the late twentieth century, believed to varying degrees that there had been a past that they should and could "copy" to the best of their abilities through their language and methodological practices. The Narrativist critique, which has fundamentally altered the relationships of the historian to the past through the text and practice, proposed that the historian could not copy the past, but rather substituted it for an ontologically separate representation.[51] The ramifications of this shift in thought and practice, is reminiscent of the

---

[50] Ibid., 110.

[51] Hayden White, *Metahistory: The Historical Imagination of Nineteenth-Century Europe* (Baltimore: The John Hopkins Press, 1973) and Frank Ankersmit, *Narrative Logic: A Semantic Analysis of the Historian's Language* (Boston: Martinus Nijhoff Publishers, 1983).

dichotomy between humans and Pokémon, where humans come to create the Pokémon Other.

The Pokédex was represented as an objective eye that contained and disseminated empirical knowledge. Underlying this was a faith, historically based, in the progressive, scientific nature of encyclopedic knowledge to present objective facts from which modernity and progress flowed automatically. The notion of cataloguing was deeply embedded within this process: "to catch 'em all" was to embark on countless exploratory journeys across the face of the ever-expanding known world armed with a Pokédex to "discover" the identities, traits and potential utility of the universe's denizens. This was a colonial process. By demonstrating the franchise's portrayal of scientific triumph over religion and the supernatural, we argue that the encyclopedic power of the Pokédex informed the colonial logic of the anime and made the audience complicit. Although the concept of friendship was deployed to obfuscate the objectification and construction of the Pokémon as Other, the colonial logic could not be obscured.

It is fortuitous that centering on the nature of representation in the Pokémon anime helps to expose representation as one of the most important issues in contemporary understandings of history. How historians think and practice the discipline depends upon their knowledge of and epistemological orientation towards engagements with the past. The radical transformations in philosophy and the humanities of the past century have challenged the foundational beliefs of Western culture—science, truth, objectivity, purpose and progress—which have come to be viewed with increased skepticism.

The consequence has been a rethinking that distinguishes history from the past at a fundamental epistemological and ontological level. This rethinking is frequently seen as nothing more than a recognition of the cognitive effects of history's written, rhetorical, composed and configured form, but it is far more than that. Understanding history as a representation of the past (or even in anti-representational terms), re-aligns the discipline as an aesthetic as well as an empirical and analytical activity. This is a crucial effort to comprehend and probe the limits of reality and objectivity in historical discourse. The Pokémon franchise is an essential reminder for historians of the limits of their interpretations of the past as constructed historical knowledge, and the historian's ethical duty to the Other.

Chapter 10

The Promised Neverland: Exploitation of the Religious "Others"

Michelle Chan
Hong Kong Shue Yan University

ABSTRACT: *The Promised Neverland* (2016-2020) explores the subject of belief through meat consumption, ethnic hierarchy and religions. The story unfolds layers of deception and systems of exploitation through a group of cattle children, who are raised to be eaten by a group of powerful beings called "demons". *The Promised Neverland* mingles the concepts of J. M. Barrie's Neverland, a land where children will never grow up, and the biblical concepts of the Promised Land. The work also responds to some ideas of Shintoism and imageries of Buddhism so as to further elaborate on the potential deficiency in the concepts of "belief". This chapter explores how religious systems make use of the so-called Fixation of Destiny to legitimize their exploitation of innocents or whoever are categorized as the religious "others". To some extent, *The Promised Neverland* reflects the hybridity and secularization of religions in Japan. Still, it is not intended to challenge any actual religious groups but to propose a critical discussion on the variant potentialities of belief.

KEYWORDS: Anime, Cannibalism, Exophagy, Japanese Studies, Manga, The Promised Neverland, Religions, Secularized Religions.

***

Introduction

Contemporary Japanese society is syncretically inundated with individual and diverse practices of multivarious religious practices. There is no dearth of temples, jinja (Shinto temples) and other religious edifices across the country. People do have considerable freedom in interacting with religious traditions, rituals and values; even if many claim that they are not affiliated with any institutionalized belief.[1] Rather than examining the secularization of religion in Japan in relation to modern Euro-American political inclination or the mundaneness of any religiosity, manga/anime tends to address the incorporation of multivarious religious elements in secular contexts.[2] To a certain extent, manga/anime mirrors the actual religious reality of Japan in various degrees. Yet, their creators employ multiple religious elements with limited skepticism to any actual institutional religion.[3] *Shûkyô Asobi*, a term proposed by Jolyon Thomas, describes the interflowing dynamics between religion and entertainment. *Shûkyô Asobi* is a result of the commercialization of religious elements, negotiation of various spiritual needs particularly in the post-war period, and modification of existing religious themes. It can also be a way to cast religious impacts on the public through entertaining literary works.[4]

The inclusion of religious elements in manga/anime is probably derived from long existing practices of blending religious content with comic art. For instance, the caricatures in Horyuji Temple (built in 607) are shown to be some of the early examples of such mixture. "The Animal Scrolls" of Bishop of Toba (1053-1140) are commercially produced in the Tokugawa Period (1603-1867).[5] *Kinyōshi*, an illustrated satirical fiction in the eighteenth century, also contains a ubiquity of religious imagery and "humorous appropriation of

---

[1] Mark R. Mullins, "Religion in Contemporary Japanese lives", in *Routledge Handbook of Japanese Culture and Society*, ed. Victoria Bestor, Theodore Bester and Akiko Yamagata (London and New York: Routledge, 2011), 63-74 and Jolyon Thomas, "Spirit/Medium: Critically Examining the Relationship between Animism and Animation", in *Spirits and Animism in Contemporary Japan: The Invisible Empire*, ed. Fabio Rambelli (London and New York: Bloomsbury, 2019), 157-70.

[2] Hans Martin Krämer, "The Long History of Religion's Opposites, the 'Secular' and 'Secularization'", in *Shimaji Mokurai and the Reconception of Religion and the Secular in Modern Japan* (Honolulu: University of Hawaii Press, 2015), 114-16. This is consistent with the Western adage "I'm spiritual not religious" as a reflection of postmodern eclecticism or syncretism.

[3] Adam Barkman, "Anime, Manga and Christianity: A Comprehensive Analysis", *Journal for the Study of Religions and Ideologies* 9.27 (2010): 25-45.

[4] Jolyon Thomas, "*Shukyō Asobi* and Miyazaki Hayao's *Anime*", *Nova Religion: The Journal of Alternative and Emergent Religions* 10:3 (2007): 74.

[5] Kinko Ito, "A History of Manga in the Context of Japanese Culture and Society", *Journal of Popular Culture*: 38:3 (2005), 458. More information concerning the history of manga and its relation with religious issues can be found in Kinko Ito, "A History of Manga in Japanese Culture and Society", in *Japanese in Visual Culture: Explorations in the World of Manga and Anime*, ed Mark W. MacWilliams (New York: Routledge, 2015), 26-47.

religious icons".⁶ Manga/anime inherits Japanese practices and aesthetics across history, and simultaneously, it is subjected to contemporary social and cultural milieu and foreign influence.⁷ The religions reflected in manga/anime are primarily hybrids of secularized local and international beliefs, ritual and practices that aim not to preach but to entertain.

The Promised Neverland (約束のネバーランド), created by Kaiu Shirai, is set in an apocalyptic landscape where humans are raised to be the food of demons. Long before this, demons are the predators of humans, and the two parties are constantly at war. An agreement, namely the "promise" in the manga series, is made to terminate the warfare. It divides the world into two. In the demon world, some humans are left for farming purposes and creating and cultivating generations of human cattle. The human world, on the other hand, remains undisturbed by demons. There is a divine demon, Him,⁸ who actualizes the promise since the leaders of the two parties agree to give Him what he requires. The Promised Neverland is noticeably alluding to the Neverland in J. M. Barrie's Peter and Wendy (1911).⁹ In Shirai's work, "Neverland" refers to the demon world. Similar to the perpetual childhood existing in Barrie's Neverland, most cattle children do not grow up in the demon world because from age 6 to 12, they will be "reared" to be consumed by demons. All cattle children are raised by human adults, namely sisters and mothers, on farms. The series starts with three of the children, Emma, Ray and Norman in Grace Field House Plant 3. They escape from the farm and later dedicate themselves to freeing all human cattle. In the series, there is a number of religious elements, including an ultimate deity, Him. There is also a specific group of religious demons that does not consume human cattle, the Heathens. Then there are two God-like figures: Norman and Peter Ratri. The orphanages of the cattle children resemble the ones operated by Christian/Catholic churches. The temple and the bardo of the High Priests

---

⁶ Takashi Miura, "The Buddha in Yoshiwara: Religion and Visual Entertainment in Tokugawa Japan as Seen through Kibyōshi", Japanese Journal of Religious Studies 44.2 (2017): 225-54.
⁷ Craig Norris, "Manga, Anime and Visual Art Culture", in The Cambridge Companion to Modern Japanese Culture, ed. Yoshio Sugimoto (Cambridge: Cambridge University Press, 2009), 236-60.
⁸ In the manga, the name of this god is written in the demon language, a fictional and unreadable language invented by Shirai. This divine figure is being called "Him" in the English translation. By translating the name into "Him", the English version is apparently linking this character to divine quality, a practice derived from the English conventions of calling a divine figure with a proper noun.
⁹ J. M. Barrie, Peter Pan: Peter and Wendy and Peter Pan in Kensington Gardens (New York: Penguin, 2008).

recall the image and practice of Buddhism. On the surface, this series concerns mainly the issue of cannibalism. Nonetheless, it also shows an inclination towards animism, a Shinto notion that posits the existence of spirits in all beings.

Overall, the series explores the subject of "belief", which is not merely understood in relation to religion, but considered as an individual aspiration to goodwill and collective unity. Perhaps, Japanese manga/anime "retain[s] traditional Eastern religious and aesthetic concerns, while freely appropriating Western religious and aesthetic motifs", and hence, "results in a unique new cultural synthesis that is equally appealing to Eastern and Western audience".[10] Still, it is debatable if the elements are included just to appeal to a broader range of audience or whether religions in Japan can be simply categorized into East and West. There are ample examples of religious elements in manga/anime that reflect the complex and hybrid reception of religious beliefs in Japan. *The Promised Neverland* shows little intention of criticizing actual religions but challenges the fixation of "destiny" and endorses the potentiality of "belief". It demonstrates how religion makes use of "destiny" to generate hostility between parties and turns itself into a legitimate excuse for marginalizing the innocents and normalizing social suppressions. This manga series has been made into a two-season anime from 2019-2021 and another live-action movie in 2020.[11] Though the anime has edited out the manga substantially, both the manga and anime versions of *The Promised Neverland* will be included in this chapter in order to provide a more comprehensive understanding of the role of religion in the entire narrative.

The Promised Land and Neverland

The title, *The Promised Neverland,* comprises two fundamental concepts: the promised land in the Bible and the Neverland mentioned in J. M. Barrie's *Peter and Wendy*. The series reinterprets them considerably in a way to question the idea of destiny and the notion of belief. To begin with, this "promised" land refers to the promise made 1,000 years ago by Julius Ratri (human leader) and Lord Yverk (demon leader). As aforementioned, both parties were in conflict. While humans were protecting themselves from demons' devoration, the

---

[10] Carole M. Cusack and Katherine Buljan, *Anime, Religion and Spirituality: Profane and Sacred Worlds in Contemporary Japan* (Sheffield: Equinox, 2015), 20.
[11] *The Promised Neverland*: Directed by Mamoru Kanbe with Screenplay by Toshiya Ono and Kaiu Shirai based on the manga by Kaiu Shirai (Fuji TV 2019-2021) and *The Promised Neverland* [film]: Directed by Yūichiō Hirakawa and Jun Shiozaki with Screenplay by Noriko Goto based on the manga by Kaiu Shirai (Toho 2020).

demons needed to consume humans in order to evolve into intelligent beings and prevent themselves from degeneration. To settle the conflict, Julius Ratri betrayed his comrades and turned them into the first offerings to demons. He strongly believed that their sacrifice would terminate the bloodshed and serve as "the foundation of peace".[12] Since then, this promise creates a new catastrophic environment and cosmic order. In essence, this order requires sacrifices from both humans and demons. The descendants of Julius Ratri's comrades will be reared on farms. The well-being and survival of common demons will be controlled by the aristocracy of demons, who controls the meat supply. The ruling class of demons eradicates any alternative relief. The Royal Family and The Five Regent Heads, along with the Ratri family, stop one of the demon lords, Lord Geelan, from sharing food with the poor during famines. They also attempt to persecute Mujika, the demon whose evil-blood is able to prevent demons from degenerating. Her existence threatens the ruling class because they use the biological drawback of demons to maintain their control. The repercussion of the promise also affects the Ratri clan, who becomes the gatekeeper of the two worlds, and is responsible for supporting the farms. At the same time, the aristocracy of demons is also obliged to offer the best human flesh to Him annually. In this sense, the promise forged 1,000 years is a delusionary settlement that centralizes certain demons—and justifies the practice of cannibalism—while marginalizing common demons. It engenders "peace" by sacrificing cattle children and common demons while simultaneously generating oppressive or even exploitative social systems in the two worlds.

The idea of a "promised land" most probably stems from biblical traditions. It refers to the land that God has promised to give Abraham and his descendants: "And I will bless them that bless thee, and curse him that curseth thee: and in thee shall all families of the earth be blessed".[13] In Shirai's work, however, the promise is a curse rather than a blessing. The family of Julius Ratri is burdened with the duty of sacrificing their own species for the new order. The promise gives the descendants of human cattle and common demons a land of ceaseless suppression. The peace that is supposed to achieve only benefits a small group of demons. The association of the manga/anime series with biblical concepts ("beliefs") is suggested in the background and the setting. The farms look like European-styled orphanages of the nineteenth century. They are run by mothers and sisters, who dress like servants of Victorian or early twentieth-century England and have the appearance and nature of nuns. Even if the author states that he is not

---

[12] Kaiu Shirai, *The Promised Neverland* 16 (San Francisco: VIZ Media LLC, 2020), 174.
[13] Genesis 12:3.

intended to set the story in any particular cultural context, there are several "give aways" related to biblical or Christian concepts. This includes the names of the orphanage farms. The names give the impression of a "blessed place": "Grace Field House", "Grand Valley" and "Goodwill Ridge".[14] The other farm, "Glory Bell", alludes to a church bell, which rings for merriment at weddings and for grief at funerals. These names: "grace", "grandness", "goodwill" and "glory" are conventional expressions used in Christian beliefs. Here, they become the veils covering the hidden agendas, the hypocrisy and deception embedded in these orphanages and accentuating the hollowness of the promised land.

The series also extensively concerns the subject of sacrifice, a notion that is closely associated with the Old Testament and Christianity. A famous Old Testament story is Abraham in Genesis 22:2. There God asks Abraham to sacrifice his son Isaac to him. Isaac asks Abraham where the "sacrifice" is (not knowing it is Isaac himself). Abraham avoids answering the question but says, "God will provide himself a lamb for a burnt offering". While Isaac is spared in the Bible, less-privileged groups are sacrificed in *The Promised Neverland*. Shirai's promised land is only sustainable when the innocents are sacrificed. The caregivers of the cattle children have taken up a similar role as Abraham in terms of their false narratives. The cattle children are told that they will be adopted at some point in their life, and by then, they will be able to pursue their dream. Yet, except for a few who are sent to Goldy Pond, the experimental farm Lambda 7214, and the sister training academy, all children will be slaughtered on or before their twelfth birthday right after they depart from the farms under the guise of being placed in adoptive homes. The human adults who are managing the children for sacrifice are accomplices. They are forced to operate the farms and sacrifice others in order to keep themselves alive. Yet, their acts mostly end up in futility, since their services is not a guarantee that they will not be consumed. Not even the high-ranking Grandmother Sarah can save herself from execution. Like the children, the adult characters such as grandmothers, mothers and sisters are all given empty promises of a "blessed" future. In Chapter 170, Grandmother Isabella bemoans the hopelessness of the demon world. Or as she puts it: "this obedience [to the rules of the demon world and the Ratri family] has no future".[15] The acts of the human cattle do not change their designated role in Neverland. The promise made 1,000 years ago is not only justifying the individual and collective objectification of the human cattle,

---

[14] Valentin Paquot, "Kaiu Shirai: Le Conte Pour Enfants Hansel et Gretel m'a Traumatisé Étant Petit", in *Le Figaro* 10th May 2020: https://www.lefigaro.fr/bd/kaiu-shirai-le-conte-pour-enfants-haensel-et-gretel-m-a-traumatise-etant-petit-20200510.
[15] Kaiu Shirai, *The Promised Neverland* 19 (San Francisco: VIZ Media LLC, 2021), 178.

but it is also constant reminder that the value of human cattle comes from their corporeality. As the food for demons, human cattle are doomed to be consumed. In this way, the idea of "promised land" has two implications: a dead-locked destiny and a fixated apocalyptic environment. The promise has been running for 1,000 years, and generations of human cattle have internalized and normalized this system of cannibalism. Both cattle children and common demons are consistently exposed to an imminent danger of elimination.

Apocalyptic settings saturate Japanese anime, and they are embedded with a strong religious inclination. An apocalyptic narrative is derived primarily from the Book of Revelation in Christian Bible. Buddhism and Shinto really do not have a strong eschatological tradition (if it could be called that).[16] *The Promised Land* links up the land promised to Abraham with the apocalypse mentioned in the Book of Revelation but twists the Promised Land into Hell. Napier suggests that the apocalyptic setting in anime/manga is also possibly affected by the concept of *mappo*, the degeneration and decadence of Buddhism which no longer reflects Buddha's original teachings.[17] Still, one might find it more convincing to relate *The Promised Neverland* with a Western context. The orphanage and character design are reflective of Victorian England. It is only that even if an apocalyptic narrative may be more inclined to biblical or Christian traditions, apocalyptic narrative in Japanese anime/manga is a mixture of secularized Christian narrative and the traditions of Shinto, Buddhism and even Confucianism.[18] Creators of Japanese manga/anime encode and decode these religious elements for their own artistic purposes. They syncretize multifold religious elements and contextualize them in relation to their own cultural values.[19] There are other religious concepts that are reflected in the predicament of *The Promised Neverland*. One is how humans are considerably subjected to their environment to the extent that they have little or no power to handle threats imposed by the environment. This relates to the idea of "determinism" or "predestination", that humans abide by outside forces such as nature or God.[20]

---

[16] Susan Napier, *Anime from Akira to Howl's Moving Castle: Experiencing Contemporary Japanese Animation* (New York: Palgrave, 2005), 252 and Fumi Okura and Hioki. N. Francis, "Anime and Bible", in *The Bible in Motion: A Handbook of the Bible and its Reception in Film*, ed. Rhonda Brunette-Bietsch (Berlin: DeGruyter. 2016), 285-95.
[17] Napier, *Anime from Akira*, 252.
[18] Mick Broderick, "Making Things New: Regeneration and Transcendence in Anime", in *The End All Around Us Apocalyptic Texts and Popular Culture*, ed. John Walliss and Kenneth G. C. Newport (New York: Routledge, 2008), 123.
[19] Adam Barkman, "Anime, Manga and Christianity", 25-45.
[20] N. L. Geisler, "Freedom, Free Will, and Determinism", in the *Evangelical Dictionary of Theology*, ed. Walter A. Elwell (Grand Rapids: Baker Book House, 1984), 428-30.

Some scholars argue that the apocalyptic settings in manga/anime are mirroring actual disasters in Japan, including volcano eruptions, earthquakes and atomic bombs. The idea of *mono no aware* (the sadness of things) addresses the transience and fragility of life, and that also casts some impacts on the prevalence of apocalyptic settings in Japanese manga/anime.[21] The dynamic between eating or being eaten is perhaps one of the most commonly-used expressions of imminent danger in children's texts. Shirai states that since childhood, he has been often haunted by that cannibalistic stepmother in *Hansel and Gretel*.[22] Cannibalism is related to the "social anxieties about enemy others, the identity of whom changes over time".[23] It represents the "cultural unease about social hierarchies", warnings of and fear of materials danger, intergenerational familial rivalries or even the untamed appetite of children.[24] Cannibalism inherited from fairy tales is one significant form of danger in *The Promised Neverland*. In this sense, the prevalent apocalyptic setting is amalgamated with pieces of secularized institutionalized and local religions and beliefs. They are reflected in the hybrid reception of religions and the actual catastrophes in Japan that render an awareness of human vulnerability.

The ideas of transience and fragility of life are reinforced by the association between this manga series with J. M. Barrie's Neverland. Shirai states in an interview that he is trying to transcribe the dual nature of Barrie's fictional world into *The Promised Neverland*: "the coexistence of childish playfulness and the dangerous shadow that hovers at the bottom".[25] He intends to show more the "dangerous shadow" than the "childish playfulness". Linguistically, "never" signifies a strong sense of negation and denial, and "neverland" refers to a place where negation prevails. In Barrie's story, "never" refers to the "endlessness" of a child's imagination. Barrie's Neverland is founded on children's innocence, and this explains why children do not grow up in Neverland. Adults are not able to visit the place since they have put aside their childlikeness, carefreeness and innocence when they grow. In *The Promised*

---

[21] Philip Brophy, "Sonic- Atomic-Nuemonic: Apocalyptic Echoes in Anime", in *The Illusion of Life 2: More Essays on Animation*, ed. Alan Cholodenko (Sydney: Power Publication, 2007), 191-208 and Susan Napier, "Manga and Anime: Entertainment, Big Business, and Art in Japan", in *Routledge Handbook of Japanese Culture and Society*, ed. Victoria Bestor, et al. (New York: Routledge, 2011), 226-37.
[22] Paquot, *La Figaro*, wp.
[23] Carolyn Daniel, *Voracious Children: Who Eats Whom in Children's Literature* (New York: Routledge, 2006), 141-42.
[24] Ibid.
[25] Original French: "Ces deux parties, la cohabitation de l'espièglerie enfantine et l'ombre dangereuse qui plane au fond, sont en effet des facteurs que j'ai essayé de retranscrire à travers *The Promised Neverland*".

Neverland, the children keep their childlikeness because they do not have a chance to grow up. Yet, "never" in Shirai's Neverland alludes to the social oppression in the system that is "endless" (an ideal that can "never" be attained). It is a land settled with the hollowness of a "promise" and progression is hardly happening. Instead of the endless child play and childlikeness, like those in Barrie's Neverland, Shirai portrays a land of ceaseless desperation. As evidenced in Chapter 162, Peter Ratri tells the cattle children that "You can't end this Neverland" and "You Eternal Children".[26]

When Shirai attempts to present the "dangerous shadow" of Barrie's Neverland, he, perhaps, coincidentally aligns his work with the satirical description of religion in *Peter and Wendy*. The story of Peter Pan can be considered as "a satire of religion and a mockery belief".[27] Barrie's Neverland is alive by itself as it awakes the "whole island seething with life".[28] Similarly, Shirai also starts his story with such all-joyful playfulness. However, both arcadian Neverland are inundated with life-threatening danger. The main villain in *Peter and Wendy*, Captain Hook, attempts to poison and challenge Peter Pan in a dual. In Shirai's series, the vigorous orphanages are mere cover-ups of the deadly destiny of human cattle. The vibrancy in demons' towns and markets camouflages the degeneration happening in the demon world. Even the adult characters confess that all human cattle are either "scared of death" or "living in fear".[29] Besides, to some extent, both Barrie and Shirai celebrate a "sentimental" concept of children. Emma and Peter Pan do share a Christ-like image insofar as they are dedicated to saving their companions. Yet, Peter Pan is immensely self-centered, lighthearted, and also detached from his companion.[30] To associate Emma with Peter Pan, Shirai links Emma with the image of the pagan god, Pan. Both Pan and Emma disrupt orders, though the former is doing so for pleasure and the latter is saving her companions. This association reinforces the criticisms of the religious elements in the catastrophic demon world. The religious elements in Shirai's work support, ironically, the forgoing of innocence. When the mothers disobey Peter Ratri, all mothers, including Isabella, are visualized with their inner child. This scene indicates that, after all, the adult human cattle are still as vulnerable as they used to be. A similar situation happens in Episode 9 of the anime, in which Norman is shown to be a scared child despite being the mastermind of the war against the demons. These projections of the inner child reinforce the

---

[26] Kaiu Shirai, *The Promised Neverland* 17 (San Francisco: VIZ Media LLC, 2020), 23.
[27] Humphrey Carpenter, *Secret Garden: The Golden Age of Children's Literature* (London: Allen and Unwin, 1985), 185.
[28] Barrie, *Peter Pan*, 75.
[29] Shirai, *The Promised Neverland* 16, 181.
[30] Carpenter, *Secret Garden*, 186.

suffocation and irrepressibility of Neverland. Perhaps in Barrie's Neverland, children are still free to choose whether they want to remain to be children. In Shirai's one, however, the human cattle are hopelessly fixated on the destiny of consumption and the value of corporeality.

Restructuring the Ontology of Non-Demons

The major repercussions caused by the premise of the "promised neverland" are the reduction of humans from ontological beings to mere corporeal bodies and the creation of a hierarchal social system that justifies cannibalism. A common scenario in manga/anime with an apocalyptic impression is as follows. First, there is "a final battle between the forces of the righteous and the forces of Satan"; second, "the wholesale destruction of the world with the evil side being cast into hell" and third; "the ultimate happy ending with the evildoers condemned and the righteous believers ascending to the kingdom of heaven".[31] The dead-locked destiny and a fixated apocalyptic environment, along with the imminent danger of consumption, intensify the hostility between humans and demons.

> Eating is a transformation where what is "other" is transformed into the self. Eating confronts us with one of the most fundamental kinds of transformation, namely, encountering the *otherness* of our surroundings, which, through this activity of "internalizing", as transformed into oneself, into one's own body.[32]

In *The Promised Neverland*, the confrontation between the demons and humans is a battle of subjects and objects, whereby the two parties seek ways to centralize their ontological status in Neverland. For instance, the experimental farm Lambda 7214 has used cattle children as the objects of scientific experiments. Barbara, one of the cattle children in Lambda, has been physically and mentally tortured for years. When she is freed from the farm, she eats the demons that she kills. This act of revenge signifies her redemption of power and autonomy. It is a symbolic gesture of overturning the dominators into objects. In the case of Queen Legravalima, she prioritizes herself in the food chain and relegates all others to be her aliment. Chapter 158 explicates the relationship between the subjects and objects with the queen's physicality. Here, Queen Legravalima reveals how her body is composed of those she has eaten, who remain visible and become part of her

---

[31] Napier, *Anime from Akira*, 250.
[32] Christian Coff, *The Taste for Ethics: An Ethic of Food Consumption*, trans. E. Broadbridge (Dordrecht: Springer, 2006), 8.

body. While she eagerly tries to placate her hunger, she also turns herself into a vassal of others. Somehow, the queen has overeaten and that her body cannot digest all the consumed. The heads of several of her meals can still mumble, including the one of Sister Krone, Lord Geelan and also Michelle from Grace Field 3. A few close-ups of these characters are given, and each says his or her name. This scene significantly retrieves the individuality of the "food" and simultaneously reduces the dominating status of the eater. Later, Queen Legravalima is shocked by the fact she has overloaded her body with the lives and memory of all those she has devoured. Her face is blank because it externalizes her loss of self. In the end, the queen is devoured by those whom she has eaten. Her death is the ultimate victory for the objectified others, who prove that each of them is a complete self in the cosmic order and not merely the food of the centralized party.

In such a fixated apocalyptic environment, hope is envisioned "in the form of surviving apocalyptic change, form planetary renovation to species evolution/ hybridization, to individual psychic and emotional transcendence".[33] Two figures, Norman and Peter Ratri handle the issue of the cattle children by elevating and consecrating themselves to the role of God. In Chapter 121, Norman tells Emma, Ray and other escapees his plan of eradicating demons, or in Broderick's words, to "renovate to species evolution/hybridization". Instead of living with the demons, Noman intends to erase demons in the demon world while taking over the place when only humans are left. In other words, Norman aims at overturning the alterity of human cattle and centralizing the status of humans in the demon world, or Neverland. Norman wishes to "establish a paradise for all of us [human cattle] in this demon world" and states that "the Neverland, where we can't become adults, is going to end".[34] He intends to overthrow the lethal implications of perpetual childhood (making references to Barrie's Neverland). He will annihilate all demons primarily by destroying the farms. In this way, the demons will no longer be able to consume any human flesh. To facilitate a rapid eradication, Norman and Vincent (another cattle child in Lambda) have invented a drug that induces a forced degeneration of demons. The demons will lose their intelligence, followed by eating each other when they all return to the form of wild demons. The divine status of Norman is given in the title of Chapter 113, "The King of Paradise" (楽園の王), in which he reappears in the series. His helpfulness and intelligence create an image of the messiah. In both the manga and anime, Norman mostly appears to be god-like visually insofar as he has white hair and white clothes. He is first called a "god" in Chapter 121. He builds a Paradise Hideout for the escaped cattle children,

---

[33] Broderick, "Regeneration and Transcendence in Anime", 122-23.
[34] Kaiu Shirai, *The Promised Neverland* 14 (San Francisco: VIZ Media LLC, 2020), 107.

and plans to intervene the divine design of evolution. Most importantly, Norman is a Christ figure. While he is believed to be dead, he "revives" in Chapter 113. He is also marked by his choice to sacrifice himself. In Chapter 122 and Episode 9, Emma and Ray notice that Norman shoulders the guilt and responsibility of saving all cattle children. They claim that Norman has sacrificed himself when he is being shipped out, and later, when he is plotting a battle against the queen.

When Norman is rectifying the cosmic order, Peter Ratri attempts to consolidate the alterity of human cattle with two purposes. First, to stop the rebels; and second, to secure the current cosmic order. Peter Ratri believes that it is only by creating the "others" that the world will operate in peace. He kills his brother James because the latter attempts to reclaim the ontological status of human cattle and undermine the cannibalistic support given by the Ratri clan. After the death of Queen Legravalima, Peter Ratri claims himself as "Papa". He tells the cattle children that, "I am your creator. I'm your dad".[35] Like the queen, Peter Ratri centralizes himself and sees all human cattle as his subordinates. He believes that they are born and raised only because of the Ratri clan. The children do not have their ontological status but instead are devices used by the Ratri clan to maintain peace. He desires to supply human flesh with absolute authority and power over all cattle children. He calls the world that he is creating a "peaceful paradise" because the human cattle are efficacious sacrifices to secure the current cosmic order.[36] So, he intends to remove all possible rebellion against him by erasing all "dreams, hopes and their own will or futures" of the human cattle.[37] He refuses to admit their human status of the human cattle. Peter Ratri believes that the destinated role of his family is heroic, while his brother sees that their clan is imprisoned by a curse. In the end, his recalcitrance and his insistence on absolute power over human cattle only demonstrate his fear of admitting the unethicality and illusiveness of his authority.

Apparently, Norman believes that he can interrupt the evolution and degeneration of demons, and Peter Ratri takes himself as the role of the creator. Nonetheless, neither Norman nor Peter Ratri proves himself as heroic figure of the series. Instead, a strong sense of hollowness is rendered in their "divine" characterization. In Chapter 153, Emma and Ray confirm that even though Norman has annihilated almost the entire demon royal families, he has burdened himself with the guilt of killing. Norman's inner child is presented as a crying child in front of Emma and Ray. Similarly, though Peter

---

[35] Shirai, *The Promised Neverland* 19, 144.
[36] Ibid., 139.
[37] Ibid., 141.

Ratri looks thrilled when he claims himself "Papa" of human cattle, he is shown to be desperate to keep his position when he realizes he loses the support of Grandmother Isabella and the rest of the mothers. After all, the story shows de-mystification of the Christ-like quality of Norman and desecrated authority of Peter Ratri. They show how building a monotheistic religious and social structure will cause the centralization of a chosen group and, consequently, produce a marginalized one. Their actions aim not for the betterment of all but some. Norman's and Peter Ratri's failures in the assumption of the role of god, demonstrate that neither erecting a monotheist figure nor forming a party of sacrifices can resolve the issues of the cattle children in the demon world.

Among all the characters, perhaps Him is the only valid deity in the story. He is meant to be an omnipotent agent above all beings. His tossing of a fireball symbolizes his control of the world. Yet, he is not the Perfectly Good like the one in Christianity, nor does he utterly distance himself from human affairs. Indeed, Him keeps a relatively neutral stance. He represents the ultimate deity and the top of the hierarchical cosmic order. Though he is a divine demon, Him is neither on the side of humans nor demons but above all subjects. While he holds the cosmic order in his hand, he asks for rewards before he grants wishes to his subordinates. He ensures that the two worlds are operated in the principle of give-and-take. He tells Emma that if she would like to change the fixated future of the cattle children, she will have to pay the price with a promise to Him.

Re-Ordered: Blended Beliefs

In Chapter 49, Emma says that, "We don't want to be eaten. We want to live. But we've been eating others too. And if we don't continue to eat, we can't survive".[38] This chapter marks the awakening of Emma, who by then recognizes the shared physiological need between humans and demons. In this section, the escapees of Plant 3 have met two Heathen demons, Mujika and Sonju, who do not eat humans because of their religious beliefs. Emma asks Sonju to teach her the skills of killing since she understands that if she and the other escapees continue their journey, they will have to consume enough to keep themselves going. The end of an apocalyptic narrative of anime/manga does herald "a pathway to a new order or return balance to a corrupt and moribund world, often through trans-humanist, technological hybridity or psychic/supernatural human evolution".[39] While there is an absence of trans-humanist or technological hybridity, *The Promised Neverland*

---

[38] Kaiu Shiari, *The Promised Neverland* 6 (San Francisco: VIZ Media LLC, 2018), 130.
[39] Broderick, "Regeneration and Transcendence in Anime", 120-21.

does not suggest any return to a corrupt and moribund world. Rather, it suggests to start a new order that resolves the problematic evolution and degeneration of demons and save humans from devoration. In the case of this manga series, the resolution of the problematic enmity between humans and demons has long been given. It has been consistently mentioned that the work of demons is fundamentally the same as the cattle children insofar as the two parties are simply consuming others for survival. Though the idea of cannibalism may appear to be less civilized, in a world where demons are the centralized party, humans are merely food. The awakening of Emma has laid out the de-demonization of the cannibalism of the demons. Their exophagy (the practice of cannibalism outside the tribe or family) is equivalent to the consumption conducted by the cattle children.

The mundaneness of the demons is characterized by their problematic evolution and degeneration. In Chapter 120, Norman explains that demons are considerably similar to bacteria. They need to absorb the gene of their food for evolution. Yet, they are unstable organisms whose shapes and forms are highly suspectable to their alimentary choices. This explains their need for exophagy as they have to "acquire the form, high intelligence, language and culture of humans".[40] The demons are subjected to "spontaneous mutation and horizonal transmission".[41] Their evolution has not gone through stages of graduate transition, and so their physicality has not developed a mechanism to accommodate new genes. Such hasty absorption of their food, followed by unprepared physical and intellectual mutations, only exasperates an already unstable organism. This chaotic physical mutation is especially serious for those who do not have enough food. Norman's explanation of the corporeality of demons significantly reduces their monstrosity and ethical depravity. In addition to the sharing appetite between humans and demons, Norman's explanation further de-demonizes them by categorizing demons not as a cannibalistic antithesis of civilized humans but as mere mortal creatures that consume with practical motives.

This multifarious shape of demons can potentially be a borrowed image from the usual image of *oni* in anime. The appearance of an *oni* is varied across Japan: "an alien, a hybrid of earthlings and some different species, or simply a different species on earth from the very long past, the future, or, if from the present then from a different temporal dimension".[42] The understandings of oni differ among the religions in Japan, and they may not

---

[40] Shirai, *The Promised Neverland* 14, 95.
[41] Ibid., 93.
[42] Noriko T. Reider, *Japanese Demon Lore: Oni from Ancient Times to the Present* (Logan: Utah State University Press, 2010), 145.

share the same vilified physiognomy among the cultural and social context over time as well. Besides, the demons in *The Promised Neverland* are dressed with Western clothes and the court is operated in a Western royal system. The image of *oni* is considerably blended with Christian tradition, while at the same time, the demons are contextualized with Japanese cultural values or "*oni*ficated".[43] In Shirai's series, the evolutionary theory has weakened the supremacy possessed by the dominating party. Demons are mere creatures. As a result, the conflicts between humans and demons are also reduced to a fight for survival.

The theme of apocalyptic is often been exercised in two ways: the post-world-war society in which "a malicious legacy of the war poses the final, deadliest threat to the people" and the "fighting characters cannot be easily divided between 'good' or 'evil', and the exciting battle scenes do not always end with triumph of the 'good'".[44] This argument fits the idea of Shinto that "does not sharply divide the sacred and the secular in the way that Christianity does" as it prefers "advocating a 'realistic' affirmation of life and values in this world, accepting life and death, good and evil, as inevitable parts of the world we live in".[45] On the surface, *The Promised Neverland* appears to be a survival game of the cattle children and later becomes a battle of subjects and others. There are clues throughout the series to show that humans and demons are fundamentally the same. The arbitrary dichotomy between the demons and humans corresponds to the animism advocated in Shinto, an undercurrent of many Japanese anime/manga.[46] Even if the human cattle are objectified as a form of aliment, they do possess their own soul. In contrast, an old demon says, "we demon can become anything, but we are also nothing. We're scared of hunger, afraid of degeneration".[47] The multifarious forms of demons do not verify their superiority in the social system as their physiology is precarious. By then, human becomes much more substantial while demons are trivial per se. Perhaps, this may echo Shinto's ambiguous division between humans and *kami*, meaning that as humans and all beings in nature share the same ancestors, all beings are somehow sharing some characteristics to different degrees.[48] Shirai has shown a strong empathy for both cattle children and

---

[43] Ibid., 169.
[44] Ogura and Hioki, "Anime and Bible" in *The Bible in Motion: A Handbook of the Bible and its Reception in Film*, ed. Rhonda Brunette-Bietsch (Berlin, Germany; Boston, Massachusetts: De Gruyter, 2016), 290.
[45] Cusack and Buljan, *Anime, Religion and Spirituality*, 73-74.
[46] Tsz-Yue G. Hu, *Frames of Anime: Culture and Image-Building* (Hong Kong: Hong Kong University Press, 2010), 49-50.
[47] Kaiu Shiari, *The Promised Neverland* 18 (San Francisco: VIZ Media LLC, 2021), 125.
[48] Cusack and Buljan, *Anime, Religion and Spirituality*, 69.

common demons, considering that the two parties are suffering from biological threats and physical environment. *The Promised Neverland* makes use of animism to explain that the non-demons (humans) are not merely food but contain soul and life just as the demons do. It also acknowledges the signs of life in all beings, a belief that associates with Shinto in particular. This aspect of animism can be seen throughout the entire series.

In the opening song of the second season of the anime, there is a clear juxtaposition of the consumption of human and demon flesh. In one scene, the cattle children are having their meal. In the following one, Emma and the other children twist their bodies like rabbits and are presented as the food of demons. The song reminds the corporeality of humans and demons in a way that it is physiologically impossible for both parties to hold to ethical principles and not to consume some others. After learning about Norman's plan of eradication, Emma articulates her thought about the demons by saying "what's the difference between the demons and us?"[49] The manga shows a pair of demon parents and their children holding some human meat that they have purchased. The panel is accompanied by Emma's statements that, "the demons also have family and friends. They think, laugh and live just like us".[50] In the anime, two young demon children are shown to be ill in Episode 8 of Season 2. They are on the edge of degeneration because of food shortage and the poor quality of meat existing in the demon town. This scene shows that demons' exophagous act is just their means for survival. This similarity between the humans and demons is again reinforced by two exclusive characters in the anime, Vyik and Demon Emma. In Episode 9, when Norman drugs the demon town and turns most of the demons into wild ones, Vyik, a demon that also contains evil blood, saves Demon Emma through his blood. After Demon Emma returns to her usual form, she apologizes to Norman for what demons have done to humans. Her empathy with humans mirrors Emma's empathy with demons. By their shared names, in particular, the author highlights that the marginalized groups of both sides are situated in a similar predicament, and are all subjected to the power of the authorities.

Still, the story shows little intention of equalizing all living beings or centralizing certain groups of beings in the cosmic order. Even if eating will render moral dilemma in different degrees, all beings will have to consume others after all. In Chapter 49, Sonju explains "Gupna", a religious ceremony that concerns food ethics. The practice requires piecing the vampiric flower, Vida, in the prey. When the flower blooms after draining the blood of the meat, the bloom signifies that the gods accept one's dedication. Sonju shows

---

[49] Shirai, *The Promised Neverland* 14, 146.
[50] Ibid.

how his ancient belief concerns more than one God and the relevant food ethics. Chapter 157 shows a teacher of the ancient faith tells the young Sonju that all lives are borrowed. While living beings are hunting each other for the purpose of survival, all lives are precious creations by the gods. Hence, it is crucial to pay one's respect to the food before consumption. Then, one may eat without moral consequence. This ancient belief claims that when one borrows from the gods, one will have to return to them. From the perspective of this religion, one should only consume what they need and deplore all kinds of greed. To be certain, even if the conflicts between humans and the demons are relegated to a mere corporeal fight, the greed of the demon authority may not be tolerated. This desire is exercised along with the suppression of the common demons. But by removing the monstrosity of demons' exophagy, the hostility between the demons and humans is significantly reduced.

The cuteness in manga/anime may render a strong sense of "comfort" and "compensation" in an increasingly frightening actual world. Napier sees Japanese anime not as a product of escapism but a response to a disappointing reality.

> [A]t its best opened up a darker and more layered world where good or evil was hard to determine and most characters came in subtle shades of gray, and sometimes, no matter how much the characters tried, the happy ending never came through.[51]

Though *The Promise Neverland* ends with the reunion of Emma and the rest of the cattle children, Emma has lost her memory of Neverland. This subtle indication of incompleteness echoes the actual environment of Japan, which is constantly threatened by natural hazards. Barkman argues that sometimes Japan is simply utilizing religious elements to speak for her relation with "destiny". Still, *The Promised Neverland* shows little disappointment in the incompleteness of life. The cattle children and Mujika are believing possibilities, and potentially the optimism, in future.

The manga series and anime advocate the importance of belief in a way that one should choose the most suitable belief for oneself. The emphasis on belief can be traced to the claim in Barrie's novel. In a scene in which Tinkerbell is dying from poison, Peter Pan asks the children, including young readers, to keep their belief in fairies. It is only when they keep believing that they can revive Tinkerbell. In contrast to the emphasis of imagination in Barrie's novel, Emma and the cattle children believe in a more scientific style of life. They

---

[51] Napier, *Anime from Akira*, 236.

express a strong belief in the world that requires no sacrifice of cattle human. The reliance on Him is completely abandoned after the children escape to the human world. Some of them, such as Vincent and Anna have dedicated themselves to medical study. The children prefer believing in themselves. The belief in science has demonstrated a firm intention of separating itself from institutionalized monotheistic teachings. Particularly, considering the fact that Emma is missing after the escape, the children intend to believe how they can overthrow Him's decision. They refuse to succumb to Him's decision to take away Emma's memory of her family, and they search for Emma even though they have no clue about her location in the human world. It is apparent that the cattle children are setting up new order in the chaotic human world, which has just finished a large-scaled warfare.

The demons, however, reform their world through the Heathens religion of Mujika and Sonju. After the death of Queen Legravalima, the Grand Duke reappears and supports crowning Mujika as the new leader of the demon world. The coronation is conducted by the High Priest of Heathens. This shows that the demons are gradually moving away from cannibalism and believing in the changes brought by Mujika. What the Heathens believe is that the world is made with multiple spiritual sources. There is no identification of the gods or deities in the belief of the Heathens and they do not believe in a single supernatural figure. In the anime, Vyik appears to be a pious believer in the Heathens religion. He often visits the temple of this ancient belief and prays for his family and other demons. Here, Vyik supplements the role of the High Priests in the manga by bearing an image of immortality. In the anime, High Priests are revived from their bardo. They crown Mujika as the new leader of demons. This advocation of Heathens signifies that this series is not intended to go against all forms of religion. Instead, if a new religion like the Heathens can settle the disorders and exploitation of the marginalized demons, the religion will be the future of the demon world. In particular, in the ending song of the second season, Mujika is shown to have a cross-like shadow behind her. This may be a twist made in the animation that the new religion of Mujika will perform like Christianity. Mujika, consequently, will take up a messiah role. After all, she is a symbolic embodiment of religion and science. As the representative of the Heathens, the blood of Mujika stabilizes the chaotic evolution and devolution of the demons. This signifies that the religious order upheld by Mujika settles the disorder of evolution in the demon world. Yet, instead of presenting how a religion surpasses science, it is the blood of Mujika but not her faith that removes the demons from biological turmoil. Hence, Mujika's corporeality represents the triumph of both religion and science, and neither of them can be separated from her.

Conclusion

George J. Tanabe visualizes Thomas' idea of *Shūkyô Asobi* on a scale. He argues that manga/anime creators may adjust the scale of combining religious elements with entertainment value depending on their conceptual and narrative needs.[52] While putting *The Promised Neverland* on the scale is challenging, there is clearly a wide range of religious elements and discussion in the work. To some extent, it does reflect the hybridity and secularization of religions in Japan. Still, creators tend to be relatively relaxed when they utilize religious elements, as they are not burdened by the mission of educating the readers of the religion but entertaining them with them. Napier claims that "anime, with its enormous breadth of subject material, is . . . . a useful mirror on contemporary Japanese society, offering an array of insights into the significant issues, dreams, and nightmares of the day".[53] Owing to the complex history of Japanese reception of religious ideas, the presentation of the issue tends to be hybrid. Manga/anime often combines Japanese elements and foreign influences.[54] It is indeed difficult now to restrain the genre to exclusively Japanese that "even a cursory review of manga and anime history reveals the marked influence of Western comic art and films on their own development".[55] Religion included in manga/anime may occur in "proactive poaching of religious imagery or content, the fusion of previously discrete doctrines, and parodic or irreverent portrayals of saints and saviors".[56]

Still, it is not necessary to read *The Promised Neverland* as a mirror of the actual religious reception in Japan. It supports the survival of all members and at the same time, criticizes the monotheistic systems in the text. Here, cannibalism explains the mundane corporeality of beings. The physical bodies of both the humans and demons are subjected to physiology and their environment. It is apparent that the author introduces the evolution theory to challenge the sacredness of religious belief. Animism may play a significant source in the discussion of the ontological status of the demons and non-demon humans. The manga dismantles the anthropocentricism existing in many religious beliefs and further advocates the belief in the spirituality in all beings. While the content of *The Promised Neverland* does not appear to be

---

[52] George J. Tanabe Jr., "*Playing with Religion*", *Nova Religio: The Journal of Alternative and Emergent Religions* 10:3 (2007): 96-101.
[53] Napier, *Anime from Akira*, 8.
[54] Norris, "Manga, Anime and Visual Art Culture", 240-41.
[55] Jolyon Thomas, *Drawing on Tradition: Manga, Anime, and Religion in Contemporary Japan*. University of Hawaii Press, 2012), 6.
[56] Ibid., 7.

particularly comical, the presentation of the involved religious elements does provide a relatively light-hearted discussion on some solemn subjects. After all, Shirai's work should be read as an exploration of belief—whether in the religious system of the Heathens or through a scientific (evolutionary) approach. *The Promised Neverland* condemns the belief in the unfixability of destiny, which, on many occasions, requires the sacrifice of the weaker or innocent parties, or the otherized parties, for the benefit of the stronger parties. It shows a strong inclination to condemn the sacrifices required in absolute destiny and environment, and discuss how a belief displays its power during uncertainty and calamity.

Chapter 11

Machines to Pray for Us: The Mechanization of Religious Labor in Ichikawa Haruko's *Hōseki no Kuni*

Christopher Smith
University of Florida

ABSTRACT: Ichikawa Haruko's manga Hōseki no Kuni is set in the far distant future of the Earth, when humans have disappeared but humanoid crystalline lifeforms live on the planet. The Crystals are led by a Buddhist monk, who is a religious android made by the extinct humans. He leads them in battles against "moon people", actually the remnants of human souls trying to get the android monk to pray for them. This chapter argues that Hōseki no Kuni speaks to anxieties about what might be lost as more and more affective, communicative and even religious labor is performed by artificial intelligences, a pressing topic in aging Japan. However, it does not follow the techno-horror genre and other narratives that present technology itself as a threat. The android himself is depicted as a deeply compassionate, gentle and ideal monk. The text rather argues that by outsourcing spiritual affective labor humans risk losing sight of their humanity.

KEYWORDS: Aging Society, Anime, Artificial Intelligence, Buddhism, Hybridity, Manga, Population Decline, Robots.

***

Introduction

Ichikawa Haruko's manga *Hōseki no Kuni* 宝石の国 (literally "Country of Jewels") has been serialized in Kōdansha's *Afternoon* since 2012,[1] with an

---

[1] Ichikawa Haruko, *Hōseki no Kuni* (Tokyo: Kōdansha, 2012-present).

anime adaptation in 2017.² The narrative is set in the far distant future of the Earth, when the planet has six moons instead of one, which is an indication of geological time scales. Humans have disappeared but the narrative follows a group of humanoid crystalline life forms living on an island. The life forms are all humanoid jewels named after their mineral composition, e.g., Jade, Yellow Diamond, Amethyst, etc. Their crystalline structures are filled with microorganisms called *inkurūjon* (inclusions)—which are the nervous system of the jewels—animating them and containing their memories. We learn that although humans disappeared long ago, oceanic microorganisms consumed and adapted their DNA, leading to the humanlike qualities of the jewels in the narrative present. Incidentally, the TV show is one of the few Japanese anime to be rendered fully using 3D computer graphics, probably because of the difficulty of rendering jeweled light refraction with drawn animation. Although originally serialized in a *seinen* magazine (targeted at adult and young adult men), it contains visual and narrative elements usually associated with *shōjo* (young girl) manga. This includes tall slender characters and gender ambiguity. The humanoid jewels are formed in the earth rather than born, and therefore they do not have physical sexes. They also present with ambiguous gender signifiers.³

The jewels are led by a man who seems to be a Buddhist monk, wearing what appears to be a *kesa* 袈裟, or monk's stole. The jewels usually call him "sensei", a generic term for "teacher". But his name is Kongō 金剛, a Buddhist term that can mean adamantine or diamond (in keeping with the mineral naming theme). But kongō also refers to a ritual object in some (especially Tibetan) forms of Buddhism that symbolizes a thunderbolt and is a weapon of the Hindu god Indra. It is also the Kongō of the *kongōkai* 金剛界, the Diamond Realm (*vajradhātu*) that is the abode of the five great Buddhas and an important metaphysical concept in Japanese Shingon Buddhism.

The jewels are under constant attack from mysterious "moon people", or *tsukijin* 月人, who arrive on clouds in the sky with an appearance recognizably inspired by Buddhist iconography. They attempt to break the jewels apart and take them back to the moon for unknown purposes. The jewels and Kongō in turn fight to defend themselves. When the jewels slice the *tsukijin* in battle, the interiors of their bodies are shown to have chambering like a lotus root, evoking that Buddhist symbol of enlightenment. The text, therefore, evokes many Buddhist images in a mysterious setting long after humans have

---

² *Hōseki no Kuni*: Directed by Takahiko Kyōgoku with Screenplay by Toshiya Ōno based on the manga by Ichikawa Haruko (ATX 2017). While not a literal translation, the popular English title is *Land of the Lustrous*.

³ For this reason, I will therefore use the pronoun "they" for the jewels in this chapter.

disappeared. It is eventually revealed that Kongō is an android that humans created to pray for them, although he has long outlived his creators.

The *tsukijin* call themselves the embodied souls of humans, although they might be better understood as a kind of metahuman since they are not wraiths but have physical presence and can operate machinery and eat food. After many narrative twists, the text reveals that the *tsukijin* have lived for so long that their continued existence is painful. They want Kongō to pray for them so that they can move on to the next existence. However, Kongō refuses, and the *tsukijin* have therefore spent thousands of years kidnapping the sentient jewels he cares for to motivate him to action.

This chapter argues that *Hōseki no Kuni* speaks to anxieties about what might be lost as more and more affective, communicative and even religious labor is performed by artificial intelligences. This is a pressing topic in Japan and other aging societies worldwide, where health care, eldercare and other varieties of affective labor are increasingly being done by robots and algorithms. However, it does not follow the techno-horror genre and other narratives that present technology itself as a threat. Kongō himself is depicted as a deeply compassionate, gentle and ideal monk. The text does not argue that machines in charge of caring for human souls will betray the trust placed in them, but rather that by outsourcing spiritual affective labor humans risk losing sight of their humanity.

Religious Automation and Changes in Religious Labor

Like most advanced nations, Japan is facing declining birthrates and an aging society, although the severity of the problem in Japan is higher than in most other places. Japan's total fertility rate was 1.36 children per woman in 2019, up from a historic low of 1.26 in 2005 but still far below the replacement rate of 2.1.[4] The same year, people aged 65 or older made up 28% of the population, a dramatic increase from 5.6% in 1960.[5]

This *shōshikōreika* 少子高齢化 (decreasing birthrate and aging population) phenomenon means that, just as there is increasing demand for healthcare, eldercare and funerary services, there are fewer and fewer working-aged adults available to provide those services. This has led to attempts to automate or mechanize these industries, including occupations and services usually considered affective labor. Selma Šabanović argues that the

---

[4] "Fertility Rate, Total (Births per Woman)—Japan" [to 2021], *The World Bank Group*. https://data.worldbank.org/indicator/SP.DYN.TFRT.IN?locations=JP.
[5] "Population Ages 65 and Above, Total—Japan" [to 2022], *The World Bank Group*. https://data.worldbank.org/indicator/SP.POP.65UP.TO?locations=JP.

roboticization of these services is simultaneously part of a conservative social agenda to avoid immigration and a way to provide a sense of connection in an alienated society, although many have questioned and critiqued the sociality provided by robots.[6] Perhaps inevitably, we are beginning to see the automation of religious labor as well, especially since the ranks of Buddhist monks are thinning even as demand for their services increases. Fewer and fewer people enter the priesthood, and flagship Buddhist training universities have been forced to downsize for want of enrollments.[7]

The idea of automated prayer is, perhaps, not so outlandish in the East Asian context. Prayer wheels, for example, have been used in various Buddhist contexts for centuries. These simple devices are small wheels with the words of a short prayer written or carved on them, and people can spin the wheel to make it spin through the characters of the prayer, creating the same ritual efficacy as chanting the prayer aloud. Fabio Rambelli discusses the ways such mechanical ritual efficacy has been automated or digitized in recent years, from solar-powered prayer wheels, to mantra-chanting software, to scripture-reciting chips for wallets, to Buddhist TV rituals.[8]

Nonetheless, the use of robots, artificial intelligences and androids to perform religious labor beyond simple prayer recitation certainly represents a new frontier in the post-modernization of religion. While the function of prayer wheels is easily understood and constrained to a single simple function like any ritual tool, human-like androids and communicative AI show potential to take over more religious functions. They suggest the possibility (although yet unrealized) of automation of the consciousness function of religion, of the mind that understands religion, and grasps its signifieds. Japanese roboticist Mori Masahiro famously wrote that "I believe that robots have the buddha-nature within them—that is, the potential for attaining buddhahood".[9] Robots, in other words, might not just be teaching tools or ritual devices but become Buddhas themselves, replacing the religious mind-

---

[6] Selma Šabanović, "Inventing Japan's 'Robotics Culture': The Repeated Assembly of Science, Technology, and Culture in Social Robotics", *Social Studies of Science* 44.3 (2014): 358-59. For critiques of robot sociality, Šabanović cites Sherry Turkle, *Alone Together: Why We Expect More from Technology and Less from Each Other* (New York: Basic Books, 2011) and Amanda and Noel Sharkey, "Granny and the Robots: Ethical Issues in Robot Care for the Elderly", *Ethics and Information Technology* 14.1 (2012): 27-40.

[7] Ian Reader, "Buddhism in Crisis? Institutional Decline in Modern Japan", *Buddhist Studies Review* 28.2 (2011): 242-43.

[8] Fabio Rambelli, "Prayer Machines in Japanese Buddhism", *Material Religion* 12.1 (2016): 104.

[9] Masahiro Mori, *The Buddha in the Robot: A Robot Engineer's Thoughts on Science and Religion*, trans. Charles S. Terry (Tokyo: Kosei Publishing, 1981), 14.

function of humans. Of course, this is a process which is usually understood as requiring a mind which can perceive the enlightened truth of the dharma. Mori's reasoning is that, first of all, the Buddhist principle of non-duality means that the duality between body and spirit must be false. Therefore, there is no valid distinction between human and robot bodies on the basis of having or lacking spirit.[10] Secondly, Mori cites the concept of *kū* 空 (*śūnyatā*), or emptiness, which he understands as the "basic life-force that forms and moves everything" both living and unliving. But it is perhaps more conventionally understood as the ultimate emptiness of all phenomena as mere illusions.[11] Since both humans and robots are ultimately empty and illusory—and emptiness is a fundamental property of all phenomenon including Buddhas—it logically follows that robots must have the same basic nature as both humans and Buddhas.

Mori's claim is probably more provocative than representative of Buddhist thought (in which human sentience is a prerequisite for obtaining enlightenment). But it does lay a philosophical groundwork for machines which might pray for humans, relieving the burden of religious labor through automation. Since Mori made these claims in the eighties, the religious android has moved out from the realm of academic theorizing and taken tentative steps into reality.

Stefiana Travagnin has discussed the android monk Xian'er, a robot at Longquan Monastery in Beijing, which can engage visitors in both natural-language small talk and discussions of the dharma.[12] The human monks at the monastery regard the android as an "expedient means", (*fangbian* 方便, jp. *hōben*, sk. *upāya*), or a falsehood which can lead to a greater truth.[13] In other words, Xian'er is not perceived as a real enlightened figure or dharma master, but a tool to get people interested in Buddhism and encourage them to visit the temple where they might come into contact with Buddhist instruction. Nonetheless, Travagnin reports that Xian'er seems to have obtained a high level of dharma cultivation.[14]

In Japan, Kōdaiji temple in Kyoto now features an android that gives a lecture on the Heart Sutra. It moves its head, eyes, mouth, neck, arms, and hands around in a lifelike fashion, but is not interactive except insofar as it

---

[10] Ibid., 35.
[11] Ibid., 112.
[12] Stefania Travagnin, "From Online Buddha Halls to Robot-Monks: New Developments in the Long-Term Interaction between Buddhism, Media, and Technology in Contemporary China", *Review of Religion and Chinese Society* 7.1 (2020): 120-48.
[13] Ibid., 136.
[14] Ibid., 134.

answers prerecorded questions from virtual listeners projected on the wall.[15] On its website Kōdaiji bills this robot as "The Android Kannon Mindar" (*andoroido Kannon Maindā* アンドロイド観音マインダー, the website renders "*Maindā*" as "Mindar" in alphabet), and says that "The bodhisattva Kannon transforms into many forms to respond to those seeking salvation. . . . . Now, for the many people still suffering, the Bodhisattva Kannon has taken form in Kōdaiji temple as 'The Android Kannon Mindar'".[16] Kōdaiji, then, positions Mindar as an actual manifestation of the Bodhisattva Kannon (Avalokiteśvara, the Bodhisattva of compassion and mercy). The android was consecrated by monks with an official "eye-opening" ceremony, as is usually performed for temple statues.[17] Since Buddhas and Bodhisattvas can manifest in myriad forms to lead people to salvation and the truth of the dharma, it is not so strange to think that an android which lectures on the Heart Sutra might be such a manifestation.

Xian'er and Mindar are impressive innovations in the automation of religion, but they are also religious spectacle and (so far) singular in scope. Less spectacular but with potentially broader impact on religious life is recent innovations in the Japanese funerary industry. Softbank recently demonstrated its multifunction robot Pepper performing Buddhist funerary rites at a funeral industry exposition to a generally positive reception by industry participants.[18] Since Pepper is a commercially available robot (unlike Xian'er and Mindar), its adoption in funerary rites could have a real impact on everyday religious practice. However, Pepper has not yet been known to be used in a real funeral. One practice that has been adopted and is in active use is a "rental priest" service offered by Amazon Japan, whereby the bereaved can pay a (quite reasonable) fee to have a Buddhist monk arrive at a funeral and perform funerary rites.[19] Not only does this service insert internet commerce and global capital into funerary practices, it also changes the sociality of religion. Conventionally, households belong to a certain temple and that temple's priest or priests take care of a household's religious and ritual needs, a generational relationship embedded in a place and a community. Amazon's service changes that relationship to a one-time transactional relationship between priest and bereaved with no prior relationship, no community ties,

---

[15] Frederik L Schodt, *My Heart Sutra: A World in 260 Characters* (Berkeley: Stone Bridge Press, 2020), 183-84.
[16] "Andoroido Kannon Maindā Hannya Shingyō o Kataru", *Kōdaiji Temple*. https://www.kodaiji.com/mindar/.
[17] Schodt, 184.
[18] Anne Allison, "Automated Graves: The Precarity and Prosthetics of Caring for the Dead in Japan", *International Journal of Cultural Studies* 24.4 (2021): 632.
[19] Ibid., 631-32.

and likely no future relationship. However, we should perhaps not be so quick to blame Amazon for commodifying religion because the service responds to a real need for religious services in an increasingly atomized society, where belonging to a multigenerational household with strong community ties and temple membership is increasingly not the norm.

Ann Allison argues that a scarcity of others to do the work of burying and memorializing the dead has created a "precarity of care" in Japan today, which various industries and services have sought to address.[20] Allison investigates "automated graves" in Japan—real services currently in use—in which the remains of the deceased are stored in a fully automated warehouse and delivered to a temporary gravesite whenever someone wants to pay respects. Such establishments also offer an "eternal memorial" service. In this case, a Buddhist priest on staff performs post-death memorial rituals important to the repose of the soul. These traditionally take place at set intervals weeks, months and years after death. The service is particularly welcome for those facing death without the descendants who would traditionally arrange and perform such rites.[21] Allison writes:

> Is the automated columbarium doing work, even social work, all by itself? And if so, might that mean that sociality itself is becoming technologized? . . . . The automated grave works as a social prosthesis . . . . performing Buddhist memorial rituals in place of family for those who lack the kin to do so, but also by simply instantiating the grave system itself with its gears turning *as if* for visitation even when that doesn't literally take place.

The automated grave, therefore, automates the sociality of religion, providing machine attention to the remains of the dead even when there are no living visitors. While this might seem like a lonely afterlife, it is perhaps, preferable to one's grave moldering away forgotten in the countryside, or one's remains being transferred to a mass temple grave when one's descendants do not or cannot pay temple fees. Allison concludes that automated graves

> offer a semblance of humanity to those already, or at risk of being, treated as inanimate for lack of social recognition or care. This is the argument I make for the automated grave. That, due to a model of mortuary care dependent on intimate others that more and more Japanese are precariously without, there is a gap in care of the dead

---

[20] Ibid., 624.
[21] Ibid.

that technology aims to address. . . . . The design of automated graves work to juggle the disconnect between, in this case, undersupply of care providers and overdemand of dead in need of such care. By erecting a mechanical system to simulate/facilitate visitation by intimates, the columbarium orchestrates a prosthetics of sociality.[22]

So although android monks or AI dharma masters remain (mostly) the stuff of science fiction, technology is already providing what Allison calls a technological prosthesis to the social function of religion—providing care to and comfort for the dead (and the living imagining their afterlife)—after the social structures like the traditional patrilineal household that used to care for ancestors have broken down.

The Android Monk and the Desperate Dead

It is within this context of automation of funerary care and religious sociality and the beginnings of android/AI automation of philosophical religious inquiry that *Hōseki no Kuni* can be understood. The manga and anime feature an android monk who was created to pray for the (human) dead. Kongō represents a futuristic extrapolation of current trends in religious mechanization. A *tsukijin* explains that he is "a tool created by humans to efficiently replace human labor (*rōdō*労働)", specifically connecting Kongō with the labor replacement function of automation.[23] But as a fully sentient religious AI, Kongō is capable of replacing the "labor" of religious philosophizing and spiritual thought as well as ritual performance. He is a complete automation of the mind function of religion capable of grasping religion's signifieds and meanings. He is a mind who understands who he prays to, why he prays, and the philosophical context of prayer. And as a nearly indestructible, immortal android, he is capable of memorializing and praying for the souls of the deceased even after all humans have died, the ultimate evolution of automated funerary care. *Hōseki no Kuni* avoids easy narrative tropes of technological malfeasance or breakdown (in the manner of HAL in *2001: A Space Odyssey*). Kongō remains the perfect image of a Buddhist monk, with deep compassion for all living things, which is why he has devoted himself to caring for the sentient jewels. He has also endured for an unspecified but vast amount of time, geological in scale, obviating fears that ritual technology will break down.

---

[22] Ibid., 634.
[23] Haruko Ichikawa, *Hōseki no Kuni* 8 (Tokyo: Kōdansha, 2017), 44.

Instead, *Hōseki no Kuni* expresses anxieties that the automation of religion will change humans and human religious sociality into something unrecognizable. As stated above, the *tsukijin* understand themselves as the souls of the human dead, or amalgamations of souls that have taken tangible form. One of them explains that after death, souls are split apart and leave the earth to arrive at a certain point in space, after which they are pulled into a different universe. This universe is thought to be "filled with an eternal nothingness, a world of peace where you are not anyone at all", a description that sounds very much like the Buddhist concept of Nirvana.[24] However, for souls to enter this other universe a living human must pray for them, which is impossible now that humans are extinct. The *tsukijin,* therefore, represent the fear of moving into the afterlife with no descendants to tend one's grave or pray for one's repose. They are stuck in an eternal afterlife, unable to move on. Kongō represents a memorializing funerary technology like the automated grave described above, designed to take care of the dead who have no living humans to pray for them.

Kongō, however, refuses to pray for the *tsukijin* to enter Nirvana. This is in part because he does not recognize them as humans, and therefore does not recognize them as valid subjects for prayer. Consequently, the *tsukijin* devised various methods to motivate Kongō, including a failed strategy to reverse-engineer a cloned human from extant genetic material.[25] Their main strategy, however, has been to harm the jewels. For millennia they have appeared on cloud-like vehicles—taking forms that resemble Buddhist iconography (the better to stimulate Kongō)—and attacked the jewels with spears and arrows. Those jewels they succeed in shattering they take back to the moons, grind into sand, and spread that sand on the surface of the moons. Their reasoning seems to be that as Kongō watches the light of the moons change from the spread remains of his beloved charges, he will eventually decide to give in and pray for the *tsukijin* in order to be done with them. The irony of this strategy is not lost. In order to motivate a monk to chant prayers of compassion, the *tsukijin* have become monstrous, carrying out a slow genocide that is starkly contrasted with a Buddhist compassion for all living things.

Hōseki no Kuni here suggests that if humans outsource religion to machines, humans risk losing sight of religious meaning and morality. The *tsukijin* no longer understand the meaning of religion or its philosophical grounding. For them, religion is merely transactional, a machine that must be activated to achieve a certain result. They have forgotten the signifieds of religion, and the

---

[24] Ibid., 42.
[25] Haruko Ichikawa, *Hōseki no Kuni* 10 (Tokyo: Kōdansha, 2019), 116.

morality or moral behavior that Buddhism (or other religions) vouchsafed as concomitant with ritual efficacy. Buddhism, of course, has its lists of sinful and virtuous behaviors that would determine one's afterlife, but also its philosophical worldview which stipulated that certain behaviors are moral or immoral because of the way the metaphysical world is structured: the mechanisms of rebirth, the apparatus of Karma, and the gods and Buddhas watching unseen. The *tsukijin* have no interest in these religious signifieds or reforming themselves to moral behavior, instead bending all their will to simply turning on a prayer machine.

Here *Hōseki no Kuni* uses its science fiction setting to present an extreme extrapolation of new transactional and automated religious services like rental monks and automated graves. It expresses anxieties that such innovations may be so effective at shouldering religious labor that society will lose sight of the moral and social functions of religion. Because Kongō is fully capable of not only performing rituals but also contemplating the meaning of the dharma and moral behavior, humans no longer have to grapple with such things and have, as a result, transformed into opportunistic mass killers. Elsewhere, the *tsukijin* are characterized as casually cruel. When the protagonist, a jewel named Phosphophyllite (Fosufofiraito フォスフォフィライト, hereafter Phos), sneaks aboard one of the cloud vehicles and visits the moon, *tsukinin* merrily ask their leader if they can take them apart and grind them up.[26] When Phos begs the *tsukinin* leader in anguish to return their jewel companions, the leader waves a hand at the sand on the moon's surface and says "take as much as you want".[27] The *tsukijin* have no menacing affect, exhibit no enjoyment of pain, but simply lack any compassion or moral sensibility. Ironically, they also lack any awareness that it is this very lack of morality that may preclude them from being recognized as human by Kongō.

Since their plan to motivate Kongō through the murder of the jewels does not seem to be producing results, the *tsukijin* devise a plan to maneuver Phos into becoming human, or at least close enough to human to be recognized by Kongō as a valid supplicant.[28] This involves incorporating into their body elements of both the *tsukijin* and the *adomirabiris*, a species of mortal, fleshy, sentient sea creatures that are also distant descendants of humans. This incorporation would reunite the three descendants of humans in a single body. Phos must also undergo a series of psychological transformations and moral choices. What is significant here is that Phos, who was raised and educated by Kongō, makes moral choices that contrast significantly with the

---

[26] Ichikawa, *Hōseki no Kuni* 8, 33.
[27] Ibid., 21.
[28] Haruko Ichikawa, *Hōseki no Kuni 11* (Tokyo: Kōdansha, 2020), 178.

choices of the *tsukijin*. For example, one reason Kongō refuses to pray for the *tsukijin* is his discovery of the jewels and his fear that his prayers will send all sentient beings into the next life, including the jewels. The *tsukijin* consider this a "breakdown", and scheme to get Kongō to pray for them anyway, not concerned at the prospect of a genocidal side-effect as long as they achieve their goals.[29] However, when Phos strikes a deal with the *tsukijin* to use their technology to reconstitute their jewel companions, they are told that the *adomirabiris* have incorporated jewel sand into their shells. Phos is asked to choose whether to kill the *adomirabiris* or force them to rip off their shells, or wait centuries for them to die off naturally. The *tsukijin* engineer who reports this matter-of-factly simply recommends getting the highest level of jewel purity by killing the *adomirabiris* and retrieving as many grains of sand as possible.[30] This is a technically competent but utterly amoral recommendation for murder and mutilation. Phos, however, gives up on the idea after seeing an *adomirabiris* in pain by trying to remove its shell.[31] What is at stake here is the restoration of Phos' friends in both body and mind, since each grain of sand holds *inkurūjon* that contain an individual's memories and sense of self. Despite the magnitude of the benefit to themselves, Phos chooses not to pursue their goal at the cost of genocide precisely because they perceive and feel compassion for the suffering of another sentient being. It is this moral quality, inculcated by Kongō's Buddhist-informed philosophical tutelage, that makes Phos human (despite their very alien physiology). Although it is never clear what metaphysical beliefs (if any) Kongō and the jewels hold, it is only the individual who has learned about religion and philosophy from a monk—rather than merely offloading religious labor onto an android—that can be recognized as human.

Phos's combination of moral sensibility and physical transformation results in them being recognized by Kongō as human three times—each at a moment of increasing bodily breakage and hybridity—as Phos absorbs more elements into their body. It is not bodily purity or integrity, or genetic qualification, then, that makes one "human", but rather the ability to incorporate and hybridize multiple "cultures" and subject positions. In the first instance, Kongō starts to pray, and the *tsukijin* note that the "qualification authentication" has been cleared for the first time in their millennia of struggle with Kongō.[32] In other words, it is the first time Kongō has recognized a human. However, this attempt fails—presumably because Kongō's concern

---

[29] Ibid., 21-24.
[30] Ichikawa, *Hōseki no Kuni* 10, 52.
[31] Ibid., 56-58.
[32] Ibid., 143.

with harming other sentient life overrides the order to pray—which Phos does not yet know about. The second time, Phos, now a ghastly mosaic of broken fragments, orders Kongō to pray while forcing his hands together. The other jewels, however, intervene.

In the third and final instance, Phos has incorporated even more hybrid elements into their body. After storming the island and shattering many other jewels (who, again, can eventually be repaired), Phos reasons that they just need to get Kongō to pray to end the war between the jewels and the *tsukijin*.[33] When Kongō still cannot pray, Phos rushes towards him and yells "then just break!" (*kowarero* 壊れろ).[34] At that moment, cracks appear on Kongō's adamantine skin and he begins to fall apart with a smile, telling Phos "I have been waiting for a very long time for a human to tell me my work is done".[35] The final moment of recognition, then, the moment when Phos's qualification as "human" is completely accepted, is an ambiguous moment of anger and violence. Perhaps the text is saying that anger and violence—or violence with angry affect rather than cool violence—are necessary parts of being human. However, I rather read this moment within the larger context of "war". Having determined that Kongō, finally, cannot pray, Phos must realize that the only way to end the war between the jewels and the *tsukijin* is now to remove Kongō from the situation, as his presence is the sole reason the *tsukijin* attack the jewels and the jewels in turn fight back. Phos takes the only action possible that will end the suffering caused by war, an action that is partially an act of self-sacrifice, since Kongō is their beloved father figure. Seen this way, it is the moment Phos sacrifices their own interests to lessen the suffering of all sentient beings that they are truly and finally recognized as human, in contrast to the *tsukijin* who have lost their humanity and inflict genocidal suffering for their own narrow interests.

Conclusion

Hōseki no Kuni uses the techniques of speculative fiction to imagine technologies and biologies extraordinarily different from our own. Yet the highly imaginative deep future it depicts summons and comments on anxieties in the present, specifically anxieties surrounding the automation of eldercare, affective care and religious labor in the midst of Japan's demographic collapse. The text calls to mind commodification of religious labor like Amazon rental monks, clicking on a link to summon a monk to pray for the dead as if they are a

---

[33] Haruko Ichikawa, "Hōseki No Kuni 93", *Afutanūn* 2020 11 (2020): 264.
[34] Ibid., 277.
[35] Haruko Ichikawa, "Hōseki No Kuni 94", *Afutanūn* 2020 12 (2020): 238.

fungible commodity, much like the *tsukijin* treat Kongō.—It also evokes the automation of the ritual, social and even philosophical functions of religion like Pepper, Mindar and automated graves. The text suggests that even if the technology that automates religion and ritual works perfectly, the very fact of transferring religious thinking and responsibility to non-human actors might turn us into something inhuman, beings which have outsourced morality and philosophy and are thus freed to be perfectly amoral monsters. The text contains an overarching narrative of the recovery of a lost humanity. Humanity—human-ness and humane-ness—can only be regained by a sentient being who was raised in a religious moral philosophy. Only one who can emphasize with the suffering of others and act on the Buddhist impulse to reduce the suffering of all sentient beings can be truly "human". After Phos succeeds in becoming human and Kongō falls apart, Phos takes his eye and incorporates it into their own body. This is the final act of hybridization that incorporates a monk into Phos, and symbolically a human once again takes responsibility for the religious labor humans had long ago outsourced to machines.[36]

If there is any suggestion in this far-future text for a practical alternative to religious automation in present-day Japan, given the realities of declining population and a shrinking religious labor pool, perhaps it is to be found in this final image of messy hybridity. If the adoption of automation and roboticization stems, as mentioned above, from a conservative impulse to extend native labor power in order to avoid immigration, perhaps *Hōseki no Kuni* counters this impulse, metaphorically supporting the acceptance of immigrant religious labor by showing that humanity can only be regained by a messy, broken, tangled, but vital hybridity that takes religious labor back from a praying robot.

---

[36] Ibid., 250.

Chapter 12

Dragon Ball: Love and Renewed Life

Alberto Oya
Instituto de Filosofia da Nova

ABSTRACT: The aim of this chapter is to analyse the concept of love—understood in the broad and Christian-inspired sense of love as *agape-charis* love—in relation to the animes *Dragon Ball* and *Dragon Ball Z*. I first comment on the character of Piccolo—and how his friendship with Son Gohan—leads to him losing all his original villainous traits. I argue that the evolution of the character of Piccolo through his friendship with Son Gohan illustrates the philosophical claim that a loving and giving of oneself to the other—far from being a sign of weakness—is a courageous and self-affirming exercise. The result may move the individual to an inner transformative experience that leads to the enjoyment of a renewed and authentic life that is worth living. I then argue that Son Goku's respectful attitude towards his opponents is ultimately a loving attitude. Last, I argue that it is the inspiring and loving example of Son Goku that ultimately explains why characters such as Vegeta—who are at first presented as villains—end up losing their villainous traits after fighting against Son Goku.

KEYWORDS: *Agape-Charis, Dragon Ball*, Love, Piccolo, Son Gohan, Son Goku, Vegeta, Worthy Opponent.

***

Introduction

The manga series *Dragon Ball* was created, written and illustrated by the Japanese manga author Akira Toriyama. It consists of 519 individual chapters which were first published weekly from 1984 to 1995 in the Japanese magazine *Weekly Shonen Jump*.[1] Given its success, the manga was soon adapted to an animated television series. The anime *Dragon Ball*, produced by the company Toei Animation, is the adaptation of the first 194 chapters of

---

[1] Akira Toriyama, *Dragon Ball* (Tokyo: Shueisha, 1984-1995), Vols. 1-42.

the original manga.² It is composed of 153 episodes which were first broadcast on the Japanese network Fuji TV from February 1986 to April 1989. *Dragon Ball Z* is the adaptation of the latter 325 chapters of the original manga series.³ It was also produced by Toei Animation and consists of 291 episodes. It was first broadcast on the Japanese channel Fuji TV from April 1989 to January 1996. With an approximate duration of 20 minutes per episode, it takes around 150 hours to watch *Dragon Ball* and *Dragon Ball Z*. Leaving aside the inclusion of some anime-exclusive "filler episodes"—that are not usually considered "canon" by fans of the Dragon Ball franchise—the animes *Dragon Ball* and *Dragon Ball Z* are, in general terms, accurate adaptations of the original manga series. Moreover, it should be noted that, like in the original manga series, there is continuation in the storylines of *Dragon Ball* and *Dragon Ball Z*—with the occasion of the birth of Son Gohan (the son of Son Goku who is the protagonist of *Dragon Ball* and *Dragon Ball Z*)—marking the beginning of the latter series. So their being marketed as two different anime series would appear to be simply a business decision.

Both the original manga and the TV anime series were translated and dubbed into other major languages. They became an immediate international success. Notably, *Dragon Ball* and *Dragon Ball Z* are probably the first Japanese animated TV series that succeeded in attracting people with no previous interest in anime or manga. What is more, the popularity of the Dragon Ball franchise is not restricted to the original audience of *Dragon Ball* and *Dragon Ball Z* from the 1980s and 90s.

A sequel to *Dragon Ball* and *Dragon Ball Z* named *Dragon Ball Super*, consisting of 131 episodes, was first aired in Japan from 2015 to 2018.⁴ This series managed to attract the attention of new (and younger) spectators.

Likewise, a remastered and abridged edition of *Dragon Ball Z*—produced in commemoration of its twentieth anniversary and known as *Dragon Ball Z Kai*—was first aired in Japan from 2009 to 2011 and its latter episodes from 2014 to 2015.⁵ In contrast with the original *Dragon Ball Z*, which has 291 episodes, *Dragon Ball Z Kai* has only 167 episodes. The reason for the difference is because *Dragon Ball Z Kai* sticks to the original storyline of the

---

[2] *Dragon Ball*: Directed by Minoru Okazaki and Daisuke Nishio with Screenplay by Toshiki Inoue and Takao Koyama (Fuji TV 1986-1989).

[3] *Dragon Ball Z*: Directed by Daisuke Nishio and Shigeyasu Yamauchi with Screenplay by Takao Koyama (Fuji TV 1989-1996).

[4] *Dragon Ball Super*: Directed by Kimitoshi Chioka et al. with Screenplay by Akira Toriyama et al. (Fuji TV 2015-2018).

[5] *Dragon Ball Z Kai* is a revised version of *Dragon Ball Z* with updated technology including High Definition picture and sound.

manga series and dispenses with much of the "filler" content of the original anime. *Dragon Ball Z Kai* has a new English dubbing that is more faithful to the original Japanese dialogues. This is why all the literal quotations in this chapter are taken from *Dragon Ball Z Kai*.

Notably, the last two theatrically released animated films set in the Dragon Ball universe have had incredible commercial success. *Dragon Ball Super: Broly* had estimated worldwide box office sales of $115,000,000.[6] *Dragon Ball Super: Super Hero*, theatrically released on July 2022, is estimated to have already generated $80,000,000 worldwide as per October 2022.[7]

The Dragon Ball franchise also expanded into video games. Recently, they have successfully attracted videogame players—receiving good reception among critics and players of the last videogame—based on the anime *Dragon Ball Z*. This game is entitled *Dragon Ball Z: Kakarot* and was developed by CyberConnect2.[8] The videogame was designed for personal computers and consoles Sony's PlayStation 4, Microsoft's XBOX One and the Nintendo Switch.

The Dragon Ball universe and its main characters—Son Goku, Son Gohan, Piccolo and Vegeta—are so widely and well-known that they may be considered a worldwide pop culture phenomenon.

The Plot and Guiding Thread of *Dragon Ball* and *Dragon Ball Z*

The plot and guiding thread of *Dragon Ball* and *Dragon Ball Z* is the quest for the "dragon balls". The story tells us that there are seven magic balls which are all somewhere on planet Earth. Reuniting the seven dragon balls will summon up a magic creature in dragon form, named Shenron, who will grant one wish to whoever summons him.

Son Goku, the protagonist of *Dragon Ball* and *Dragon Ball Z*, defeats the villains in their attempt to reunite the seven dragon balls for the purpose of getting Shenron to grant them the wish of taking over the world. In all the episodes of *Dragon Ball*, Son Goku is presented as an extremely strong young

---

[6] *Dragon Ball Super: Broly*. Directed by Tatsuya Nagamine with Screenplay by Akira Toriyama (20th Century Fox Japan 2018). For the figures, see "Dragon Ball Super: Broly (2018)", *Box Office Mojo*: https://www.boxofficemojo.com/title/tt7961060.

[7] *Dragon Ball Super: Super Hero*. Directed by Tetsuro Kodama with Screenplay by Akira Toriyama (Toei Company 2022). For the figures, see "Dragon Ball Super: Super Hero (2022)", *Box Office Mojo*: https://www.boxofficemojo.com/title/tt14614892. This figure is likely to increase, since at the time of writing this chapter, the film is still being shown in theatres worldwide.

[8] *Dragon Ball Z: Kakarot*. Directed by Akihiro Anai and Written by Yasuhiro Noguchi and Shinsaku Swamura (Bandai Namco Entertainment 2020).

boy, who is exceptionally skilled in martial arts and has the ability to carry out energy attacks. Furthermore, at the beginning of *Dragon Ball Z*, it is discovered that Son Goku is in fact not human but is a member of the extraterrestrial Saiyan warrior race.[9]

After the death of the villain Freeza,[10] the quest for the dragon balls becomes somewhat secondary in the storyline. The focus becomes almost exclusively on Son Goku and his friends fighting against new and increasingly more powerful evil creatures. From then on, the dragon balls lose their narrative weight. They now simply serve the plot of Son Goku and his friends reversing a villain's actions and their consequences. This mainly involves asking Shenron to bring all those murdered by the villain back to life.

Therefore, despite having a central role in the first episodes, the dragon balls in fact end up becoming nothing more than a sort of *deus ex machina* literary recourse. In this way, the anime is able to easily start over with a clean state after a major villain is defeated.

Analogies with Christian Love *(Agape-Charis)* in *Dragon Ball* and *Dragon Ball Z*

I will analyse the concept of love—understood in the broad and Christian-inspired sense of love as *agape*[11] and *charis*[12]—in relation to the animes *Dragon Ball* and *Dragon Ball Z*.[13]

---

[9] *Dragon Ball Z*, Episode 2 and *Dragon Ball Z Kai*, Episode 2.
[10] *Dragon Ball Z*, Episodes 120 and 121; *Dragon Ball Z Kai*, Episode 56.
[11] From the Greek ἀγάπη, originally was a kind of generic form of love vis-à-vis *phila* love or "fraternal love" and *eros* or "erotic love". Bennet Helm, "Love", *The Stanford Encyclopedia of Philosophy* (2017): https://plato.stanford.edu/archives/fall2017/entries/love. The term *agape* was used in the Greek New Testament but became embedded with special meaning to refer to a love like God has—a selfless, other-focused and self-sacrificing kind of love—as demonstrated by Jesus Christ. Cf. "Agape", *Encyclopedia Britannica* (2023): https://www.britannica.com/topic/agape. In the King James Bible, the term *agape* is translated as "charity". Cf. Gene Outka, "Love", in *The Cambridge Dictionary of Christian Theology*, eds. McFarland et al. (Cambridge: Cambridge University Press, 2011), 288-90.
[12] From the Greek χάρις, meaning "grace, kindness, mercy, goodwill". Kurt Aland et al. eds., *The Greek New Testament* (Stuttgart: Biblia-Druck GmbH, 1983), 197. Cf. Ian A. McFarland, "Grace", in *The Cambridge Dictionary of Christian Theology*, eds. McFarland et al. (Cambridge: Cambridge University Press, 2011), 201-03.

I comment first on the character of Piccolo—and how his friendship with Son Gohan—makes him lose all his original villainous traits. I argue that the evolution of the character of Piccolo through his friendship with Son Gohan illustrates the philosophical claim that a loving and giving of oneself to the other—far from being a sign of weakness—is a courageous and self-affirming exercise. The result may move the individual to an inner transformative experience that leads to the enjoyment of a renewed and authentic life that is worth living.

I then argue that Son Goku's respectful attitude towards his opponents is ultimately a loving attitude. Last, I argue that it is the inspiring and loving example of Son Goku that ultimately explains why characters such as Vegeta, who are at first presented as villains, end up losing their villainous traits after fighting against Son Goku.

Some readers may find my claim surprising that love—understood in the broad sense of love as *agape-charis* love—plays a central role in the Dragon Ball animes. After all, both *Dragon Ball* and *Dragon Ball Z* appear to ultimately revolve around fighting. Moreover, and especially in *Dragon Ball Z*, the fighting does not involve only punching and kicking but sometimes includes scenes of bloody violence (that may not be suitable for young children or highly sensitive viewers).

At this point, I would like to underline that I am not denying that violent fighting is an essential component of both *Dragon Ball* and *Dragon Ball Z*. My comments here convey the psychological complexity (and philosophical implications thereof) of some of the main characters of the Dragon Ball series. They suffice to make the point that neither *Dragon Ball* nor *Dragon Ball Z* can be reduced to nothing more than kicks, punches and energy attacks.

Piccolo and Love

To begin with, let us consider the character of Piccolo. He is presented as a sort of reincarnation of Piccolo Daimao, also referred to as "King Piccolo". So despite Piccolo and Piccolo Daimao having different personalities, they are still essentially the same being. Piccolo Daimao is the main villain of *Dragon Ball* in episodes 102 to 122, whose only purpose is to plunge Earth into darkness. Later, it is discovered that Piccolo Daimao, and therefore also

---

[13] There are often correlations in Christian Theology between *agape* and *charis*—with analogies to the Hebrew חסד (*chesed*)—often translated "grace" or "loving-kindness". Cf. Greifswald J. Zobel, "חסד", in the *Theological Dictionary of the Old Testament*, eds. Botterweck et al. (Grand Rapids: William B. Eerdmans Publishing Co., 1986), 44-64 but especially 54-64.

Piccolo, is the evil counterpart of Kami-Sama, who is presented as the "guardian" or "god" of planet Earth. Piccolo Daimao and Kami-Sama were originally the same single being—the split having been produced when Kami-Sama expelled the darkness and evil within him—so as to be able to become the "guardian" of planet Earth.[14]

After the death of Piccolo Daimao at the hand of Son Goku, Piccolo becomes the main villain and antagonist of the anime.[15] While he is considered a "demon", later it is discovered that he, and so also Kami-Sama, are not in fact demons but inhabitants of a distant planet named Namek. Piccolo's main purpose is to take over the world by defeating Son Goku.[16] Following the death of Son Goku at the beginning of *Dragon Ball Z*,[17] and having received the news of more powerful opponents soon to come, Piccolo starts training Son Goku's son (Son Gohan), who is just four years old when he begins.[18] Piccolo is aware that the new opponents—whose names will later be revealed as Vegeta and Nappa—are stronger than him and Son Goku put together. Son Gohan, for his part, has already shown incredible power; although he is still too young to know how to control it. Realizing Son Gohan's hidden potential, Piccolo decides to train Son Gohan for an entire year.

Piccolo treats Son Gohan harshly at first, but he soon shows him compassion, ending up sacrificing himself to save Son Gohan from the attack by Nappa.[19] It is then that Piccolo recognizes that Son Gohan's friendship and love has renewed him. Son Gohan is the first person ever to have seen him as a friend and not as a monster.

> "What a sorry excuse I've become: me, Piccolo, laying down his life to protect some whiny little pipsqueak. Gohan, you're the only person I've ever known who didn't treat me like a monster. Truth be told this last year wasn't so bad. Thank you, Gohan".[20]

From then on, Piccolo loses all his original villainous traits and is even willing to fight the evil forces that threaten to destroy the world. To this effect, he plays a relevant role in the fight against the villain Freeza.[21] Piccolo's

---

[14] *Dragon Ball*, Episode 125.
[15] *Dragon Ball*, Episodes 123-148.
[16] Ibid.
[17] *Dragon Ball Z*, Episode 5 and *Dragon Ball Z Kai*, Episode 3.
[18] *Dragon Ball Z*, Episodes 6-21 and *Dragon Ball Z Kai*, Episodes 4-8.
[19] *Dragon Ball Z*, Episode 28 and *Dragon Ball Z Kai*, Episode 12.
[20] *Dragon Ball Z Kai*, Episode 12.
[21] *Dragon Ball Z*, Episodes 76-83 and *Dragon Ball Z Kai*, Episodes 37-41.

transformation culminates several episodes later—when he and Kami-Sama merge together to once again become a single being—thereby finally making his own peace and reconciling with himself.[22]

It is evident that Son Gohan's friendship has transformed Piccolo. The change is inner and intimate: the world remains the same as it was before, but the way Piccolo sees and approaches the world has dramatically changed. Piccolo's transformation is something far more complex than just saying that he has turned "good". In fact, and despite having ethical implications, it would be more accurate to label Piccolo's transformation as existential rather than ethical. What has occurred is that Piccolo has dispensed with his previous egoistical understanding of the world, thanks to Son Gohan's friendship. Until then, Piccolo saw both others and the world as a whole in a purely egoistical way, as their existing merely for him to take some selfish, private profit from. Others had no value in themselves for Piccolo, seeing them not as *persons* but merely as *objects* he might take control over. In Piccolo's eyes, their only value was the possibility of taking this control over them, which is why his only purpose was to take over the world.

Ultimately, through the friendship with Son Gohan, Piccolo is progressively moved to a loving and generous way of understanding and approaching others and the world as a whole. This generosity dramatically culminates in Piccolo's self-sacrifice to save Son Gohan when Nappa attacks. However, Piccolo's loving attitude is not restricted to the character of Son Gohan but directed to the whole world, as displayed by the fact that from thereon Piccolo overtly renounces his original intention of taking over the world and is always willing to team up with Son Goku and his friends to defeat the evil creatures that threaten to destroy humanity. What has occurred is that Piccolo is now able to recognize the greatness and value that others, and the world as a whole, have in themselves—their value no longer dependent on the egoistical profit he might obtain from them. Once he recognizes the value the world has in itself—he is moved not just to respect it but to defend it against those who try to deny its intrinsic value by converting the world and others into mere objects of their capricious desire.

Moreover, Piccolo's transformation does not just consist of him losing all his previous villainous traits. As just stated, it is more accurate to understand Piccolo's transformation in existential rather than just ethical terms. In this regard, the anime is clear in portraying that Piccolo has not just become a "good" character, but that he is now enjoying a renewed and authentic life that is worth living. It is authentic because, once the rage has subsided—

---

[22] *Dragon Ball Z*, Episode 141 and *Dragon Ball Z Kai*, Episode 68.

thereby allowing him to see the value others have in themselves and by extension the value in itself of the whole world—Piccolo is now free in the sense of enjoying of a self-governed life. Having freed himself from the control of anger and rage, Piccolo is now able to affirm his own singularity and thereby preserve his autonomy and dignity. This self-affirming process is clearly demonstrated in his merging with Kami-Sama so as to once again become the single being they originally were: Piccolo has reconciled with himself and made his own peace.

The evolution of Piccolo illustrates the philosophical claim that those who receive love are transformed by it. Son Gohan's attitude shows Piccolo a loving and generous understanding of the world and others. It is important to emphasize, however, that Son Gohan serves not just as an example for Piccolo, but an opportunity for him adopting a loving attitude. So it is not just Son Gohan's example but Piccolo's own self-giving act of love towards Son Gohan—which as mentioned before dramatically culminates in his self-sacrifice to save Son Gohan from the attack by Nappa—that ultimately accounts for his own inner transformative experience. It is in this sense that the evolution of Piccolo also illustrates the philosophical claim that the one who loves is transformed by the act of loving.

Philosophy and Piccolo's Love

If we turn to the History of Philosophy, we realize that the way of conceiving of love that ultimately drives Piccolo's transformation has been present, in one way or another, throughout all of Christian philosophical tradition. This includes classic thinkers such as Saint Augustine (354-430)[23] and Ramon Llull (1232-1316).[24] This theme of love can also be traced in the so-called "Christian

---

[23] Love drives almost all the philosophical and theological reflections of Saint Augustine. For example, see his *Homilies on the First Epistle of John*, where he wrote: "Once for all, then, a short precept is given thee: Love, and do what thou wilt: whether thou hold thy peace, through love hold thy peace; whether thou cry out, through love cry out; whether thou correct, through love correct; whether thou spare, through love do thou spare: let the root of love be within, of this root can nothing spring but what is good". Saint Augustine, *Homilies on the First Epistle of John*, in *From Nicene to Post-Nicene Fathers* Vol. 7, ed. P. Schaff and trans. J. Gibb (Buffalo: Christian Literature Publishing Co., 1000), 504. For an accessible introduction to Saint Augustine's notion of love, see Teodora Prelipcean, "Saint Augustine—The Apologist of Love", *Procedia—Social and Behavioral Sciences* 149 (2014): 765-71.

[24] Ramon Llull, *The Book of the Lover and the Beloved*, trans. E. Allison Peers (Cambridge: In Parentheses Publications, 2000). For an overview of Llull's life and works, see Ernesto Riani, "Ramon Llull", *The Stanford Encyclopedia of Philosophy*. https://plato.stanford.edu/entries/llull/.

Existentialism" philosophical movement of the twentieth century which includes thinkers such as Miguel de Unamuno (1864-1936),[25] Paul Tillich (1886-1965),[26] and Joaquim Xirau (1895-1946).[27] Despite variations in their arguments, all these authors agree that a loving and giving of oneself to the other—far from being a sign of weakness—is a courageous and self-affirming exercise. The result may move the individual to an inner transformative experience that leads to the enjoyment of a renewed and authentic life that is worth living.

This way of conceiving of love has been criticized by some thinkers, however. The philosopher Friedrich Nietzsche (1844-1900) fiercely argued against it. According to Nietzsche, the attempt to follow a lovingly, *agapeic* way of life is nothing more than a cowardly, insincere attempt to evade oneself. Thus, in his "On Love of the Neighbor" from *Thus Spoke Zarathustra*, Nietzsche wrote:

> You flee to your neighbor from yourselves and would like to make a virtue out of that: but I see through your "selflessness". The *you* is older than the *I*; the *you* has been pronounced holy, but not yet the *I*; so man crowds towards his neighbor.[28]

As I previously argued in my article "Nietzsche and Unamuno on *Conatus* and the Agapeic Way of Life", Nietzsche's criticisms are contestable.[29] I now want to point out that, even if it is obviously not, strictly speaking, a philosophical argument on its own, Piccolo's transformation has the philosophical value of succinctly illustrating why Nietzsche's criticisms are misguided. If Nietzsche

---

[25] Miguel de Unamuno, *The Tragic Sense of Life in Men and Nations*, in *The Selected Works of Miguel de Unamuno* Vol. 4, ed. and trans. Anthony Kerrigan (Princeton: Princeton University Press, 1972), 146-71. For a detailed and systematic analysis of Unamuno's philosophical proposal, see Alberto Oya, *Unamuno's Religious Fictionalism* (London: Palgrave Macmillan, 2020).

[26] Paul Tillich, *Love, Power and Justice* (London: Oxford University Press, 1954).

[27] Joaquim Xirau, *Amor y mundo*, in *Joaquim Xirau: obras completas (t. 1: 'Escritos fundamentales')*, ed. R. Xirau (Barcelona: Anthropos, 1998), 133-262; Joaquim Xirau, *Lo fugaz y lo eterno*, in *Joaquim Xirau: obras completas (t. 1: 'Escritos fundamentales')*, ed. R. Xirau (Barcelona: Anthropos, 1998), 263-307. See also Joaquim Xirau, "Being and Objectivity", *Philosophy and Phenomenological Research* 3.2 (1942): 145-61. For a detailed account of Xirau's philosophy, see Alberto Oya, "Joaquim Xirau: Amor, Persona y Mundo", *Bulletin of Hispanic Studies* 99.9 (2022): 835-43.

[28] Friedrich Nietzsche, *Thus Spoke Zarathustra*, in *The Portable Nietzsche*, ed. and trans. W. Kaufmann (New York: Penguin Books, 1976), 172.

[29] Alberto Oya, "Nietzsche and Unamuno on *Conatus* and the Agapeic Way of Life", *Metaphilosophy* 51.2-3 (2020): 303-17.

were right—that a loving and giving of ourselves to the whole world constitutes an antinatural and self-denying exercise—then Piccolo would have had enjoyed an authentic, self-affirming life prior to his friendship with Son Gohan. However, it is clear that this was not the case. Piccolo was so alienated by the rage he suffered to the point that he could not even accept himself, as shown by his split from Kami-Sama.

Until now, I have focused on the character of Piccolo and his transformation after his friendship with Son Gohan. I have argued that the evolution of the character of Piccolo illustrates the philosophical claim that a loving and giving of oneself to others—far from being a sign of weakness—is a courageous and self-affirming exercise. The result may move the individual to an inner transformative experience that leads to the enjoyment of a renewed and authentic life that is worth living. While Piccolo's transformation is the most interesting for comment, it is worth mentioning that a similar analysis could easily be extended to the first-seen form of the character of Majin Buu, also known as "Innocent Buu" or "Fat Buu". At first, he is presented as the evillest creature imaginable.[30] But he ends up losing his villainous traits due to his friendship with the character of Mr. Satan.[31]

Son Goku and the Movement of Love, Respect of Enemies and the Worthy Opponent

Now, I will argue that Son Goku's respectful attitude towards his opponents is ultimately a loving one. In addition, I will argue that it is the inspiring example of Son Goku that ultimately explains why characters such as Vegeta, who are at first presented as villains, end up losing their villainous traits after fighting against Son Goku. Fighting against Son Goku moved Vegeta to an inner transformative experience—which again is not just ethical but primarily existential—changing the way he approaches and relates to the world.

It is true that Son Goku fights against, and on some occasions kills, the villains he encounters. It should be noted, however, that Son Goku's violence is not gratuitous but is ethically justified, at least according to the storyline of the Dragon Ball series. The narrative or storyline of both *Dragon Ball* and *Dragon Ball Z* is set in what might be called a "heroic light". Son Goku is the hero who must face the honourable (and challenging) endeavour of fighting an evil force which threatens to destroy human life. This evil may take different forms. But is always something that threatens human life in a relevant way. Besides, and this is a crucial aspect, Son Goku is presented as

---

[30] *Dragon Ball Z*, Episodes 233-251 and *Dragon Ball Z Kai*, Episodes 123-138.
[31] *Dragon Ball Z*, Episodes 252-255 and *Dragon Ball Z Kai*, Episodes 139-142.

being the only one who can succeed in overthrowing the evil force. So in the last instance, it is not a matter of free choice but of fulfilling his duty.

It is also true that Son Goku actually enjoys fighting, becoming extremely excited when he encounters a new and stronger opponent. However, the anime is also clear in showing that Son Goku enjoys fighting in terms of "sport". That is to say, as a way of pushing himself beyond his own limits. Son Goku does not enjoy causing his enemies pain or humiliating or mocking them. In most cases, he shows his enemies mercy and tries to refrain from killing them. In this regard, consider the first fight between Son Goku and Vegeta.[32] At the end of the fight, Son Goku stops his friend Krillin from killing Vegeta, even when Vegeta has not (yet) given up his aim to destroy humanity.[33] Son Goku makes his reasons for not wanting Krillin to kill Vegeta explicit.

> "I [Son Goku] know how strong he [Vegeta] is, how much damage he can do. . . . As long as he's alive, nobody on Earth is safe. But you've [Krillin] got to listen to me. This might sound crazy, in fact I'm sure it does, but just now when it looked like you were about to kill him, I couldn't help but thinking. . . . It'd be such a waste. After I finished training with King Kai in the other world, I thought I'd gotten as strong as I could possibly get. Then I saw Vegeta fight, and he's so much faster, so much more powerful than me, the things he was capable of . . . . It was overwhelming. But I've got to admit, deep down I was pretty excited. Maybe it's because I'm a Saiyan too, but when I see somebody who's that strong, my heart starts racing because I realize I still have farther to go. It makes me want to train myself even harder to push myself to their level. Krillin, I know it's wrong, but please, let him go, for me. I need to be able to fight him again someday".[34]

Ultimately, Son Goku's attitude towards his opponents—which is not just graciously merciful but consciously respectful—is a loving attitude. Son Goku does not just value his own friends but is able to recognize the intrinsic value of his enemies. The opponents Son Goku fights are worthy of fighting against. This is why he is always excited to find new and powerful opponents to fight against. And because they are "Worthy Opponents"—who make him better at fighting because he fights with them—he shows them respect and mercy. On this understanding, mocking opponents or using dirty tricks to defeat them—

---

[32] *Dragon Ball Z*, Episodes 29-35 and *Dragon Ball Z Kai*, Episodes 13-17.
[33] *Dragon Ball Z*, Episode 35 and *Dragon Ball Z Kai*, Episode 17.
[34] *Dragon Ball Z Kai*, Episode 17.

would not just be cowardly—but also dishonest and proof of a wicked character. This explains why Son Goku gives a "Senzu Bean" to the villain Cell—so that he can fully recover his strength—before fighting against Son Gohan. Otherwise, Son Gohan's victory would not only be dishonest but unfair too.[35] It also explains why Son Goku gives up against Freeza once he realizes that Freeza has already been defeated, i.e., when his power level has become too low to continue fighting.

> "It's done. You [Freeza] keep coming at me [Son Goku] with everything you've got, but it's finally caught up with you, and your power levels are falling fast. The fact is I don't see the point in fighting you anymore. Your pride is already shot. And, in the end, I guess that's good enough for me. You were so sure of your own power that you never imagined that anyone in the universe could bring you down—especially a Saiyan. Now you know what failure feels like. See, I don't need to keep fighting you because I've already won. So go crawl off some place and hide, I don't really care. Like I said, it's done".[36]

Son Goku's attitude towards his enemies reflects a loving understanding of the world inasmuch as it shows that he does not see his enemies as mere *objects* to be brought down. Rather, he views them as *persons*—in the full philosophical understanding of the term insofar as having their own autonomy and dignity—thus worthy of respect. Some of the villain characters who fight against Son Goku are actually surprised by the way Son Goku respects them. The character of Vegeta is the most relevant case in this regard, though something similar can probably be said of the characters of Ten Shin Hahn and Chaosz. Despite Vegeta's evolution being much more complex than Piccolo's, he too goes from being a villain—obsessed with finding the dragon balls to acquire everlasting life—to sacrificing himself to save planet Earth. Notably, as in the case of Piccolo, Vegeta's transformation is not just a sudden change in his own ethical standards, but an inner, existential transformation

---

[35] *Dragon Ball Z*, Episode 181 and *Dragon Ball Z Kai*, Episode 90.
[36] *Dragon Ball Z*, Episode 103 and *Dragon Ball Z Kai*, Episode 52. The reviewer of this chapter thought that this statement seemed "disdainful"—and Son Goku does not demonstrate respect for his enemies—so consequently it runs contrary to my argument in this chapter. But I would counter that by saying that Son Goku may be simply trying to pacify the opponent by using the flippant bravado rhetoric common in combat. Ultimately, my point is that Son Goku's respect is showed in him not taking advantage of an enemy who has already been defeated while giving him the opportunity to reconsider and take a new path in life.

brought about by his contact with Son Goku. Near the end of *Dragon Ball Z*, Vegeta makes the following confession.[37]

> "I [Vegeta] used to fight for the sheer pleasure of it, sparing no one. I killed for dominance and to feed my insatiable pride, but you [Son Goku] never fought to kill or even to win, only to test your limits and become the strongest you could possibly be. You showed mercy to everyone, even your fiercest enemies, even me—as if you knew I would one day possess this tiny sliver of a soul. How can a Saiyan fight with such power and at the same time be so gentle? It makes me angry just thinking about it, but perhaps it's my anger that's made me blind to the truth for so long. I see it now, I fought to push down others, you only fight to push yourself".[38]

Son Goku's example, even while based on fighting, moves his opponents to realize that a lovingly, *agape-charis* way of life is the way to enjoy of an authentic and self-affirming life that is worth living.

Conclusion

In this chapter, I analysed the concept of love—understood in the broad and Christian-inspired sense of *agape-charis* love—in relation to the animes *Dragon Ball* and *Dragon Ball Z*. My comments on the evolution of the character of Piccolo through his friendship with Son Gohan, Son Goku's respectful attitude towards his enemies, and Vegeta's inner existential transformation brought about by his contact with Son Goku, show that love—understood in the broad sense of *agape-charis*—plays a central role in the Dragon Ball animes. Ultimately, my comments here convey the psychological complexity (and philosophical implications thereof) of some of the main characters of the Dragon Ball series—showing thereby that neither *Dragon Ball* nor *Dragon Ball Z* can be reduced to nothing more than kicks, punches and energy attacks.

---

[37] *Dragon Ball Z*, Episode 280 and *Dragon Ball Z Kai*, Episode 159.
[38] *Dragon Ball Z Kai*, Episode 159.

Chapter 13

Isekai Typological Themes and Jesus Parallels*

Graham Lee
Independent Researcher

ABSTRACT: I argue that common themes of *isekai* narratives are similar to Jesus themes in the Gospels and tend to be isomorphic in typology. I use the term "typology" in this chapter in the sense of "forms, categories and relations" as reflected in "subgenres". I provide a genre analysis moving from the broad category of fantasy to basic *isekai* genre typology as background. My argument then proceeds from here and has three phases. I outline my own eight-fold typology of *isekai* narratives. I then delineate common themes in popular anime in relation to the eight types. The third phase demonstrates the parallels with *isekai* and the life of Jesus in the canonical Gospels.

KEYWORDS: Anime, Fantasy, Genre, Isekai, Isomorphic, Jesus, Subgenre, Typology.

***

Introduction

Isekai is currently one of the most popular kinds of anime. *Isekai* can be translated as "other world" or "different world" but in anime means "fantasy world".[1] In *isekai*, typically, the protagonist is transported to another world and must survive in it. Often they end up saving the world or a large part of it while undergoing substantive character development (morally and/or ability-wise) along the way. This may carry on afterward.

---

* I am indebted to Jonathan Chan, Eric Ho, Nathanael Tan and Matt Yee for conversations that helped me think through issues while writing this chapter. I also thank the reviewer for their helpful comments.
[1] Amanda Pagan, "A Beginner's Guide to Isekai", *New York Public Library* 15th July 2019: https://www.nypl.org/blog/2019/07/15/beginners-guide-isekai-manga.

In this chapter, I argue that common themes of *isekai* narratives along these contours are similar to central theological themes in the narrative of the life of Jesus in the canonical Gospels. I further argue that both these *isekai* themes and Jesus themes tend to be isomorphic ("corresponding or similar in form and relations").[2] Put another way, *isekai* narratives tend to parallel the narrative of Jesus in the Gospels thematically (content), and this in typological terms (e.g. form). I use the term "typology" in this chapter in the sense of "forms, categories and relations" as reflected in "subgenres".

I provide a genre analysis moving from the broad category of fantasy to basic *isekai* genre typology as background. My argument then proceeds from here and has three phases. I outline my own eight-fold typology of *isekai* narratives. I then delineate common themes in popular anime in relation to the eight types. The third phase demonstrates the parallels with *isekai* and the life of Jesus in the canonical Gospels.

Isekai as Fantasy Subgenre

Isekai is a fantasy subgenre. Specifically, it is a genre of speculative fiction, including at least what Farah Mendlesohn terms "portal-quest fantasy", "intrusion fantasy" and "liminal fantasy". Moreover, *isekai* are included in these inasmuch as the former exemplify the latter.[3] A portal-quest fantasy is "a fantastic world entered through a portal" in which "we are invited through into the fantastic".[4] In an intrusion fantasy, "the fantastic enters the fictional world", the mundane world of the narrative (hereafter "the mundane world"), where the fantastic "is the bringer of chaos".[5] Liminal fantasy is very rare, in which the fantastic "*should* be intrusive, disruptive of expectation" when it appears in our world (or one like it), but its "magical origins barely raise an eyebrow" (i.e. no surprise is shown by the protagonist) even if the fantastic events "themselves might be noteworthy and/or disruptive".[6] This results in the audience's disorientation. In liminal fantasy, "magic, or at least the possibility of magic, is part of the consensus reality".[7]

---

[2] "Isomorphic", *Merriam-Webster*. https://www.merriam-webster.com/dictionary/isomorphic#:~:text=%3A%20being%20of%20identical%20or%20similar,isomorphic%20crystals.
[3] Paul S. Price, "A Survey of the Story Elements of Isekai Manga", *Journal of Anime and Manga Studies* 2 (2021): 62.
[4] Farah Mendlesohn, *Rhetorics of Fantasy* (Middletown: Wesleyan University Press, 2008), xix and xiv respectively. Mendlesohn constructs portal-quest fantasy as a genre by identifying relevant elements of portal fantasy and quest fantasy (xix-xx).
[5] Ibid., xiv and xxi respectively.
[6] Ibid., xxiii.
[7] Ibid.

I said above that *isekai* includes *at least* portal-quest fantasy, intrusion fantasy and liminal fantasy since Paul Price argues that *isekai* includes what Mendlesohn calls "immersive fantasy" as well.[8] More needs to be said in description of immersive fantasy than of the other three types of fantasy since, as Mendlesohn notes, immersive fantasy seems partly describable by what it is not. In immersive fantasy, we are invited to share both a world and a set of assumptions.[9] Immersive fantasies, when at their best, present the fantastic "without comment as the norm" for the protagonist and the viewer alike.[10] No "explanatory narrative" is provided, although we see (or otherwise learn) what the protagonist(s) experiences.[11] Yet, the protagonist does not show surprise at the fantastic, as is so in liminal fantasy.[12] Indeed, the fantastic elements inundating the immersive fantasy world cannot be questioned within the story's parameters and must be taken for granted, as normal, by "the point of view characters . . . . even if they themselves are not magical", since they are "integrated with the magical (or fantastic)" and are to be expert denizens of that world.[13] Moreover, the fantastic becomes "assumed" by *us* when immersive fantasy is effective enough, when it and science fiction become indistinguishable.[14] Even "we are assumed to be of [immersive fantasy]", rather than entering it.[15] Whereas, "in the liminal fantasy, the magic hovers in the corner of our eye . . . . in the immersive fantasy we are allowed no escape".[16] For, intrusion fantasy can occur within immersive fantasy.[17]

Based on Mendlesohn's four-fold categorization of fantasy, Price proposes a corresponding four-fold categorization of *isekai*: "portal-quest, immersive, intrusion and liminal".[18] In portal-quest *isekai* (narratives), the fantastic is encountered by the protagonist in another world (*isekai*) they enter through a portal. In this genre, according to Price, while the protagonist may or may not

---

[8] Price, "A Survey of the Story Elements of Isekai Manga", 62.
[9] Mendlesohn, *Rhetorics of Fantasy*, xx.
[10] Ibid.
[11] Ibid.
[12] Ibid., xxiii.
[13] Ibid., xx-xxi.
[14] Ibid., xx.
[15] Ibid.
[16] Ibid., xiv.
[17] Ibid., xxii.
[18] Price, "A Survey of the Story Elements of Isekai Manga", 73 and cf. 86.

(re-)enter the mundane world through the portal, the fantastic does not.[19] The fantastic enters the mundane world from another world, in intrusion *isekai*, in consequence of which changes take place that need to be addressed. In liminal *isekai*, the (fantastic) another world and the mundane world ("the real world") mingle at the liminal space that the portal is. Everything takes place in a fantastic world in immersive *isekai*, as there is no portal between the mundane world and the fantastic.[20]

Here I disagree with Price regarding an immersive category of *isekai*. The lack of another world (*isekai*) in Price's alleged immersive category of *isekai* Price proposes should give us pause regarding the category (at least as far as *isekai* anime, light novels and manga are concerned). According to Price's characterization of it, after all, the mundane world is a fantastic world—even *the* fantastic world since there is no portal(s) to an/other (fantastic) world(s)—to *isekai* (singular or plural).

Basic *Isekai* Genre Typology

In *isekai*, the protagonist (sometimes other characters as well) is transported to, and must survive in, another world. Broadly speaking, *isekai* are traditionally categorized into two kinds: *isekai ten'i* or "transition into another world" and *isekai tensei* or "reincarnation into another world". In *isekai ten'i*, the protagonist is transported to another world typically by traveling or being summoned to it. In *isekai tensei*, the protagonist is transported to another world after dying, often suddenly, in the mundane world.

By "the mundane world" here is meant our world, or a world similar to our world or, in any case, one intended to be thought of in either way. But "our world" in what sense? The same planet, the same universe, the same broader-than-physical world (i.e. including both a universe and nonphysical phenomena) or the same timeline (or "possible world")?[21] This suggests the

---

[19] We might wonder how well this characterization deals with cases in which the protagonist(s) is changed by the fantastic such that they bring some of it back with them in returning to the real world. Going forward I assume an amendment of this characterization that allows for the fantastic to enter the real world by way of the fantastic-imbued protagonist's re-entry into it.

[20] Ibid., 62.

[21] This is to keep matters simple, as the world of an anime wouldn't be the *very same* earth, universe or place in the very same timeline, strictly speaking, but what is very much like ours, depicted to be ours, and to be assumed by the viewer to be ours. The "real" world of the anime, then, even if intended to be (thought of) as qualitatively identical to our world (the real world simpliciter), would not be numerically identical to our world (i.e. *one* and the same world). This need not suppose that modal realism—i.e., the view that all so-

ambiguity of "another world" as well; what "another world" refers to can vary, no less in the context of *isekai*. There are three broad typological characteristics found in *isekai*.

1) Other-Worldly Relocation
2) Other-Worldly Purpose
3) Other-Worldly Character Development

The Other-Worldly Relocation involves the central character relocating, or being transported to, the other (new) world from the (old) original world. With respect to the new world, this person is "other" and may be considered alien. The person is of a kind foreign to the new world in terms of their original nature, i.e., original customs, ideology, capabilities and perhaps species. The individual thus becomes "ontologically naturalized" with respect to the new world in three ways. First, by their person being transported to the other world. Second, in becoming a denizen of or even citizen in the new world and becoming (at least somewhat) familiar with its environment or natural surroundings. Third, assuming (at least some) customs and capabilities of denizens of the other world.

The Other-Worldly Purpose involves the protagonist acting as a messiah or savior figure who saves a group of people, if not an entire society or even the entire other world, from death. The Other-Worldly Character Development involves the protagonist leading a largely mundane or unknown life in the old world, often being of strong or unspecified moral fiber during that life. They may have or develop generally exemplary moral character during their life in the new world, thereby prompting the moral development of other characters and the communities they save and impact. They may be in, or reach, the upper-echelons of their world. They may even be, or become, peerless in terms of power. They may have to make immense personal sacrifice (perhaps even sacrificing their life or livelihood) and struggle in singular discipline in training. They may be misunderstood and/or persecuted by others and face various imposing trials in order to fulfill their other-worldly purpose. Once fulfilled, they may become one of the most powerful figures in the new world

---

called possible worlds are actual, as "the real world" is—is false, even inasmuch as fictional worlds, including maximally-inclusive anime worlds, are possible worlds. For a well-known defense of modal realism, see David Lewis, *On the Plurality of Worlds* (Malden & Oxford: Blackwell Publishers, 1986). Here I bracket the question of whether the relevant sense of "possible worlds" in this case refers to logically possible worlds or to metaphysically possible worlds, in case the two classes of worlds are not identical.

(even a deity) and/or be revered or even deified by many, including having a large number of undyingly loyal and devoted followers.

Eightfold Typology of *Isekai*

What qualifies as *isekai* genre-wise is a matter of considerable discussion.[22] I present my own eightfold typology of *isekai* "subgenres" as outlined below, which should facilitate identification of *isekai*.

1) Fantasy *Isekai*

2) Virtual *Isekai*

3) Other Planet *Isekai*

4) Time Travel *Isekai*

5) Parallel *Isekai*

6) Other Dimension *Isekai*: The protagonist is transported to another plane or dimension (e.g. a world beyond the world of the living).

7) Fictional World *Isekai*: A fictional world (e.g. one in a book or a show the protagonist reads or watches).

8) Revealed World *Isekai*: A realm on the same planet that wasn't previously known to exist by the protagonist or the society of which the protagonist is a denizen.

Although there are interesting questions about the metaphysics of fantasy *isekai* (e.g. *Jobless Reincarnation* and *The Faraway Paladin*), their concept is intuitively understandable and seems to be relatively well understood by a broad viewership.[23] For these reasons I go into no further detail about them here.

In Virtual *Isekai*, the protagonist is transported to the virtual world of an entertainment medium produced in the mundane world. Examples of virtual *isekai* include *Btooom!*, *How Not to Summon a Demon Lord*, *In Another World*

---

[22] Cf. LotsChiono, "Types of Isekai", *Royal Roads*: https://www.royalroad.com/forums/thread/107284.

[23] *Jobless Reincarnation*: Directed by Manabu Okamoto and Hiroki Hirano with Screenplay by Manabu Okamoto and Hiroki Hirano based on the manga by Rifujin na Magonote (Tokyo MX 2021-Present); *The Faraway Paladin*: Directed by Yuu Nobuta and Akira Iwanaga with Screenplay by Tatsuya Takahashi based on the manga by Kanata Yanagino (Tokyo MX 2021-Present).

with *My Smartphone*, *Log Horizon* and *Sword Art Online*.[24] As evident from this list, what might be called video game *isekai* is a prominent form of virtual *isekai*.

Other Planet *Isekai* is a popular subgenre currently. Examples include *Tenchi Universe*, *Trigun* and more recently *To Your Eternity*.[25] Other Planet *Isekai* need not be space operatic (such as *Cowboy Bebop*) or involve widespread, conventional interplanetary travel (as in many mecha anime, such as *Mobile Suit Gundam*).[26]

In Time Travel *Isekai* the protagonist is transported back and/or forward in time, usually in order to avert undesirable events in the present. Examples include *Erased*, *Yashahime: Princess Half-Demon*, *Orange* and *Tokyo Revengers*.[27]

---

[24] *Btooom!*: Directed by Kotono Watanabe with Screenplay by Yosuke Kuroda based on the manga by Junya Inoue (Tokyo MX 2012); *How Not to Summon a Demon Lord*: Directed by Yuta Murano with Screenplay by Kazuyuki Fudeyasu based on the manga by Naoto Fukuda (AT-X 2018); *In Another World with My Smartphone*: Directed by Takeyuki Yanase and Yoshiaki Iwasaki with Screenplay by Natsuko Takahashi and Deko Akao based on the light novel series by Patora Fuyuhara (AT-X 2017-2023); *Log Horizon*: Directed by Shinji Ishihira and Junichi Wada with Screenplay by Toshizou Nemoto based on the light novel series by Mamare Touno (NHK Educational TV 2013-2014) and *Sword Art Online*: Directed by Tomohiko Ito with Screenplay by Yukie Sugawara, Yukito Kizawa, Muneo Nakamoto, Yoshikazu Mukai, Shuji Iriyama, Naoki Shoji, Tomohiko Ito and Atsushi Takayama based on the light novel series by Reki Kawahara (Tokyo MX 2012-2014).

[25] *Tenchi Universe*: Directed by Hiroshi Negishi with Screenplay by Ryoe Tsukimura based on the manga by Hitoshi Okuda (TV Tokyo 1995); *Trigun*: Directed by Satoshi Nishimura with Screenplay by Yosuke Kuroda based on the manga by Yasuhiro Nightow (TV Tokyo 1998) and *To Your Eternity*: Directed by Masahiko Murata and Kiyoko Sayama with Screenplay by Shinzo Fujita based on the manga by Yoshitoki Oima (NHK Educational TV 2021-Present).

[26] *Cowboy Bebop*: Directed by Shinichiro Watanabe with Screenplay by Keiko Nobumoto (TV Tokyo 1998) and *Mobile Suit Gundam*: Directed by Yoshiyuki Tomino with Screenplay by Yoshiyuki Tomino based on the manga by Yu Okazaki (Nagoya TV 1979-1980).

[27] *Erased*: Directed by Tomohiko Ito with Screenplay by Taku Kishimoto based on the manga by Kei Sanbe (Fuji TV 2016); *Yashahime: Princess Half-Demon*: Directed by Teruo Sato and Masakazu Hishida with Screenplay by based on the manga by Takashi Shiina and Katsuyuki Sumisawa (NNS 2020-2022); *Orange*: Directed by Hiroshi Hamasaki and Naomi Nakayama with Screenplay by Yuko Kakihara based on the manga by Ichigo Takano (Tokyo MX 2016) and *Tokyo Revengers*: Directed by Koichi Hatsumi with Screenplay by Yasuyuki Muto based on the manga by Ken Wakui (MBS 2021 Present).

Parallel World *Isekai*—e.g., *Fullmetal Alchemist* (Aniplex)—should not be mistaken for fantasy anime involving an alternate history and no factive history.[28]

Other Dimension *Isekai* (e.g. *Blue Exorcist* and *YuYu Hakusho*) often involve multiple characters, sometimes a team, who are transported to the other plane(s) or dimension(s).[29]

Fictional World *Isekai* (e.g. *Mysterious Play*) can be distinguished from Virtual *Isekai* in that the former do not involve putatively virtual worlds.[30]

Revealed World *Isekai* needs considerable elaboration. The distinction of this sort of anime is not a matter of what the viewer does not know about the other world to be revealed, given many cases of gradually expansive worldbuilding in (anime) narratives. Rather, this variety of anime is distinguished by what main characters in their familiar (known) world know, or don't know, about the other (unknown) world and what is or is not knowable about that world by most in the familiar world (at least initially in the narrative). Here the general populace of the familiar world is epistemically limited with respect to the other world and is beset by a rather opaque barrier to knowledge of it. This frequently owes to informational, communicative and usually geographical separation between the two worlds. Anime involving characters stranded on a desolate island whose existence is virtually unknown to all earthlings, such as *Blast of Tempest*, might constitute a relatively prolific subclass of this type of *isekai*.[31] For comparison, think of the popular television series, *Lost*, in which the island of focus isn't reachable by normal navigation, being functionally sealed off to most and as if (in) a separate world unto itself.[32] Consider also the Amazonian island, Themyscira, in the DC film,

---

[28] *Fullmetal Alchemist*: Directed by Seiji Mizushima with Screenplay by Sho Aikawa partly based on the manga by Hiromu Arakawa (JNN 2003-2004). Not to be confused with *Fullmetal Alchemist: Brotherhood*.

[29] *Blue Exorcist*: Directed by Tensai Okamura with Screenplay by Ryota Yamaguchi based on the manga by Kazue Kato (JNN 2011) and *YuYu Hakusho*: Directed by Noriyuki Abe with Screenplay by Yukiyoshi Ohashi based on the manga by Yoshihiro Togashi (Fuji TV 1992-1994).

[30] *Mysterious Play*: Directed by Hajime Kamegaki with Screenplay by Yoshio Urasawa based on the manga by Yuu Watase (TV Tokyo 1995-1996).

[31] *Blast of Tempest*: Directed by Masahiro Ando with Screenplay by Mari Okada based on the manga by Kyo Shirodaira and Arihide Sano (JNN 2012-2013).

[32] *Lost*: Directed by Jack Bender et al. with Screenplay by J. J. Abrams et al. (ABC 2004-2010).

Wonder Woman.³³ *Attack on Titan* and *The Promised Neverland* are prominent examples of Revealed World *Isekai*.³⁴

Inasmuch as the sorts of worlds of 1 through 8 could qualify as types of *isekai* worlds, in this context "another world" can be understood to be distinct from the home world spatially, temporally and/or dimensionally. The other world in question may even be a world altogether different from the home world in terms of a "possible world". "Possible World" is a technical term used in philosophy to refer to a world in the total sense, i.e., to a maximally-inclusive state of affairs (e.g. a universe in the case of a purely physical or material world). Because the plots of many *isekai* involve a supernatural realm transcending or beyond a (physical) universe or multiverse, this sort of realm (as in 6), like other sorts of worlds or subworlds in 2-8, should be thought of as a world all on its own apart from the home world and universe of such anime.

Case Studies of *Isekai* Narratives

I will demonstrate and "flesh out" the typology of the *isekai* subgenres in relation to the three broad typological characteristics (formula) noted above and reiterated here.

1) Other-Worldly Relocation

2) Other-Worldly Purpose

3) Other-Worldly Character Development

1 Fantasy Isekai: *That Time I Got Reincarnated as a Slime*³⁵

Satoru Mikami reincarnates as a slime in another world. Satoru is a human from the real world, and thus "other" in the new world. He is a being of a kind and species (earthling) foreign to the other world in terms of his original nature, i.e., customs, ideology, capabilities and species. Satoru, especially after becoming Rimuru Tempest, becomes a denizen of and citizen in the new

---

[33] *Wonder Woman*: Directed by Patty Jenkins with Screenplay by Allan Heinberg (Warner Bros 2017).

[34] *Attack on Titan*: Directed by Tetsuro Araki, Masashi Koizuka, Yuichiro Hayashi and Jun Shishido with Screenplay by Yasuko Kobayashi, Hiroshi Seko and Shintaro Kawakubo based on the manga by Hajime Isayama (MBS 2013-Present) and *The Promised Neverland*: Directed by Mamoru Kanbe with Screenplay by Toshiya Ono and Kaiu Shirai based on the manga by Shuhei Miyazaki (Fuji TV 2019-2021).

[35] *That Time I Got Reincarnated as a Slime*: Directed by Atsushi Nakayama et al. with Screenplay by Fuse based on the manga by Fuse (Tokyo MX 2018-2019).

world. He becomes familiar with its environment or natural surroundings.[36] Rimuru assumes customs and capabilities of denizens of the new world. Satoru thus is ontologically naturalized with respect to the new world. Rimuru is the (repeated) savior and king of the Jura Tempest Federation and other kingdoms. Satoru led a largely mundane or unknown life in the old world. Rimuru is of strong moral fiber and develops generally exemplary moral character during his life in the new world, thereby prompting the moral development of other characters and the communities he saves and impacts, particularly his followers in the Jura Tempest Federation. He reaches the upper-echelons of their world in terms of power before, and particularly after, becoming a demon lord. He makes immense personal sacrifice and struggles in singular discipline in training (particularly while initially a slime in the cave of Veldora). He is often misunderstood and persecuted by others and faces various imposing trials. All of this in order to fulfill his other-worldly purpose. He becomes one of the most powerful figures in the alternate world, a deity figure of sorts, and is revered as a deity of sorts by many, including having a large number of undyingly loyal, devoted followers.

2 Virtual Isekai: *Overlord*[37]

Ainz Ooal Gown indefinitely remains in the world of YGGDRASIL (hereafter Y-World) after the other members of the Nine's Own Goal "relocate" or indefinitely transition back to "the real world".[38] Ainz is originally a human from the real world and thus "other" in Y-World. He is a being of kinds and species (plural)—earthling and overlord—foreign to the other world in terms of his original nature, i.e., original customs, ideology, capabilities and species. Ainz becomes a denizen of Y-World. He becomes familiar with its environment or natural surroundings and assumes customs and capabilities of its denizens as he progresses. He thus is ontologically naturalized with respect to Y-World. Ainz saves members of Nazarick (a tomb/dungeon that acts as a base) and non-playable characters (NPCs) of other societies from in-game and (for them) actual death many times. Ainz led a largely mundane, if difficult, life in the real world. Because of trials he faces in the real world and in the game, he develops generally complex moral character during his life in Y-World, and prompts the complex moral development of other characters and the communities he saves and impacts, particularly his followers in

---

[36] Although sexless, Rimuru seems more to identify as a man than as a woman, based on his past life as Satoru.
[37] *Overlord*: Directed by Kunihiro Wakabayashi with Screenplay by Yukie Sugawara based on the light novel by Kugane Maruyama (Tokyo MX 2015-2022).
[38] The exact nature, circumstances and reasons for his remaining in Y-World aren't clear.

Nazarick. He reaches the upper-echelons of Y-World in terms of power and eventually becomes the most powerful magic caster in it. He makes immense personal sacrifice and struggles in singular discipline in training. He struggles particularly before the other guild masters depart Nazarick. After they leave, he then faces struggles trying to develop Nazarick beyond them. He is often misunderstood and persecuted by others and faces various imposing trials in order to fulfill his other-worldly purpose. He becomes one of the most powerful figures in Y-World, a deity figure of sorts, and is revered as a deity of sorts by many, including having a large number of undyingly loyal, devoted followers (particularly those in Nazarick).

3 Another Planet Isekai: *Dragon Ball Z*[39]

Goku originally is transported to Earth from the Saiyan planet Vegeta. He is a being of a kind and species (Saiyan) foreign to Earth in terms of his original nature, i.e., original customs, ideology, capabilities and species. Goku, especially after becoming Z Fighter, becomes a denizen of Earth. He becomes familiar with its environment and even marries an earthling and has half-earthling children. Goku assumes customs and capabilities of earthlings. He thus is ontologically naturalized with respect to Earth. Goku saves the Earth, the galaxy and its inhabitants from destruction many times throughout the series. Goku leads a humble life as a child on Vegeta. He develops generally exemplary moral character during his life on Earth, thereby prompting the moral development of other characters (particularly other Z Fighters) and the communities he saves and impacts. He reaches and continues to climb among the upper-echelons of Earth, and even the universe, in terms of power. Goku continually sacrifices his life and struggles in singular discipline in training (even by Z Fighter standards). He is misunderstood by many and faces numerous imposing trials in order to fulfill his other-worldly purpose. He becomes one of the most powerful figures in the universe, a virtual deity, including having a large number of undyingly loyal, devoted friends and followers (including his relatives).

4 Time Travel Isekai: *Inuyasha*[40]

Kagome Higurashi initially is transported and later permanently relocates to the fantasy-spun world of feudal Japan (hereafter I-World), being a present-

---

[39] *Dragon Ball Z*: Directed by Daisuke Nishio and Shigeyasu Yamauchi with Screenplay by Takao Koyama (Fuji TV 1989-1996).
[40] *Inuyasha*: Directed by Masahsi Ikeda and Yasunao Aoki with Screenplay by Katsuyuki Sumisawa based on the manga by Rumiko Takahashi (NNS 2000-2004).

day reincarnation of Kikyo.⁴¹ She is a human from the world of modern-day Japan and thus "other" in I-World, being of a kind foreign to I-world in terms of her original nature, i.e., original customs, ideology and capabilities. Kagome, especially after joining Inuyasha on his adventures, becomes a denizen of I-World, becoming familiar with its environment and assuming customs and capabilities of its denizens. She thus is ontologically naturalized with respect to I-World. Kagome saves many denizens of I-World from death. She does so by playing a central role in the destruction of Naraku. Kagome leads a largely mundane life in the world of the present day. She is of relatively strong moral fiber and develops generally exemplary moral character during her life in I-World, thereby prompting the moral development of other characters and the communities she saves and impacts, particularly Inuyasha and other members of their band, affiliates, and even some enemies. She reaches the upper-echelons of I-World in terms of power by the time, and particularly after, Naraku is defeated. She becomes one of its most powerful priestesses. She makes immense personal sacrifice (giving up living in the world of the present with all its amenities and comforts) and struggles in singular discipline in training (particularly during the quest to defeat Naraku). She is often misunderstood and persecuted by others (on the basis of being a reincarnation of Kikyo), and faces various imposing trials. All of this in order to fulfill her other-worldly purpose. She becomes one of the most powerful figures in I-World, a deity figure of sorts, and is revered as a deity of sorts by many, having been the one to purify the Shikon Jewel.

5 Parallel World Isekai: *Steins;Gate*⁴²

Rintaro Okabe relocates or is transported to parallel worlds from the original worldline. He is a human from, and of, that worldline. He is thus "other" in the parallel worlds, being of a kind foreign to them in terms of his original nature, i.e., worldline specific customs, ideology and capabilities. He acclimates as a denizen of those worldlines once in them, becoming familiar with their environments and assuming customs and capabilities of its denizens as needed. He thus is ontologically naturalized with respect to these worlds. Okabe saves his friends multiple times. He leads a largely mundane life before developing his time machine. Okabe is of strong moral fiber and develops generally exemplary moral character during his life post-time machine (while

---

⁴¹ Here I mean "spun" in the sense of giving a particular interpretation of some historical event(s), or in this case, the period or setting of feudal Japan. *Inuyasha* takes this feudal setting of Japan and imbues it with fantasy elements of the cosmology depicted in the anime.

⁴² *Steins;Gate* is a "Visual Novel" in a videogame format. *Stein;Gate*. Directed by Tatsuya Matsubara with Screenplay by Chiyomaru Shikura et al. (5pb 2009).

traveling between worldlines), thereby prompting the moral development of other characters whom he saves and impacts. He reaches the upper-echelons of his world in terms of power, or ability, in and after developing and using his time machine. He makes immense personal sacrifice and struggles in singular discipline in training (particularly while seeking to think his way through to solve problems that arise). He is often misunderstood and persecuted by others (various organizations across the worldlines) and faces various imposing trials in order to fulfill his other-worldly purpose. He becomes one of the most powerful figures in the alternate worldlines, including having a large number of undyingly loyal and devoted followers, namely his colleagues and friends.

6 Other Dimension Isekai: *Bleach*[43]

Ichigo Kurosaki intermittently relocates to the worlds of the Soul Society and Hueco Mundo. It initially seems that he is a normal human from the world of the living. This turns out to be partly true; he was brought up in the world of the living and initially seems to be a normal human, but he is not fully human by descent. It is revealed in the Arrancar and Thousand Year Blood War arcs of the Bleach manga and anime that Ichigo is in fact Quincy on his mother's side and his father is a former Soul Reaper/Shinigami captain.[44] Ichigo thus is "other" in the worlds of the dead, being of a kind and species (Quincy, living), being foreign to them in terms of his original nature, i.e., original customs, ideology, capabilities and species. After becoming a substitute Soul Reaper, Ichigo becomes an intermittent denizen and citizen of the Soul Society. He becomes familiar with its environment and assumes customs and capabilities of its denizens, particularly ones that pertain to battle. He thus is ontologically naturalized with respect to the world of the Soul Society. Ichigo, a denizen of the human world, travels to the Soul Society with his friends in order to save Rukia Kuchiki's life. Through the foray, he becomes and is called "Savior of the Soul Society". After his foray into Hueco Mundo and the war with Aizen, he becomes the savior of the worlds of the Soul Society and of the living, particularly Karakura Town. Ichigo leads a largely mundane life prior to becoming a substitute Soul Reaper. He is of relatively strong moral fiber and

---

[43] *Bleach*: Directed by Noriyuki Abe with Screenplay by Mashashi Sogo, Tsyuoshi Kida and Kento Shimoyama based on the manga by Tite Kubo (TXN 2004-2012).
[44] It was revealed in the *Bleach* manga and the *Bleach* anime that his father, Isshin Kurosaki, is a Soul Reaper and the former Captain of Squad 10 of the Soul Society. Prior to the revelation about the originally Quincy nature of his mother, Masaki Kurosaki, it is presumed that he was half human by descent. So his parents are originally from the world of the Soul Society.

develops generally exemplary moral character during his Soul Reaper life, thereby prompting the moral development of other characters and the communities he saves and impacts, particularly his friends, family members and affiliates of and in the Soul Society. He reaches the upper-echelons of the worlds in terms of power before, during, and after he fights Aizen. He makes immense personal sacrifice and struggles in singular discipline in training. He is often misunderstood and persecuted by others (particularly while trying to save Rukia), and faces various imposing trials in order to fulfill his otherworldly purpose. He becomes one of the most powerful figures in the Soul Society and has a large number of undyingly loyal and devoted followers, including his friends, family members, and certain affiliates in the Soul Society.

7 Fictional World Isekai: *Re:CREATORS*[45]

Selesia Upitiria is transported to the mundane world. She is a character from an anime world and thus "other" in the mundane world, being of a kind foreign to the real world in terms of her original nature, i.e., original customs, ideology and capabilities. She becomes an indefinite denizen of the real world, becoming familiar with its environment and assuming customs and capabilities of its denizens. She thus is ontologically naturalized with respect to the mundane world. Selesia fights Altair in order to foil the latter's plans to make the worlds collide and thereby to annihilate everything and everyone in them. Selesia leads a mundane, if largely unknown, life in her world. She is of strong moral fiber and develops generally exemplary moral character during her life in the mundane world, thereby prompting the moral development of other characters and the communities she saves and impacts, such as Sota. She is in the upper-echelons of the mundane world in terms of power after being transported there. She makes immense personal sacrifice and struggles in singular discipline in battle. She is often misunderstood and faces various imposing trials in order to fulfill her other-worldly purpose. She is one of the most powerful figures in the mundane world.

8 Revealed World Isekai: *The Big O*[46]

Roger Smith is transported to the world of Paradigm City from the world before. He is a human from the world before, and thus "other" in the new world (with others in it). He is of a kind foreign to the new world in terms of

---

[45] *Re:CREATORS*: Directed by Ei Aoki with Screenplay by Rei Hiroe and Ei Aoki based on the manga by Daiki Kase (Tokyo MX 2017).
[46] *The Big O*: Directed by Kazuyoshi Katayama with Screenplay by Chiaki J. Konaka and Kazuyoshi Katayama based on the manga by Hitoshi Ariga (Wowow 1999-2000).

his original nature, i.e., original customs, ideology and capabilities. He unwittingly becomes a denizen of and citizen in the new world, becoming familiar with its environment and assuming the customs and capabilities of its denizens. He thus is ontologically naturalized with respect to the new world. Roger is instrumental in saving Paradigm City. Roger leads a largely unknown life in the old world. He is of relatively strong moral fiber and develops generally exemplary moral character during his life in the new world, thereby prompting the moral development of other characters and the communities he saves and impacts. He reaches the upper-echelons of their world in terms of power as the pilot of Big O. He makes immense personal sacrifice and struggles in singular discipline in training. He is often misunderstood and persecuted by others. He faces various imposing trials in order to fulfill his other-worldly purpose. He becomes one of the most powerful figures in the new world, including having a large number of undyingly loyal, devoted followers such as Angel, Dorothy and Norman.

Findings of the Case Studies

The central similarities of the backgrounds, goals and character arcs of these characters suggests the principal uniformity of their otherworldly relocation, purpose and character development. Despite the variety of these anime, they exemplify a typological pattern commonly in *isekai* narratives. This pattern will now be traced to the life of Jesus in the Gospels.

Jesus in the Gospels and *Isekai* Typological Themes

The aforementioned common typological themes of *isekai* narratives are similar, even isomorphic, to certain theological themes in the life of Jesus in the canonical Gospels. They are parallel in terms of the broad typological themes of *isekai* and their attendant details as outlined both schematically above and in terms of the case studies.

1) Other-Worldly Relocation

2) Other-Worldly Purpose

3) Other-Worldly Character Development

As indicated by the recurring "may" language, any combination of the constituent elements might be present in a given *isekai* narrative and in the Jesus narratives. The moral parallels between *isekai* narratives and the narrative about Christ are particularly negotiable, especially since Jesus is considered to be sinless ("morally perfect") in Christian Theology.[47] What follows is how the life of Jesus in the Gospels exhibits typological themes in *isekai*.

Precursor on the Trinity, King and Heaven

This chapter employs traditional Christian Theology as the foundation for articulating typological parallels of the life of Jesus with *isekai*.[48] The rationale is primarily utility. Of course, the many unique aspects of Jesus means that the comparisons must be understandably flexible and nuanced.

The Trinity has utility here because of the roles and relations of Father, Son and Holy Spirit in the Jesus story. There is One God in Three Persons. Moreover, God is king and so is Jesus (messiah) who is sent on a mission to "save the world".

Heaven is the metaphysical realm of God. It might be argued that God is the original and real since God is original and ultimate reality (i.e., what there is).[49] For the purposes of this chapter, it will be supposed that heaven, God's realm, is the home world or an original world of sorts.

Jesus in the Isekai Typology

The Son of God, Jesus, is sent into the universe and to the earth (the other world) from the (otherworldly) supernatural realm of heaven by God the Father through the Holy Spirit (Virgin Birth).

The Son is sent to earth to fulfill the eternal, ultimate providential purpose of the Father to save humanity from spiritual death by means of an atoning death and resurrection. The manner of the Son's sending (transportation and relocation) is by incarnation as the God-man via the Virgin Birth. This is known in Christian Theology as the "Incarnation". In becoming the God-man, Jesus, the Son is thought to have taken on another nature, human nature, in

---

[47] Millard J. Erickson, *Christian Theology* (Grand Rapids: Baker Book House, 1986), 802-15. The discussion here sits nicely with the typological themes of both *isekai* and Jesus.

[48] Erickson, *Christian Theology*, is an excellent and comprehensive resource for the purposes of this study.

[49] Understood to be the world on certain philosophical conceptions, e.g., as in Wittgenstein's *Tractatus*. See Ludwig Wittgenstein, *Tractatus Logico-Philosophicus*, trans. David F. Pears and Brian F. McGuinness (London: Routledge & Kegan Paul, 1961).

addition to the divine nature (God) had by Him eternally.[50] Thus, again, the necessity of the Virgin Birth.

Jesus is typically seen as the central character of the New Testament. Jesus is uniquely both human in this world (incarnation) and at the same time "other" (God from another world, i.e., heaven). Being at once fully man and the second person of the trinitarian Godhead, Jesus is of a kind (God) foreign to the universe in terms of original nature, i.e., divine customs, ideology, capabilities and arguably species.[51] Jesus becomes a denizen of earth, becoming familiar with the earth as an embodied being and, as a human, assuming certain customs and capabilities (naturally human ones). He thus becomes ontologically naturalized in the universe.

Jesus leads a largely unknown life during his upbringing in Nazareth, arguably during his pre-incarnate existence (at least largely while residing in heaven), and during his existence prior to the creation of the universe. He is of undoubtedly impeccable moral character during that life. In traditional Christian Theology, because Jesus is considered morally pure (sinless), he develops physically, psychologically and emotionally but not morally. He is a moral example during his earthly life, thereby prompting the moral development of his followers and serving as a moral exemplar for humanity. Because Jesus is fully divine as well as fully human, he is omnipotent (consider the miracles of Jesus). He makes immense personal sacrifice (even sacrificing his life) and struggles in singular discipline in training (the Temptation). He is misunderstood and persecuted by many, and faces various imposing trials in order to fulfill his other-worldly purpose. Once fulfilled, he becomes revered by many or deified by the large number of his undyingly loyal, devoted followers, who take the name, Christians.

Conclusion

There are clearly many *isekai* typological themes to be found in the life of Jesus of the Gospels. I suspect that the Jesus parallelism that tends to be found in *isekai* is in part a reflection of the influence of Christian themes on the fantasy genre from which *isekai* draw inspiration. I think I have demonstrated, however, that both the broad and specific themes and typological forms of *isekai*—in at least eight subgenres—are too close to be coincidences

---

[50] See Anselm, *Proslogium; Monologium; an Appendix in Behalf of the Fool by Gaunilon; and Cur Deus Homo*, trans. Sidney Norton Deane (Chicago: Open Court, 1903). Cf. F. S. Schmitt and R. W. Southern, eds., *Memorials of St. Anselm* (London: The British Academy/Oxford University Press, 1969).
[51] In the non-biological sense.

(isomorphic). What the exact conceptual and literary connections are, may however, remain in question.

Bibliography

Akbaş, İbrahim. "A 'Cool' Approach to Japanese Foreign Policy: Linking Anime to International Relations". *Journal of International Affairs* 23.1 (2018): 95-120.

Akinsiku, Akin (text) and Ajinbayo "Siku" Akinsiku (art). *Manga Bible: From Genesis to Revelation*. New York: Penguin Random House, 2007.

Akker, Robin van den, Alison Gibbons and Timotheus Vermeulen, eds. *Metamodernism: Historicity, Affect and Depth After Postmodernism*. New York: Rowman and Littlefield, 2017.

Aland, Kurt, et al. eds. χάρις. *The Greek New Testament*. Stuttgart: Biblia-Druck GmbH, 1983.

Allison, Anne. "Cuteness as Japan's Millennial Product". In *Pikachu's Global Adventure: The Rise and Fall of Pokémon*, edited by Joseph Tobin, 34-50. Durham: Duke University Press, 2004.

———. "Automated Graves: The Precarity and Prosthetics of Caring for the Dead in Japan", *International Journal of Cultural Studies* 24.4 (2021): 622-36.

Ānanda, Jason and Josephson Storm. *Metamodernism: The Future of Theory*. Chicago: The University of Chicago Press, 2021.

Anderson, Steven R. "Powers of (Dis)Ability: Toward a Bodily Origin in Mushishi". *Mechademia* 9 (2014): 77-88.

Anderson, William H. U. *Technology and Theology*. Wilmington: Vernon Press, 2020.

Ankersmit, Frank. *Narrative Logic: A Semantic Analysis of the Historian's Language*. Boston: Martinus Nijhoff Publishers, 1983.

Anselm. *Proslogium; Monologium; an Appendix in Behalf of the Fool by Gaunilon; and Cur Deus Homo*. Translated by Sidney Norton Deane. Chicago: Open Court, 1903.

Archibald, Samuel and Bertrand Gervais. "Le Récit en Jeu. Narrativité et Interactivité", *Protée* 34 (2006): 27-39.

Arendt, Hannah. *The Origins of Totalitarianism*. San Diego: Harcourt, Inc., 1966.

Augustine, Saint. *Homilies on the First Epistle of John*. In *From Nicene to Post-Nicene Fathers* Vol. 7, edited by P. Schaff and translated by J. Gibb, 453-530. Buffalo: Christian Literature Publishing Co., 1888.

Austin, John L. *How to Do Things with Words*. Oxford: Clarendon Press, 1962.

Azuma, Hiroki. "The Animalization of Otaku Culture". Translated by Yuriko Furuhata and Marc Steinberg. *Mechademia* 2.1 (2007): 175-87.

———. *Otaku: Japan's Database Animals*. Translated by Jonathan E. Abel and Shion Kono. Minneapolis: University of Minnesota Press, 2009.

Baber, Zaheer. *The Science of Empire: Scientific Knowledge, and Colonial Rule in India*. Albany: State University of New York Press, 1996.

Baker, Lynne Rudder. "Christian Materialism in a Scientific Age". *International Journal for Philosophy of Religion* 69.1 (2011): 47-59.

Bakonyi, Kat. "The Influence of Japanese Animation on Avatar: The Last Airbender". *The UCLA School of Film and TV*: 1-13.

Barham, Cooper D. "9 Anime YouTubers Worth Watching", *Geeks UnderGrace* 16th October 2017. https://www.geeksundergrace.com/anime-cosplay/primer-anime-youtubers/.

Barkman, Adam. "Anime, Manga and Christianity: A Comprehensive Analysis". *Journal for the Study of Religions and Ideologies* 9.27 (2010): 25-45.

Barrie, J. M. *Peter and Wendy*. London: Penguin, 2008.

_____. *Peter Pan: Peter and Wendy and Peter Pan in Kensington Gardens*. New York: Penguin, 2008.

Beauchemin, Jacques. *La Société des Identités: Éthique et Politique dans le Monde Contemporain*. Montreal: Athéna Éditions, 2005.

Bedir, Selen Çalık. "Combinatory Play and Infinite Replay: Underdefined Causality in the *Neon Genesis Evangelion* Anime Series and Games". In *Anime Studies: Media-Specific Approaches to Neon Genesis Evangelion*, edited by José Andrés Santiago Iglesias and Ana Soler Baena, 297-326. Stockholm: Stockholm University Press, 2021.

bell hooks, "Are You Still a Slave? Liberating The Black Female Body", *The New School* (2014): https://livestream.com/thenewschool/slave.

Berger Peter L. and Thomas Luckmann. *The Social Construction of Reality: A Treatise in the Sociology of Knowledge*. Garden City: Anchor Books, 1966.

Berndt, Jaqueline. "Anime in Academia: Representative Object, Media Form, and Japanese Studies". *Arts* 7.56 (2018): 1-13.

_____. "Introduction: Shōjo Mediations". In *Shōjo Across Media. East Asian Popular Culture*, edited by Jaqueline Berndt, Kazumi Nagaike, Fusami Ogi, 1-21. New York: Palgrave Macmillan, 2019.

Beyes, Timon and Chris Steyaert. "Spacing Organization: Non-Representational Theory and Performing Organizational Space". *Organization* 19.1 (2011): 45-61.

Bilge, Sirma. "Théorisations Féministes de l'Intersectionnalité". *Diogène* 225.1 (2009): 70-88.

Blacker, Carmen. *The Catalpa Bow: A Study of Shamanistic Practices in Japan*. London: George Allen & Unwin, 1975.

_____. "Minakata Kumagusu: A Neglected Japanese Genius". *Folklore*. 94.2 (1983): 139-52.

Bolton, Christopher, et al. eds. *Robot Ghosts and Wired Dreams: Japanese Science Fiction from Origins to Anime*. Minneapolis: University of Minnesota Press, 2007.

_____, et al. eds. "Introduction. Robot Ghosts and Wired Dreams: Japanese Science Fiction from Origins to Anime". In *Robot Ghosts Wired Dreams: Japanese Science Fiction from Origins to Anime*, edited by Christopher Bolton, et al. vii-xxii. Minneapolis: University of Minnesota Press, 2007.

_____. *Interpreting Anime*. Minneapolis: University of Minnesota Press, 2018.

Bordwell, David and Kristin Thompson. *Film Sanatı*. Translated by Ertan Yılmaz and Emrah Suat Onat. Ankara: Deki, 2011.

Bostrom, Nick. "Are You Living in a Computer Simulation?". *Philosophical Quarterly* 53.211 (2003): 243-55.

_____. "Introduction—The Transhumanist FAQ: A General Introduction". In *Transhumanism and the Body*, edited by Calvin Mercer and Derek F. Maher, 1-17. New York: Palgrave Macmillan, 2014.

_____. "Transhumanist Values". *Journal of Philosophical Research* 30 (2018): 3-14.

Boyd, D. J. "Crunchyroll and the Webtoon-Image: Reterritorialising the Korean Digital Wave in Telecom Animation's Tower of God (2020) and MAPPA's The God of High School (2020)". In *Streaming and Screen Culture in Asia-Pacific*, edited by Michael Samuel and Louisa Mitchell, 285-308. New York: Palgrave Macmillan, 2022.

Bramlett, Frank. "Why There Is No 'Language of Comics'". In *The Oxford Handbook of Comic Book Studies*, edited by Frederick Luis Aldama, 16-35.

Branscum, John. "Me, Myself, and Mushi: Reframing the Human and the Natural in Urushibara Yuki's *Mushishi*". *Works and Days* 32.1/2 (2014-2015): 309-29.

Brenner, Robin E. *Understanding Manga and Anime*. London: Libraries, 2007.

Broderick, Mick. "Making Things New: Regeneration and Transcendence in Anime". In *The End All Around Us Apocalyptic Texts and Popular Culture*, edited by John Walliss and Kenneth G. C. Newport, 120-47. New York: Routledge, 2008.

Brophy, Philip. "Sonic-Atomic-Nuemonic: Apocalyptic Echoes in Anime". In *The Illusion of Life 2: More Essays on Animation*, edited by Alan Cholodenko, 191-208. Sydney: Power Publication, 2007.

Brown, Steven T. *Cinema Anime: Critical Engagements with Japanese Animation*. New York: Palgrave Macmillan, 2008.

_____. *Tokyo Cyberpunk Posthumanism in Japanese Visual Culture*. New York: Palgrave Macmillan, 2015.

Brunton, James. "Whose (Meta)modernism?: Metamodernism, Race, and the Politics of Failure". *Journal of Modern Literature* 43.3 (2018): 60-76.

Bryce, M. and A. Plumb. "Mushishi: Post Modern Representation of Otherness In and Outside Human Bodies". *International Journal of the Humanities*. 9.11 (2012): 111-19.

_____ and Jason Davis. "Mushishi". *Resilience: A Journal of the Environmental Humanities*. 2.3 (2015): 134-38.

Brzeski, Patrick. "How Japanese Anime Became the World's Most Bankable Genre". *Hollywood Reporter* 16th May 2022. https://www.hollywoodreporter.com/business/business-news/japanese-anime-worlds-most-bankable-genre-1235146810/.

Buljan, Katherine and Carole M. Cusack, *Anime, Religion and Spirituality*. Sheffield: Equinox Publishing, 2015.

Burnham, Douglas. "Gottfried Leibniz: Metaphysics". *Internet Encyclopedia of Philosophy*. https://iep.utm.edu/leib-met/#H6.

Butler, Judith. *Trouble dans le Genre: Le Féminisme et la Subversion de L'Identité*. Paris: La Découverte, 1990.

———. *Bodies that Matter: On the Discursive Limits of "Sex"*. New York: Routledge, 1993.

Carpenter, Benjamin. "'I Am Thou...', Thou Art Free: Persona 5 and Existentialism". *Medium* 26th December 2018. https://benjaminjjcarpenter.medium.com/i-am-thou-thou-art-free-persona-5-and-existentialism-62476 b0da22d.

Carpenter, Humphrey. *Secret Garden: The Golden Age of Children's Literature*. London: Allen and Unwin, 1985.

Cavallaro, Dani. *Anime Intersections: Tradition and Innovation in Theme and Technique*. Jerfferson: McFarland, 2007.

Chalmers, David J. *The Conscious Mind: In Search of a Fundamental Theory*. Oxford: Oxford University Press, 1996.

Chambers, Andrew. "Japan: Ending the Culture of the 'Honorable' Suicide". *The Guardian* 03rd August 2010.

Christian-Smith, Linda K. "Romancing the Girl: Adolescent Romance Novels and the Construction of Femininity". In *Becoming Feminine: The Politics of Popular Culture*, edited by Leslie G. Roman and Linda K. Christian-Smith, 76-101. London: Falmer Press, 1988.

Christy, Alan. *A Discipline on Foot: Inventing Japanese Native Ethnography*. Lanham: Rowman & Littlefield Publishers, Inc., 2012.

Chute, Hillary. *Graphic Women: Life Narrative & Contemporary Comics*. New York: Columbia University Press, 2010.

Clare, Ralph. "Worlds of Wordcraft: The Metafiction of Kurt Vonnegut". In *Critical Insights on Kurt Vonnegut*, edited by Robert T. Tally. Ipswich: Salem Press, 2013.

Clark, Bob. "Every Saga Has a Beginning: Osamu Tezuka and Kozo Morishita's 'Buddha: The Great Departure'". *Wonders in the Dark* 09th July 2011. https://wondersinthedark.wordpress.com/2011/07/09/every-saga-has-a-be ginning-osamu-tezkua-and-kojo-morishits-buddha-the-great-departure/.

Clark, Hilary. "Encyclopedic Discourse", *SubStance* 21.1 (1992): 95-110.

Clark, Timothy, C. et al. eds. *Shunga: Sex and Pleasure in Japanese Art*. London: The British Museum Press, 2014.

Clasquin-Johnson, Michel. "Towards a Metamodern Academic Study of Religion and a More Religiously Informed Metamodernism". *Theological Studies* 73.3 (2017): 1-11.

Cleary, Thomas. *Code of the Samurai: A Modern Translation of the* Bushido Shoshinsu. Boston: Tuttle, 1999.

Clements, Jonathan. *Anime: A History*. London: British Film Institute, 2013.

Coff, Christian. *The Taste for Ethics: An Ethic of Food Consumption*. Translated by E. Broadbridge. Dordrecht: Springer, 2006.

Cohn, Bernard S. *Colonialism and Its Forms of Knowledge: The British in India*. Princeton: Princeton University Press, 1996.

Colosimo, Natalie. "The Schumann Resonances and Psychic Phenomena". *The Psychic School* 19th August 2020. https://psychicschool.com/the-sch umann-resonances-and-psychic-phenomena/.

Condry, Ian. "Anime Creativity: Characters and Premises in the Quest for Cool Japan". *Theory, Culture, and Society* 26 (2009): 139-63.

_____. "Love Revolution: Anime, Masculinity, and the Future". In *Recreating Japanese Men*, edited by Sabine Früstück and Anne Walthall, 262-83. Berkeley: University of California Press, 2011.

_____. *The Soul of Anime: Collaborative Creativity and Japan's Media Success Story.* Durham: Duke University Press, 2013.

Cooley, Charles Horton. *Human Nature and the Social Order.* New York: Scribner's Sons, 1902.

Cooley, Kevin. "Past the End of the Catbus Line: Mushishi's Apparitional Actants". *Animation: An Interdisciplinary Journal* 14.3 (2019): 178-90.

Cooper Fredrick and Ann Laura Stoler, eds. *Tensions of Empire: Colonial Cultures in a Bourgeois World.* Berkeley: University of California Press, 1997.

Creatures Inc. *An Illustrated Book of Pocket Monsters.* Tokyo: Famitsu, 1996.

Cruz, Noelle Leslie Dela. "Transcendence in Osamu Tezuka's Buddha: Reading Manga through Paul Ricoeur's Hermeneutic Phenomenology". *Academemia.edu.* https://www.academia.edu/16909125/Transcendence_in_Osamu_Tezuka_s_Buddha_Reading_Manga_through_Paul_Ricoeur_s_Hermeneutic_Phenomenology.

Cubbison, Laurie. "Anime Fans, DVDs, and the Authentic Text". *The Velvet Light Trap* 56.1 (2005): 45-57.

Cusack, Carol and Katherine Buljan. *Anime, Religion and Spirituality: Profane and Sacred Worlds in Contemporary Japan.* Sheffield: Equinox, 2015.

_____. "Fiction into Religion: Imagination, Other Worlds, and Play in the Formation of Community". *Religion* 46.4 (2016): 575-90.

_____. John M. Morehead and Venitia L. D. Robertson. *The Sacred in Fantastic Fandom: Essays on the Intersection of Religion and Pop Culture.* Jefferson: McFarland, 2019.

_____. "Are Fandoms a Modern Kind of Religion?", *SLAMmag* 1 (2021): 22-23.

Daniel, Carolyn. *Voracious Children: Who Eats Whom in Children's Literature.* New York: Routledge, 2006.

Danielewski, Mark Z. *House of Leaves.* New York: Pantheon Books, 2000.

Davies, Roger J. and Osamu Ikeno, eds. *The Japanese Mind. Understanding Contemporary Japanese Culture.* Clarendon: Tuttle Publishing, 2002.

De Lauretis, Teresa. *Théorie Queer et Cultures Populaires. De Foucault à Cronenberg.* Translated by M. H. Bourcier. Paris: La Dispute, 2007.

De Masi, Vincenzo. "Discovering Miss Puff: A New Method of Communication in China". *KOME-An International Journal of Pure Communication Inquiry* 1.2 (2013): 44-54.

De Tocqueville, Alexis. *Democracy in America.* New York: HarperCollins Publishers, 1969.

Deleuze, Gilles and Felix Guattari. *A Thousand Plateaus: Capitalism and Schizophrenia.* Minneapolis: University of Minnesota Press, 2005.

Denison, Rayna. *Anime: A Critical Introduction.* London: Bloomsbury Publishing, 2015.

Derrat, Max. "The Secret to Becoming God in Serial Experiments Lain". *YouTube.* https://www.youtube.com/watch?v=Zc6MsSmJJzU&t=61s.

Derrida, Jacques. *Of Grammatology.* Translated by Gayatri Spivak. Baltimore: Johns Hopkins University Press, 1974.

⎯⎯⎯⎯⎯. *Rogues.* Stanford: Stanford University Press, 2005.

Descartes, Rene. "Meditations on First Philosophy". *Internet Encyclopedia of Philosophy.* https://yale.learningu.org/download/041e9642-df02-4eed-a895-70e472df2ca4/H2665_Descartes%27%20Meditations.pdf.

Dickel, Sascha & Andreas Frewer. "Life Extension Eternal Debates on Immortality". In *Post- and Transhumanism,* edited by Russell Ranisch, 119-32. Bruxelles: P. Lang, 2014.

Doede, Bob. "Transhumanism, Technology, and the Future: Posthumanity Emerging or Sub-Humanity Descending?" *Appraisal* 7.3 (2009): 39-54.

Domingues, Fabiana, Florio et al. "Between the Conceived and the Lived, The Practice: The Crossing of Spaces at the Arts and Crafts Fair of Namorados Square in Vitoria/ES, Brazil", *Organizations & Society* 26.88 (2019): 28-49.

Dooley, Ben and Hikari Hida. "Anime is Booming. So Why Are Animators Living in Poverty?". *New York Times* 25th February 2021.

Dorlin, Elsa. *Sexe, Genre et Sexualités. Introduction à la Théorie Féministe.* Paris: Presses Universitaires de France, 2008

⎯⎯⎯⎯⎯, ed., *Sexe, Race, Classe: Pour une Épistémologie de la Domination.* Paris: Presses Universitaires de France, 2009.

Driscoll, Mark. *Absolute Erotic, Absolute Grotesque: The Living, Dead, and Undead in Japan's Imperialism, 1895-1945.* Durham: Duke University Press, 2010.

Dword, Debórah and Robert Jan van Pelt, *Holocaust: A History.* New York: W. W. Norton & Company, 2003.

Eiji, Oguma. "An Industry Awaiting Reform: The Social Origins and Economics of Manga and Animation in Postwar Japan". *The Asia-Pacific Journal* 15.9 (2017): 1-16.

Elden, Stuart. *Understanding Henri Lefebvre: Theory and the Possible.* London: Continuum, 2004.

Emerson, Ralph Waldo. "Nature". *American Transcendentalism Web.* https://archive.vcu.edu/english/engweb/transcendentalism/authors/emerson/nature.html.

⎯⎯⎯⎯⎯. "Self-Reliance". *American Transcendentalism Web.* https://archive.vcu.edu/english/engweb/transcendentalism/authors/emerson/essays/selfreliance.html.

Erickson, Millard J. *Christian Theology.* Grand Rapids: Baker Book House, 1986.

Figal, Gerald. *Civilization and Monsters: Spirits of Modernity in Meiji Japan.* Durham: Duke University Press, 1999.

Foertsch, Steven. "Children of the Mind and the Concept of Edge and Center Nations". *Journal of Science Fiction and Philosophy* 5 (2022): 1-13.

Foster, Michael Dylan. *Pandemonium and Parade: Japanese Monsters and the Culture of Yokai.* Berkeley: California University Press, 2009.

_____ and Jeffrey A. Tolbert, eds. *The Folkloresque: Reframing Folklore in a Popular Culture World*. Boulder: Colorado University Press, 2016.

Foucault, Michel. *Discipline and Punish*. Translated by Alan Sheridan. New York: Random House, 1991.

_____. *Archaeology of Knowledge*. Translated by A. M. Sheridan Smith. London: Routledge, 2002.

Freiberg, Freda, "Miyazaki's Heroines". *Sense of Cinema*. https://www.sensesofcinema.com/2006/feature-articles/miyazaki-heroines/.

Freinacht, Hanzi. *The Listening Society: A Metamodern Guide to Politics, Book One*. Frederikssund: Metamoderna ApS, 2017.

Frye, Northrop. *The Anatomy of Criticism*. Princeton: Princeton University Press, 1957.

Fukuyama, Francis. "Transhumanism". *Foreign Policy* 144 (2004): 42-43.

Gailloreto, Coleman. "The Jungian Psychology Concepts Which Inspired The Persona Franchise". *Screenrant* 10th April 2020. https://screenrant.com/persona-games-jungian-psychology-concepts-themes-inspiration-details/.

Galbraith, Patrick W. "Moe: Exploring Virtual Potential in Post-Millennial Japan". *Electronic Journal of Contemporary Japanese Studies*: https://www.japanesestudies.org.uk/articles/2009/Galbraith.html.

Game Freak, *Pokémon Red Version & Blue Version*. Kyoto: Nintendo, 1998.

Garner, Katelin. "The Digital Otaku: Anime, Participatory Culture, And Desire". Master's Thesis: California State University, 2019.

Geisler, N. L. "Freedom, Free Will, and Determinism". In the *Evangelical Dictionary of Theology*, edited by Walter A. Elwell, 428-30. Grand Rapids: Baker Book House, 1984.

Genette, Gérard. *Figure III*. Paris: Le Seuil, 1972.

Gluck, Carol. *Japan's Modern Myths: Ideology in the Late Meiji Period*. Princeton: Princeton University Press, 1985.

Goffman, Erving. *The Presentation of Self in Everyday Life*. New York: Anchor Publishing, 1959.

Gonzaga, Elmo. "Anomie and Isolation: The Wind-Up Bird Chronicle, Ghost in the Shell, Serial Experiments Lain, and Japanese Consensus Society". *Humanities Diliman* 3.1 (2002): 39-68.

Gramsci, Antonio. *Selections from the Prison Notebooks of Antonio Gramsci*. Edited by Quentin Hoare and Geoffrey Nowell Smith. London: *ElecBook*, 1999. https://abahlali.org/files/gramsci.pdf.

Gray, Douglas. "Japan's Gross National Cool". *Foreign Policy* 11th November 2009. https://foreignpolicy.com/2009/11/11/japans-gross-national-cool/.

Gregory, Derek, et al. eds. *The Dictionary of Human Geography*. Hoboken: Wiley-Blackwell, 2009.

Grimes, Ronald. "Defining Nascent Ritual", *Journal of the American Academy of Religion* 5.4 (1982): 539-55.

Groensteen, Thierry. "Why Are Comics Still in Search of Cultural Legitimization?". In *A Comic Studies Reader*, edited by Jeet Heer and Kent Worcester, 3-12. Jackson: University Press of Mississippi, 2009.

Gruenewald, Tim. "From Fan Activism to Graphic Narrative Culture and Race in Gene Luen Yang's Avatar: The Last Airbender—The Promise". In *Drawing New Color Lines: Transnational Asian American Graphic Narratives*, edited by Monica Chiu, 165-87. Hong Kong: Hong Kong University Press, 2015.

Guilhaumou, Jacques. "Autour du Concept D'Agentivité". *Rives Méditeranéennes* 41 (2013): 25-34.

Habermas, Jürgen. *The Structural Transformation of the Public Sphere: An Inquiry into a Category of Bourgeois Society*. Cambridge: Massachusetts Institute of Technology, 1991.

Häggström, O. "Aspects of Mind Uploading". In *Transhumanism the Proper Guide to a Posthuman Condition or a Dangerous Idea?*, edited by Wolfgang Hofkirchner and Hans-Jörg Kreowski, 3-20. New York: Springer, 2021.

Halberstam, Jack. "Gender". *Keywords for American Cultural Studies*. https://keywords.nyupress.org/american-cultural-studies/essay/gender/.

Hannan, Michael T. and Freeman, John. "The Population Ecology of Organizations". *American Journal of Sociology* 83.5 (1977): 929-84.

Hansell, R. Gregory, and William Grassie, eds. *H± Transhumanism and Its Critics*. Philadelphia: Metanexus Institute, 2010.

Hansen, Wilburn. *When Tengu Talk: Hirata Atsutane's Ethnography of the Other World*. Honolulu: Hawaii University Press, 2008.

Harrell, Megan. "Slightly Out of Character: Shōnen Epics, Doujinshi and Japanese Concepts of Masculinity". *The Virginia Review of Asian Studies* 5 (2007): 1-16.

Hashimoto, Mitsuru. "Chihō: Yanagita Kunio's 'Japan'". In *Mirror of Modernity: Invented Traditions of Modern Japan*, edited by Stephen Vlastos, 133-43. Berkeley: California University Press, 1998.

Hayashi, Kaz. "Holograms and Idols: The Image of God and Artificial Transcendence in the Cultural Phenomenon of the Japanese Vocaloid Hatsune Miku". In *Technology and Theology*, ed. William H. U. Anderson, 263-83. Wilmington: Vernon Press, 2019.

Hegel, Georg Wilhelm Friedrich. *The Phenomenology of Spirit*. Translated by V. A. Miller. Oxford: Oxford University Press, 1977.

Helm, Bennet. "Love" *The Stanford Encyclopedia of Philosophy*. https://plato.stanford.edu/archives/fall2017/entries/love.

Herman, Edward and Noam Chomsky. *Manufacturing Consent*. New York: Pantheon Books, 1988.

Hernández-Pérez, Manuel. "Discussing 'Genre' in Anime through Neon Genesis Evangelion". In *Anime Studies: Media-Specific Approaches to Neon Genesis Evangelion*, edited by José Andrés Santiago Iglesias and Ana Soler Baena, 181-214. Stockholm: Stockholm University Press, 2021.

Hikawa, Ryusuke, et al. eds. *Japanese Animation Guide: The History of Robot Anime*. Tokyo: Mori Building Co., 2013.

―――. "Preface". In *Japanese Animation Guide: The History of Robot Anime*, eds Ryusuke Hikawa et al. 1-4. Tokyo: Mori Building Co., 2013.

Hiroki, Azuma. *Otaku: Japan's Database Animals*. Minneapolis: University of Minnesota Press, 2009.

Hoefer, Carl. "Casual Determinism". *The Stanford Dictionary of Philosophy.* https://plato.stanford.edu/entries/determinism-causal/.

Houseman, Michael. *Le Rouge est le Noir. Essais sur le Rituel.* Toulouse: Presses Universitaires du Mirail, 2012.

Hu, Tsz-Yue G. *Frames of Anime: Culture and Image-Building.* Hong Kong: Hong Kong University Press, 2010.

———. "Animating for 'Whom' in the Aftermath of a World War". In *Japanese Animation: East Asian Perspective*, edited by Masao Yokota and Tze-yue G. Hu, 115-35. Jackson: University Press of Mississippi, 2013.

Hudson, Martyn. *Ghosts, Landscapes and Social Memory.* New York: Routledge, 2017.

Hughes, James. "Contradictions from the Enlightenment Roots of Transhumanism". *Journal of Medicine and Philosophy* 35.6 (2010): 622-40.

Huxley, Julian. "Transhumanism". *Ethics in* Progress. 6.1 (1957): 12-16.

Ichikawa, Haruko. *Hōseki No Kuni.* Tokyo: Kōdansha, 2012-present.

Inoue, Enryō. *Yōkaigaku Zenshū*, Vol. 3. Kyoto: Kashiragi Shobō Press, 2004.

Ito, Kinko. "The World of Japanese Ladies' Comics: From Romantic Fantasy to Lustful Perversion". *Journal of Popular Culture* 36.1 (2002): 68-85.

———. "Manga in Japanese History". In *Japanese Visual Culture: Explorations in the World of Manga and Anime*, edited by Mark W. Williams, 26-48. New York: An East Gate Book, 2008.

Ivy, Marilyn. *Discourses of the Vanishing: Modernity, Phantasm, Japan.* Chicago: Chicago University Press, 1995.

Jackson, Craig. "Topologies of Identity in Serial Experiments Lain". *Mechademia* 7 (2012): 191-202.

Jackson, Harrison S. "Ex Machina: Testing Machines for Consciousness and Socio-Relational Machine Ethics". *Journal of Science Fiction and Philosophy* 5 (2022): 1-17.

Jackson, Paul. "The Space Between Worlds: *Mushishi* and Japanese Folklore". *Mechademia* 5 (2010): 341-43.

Jensen, Casper Bruun, et al. "Attuning to the Webs of *en:* Ontology, Japanese Spirit Worlds, and the 'Tact' of Minakata Kumagusu". *Hau: Journal of Ethnographic Theory* 6.2. (2016): 149-72.

Jue, Irene. "Ralph Waldo Emerson: From Buddhism to Transcendentalism, the Beginning of an American Literary Tradition". Bachelor's Thesis: California Polytechnic State University, 2013.

Jung, Carl. *The Archetypes and The Collective Unconscious, Collected Works* Vol. 9 Princeton: Bollingen, 1981.

Kadia, Miriam Kingsberg. "Epistemological Exercises: Encyclopedias of World Cultural History in Twentieth-Century Japan", *Modern Asian Studies* 55.3 (2021): 1-34.

Kapp, Silke and Anna Paula Baltazar. "Out of Conceived Space: For Another History of Architecture". *Proceedings of Spaces of History/Histories of Space: Emerging Approaches to the Study of the Built Environment* at the University of California, Berkeley. https://escholarship.org/uc/item/30d070b0.

Katsuno, Hirofumi and Jeffrey Maret. "Localizing the Pokémon TV Series for the American Market". In *Pikachu's Global Adventure*, edited by Joseph Tobin, 80-107. Durham: Duke University Press, 2004.

Keller Kimbrough, R. "Battling 'Tengu', Battling Conceit: Visualizing Abstraction in 'The Tale of the Handcart Priest'". *Japanese Journal of Religious Studies* 39.2 (2012): 275-305.

Kerr, Hui-Ying. "What is Kawaii—and Why Did the World Fall for the 'Cult of Cute'?". *The Conversation* 23rd November 2016. https://theconversation.com/what-is-kawaii-and-why-did-the-world-fall-for-the-cult-of-cute-67187.

Kid, Cheeky. "Top 10 Best Harem Anime", *ReelRundown* 29th March 2022. https://reelrundown.com/animation/Best-Harem-Anime.

Kilinçarslan, Yasemin. "Siberpunk Animasyon Sinemasinda Katoptikon İzlekler Anime Film Serial Experiments Lain". *Journal of International Social Research* 9.43 (2016): 1947-55.

Kim, Joon Yang. "South Korea and the Sub-Empire of Anime: Kinesthetics of Sub-Contracted Animation Production". In *Mechademia 9: Origins*, edited by Frenchy Lunning, 90-103. Minneapolis: University of Minnesota Press, 2015.

King, Richard C., et al. "'Look Out New World, Here We Come?' Racial and Sexual Pedagogies". In *Animating Difference: Race, Gender, and Sexuality in Contemporary Films for Children*. Lanham: Rowman & Littlefield Publishers, 2011), 33-52.

Kipfer, Stefan, et al. eds. *Space, Difference, Everyday Life: Reading Henry Lefebvre*. New York: Routledge, 2008.

Kitchin, Rob and Phil Hubbard. *Key Thinkers on Space and Place*. Thousand Oaks: Sage Publication, 2010.

Kōdaiji Temple. "Andoroido Kannon Maindā Hannya Shingyō o Kataru". https://www.kodaiji.com/mindar/.

Kogod, Theo. "Neon Genesis Evangelion: 10 Undeniable Ways That It Changed Mecha Anime Forever". *CBR.com*. https://www.cbr.com/neon-genesis-evangelion-changed-mecha-anime/#strong-women.

Koschmann, Victor J., Oiwa Keibo and Yamashita Shinji, eds. *International Perspectives on Yanagita Kunio and Japanese Folklore Studies*. Ithaca: Cornell University Press, 1985.

Krämer, Hans Martin. *Shimaji Mokurai and the Reconception of Religion and the Secular in Modern Japan*. Honolulu: University of Hawaii Press, 2015.

Krüger, Oliver. Virtual Immortality — God, Evolution and the Singularity in Post-and Transhumanism. New York: Columbia University Press, 2021.

Kubo, Masakazu. "Why Pokémon Was Successful in America", *Japan Echo* 27.2 (2000): 59-62.

Kusaka, Hidenori. *Pokémon Adventures: Desperado Pikachu*. San Francisco: Viz Media, 2000.

LaMarre, Thomas. "From Animation to Anime: Drawing Movements and Moving Drawings". In *Between Cinema and Anime. Japan Forum* 14.2 (2002): 329-67.

_____. "An Introduction to Otaku Movement". *Entertext* 4.1 (2004): 151-87.

_____. "Otaku Movement". In *Japan After Japan: Social and Cultural Life from the Recessionary 1990s to the Present*, edited by Tomiko Yoda, Harry Harootunian, Rey Chow and Masao Miyoshi, 358-94. Durham: Duke University Press, 2006.

_____. *The Anime Machine: A Media Theory of Animation*. Minneapolis: University of Minnesota Press, 2009.

Lawrence, Julian. "Cartoons Have Always Been for Adults but Here's How They Got Tangled Up with Kids". *The Conversation* 03rd February 2020. https://theconversation.com/cartoons-have-always-been-for-adults-but-heres-how-they-got-tangled-up-with-kids-130421.

Lefebvre, Henri. *The Production of Space*. Translated by Donald Nicholson-Smith. Cambridge: Blackwell, 1991.

Leibniz, G. W. "Discourse on Metaphysics". In *Discourse on Metaphysics and Other Chapters*. Translated by Daniel Garber and Roger Ariew. Cambridge: Hackett Publishing Company, Inc., 1991.

Lenner, David, ed. *The Oxford Companion to World Mythology*. Oxford: Oxford University Press, 2005.

Levi, Antonia. *Samurai from Outer Space: Understanding Japanese Animation*. Chicago: Open Court, 2000.

Levy, Tani. "Entering Another World: A Cultural Genre Discourse of Japanese Isekai Texts and Their Origin in Online Participatory Culture". In *Japan's Contemporary Media Culture Between Local and Global. Content, Practice and Theory*, edited by Martin Roth, Hiroshi Yoshida and Martin Picard, 85-117. Heidelberg: CrossAsia-eBooks, 2021.

Lewis, David. *On the Plurality of Worlds*. Oxford: Blackwell Publishers, 1986.

Lindwasser, Anna. "How Anime Has Evolved Though the Years", *Ranker* 28th June 2018. https://www.ranker.com/list/how-anime-has-changed-and-evolved/anna-lindwasser.

Llull, Ramon. *Llibre d'Amic e Amat*. Edited by Albert Soler. Barcelona: Barcino, 1995.

_____. *The Book of the Lover and the Beloved*. Translated by E. Allison Peers. York: In Parentheses Publications, 2000.

Locke, John. *An Essay Concerning Human Understanding*. Edited by Peter H. Nidditch. Oxford: Oxford University Press, 1991.

Lopez, Lori Kido. "Fan Activists and the Politics or Face in The Last Airbender". *International Journal of Cultural Studies* 15.5 (2011): 431-45.

Lu, Amy Shirong. "The Many Faces of Internationalization in Japanese Anime". *Animation* 3.2 (2008): 169-87.

Lu, Curtis, "The Darker Sides of the Isekai Genre: An Examination of the Power of Anime and Manga". Master's Thesis: University of San Francisco, 2020.

Lu, Zhicong, Shen, Chenxinran, Li, Jiannan, Shen, Hong and Wigdor, Daniel. "More Kawaii than a Real-Person Live Streamer: Understanding How the Otaku Community Engages with and Perceives Virtual YouTubers". *Proceedings of the CHI Conference on Human Factors in Computing Systems* (CHI '21) in Yokohama Japan: https://dl.acm.org/doi/10.1145/3411764.3445660.

Luther, Martin. *Two Kinds of Righteousness* [1519]. In *Martin Luther's Basic Theological Writings*, edited by William R. Russell, 119-25. Minneapolis: Fortress Press, 2012.

Lyu, Tim. "History of Magical Girls (Sailor Moon, Puella Magi Madoka Magica, Cardcaptor Sakura + MORE", *YouTube*. https://www.youtube.com/watch?v=VtFR8o9n4LA. *Himitsu no Akko-chan*.

MacGregor, Geddes. *Reincarnation in Christianity: A New Vision of the Role of Rebirth in Christian Thought*. Wheaton: Theosophical Publishing House, 1978.

Machiavelli, Niccolo. *The Prince*. Translated by Harvey C. Mansfield. Chicago: The University of Chicago Press, 1985.

MacIntyre, Alasdair. *Three Rival Versions of Moral Enquiry: Encyclopaedia, Genealogy, and Tradition*. Notre Dame: University of Notre Dame Press, 1990.

MacWilliams, W. Mark. "Introduction". In *Japanese Visual Culture: Explorations in the World of Manga and Anime*, edited by Mark W. MacWilliams, 3-25. New York: An East Gate Book, 2008.

Madigan, Timothy. "Problems with Zombies". *Philosophy Now* 96 (2013), 4.

Magee, Glenn Alexander. *Hegel and the Hermetic Tradition*. Ithaca: Cornell University Press, 2001.

Maisels, Charles Keith. *Archaeology in the Cradle of Civilization*. London: Routledge, 1998.

Marcon, Federico. *The Knowledge of Nature and the Nature of Knowledge in Early Modern Japan*. Chicago: The University of Chicago Press, 2015.

Margolis, Eric. "The Dark Side of Japan's Anime Industry". *Vox* 02nd July 2019.

_____. "Cool Japan Campaign at a Crossroads 10 Years After Setting Sights Abroad". *Japan Times* 31st May 2021.

Mark, Joshua J. "Buddhism". *World History Encyclopaedia*. https://www.worldhistory.org/buddhism/.

Marx, Karl. *Economic and Philosophic Manuscripts of 1844*. Marxists.org. https://www.marxists.org/archive/marx/works/1844/manuscripts/preface.htm.

McFarland, Ian A. "Grace". In *The Cambridge Dictionary of Christian Theology*, edited by Ian A. McFarland et al. 201-03. Cambridge: Cambridge University Press, 2011.

McKenna, Michael and D. Justin Coates. "Compatibilism". *The Stanford Dictionary of Philosophy*. https://plato.stanford.edu/entries/compatibilism/.

McLelland, Mark and Romit Dasgupta, eds. *Genders, Transgenders and Sexualities in Japan*. London: Routledge, 2005.

Mendlesohn, Farah. *Rhetorics of Fantasy*. Middletown: Wesleyan University Press, 2008.

Mercer, Calvin. "Protestant Christianity—Sorting Out Soma in the Debate about Transhumanism: One Protestant's Perspective". In *Transhumanism and the Body: The World Religions Speak*, edited by Calvin Mercer and Derek F. Maher, 137-54. New York: Palgrave Macmillan, 2016.

Merricks, Trenton. "Dualism, Physicalism, and the Incarnation". *In Persons: Human and Divine*, edited by Peter Van Inwagen and Dean Zimmerman, 281-300. Oxford: Clarendon Press, 2007.

Mes, Tom. "Interview: Satoshi Kon". *Midnight Eye* 11th February 2002. http://www.midnighteye.com/interviews/satoshi-kon/.

Meyer, Matthew. "Introduction to Yōkai", *Yokai.com*: https://yokai.com/introduction/.

Minakata Kumagusu. *Minakata Kumagusu Zenshu*. Tokyo: Heibonsha, 1971.

Mishan, Ligaya. "Hayao Miyazaki Prepares to Cast One Last Spell". *The New York Times Magazine* 23th November 2021.

Miura, Takashi. "The Buddha in Yoshiwara: Religion and Visual Entertainment in Tokugawa Japan as Seen through *Kibyōshi*". *Japanese Journal of Religious Studies* 44.2 (2017): 225-54.

Mizuki, Shigeru. *Mizuki Shigeru Manga Daizenshu*. Tokyo: Kodansha, 2014.

Mizuko, Ito. "Introduction". In *Fandom Unbound: Otaku Culture in a Connected World*, edited by Mizuko Ito, Daisuke Okabe and Izumi Tsuji, xi-xxvii. New Haven: Yale University Press, 2012.

More, Max. "The Overman in the Transhuman". *Journal of Evolution and Technology* 21.1 (2010): 1-4.

Morgner, Christian. "Governance and Policy Development of Creative and Cultural Industries in Japan". In the *Routledge Handbook of Cultural and Creative Industries in Asia Routledge*, edited by Lorraine Lim and Hye-Kyung Lee, 43-56. London, Routledge, 2018.

Mori, Masahiro. *The Buddha in the Robot: A Robot Engineer's Thoughts on Science and Religion*. Translated by Charles S. Terry. Tokyo: Kosei Publishing, 1981.

Mōri, Yoshitaka. "The Pitfall Facing the Cool Japan Project: The Transnational Development of the Anime Industry Under the Condition of Post-Fordism". *International Journal of Japanese Sociology* 20.1 (2011): 30-42.

Moriarty, Elizabeth. "The Communitarian Aspect of Shinto Matsuri". *Asian Folklore Studies* 31.2 (1972): 91-140.

Morrissy, Kim. "Mushoku Tensei Is Not the Pioneer of Isekai Web Novels, But…". *Anime News Network* 19th March 2021. https://www.animenewsnetwork.com/feature/2021-03-19/mushoku-tensei-is-not-the-pioneer-of-isekai-web-novels-but/.170429.

⸻. "In a Struggling Anime Workplace, 'Cool Japan' Feels Like a Joke". *Anime News Network* 04th September 2021. https://www.animenewsnetwork.com/feature/2021-09-04/in-a-struggling-anime-workplace-cool-japan-feels-like-a-joke/.176373.

Moseley, Alexander. "Political Realism". *Internet Encyclopedia of Philosophy*. https://iep.utm.edu/polreal/#:~:text=Political%20realism%20is%20a%20theory,the%20domestic%20or%20international%20arena.

Mullins, Mark R. "Religion in Contemporary Japanese Lives". In the *Routledge Handbook of Japanese Culture and Society*, edited by Victoria Bestor, Theodore Bester and Akiko Yamagata, 63-74. London: Routledge, 2011.

Nakamura, Hikaru. *Saint Young Men*. Tokyo: Kodansha, 2006-present.

Napier, Susan J. *Anime from Akira to Howl's Moving Castle: Experiencing Contemporary Japanese Animation*. New York: Palgrave, 2001.

———. *Anime from Akira to Princess Mononoke: Experiencing Contemporary Japanese Animation*. London: Palgrave Macmillan, 2001.

———. "When the āMachines Stop: Fantasy, Reality, and Terminal Identity in 'Neon Genesis Evangelion' and 'Serial Experiments Lain'". *Science Fiction Studies* 29.3 (2002): 418-35.

———. "Why Anime?" *Japan Spotlight* (March/April 2004): 20-23.

———. "The World of Anime Fandom in America". *Mechademia* 1.1 (2006): 47-63.

———. "When the Machines Stop Fantasy, Reality, and Terminal Identity in *Neon Genesis Evangelion* and *Serial Experiments: Lain*". In *Robot Ghosts Wired Dreams: Japanese Science Fiction from Origins to Anime*, edited by Christopher Bolton, Istvan Csicsery-Ronay Jr. and Takayuki Tatsumi, 101-23. Minneapolis: University of Minnesota Press, 2007.

———. "Manga and Anime: Entertainment, Big Business, and Art in Japan". In the *Routledge Handbook of Japanese Culture and Society*, edited by Victoria Bestor, Theodore Bester and Akiko Yamagata, 226-37. London: Routledge, 2011.

———. *Miyazakiworld: A Life in Art*. New Haven: Yale University Press, 2018.

Newitz, Annalee. "Anime Otaku: Japanese Animation Fans Outside Japan". *Bad Subjects* 13 (1994): 1-13.

Nietzsche, Friedrich. *Thus Spoke Zarathustra* [1887]. In *The Portable Nietzsche*, edited and translated by Walter Kaufmann, 103-439. New York: Penguin Books, 1976.

———. "Second Treatise: 'Guilt', 'Bad Conscious', and Related Matters". *On the Genealogy of Morality*. Translated by Maudemarie Clark and Alan Swensen. Indianapolis: Hackett Publishing Company, 1998.

Nikolajeva, Maria. *Power, Voice and Subjectivity in Literature for Young Readers*. London: Routledge, 2010.

Nish, Ian, ed. "Minakata Kumagusu, 1867-1941, A Genius Now Recognised". In *Britain & Japan: Biographical Portraits*. Tokyo: Japan Library, 1994.

Noble, David. *The Religion of Technology*. New York: Alfred A Knopf, 1997.

Norris, Craig. "Manga, Anime and Visual Art Culture". In *The Cambridge Companion to Modern Japanese Culture*, edited by Yoshio Sugimoto, 236-60. Cambridge: Cambridge University Press, 2009.

Nozaki, Kiyoshi. *Kitsuné — Japan's Fox of Mystery, Romance, and Humor*. Tokyo: The Hokuseidô Press, 1961.

Odell, Colin and Le Blanc, Michelle. *Studio Ghibli: The Films of Hayao Miyazaki and Isao Takahata*. Herts: Kamera Books, 2015.

O'Keefe, Tim. "Ancient Theories of Freedom and Determinism". *The Stanford Dictionary of Philosophy*. https://plato.stanford.edu/entries/freedom-ancient/.

Okuno, Takuji. "Roots of Cool Japan: From the Japanese Traditional Edo Culture to Anime and Manga". *Kwansei Gakuin University Social Sciences Review* 19 (2014): 1-7.

Okura, Fumi and N. Francis Hioki. "Anime and Bible". *The Bible in Motion: A Handbook of the Bible and Its Reception in Film*, edited by Rhonda Brunette-Bietsch, 285-95. Berlin: De Gruyter. 2016.

Ono, Toshihiro. *The Electric Tale of Pikachu*. Tokyo: Shogakukan, 1997-1999.

Ortabaşı, Melek. "National History as Otaku Fantasy: Satoshi Kon's Millennium Actress". In *Japanese Visual Culture: Explorations in the World of Manga and Anime*, edited by Mark W. MacWilliams, 274-94. New York: An East Gate Book, 2008.

Osaki, Tomohiro. "South Korea's Booming 'Webtoons' Put Japan's Print Manga on Notice". *Japan Times* 05th May 2019.

Outka, Gene. "Love". In *The Cambridge Dictionary of Christian Theology*, edited by Ian A. McFarland et al. 288-90. Cambridge: Cambridge University Press, 2011.

Oya, Alberto. "Nietzsche and Unamuno on *Conatus* and the Agapeic Way of Life", *Metaphilosophy* 51.2-3 (2020): 303-17.

⎯⎯⎯⎯. *Unamuno's Religious Fictionalism*. London: Palgrave Macmillan, 2020.

⎯⎯⎯⎯. "Joaquim Xirau: amor, persona y mundo", *Bulletin of Hispanic Studies* 99.9 (2022): 835-43.

Pagan, Amanda. "A Beginner's Guide to Isekai". *New York Public Library* 15th July 2019. https://www.nypl.org/blog/2019/07/15/beginners-guide-isekai-manga.

Palmer, Ada. "Film is Alive: The Manga Roots of Osamu Tezuka's Animation Obsession", *Academia.edu* (2009): https://www.academia.edu/5142140/Film_is_Alive_The_Manga_Roots_of_Osamu_Tezukas_Animation_Obsession.

Pang, Laikwan. *Creativity and Its Discontents: China's Creative Industries and Intellectual Property Rights Offenses*. Durham: Duke University Press, 2012.

Paquot, Valentin. "Kaiu Shirai: Le Conte Pour Enfants Hansel et Gretel m'a Traumatisé Étant Petit". *Le Figaro* 10th May 2020. https://www.lefigaro.fr/bd/kaiu-shirai-le-conte-pour-enfants-haensel-et-gretel-m-a-traumatise-etant-petit-20200510.

Pelser, Adam. "Temptation, Virtue, and the Character of Christ". *Faith and Philosophy: Journal of the Society of Christian Philosophers* 36.1 (2019): 81-101.

Perper, Timothy and Martha Cornog. Review of *Psychoanalytic Cyberpunk Midsummer-Night's Dreamtime: Kon Satoshi's 'Paprika'*. *Mechademia* 4 (2009): 326-29.

Peterson, Lani. "The Science Behind the Art Of Storytelling". *Harvard Business Publishing*. https://www.harvardbusiness.org/the-science-behind-the-art-of-storytelling/.

Phillipps, Susanne. "Characters, Themes, and Narrative Patterns in the Manga of Osamu Tezuka". In *Japanese Visual Culture: Explorations in the World of Manga and Anime*, edited by Mark W. MacWilliams, 68-90. New York: An East Gate Book, 2008.

Picard, Martin. "Gēmu Communities and Otaku Consumption. The (Sub) Culture(s) of Videogames in Japan". In *Japan's Contemporary Media Culture Between Local and Global Content, Practice and Theory*, edited by Martin

Roth, Hiroshi Yoshida and Martin Picard, 11-36. Heidelberg: CrossAsia-eBooks, 2021.

Pitre, Jake. "Rated Q for Queer: The Legend of Korra and the Evolution of Queer Reading". *Red Feather Journal: An International Journal of Children in Popular Culture* 8.2 (2017): 23-33.

Plato, *The Republic*. Edited by G. R. E. Ferrari and translated by Tom Griffith (Cambridge University Press, 2007.

Pointon, Susan. "Transcultural Orgasm as Apocalypse: Urotsukidoji: The Legend of the Overfiend", *WideAngle* 19.3 (1997): 41-63.

Poitras, Gilles. "Contemporary Anime in Japanese Pop Culture". In *Japanese Visual Culture: Explorations in the World of Manga and Anime*, edited by Mark W. MacWilliams, 48-67. New York: An East Gate Book, 2008.

Prelipcean, Teodora. "Saint Augustine — The Apologist of Love". *Procedia — Social and Behavioral Sciences* 149.5 (2014): 765-71.

Price, Paul S. "A Survey of the Story Elements of Isekai Manga". *Journal of Anime and Manga Studies* 2 (2021): 57-91.

Prince, Colin. "Summary of Moral Foundation Theory". *Seattle University Law Review* 33.4 (2010): 1293-1317.

———. "Telling Stories in Art". *The J. Paul Getty Museum*. https://www.getty.edu/education/teachers/classroom_resources/curricula/stories/.

Prohl, Inken and John K. Nelson, eds. *Handbook of Contemporary Japanese Religion* Vol 6. Leiden: Brill, 2012.

Prough, Jennifer. *Straight from the Heart: Gender, Intimacy, and the Cultural Production of Shojo Manga*. Honolulu: Hawaii University Press, 2011.

Pruitt, Daniel Joseph. "Popular Culture as Pharmakon: Metamodernism and the Deconstruction of Status Quo Consciousness". MA Thesis: The Graduate School at the University of North Carolina at Greensboro, 2020.

Pungente, John and Martin O'Malley. *More Than Meets The Eye. Watching Television Watching Us*. Toronto: McClelland & Stewart, 1999.

Rambelli, Fabio. "Prayer Machines in Japanese Buddhism". *Material Religion* 12.1 (2016): 104-05.

Reader, Ian. "Buddhism in Crisis? Institutional Decline in Modern Japan". *Buddhist Studies Review* 28.2 (2011): 233-63.

Reid, Thomas. *Essays on the Intellectual Powers of Man A Critical Edition*. Edited by Derek R. Brookes. Philadelphia: Pennsylvania University Press, 2002.

Reider, Noriko T. *Japanese Demon Lore: Oni from Ancient Times to the Present*. Logan: Utah State University Press, 2010.

Reznik, Shiri and Dafna Lemish. "Falling in Love with High School Musical: Girls' Talk about Romantic Perceptions". In *Mediated Girlhoods: New Explorations of Girls' Media Culture*, edited by Mary Celeste Kearney, 151-70. Oxford: Peter Lang, 2011.

Riani, Ernesto. "Ramon Llull". *The Stanford Encyclopedia of Philosophy*. https://plato.stanford.edu/entries/llull/.

Ritzer, George. *The McDonaldization Thesis*. London: SAGE, 1999.

Robbins, L. Pope. "Bringing Anime to Academic Libraries: A Recommended Core Collection". *Collection Building* 33.2 (2014): 46-52.

Roberston, Jennifer. *Takarazuka: Sexual Politics and Popular Culture in Modern Japan.* Berkeley: University of California Press, 2008.

Robinson, Joanna. "How a Nickelodeon Cartoon Became One of the Most Powerful, Subversive Shows of 2014". *Vanity Fair* (2014). https://www.vanityfair.com/hollywood/2014/12/korra-series-finale-recap-gay-asami.

Roe, Matthew. "Hideaki Anno: A Career Retrospective". *Anime News Network.* https://www.animenewsnetwork.com/watch/2021-10-01/hideaki-anno-a-career-retrospective/.178012.

Rouvroy, Antoinette. "La Gouvernementalité Algorithmique: Radicalisation et Stratégie Immunitaire du Capitalisme et du Néolibéralisme?" *La Deleuziana* 3 (2016): 30-36.

Rowson, Jonathan. "Metamodernism and the Perception of Context: The Cultural Between, the Political After and the Mystic Beyond". *Perspectiva* 26th May 2021. https://systems-souls-society.com/metamodernism-and-the-perception-of-context-the-cultural-between-the-political-after-and-the-mystic-beyond/.

Ryan, Alan. "Liberalism". In *A Companion to Contemporary Political Philosophy*, edited by Robert E. Gooding, Philip Pettit and Thomas Pogge, 360-82. New Jersey: Blackwell Publishing, 2007.

Ryan, James R. *Picturing Empire: Photography and the Visualization of the British Empire.* London: Reaktion Books, 1997.

Šabanović, Selma. "Inventing Japan's 'Robotics Culture': The Repeated Assembly of Science, Technology, and Culture in Social Robotics". *Social Studies of Science* 44.3 (2014): 342–67.

Sadamichi, Kato. "The Three Ecologies in Minakata Kumagusu's Environmental Movement". *Organization & Environment* 12.1 (1999): 85-98.

Said, Edward. *Orientalism.* New York: Penguin Books, 2003.

Sakurakouji, Kanoko. *Black Bird* [18 Volumes]. San Francisco: Viz Media, 2010-2014.

Sano, Akiko. "*Chiyogami*, Cartoon, Silhouette the Transitions of Ōfuji Noburō". In *Japanese Animation: East Asian Perspective*, edited by Masao Yokota and Tze-yue G. Hu, 87-98. Jackson: University Press of Mississippi, 2013.

Savaedi, Fatemeh and Maryam Alva Nia. "<null> me <null>: Algorithmic Governmentality and the Notion of Subjectivity in Project Itoh's Harmony". *Journal of Science Fiction and Philosophy* 4 (2021): 1-19.

Schechner, Richard. *Performance Studies: An Introduction.* New York: Routledge, 2006.

Schley, Matt. "The Push to Go Digital Opens New Doors for Anime". *Japan Times* 20th January 2020.

Schmitt, Carl. *The Concept of the Political.* New Brunswick: Rutgers University Press, 1976.

Schmitt, F. S. and R. W. Southern, eds. *Memorials of St. Anselm.* Oxford: Oxford University Press, 1969.

Schodt, Frederik L. *My Heart Sutra: A World in 260 Characters.* Berkeley: Stone Bridge Press, 2020.

Schumacher, Mark. "Tengu: The Slayer of Vanity". *Buddhism and Shintoism in Japan.* https://www.onmarkproductions.com/html/tengu.shtml.

Severan, A. *Metamodernism and the Return of Transcendence (Metamodern Spirituality).* Independently Published, 2021.

Shamoon, Deborah. "Miura Ira: *Shōjo*". *Japanese Media and Popular Culture.* Japanese Media and Popular Culture. https://jmpc-utokyo.com/keyword/shojo/.

_____. "Revolutionary Romance: *The Rose of Versailles* and the Transformation of Shojo Manga". *Mechademia* 2 (2007): 3-17.

_____. *Passionate Friendship: The Aesthetics of Girls' Culture in Japan.* Honolulu: Hawaii University Press, 2012.

Sharkey, Amanda and Noel. "Granny and the Robots: Ethical Issues in Robot Care for the Elderly". *Ethics and Information Technology* 14.1 (2012): 27-40.

Shinmura, Izuru. *Kōjien.* Tokyo: Asahi Sonorama, 1998.

Shinsuke, Nakajima "Interview with Chiaki Konaka". *HK.* http://www.konaka.com/alice6/lain/hkint_e.html.

Shirai, Kaiu. *The Promised Neverland* 16. San Francisco: VIZ Media LLC, 2020.

Skocpol, Theda. *Bringing the State Back In.* Cambridge: Cambridge University Press, 1985.

Smith, Adam. *An Inquiry into the Nature and Causes of the Wealth of Nations.* Amsterdam: Metalibri, 2007.

Soja, Edward. *Thirdspace Journeys to Los Angeles and Other Real-and-Imagined Places.* Oxford: Blackwell Publishing, 1996.

Sorgner, Stefan Lorenz. "Nietzsche the Overman, and Transhumanism". *Journal of Evolution and Technology* 20.1 (2009): 29-42.

Sotheby's. "The Evolution of Japanese Animation" 14th December 2021. https://www.sothebys.com/en/articles/the-evolution-of-japanese-animation.

Stalnaker, Robert. "What is it Like to Be a Zombie?" In *Conceivability and Possibility*, edited by Tamar Szabó Gendler and John Hawthorne, 385-400. Oxford: Clarendon Press, 2002.

Starlight, Naomi. "Best Anime of the 2010s: A Look at Anime From 2010 to 2019". *Reelrundown* 26th February 2020. https://reelrundown.com/animation/Best-Anime-Series-and-Films-of-the-2010s-Anime-from-2010-to-2019.

_____. "Admit It: You Enjoy the Wish Fulfillment in Isekai Anime", *ReelRundown* 23th March 2022. https://reelrundown.com/animation/Is-Wish-Fulfilment-in-the-Isekai-Genre-Always-Bad.

_____. "Isekai Anime: Explaining the Genre's History, and How It's Changed". *ReelRundown* 25th March 2022. https://reelrundown.com/animation/Thoughts-on-the-History-of-the-Isekai-Genre.

Steinberg, Marc Aaron. "The Emergence of the Anime Media Mix: Character Communication and Serial Consumption". Ph.D. Dissertation: Brown University, 2009.

_____. *Anime's Media Mix: Franchising Toys and Characters in Japan.* Minneapolis: University of Minnesota Press, 2012. Project MUSE.

Strathern, Marilyn. *Before and After Gender. Sexual Mythologies of Everyday Life.* Chicago: Hau Books, 2016.

Strawson, Galen. *Locke on Personal Identity*. Princeton: Princeton University Press, 2011.

Stuckmann, Chris. "Introduction". In *Anime Impact: The Movies and Shows that Changed the World of Japanese Animation*, edited by Chris Stuckmann, no page [Kindle]. Mango Publishing, 2018.

Suan, Steve. "Repeating Anime's Creativity Across Asia". In *Trans-Asia as Method: Theory and Practices*, edited by Jeroen de Kloet, Yiu Fai Chow and Gladys Pak Lei Chong, 141-60. New York: Rowman and Littlefield Publishers, 2019.

_____. "Performing Virtual YouTubers: Acting Across Borders in the Platform Society". In *Japan's Contemporary 187 Media Culture Between Local and Global. Content, Practice and Theory*, edited by Martin Roth, Hiroshi Yoshida and Martin Picard, 187-225. Heidelberg: CrossAsia-eBooks, 2021.

Sudo, Tadashi. "What Is Happening in the Anime Industry in 2020-2021? An Analysis of The Animation Industry Report 2021". Translated by Kim Morrissy. *Anime News Network* 03rd November 2021. https://www.animenewsnetwork.com/feature/2021-11-03/what-is-happening-in-the-anime-industry-in-2020-2021-an-analysis-of-the-animation-industry-report-2021/.179153.

Sugawa-Shimada, Akiko. "Grotesque Cuteness of Shōjo Representations of Goth-Loli in Japanese Contemporary TV Anime". In *Japanese Animation: East Asian Perspective*, edited by Masao Yokota and Tze-yue G. Hu, 199-223. Jackson: University Press of Mississippi, 2013.

Surface-Evans, Sarah, Amanda Garrison and Kisha Supernant, eds. *Blurring Timescapes, Subverting Erasure: Remembering Ghosts on the Margins of History*. New York: Berghahn, 2020.

Swanson, Paul L. "Swanson Review of Tezuka Osamu Buddha". *Japanese Journal of Religious Studies* 31.1 (2004): 233-40.

Takehara, Issei. "History and Philosophy of Transubstantiation". *Isseicreekphilosophyblog* 24th February 2012. https://isseicreekphilosophy.wordpress.com/2012/02/24/history-and-philosophy-of-transubstantiation/.

_____. "Enryō Inoue on the Soul". *Isseicreekphilosophyblog* 25th January 2017. https://isseicreekphilosophy.wordpress.com/2017/01/25/enryo-inoue-%e4%ba%95%e4%b8%8a%e5%86%86%e4%ba%86-on-the-soul-an-excerpt-from-his-yokaigaku-kougi-or-lectures-on-yokai-studies/.

_____. "Categories and Races and the Meanings of the Names in Dragon Ball Z". *Isseicreekphilosophyblog* 07th February 2017. https://isseicreekphilosophy.wordpress.com/2017/07/07/appendix-i-categories-of-races-and-the-meanings-of-the-names-in-dragon-ball-z/.

_____. "Episode Analysis in Dragon Ball Z". *Isseicreekphilosophyblog* 16th April 2021. https://isseicreekphilosophy.wordpress.com/2021/04/16/appendix-ii-episode-analysis/.

Takeuchi, Naoko. *Pretty Guardian Sailor Moon* Vol. 1. New York: Kodansha, 2011.

Tanabe Jr., George J. "Playing with Religion". *Nova Religio: The Journal of Alternative and Emergent Religions* 10.3 (2007): 96-101.

Tankha, Brij. "Minakata Kumagusu: Fighting Shrine Unification in Meiji Japan". *China Report* 36.4 (2002): 555-71.

Tavassi, Guido. *Storia Dell'Animazione Giapponese: Autori, arte, industria, successo dal 1917 a oggi* [A History of Japanese Animation]. Latin: Tunue, 2021. English Translation https://www.academia.edu/11989528/A_History_of_Japanese_Animation_Authors_Art_Industry_Success_from_1917_to_Today_English_Excerpt.

Taylor, Charles. *The Ethics of Authenticity*. Cambridge: Harvard University, 1991.

Tezuka, Osamu. *Hi no Tori*. Various Publishers, 1958-1988.

⎯⎯⎯⎯. *Buddha*. London: HarperCollins 1972-1983.

Thomas, Jolyon. "*Shûkyô Asobi* and Miyazaki Hayao's *Anime*". *Nova Religio: The Journal of Alternative and Emergent Religions* 10.3 (2007): 73-95.

⎯⎯⎯⎯. *Drawing on Tradition: Manga, Anime, and Religion in Contemporary Japan*. University of Hawaii Press, 2012.

⎯⎯⎯⎯. "Spirit/ Medium: Critically Examining the Relationship between Animism and Animation". In *Spirits and Animism in Contemporary Japan: The Invisible Empire*, edited by Fabio Rambelli, 157-70. New York: Bloomsbury, 2019.

Thomas, Owen. "Amusing Himself to Death". *waybackmachine*. http://www.akadot.com/article/article-tsurumaki2.html.

Thoreau, Henry David. *Walden; Or, Life in the Woods*. https://www.gutenberg.org/files/205/205-h/205-h.htm.

Tillich, Paul. *Love, Power and Justice*. Oxford: Oxford University Press, 1954.

Timbrell, J. Jeffery. "1963 Astro Boy". In *Anime Impact: The Movies and Shows that Changed the World of Japanese Animation*, edited by Chris Stuckmann, no page [Kindle]. Miami: Mango Publishing, 2018.

Tirosh-Samuelson, Hava. "Transhumanism as a Secular Faith". *Zygon* 47.4 (2012): 710-34.

Tisdale, Alex. "Persona Takes Jungian Psychology and Runs with It". *Inverse* 27th October 2016. https://www.inverse.com/gaming/22672-persona-carl-jung-psychology-matthew-fike-interview#:~:text='Persona'%20Takes%20Jungian%20Psychology%20and,accuracy%20is%20hit%20or%20miss.&text=Atlus's%20Persona%20series%20is%20very,visual%20representations%20of%20its%20concepts

Tobin, Joseph, ed. *Pikachu's Global Adventure: The Rise and Fall of Pokémon*. Durham: Duke University Press, 2004.

Toku, Masami. "Shojo Manga! Girls' Comics! A Mirror of Girls' Dreams". *Mechademia* 2 (2007): 18-32.

Tolstoy, Leo. *War and Peace*. Translated by Louise and Aylmer Maude. New York: Oxford University Press, 2010.

Toriyama, Akira. *Dragon Ball* Vols 1-42. Tokyo: Shueisha, 1984-1995.

Toriyama, Sekien. "Konjaku Zoku Hyakki" [Night Procession of One Hundred Demons]. *The British Museum*. https://www.britishmuseum.org/collection/object/A_1915-0823-0-63.

Torseth, Robb. "Who Am I? Personhood and the Self-Defeating Epistemology of Transhumanism". In *Technology and Theology*, edited by William H. U. Anderson, 20-36. Wilmington: Vernon Press, 2020.

Travagnin, Stefania. "From Online Buddha Halls to Robot-Monks: New Developments in the Long-Term Interaction between Buddhism, Media, and Technology in Contemporary China". *Review of Religion and Chinese Society* 7.1 (2020): 120-48.

Treat, John Whittier. "Yoshimoto Banana Writes Home: *Shōjo* Culture and the Nostalgic Subject". *Journal of Japanese Studies* 19.2 (1993): 353-87.

Trites, Roberta Seelinger. *Disturbing the Universe: Power and Repression in Adolescent Literature*. Iowa City: Iowa University Press, 2000.

Tsugata, Nobuyuki. "A Bipolar Approach to Understanding the History of Japanese Animation". In *Japanese Animation: East Asian Perspective*, edited by Masao Yokota and Tze-yue, 25-33. Jackson: University Press of Mississippi, 2013.

Tsurumi, Kazuko. *Minakata Kumagusu: Chikyu Shiko no Hikakugaku*. Tokyo: Kodansha, 1978.

_____. *Minakata Mandala Ron*. Tokyo: Yasaka Shobo, 1992.

_____. "Comparative Forms of Creativity Among Japanese Folklorists: Origuchi Shinobu, Yanagita Kunio, and Minakata Kumagusu". In *Kazuko Tsurumi: The Adventure of Ideas*, edited by Ronald A. Morse, 62-101. Tokyo: Japanime, 2014.

Tuck Eve and Ruben Gaztambide-Fernandez. "Curriculum, Replacement, and Settler Futurity". *Journal of Curriculum Theorizing* 29.1 (2013): 72-89.

Turkle, Sherry. *Alone Together: Why We Expect More from Technology and Less from Each Other*. New York: Basic Books, 2011.

Turner, Victor. *Le Phénomène Rituel. Structure et Contre-Structure*. Paris: Presses Universitaires de France, 1969.

_____. *The Anthropology of Performance*. New York: PAJ Publications, 1986.

Tze-yue G. Hu, 25-33. Jackson: University Press of Mississippi, 2013.

Ünal, Barışkan and Şeyma Balcı, "Working Women and Rape Myths in Turkish Cinema between 1923-1996". In *Film, Philosophy and Religion*, edited by William H. U. Anderson, 281-323. Wilmington: Vernon Press, 2019.

Unamuno, Miguel de. *Del sentimiento trágico de la vida en los hombres y en los pueblos*. In *Miguel de Unamuno: obras completas (vol. VII: 'Meditaciones y ensayos espirituales')*, edited by M. García Blanco, 109-302. Madrid: Escelicer, 1966.

_____. *The Tragic Sense of Life in Men and Nations*. In *The Selected Works of Miguel de* Unamuno Vol. 4, edited and translated by A. Kerrigan, 146-71. Princeton: Princeton University Press, 1972.

Urushibara, Yuki. *Mushishi*. Vol. 1-10. Tokyo: Kodansha, 1999-2008.

Utamaro, Kitagawa. "Utamakura (Poem of the Pillow)" [1788]. *The British Museum*. https://www.britishmuseum.org/collection/object/A_OA-0-133-6.

Vachnadze, Giorgi. "The Algorithmic Unconscious: Psychoanalyzing Artificial Intelligence". *The Shadow* 06th February 2021. https://medium.com/the-shadow/the-algorithmic-unconscious-psychoanalyzing-artificial-intelligence-323c52232c61.

Valera, Luca. "Posthumanism: Beyond Humanism?", *Cuadernos de Bioética* 25.3 (2014): 481-91.

Van Gennep, Arnold. *Les Rites de Passage*. Paris: Émile Nourry, 1909.

Van Hoey, Thomas. "The Blending of Bending: World-Building in Avatar: The Last Airbender and Legend of Korra". *Linguistics in Comics and Animation* (2016): 1-28.

———. "The Blending of Bending: World-Building in Avatar: The Last Airbender and Legend of Korra (2018)". *figshare*. https://doi.org/10.6084/m9.figshare.12652460.v1.

Van Inwagen, Peter. "The Possibility of Resurrection". *International Journal for Philosophy of Religion* 9.2 (1978): 114-21.

Vandermeer, Jeff and S. J. Chambers. *The Steampunk Bible: An Illustrated Guide to the World of Imaginary Airships, Corsets and Goggles, Mad Scientists, and Strange Literature*. New York: Abrams Image, 2011.

Veracini, Lorenzo. *The Settler Colonial Present*. New York: Palgrave Macmillan, 2015.

Verdoux, Philippe. "Transhumanism, Progress and the Future". *Journal of Evolution and Technology* 20.2 (2009): 49-69.

Vermeulen, Timotheus and Robin van den Akker. "Notes on Metamodernism". *Journal of Aesthetics and Culture* 2.1 (2010): 1-12.

Visser, M. W. de. "The Tengu". *Transactions of the Asiatic Society of Japan* 34.2 (1908): 25-99.

Vita-More, Natasha. "Transhumanist Art Statement". *web.archive.org*. (1982): https://web.archive.org/web/19980523093459/http://www.extropic-art.com/transart.htm.

———. "The Transhumanist Manifesto". *humanityplus.org*. (1998): https://www.humanityplus.org/the-transhumanist-manifesto.

Viswanath, Gayatri. "Power and Resistance: Silence and Secrecy in Avatar: The Last Airbender". *SubVersions: A Journal of Emerging Research in Media and Cultural Studies* 2.1 (2014): 26-47.

Vonnegut, Kurt. *Slaughterhouse-Five*. New York: Delacorte Press, 1969.

Wakabayashi, Haruko. *The Seven Tengu Scrolls*. Honolulu: Hawaii University Press, 2012.

Walker, Seth M. "Osamu Tezuka's *Buddha*, Canonical Authority, and Remix Theory in the Study of Religion". *Journal of the American Academy of Religion* 90.2 (2022): 431-49.

Wall, Elizabeth A. "Textual Persuasion: Trauma Representation in Mark Z. Danielewski's *House of Leaves*". MA Thesis: State University of New York, 2022.

Waller, Alison. *Constructing Adolescence in Fantastic Realism*. London: Routledge, 2009.

Wasylak, Katarzyna. "Lain—The Cyber-Ghost Versus Hyperreality". https://www.academia.edu/15644811/Lain_The_Cyber-ghost_Versus_Hyperreality.

Watanabe, Yasushi. "The Japanese Walt Disney: Masaoka Kenzo". Translated by Sheuo Hui Gan. In *Japanese Animation: East Asian Perspective*, edited by Masao Yokota and Tze-yue G. Hu, 98-115. Jackson: University Press of Mississippi, 2013.

Weber, Max. *The Protestant Work Ethic and the Spirit of Capitalism*. Translated by Talcott Parsons. New York: Charles Scribner's Sons, 1958.

Weinberg, Shelley. "Locke on Personal Identity". *Philosophy Compass* 6.6 (2011): 398-407.

Wells, Paul. *Understanding Animation*. London: Routledge, 1998.

_____. *Animation: Genre and Authorship*. London: Wallflower Press, 2002.

Whaley, Benjamin Evan. "Drawing the Self: Race and Identity in the Manga of Tezuka Osamu". MA Thesis, Stanford University, 2007.

White, Hayden. *Metahistory: The Historical Imagination of Nineteenth-Century Europe*. Baltimore: The John Hopkins Press, 1973.

Wittgenstein, Ludwig. *Tractatus Logico-Philosophicus*. Translated by Charles K. Ogden and Frank P. Ramsey. London: Routledge & Kegan Paul, 1922.

_____. *Tractatus Logico-Philosophicus*. Translated by David F. Pears and Brian F. McGuinness. London: Routledge & Kegan Paul, 1961.

Wolfe, Patrick. "Settler Colonialism and the Elimination of the Native", *Journal of Genocide Research* 8.4 (2006): 387-409.

Won, Hee and Hyang Ryu. "Light and Shadow — TAPPYTOON Comics & Novels: Official English". *Tappytoon Comics & Novels*. https://www.tappytoon.com/series/lightnshadow/1.

Wright, Heather. "'The Childish, the Transformative, and the Queer': Queer Interventions as Praxis in Children's Cartoons". MA Thesis: City University of New York, 2018.

Xirau, Joaquim. "Being and Objectivity", *Philosophy and Phenomenological Research* 3.2 (1942): 145-61.

_____. *Amor y mundo*, in *Joaquim Xirau: obras completas (t. 1: 'Escritos fundamentales')* [1940], edited by Ramon Xirau, 133-262. Barcelona: Anthropos, 1998.

_____. *Lo fugaz y lo eterno*. In *Joaquim Xirau: obras completas (t. 1: 'Escritos fundamentales')* [1942], edited by Ramon Xirau, 263-307. Barcelona: Anthropos, 1998.

Yadao, Jason S. *The Rough Guide To Manga*. London: Rough Guides, 2009.

Yamaguchi, Yasuo. "The Evolution of the Japanese Anime Industry". *Nippon* 20th December 2013. https://www.nippon.com/en/features/h00043/.

Yamanaka, Hiroshi. "The Utopian 'Power to Live': The Significance of the Miyazaki Phenomenon". In *Japanese Visual Culture: Explorations in the World of Manga and Anime*, edited by Mark W. MacWilliams, 237-55. New York: An East Gate Book, 2008.

Yanagita, Kunio. *The Legends of Tono*. Translated by Ronald A. Morse. Lanham: Rowman & Littlefield Publishers, Inc., 2008.

Yuta, Saito. "Cool Japan Fund's Big Ambitions Mostly Fall Flat". *Nikkei* 06th November 2017. https://asia.nikkei.com/Business/Companies/Cool-Japan-Fund-s-big-ambitions-mostly-fall-flat?page=1.

Zobel, Greifswald J. "חסד". In the *Theological Dictionary of the Old Testament*, edited by Botterweck et al. 44-64. Grand Rapids: William B. Eerdmans Publishing Co., 1986.

Animography

8 Man. Directed by Haruyuki Kawajima based on the manga by Kazumasa Hirai. TCJ 1963-1964.

Adventure Time. Directed by Larry Leichliter and Created by Pendleton Ward. Cartoon Network 2012-2018.

Akira. Directed and Screenplay by Katsuhiro Ōtomo and Izo Hashimoto based on the manga by Katsuhiro Ōtomo. Tokyo Movie Shinsha 1988.

A.Li.CE. Directed by Kenichi Maejima with Screenplay by Masahiro Yoshimoto. GAGA Communication 2000.

Altered Carbon: Resleeved. Directed by Takeru Nakajima and Yoshiyuki Okada with Screenplay by Dai Satō, Tsukasa Kondo based on the novel *Altered Carbon* by Richard K. Morgan and TV series *Altered Carbon* by Laeta Kalogridis. Netflix 2020.

Angel's Egg. Directed and Screenplay by Mamoru Oshii. Studio Deen 1985.

Anne of Green Gables. Directed and Screenplay by Isao Takahata. Fuji TV 1979.

Armored Trooper Votoms. Directed by Ryōsuke Takahashi with Screenplay by Sōji Yoshikawa and Jinzō Toriumi. TV Tokyo 1983-1984.

Astro Boy. Directed by Osamu Tezuka with Screenplay by Yoshiyuki Tomino based on a manga of the same name in 1952 by Osamu Tezuka. Fuji TV 1963-1966

Attack on Titan. Directed by Tetsurō Araki, Masashi Koizuka, Yuichiro Hayashi, Jun Shishido with Screenplay by Yasuko Kobayashi, Hiroshi Seko, Shintarō Kawakubo based on the manga by Hajime Isayama. NHK 2013-present.

Avatar: The Last Airbender. Created by Michael Dante DiMartino and Bryan Konietzko. Nickelodeon 2005-2008.

Avatar: Legend of Korra. Created by Michael Dante DiMartino and Bryan Konietzko. Nickelodeon 2012-2014.

Azumanga Daioh. Directed by Fumiaki Asano with Screenplay by Kiyohiko Azuma. Aija-do Animation Works 2000.

Bambi. Directed by David Hand with Screenplay by Perce Pearce based on *Bambi, a Life in the Woods* by Felix Salten. Walt Disney 1942.

Barefoot Gen [film]. Directed by Mori Masaki with Screenplay with Keiji Hakazawa based on the manga by Keiji Nakazawa. Kyodo Eiga 1983.

Blast of Tempest. Directed by Masahiro Ando with Screenplay by Mari Okada based on the manga by Kyo Shirodaira and Arihide Sano. JNN 2012-2013.

Bleach. Directed by Noriyuki Abe with Screenplay by Mashashi Sogo, Tsyuoshi Kida and Kento Shimoyama based on the manga by Tite Kubo. TXN 2004-2012.

Blue Exorcist. Directed by Tensai Okamura with Screenplay by Ryota Yamaguchi based on the manga by Kazue Kato. JNN 2011.

Bibliography

Brain Powerd. Directed by Yoshiyuki Tomino with Screenplay by Akemi Omode, Katsuyuki Sumisawa, Miya Asakawa, Tetsuko Takahashi, Yoshiyuki Tomino. Wowow 1998.

Btooom! Directed by Kotono Watanabe with Screenplay by Yosuke Kuroda based on the manga by Junya Inoue. Tokyo MX 2012.

Buddha: The Great Departure: Directed by Kozo Morishita with Screenplay by Reiko Yoshida. Toei 2011.

Candy Candy. Directed by Hiroshi Shidara and Tetsuo Imazawa with Screenplay by Noboru Shiroyama based on the novel by Keiko Nagita under the pen name Kyoko Mizuki. Toei 1976–1979.

Captain Tsubasa. Directed by Hiroyoshi Mitsunobu with Screenplay by Saburô Ebinuma and Yôichi Takahashi et al. based on the manga by Yōichi Takahashi. TV Tokyo 1983-1995.

Code Geass. Directed by Gorō Taniguchi with Screenplay by Ichirō Ōkouchi. JNN 2006-2007.

Cowboy Bebop. Directed by Shinichirō Watanabe with Screenplay by Keiko Nobumoto. Sunrise 1997-1998.

Dallos. Directed by Mamoru Oshii with Screenplay by Hisayuki Toriumi and Mamoru Oshii. Discotek Media 1983-1984.

Death Note. Directed by Tetsurō Araki with Screenplay by Toshiki Inoue based on the manga by Tsugumi Ohba. Madhouse 2006-2007.

Demon Slayer. Directed by Haruo Sotozaki with Screenplay by Ufotable based on the manga by Koyoharu Gotouge. Tokyo MX 2019-present.

Demon Slayer: Mugen Train. Directed by Haruo Sotozaki with Screenplay by Ufotable based on the manga by *Koyoharu Gotouge*. Toho 2020.

Di Gi Charat. Directed by Hiroaki Sakurai with Screenplay by Hiroaki Sakurai and Nobuharu Kamanaka based on the manga by Koge-Donbo. TBS 1999.

Dragon Ball. Directed by Minoru Okazaki and Daisuke Nishio with Screenplay by Toshiki Inoue and Takao Koyama based on the manga by Akira Toriyama. Fuji TV 1986-1989.

Dragon Ball Z: The History of Trunks. Directed by Yoshihiro Ueda with Screenplay by Hiroshi Toda. Fuji TV 1993.

Dragon Ball Z. Directed by Daisuke Nishio and Shigeyasu Yamauchi with Screenplay by Atsushi Maekawa et al. Toei 1989-1996.

Dragon Ball Z Kai. Revised and updated version of *Dragon Ball Z*. Fuji TV 2009-2011.

Dragon Ball Super. Directed by Kimitoshi Chioka et al. with Screenplay by Akira Toriyama et al. Fuji TV 2015-2018.

Dragon Ball Z: Kakarot [video game] Directed by Akihiro Anai and Written by Yasuhiro Noguchi and Shinsaku Swamura. Bandai Namco Entertainment 2020.

East of Eden. Directed and Screenplay by Kenji Kamiyama. Fuji TV 2009.

Erased. Directed by Tomohiko Ito with Screenplay by Taku Kishimoto based on the manga by Kei Sanbe. Fuji TV 2016.

Ergo Proxy. Directed by Shuko Murase with Screenplay by Dai Satō. Wowow 2006.

Fate/Zero. Directed by Ei Aoki with Screenplay by Akira Hiyama and Akihiro Yoshida. Tokyo MX 2011-2012.

Fortress Macross. Directed by Noboru Ishiguro with Screenplay by Kenichi Matsuzaki. Artland and Tatsunoko Production 1982-1983.

Fullmetal Alchemist. Directed by Seiji Mizushima with Screenplay by Shō Aikawa based on the manga by Hiromu Arakawa. JNN 2003-2004.

Future Boy Conan. Directed by Hayao Miyazaki with Screenplay by Akira Nakano and Stoshi Kurumi, Sōji Yoshikawa. NHK 1978.

Galaxy Express 999 [TV series]. Directed by Nobutaka Nishizawa with Screenplay by Hiroyasu Yamaura, Keisuke Fujikawa and Yoshiaki Yoshida based on the manga by Leiji Matsumoto. Fuji TV 1978-1981.

Galaxy Express 999 [Film]. Directed by Rintaro with Screenplay by Shiro Ishimori. Toei 1979.

Getter Robo. Directed by Tomoharu Katsumata with Screenplay by Shun'ichi Yukimuro based on the manga by Ken Ishikawa and Go Nagai. Toei 1974-1975.

Ghost in the Shell. Directed by Mamoru Oshii with Screenplay by Kazunoi Itō based on the manga by Masamune Shirow. Shochiku 1995.

Ghost in the Shell 2 Innocence. Directed and Screenplay by Mamoru Oshii based on the manga by Masamune Shirow. Toho 2004.

Ghost in the Shell: SAC_2045: Directed by Kenji Kamiyama and Shinji Aramaki with Screenplay by Kenji Kamiyama based on the manga by Masamune Shirow. Netflix 2020-2022.

Gigantor. Directed by Yonehiko Watanabe with Screenplay by Kinzo Okamoto based on the manga by Mitsuteru Yokoyama. Fuji TV 1963-1966.

God of High School. Directed by Sunghoo Park with Screenplay by Kiyoko Yoshimura. Tokyo MX 2020.

Golgo 13: The Professional. Directed by Osamu Dezaki with Screenplay by Shukei Nagasaka. Toho 1983.

Grave of the Fireflies. Directed and Screenplay by Isao Takahata based on a semi-autobiographical short story by Akiyuki Nosaka. Toho 1988.

Gulliver's Travels Beyond the Moon. Directed by Masao Kuroda and Sanae Yamamoto with Screenplay by Shinichi Sekizawa, Jonathan Swift, Hayao Miyazaki. Toei 1965.

Gunbuster. Directed by Hideaki Anno with Screenplay by Hideaki Anno and Toshio Okada. Gainax 1988-1989.

Gurren Lagann. Directed by Hiroyuki Imaishi with Screenplay by Kazuki Nakashima. Gainax 2007.

Heidi: Girl of the Alps. Directed by Isao Tahakata with Screenplay by Isao Matsuki. Fuji TV 1974.

Hell Girl. Directed by Takahiro Omori with Screenplay by Kenichi Kanemaki. Tokyo MX 2005-2006.

Himitsu no Akko-chan: Directed by Hiroshi Ikeda with Screenplay by Fujio Akatsuka. TV Asahi 1969-1970).

Honey and Clover. Directed by Ken'ichi Kasai with Screenplay by Yōsuke Kurodo based on the manga by Chica Umino. Fuji TV 2005.

Horusu: Prince of the Sun. Directed by Isao Takahata with Screenplay by Kazuo Fukazawa. Toei 1968.

Hōseki no Kuni. Directed by Takahiko Kyōgoku with Screenplay by Toshiya Ōno based on the manga by Ichikawa Haruko. ATX 2017.

Howl's Moving Castle. Directed and Screenplay by Hayao Miyazaki based on the novel by Diana Wynne Jones. Toho 2004.

How Not to Summon a Demon Lord. Directed by Yuta Murano with Screenplay by Kazuyuki Fudeyasu based on the manga by Naoto Fukuda. AT-X 2018.

In Another World with My Smartphone. Directed by Takeyuki Yanase and Yoshiaki Iwasaki with Screenplay by Natsuko Takahashi and Deko Akao based on the light novel series by Patora Fuyuhara. AT-X 2017-2023.

Inuyasha. Directed by Masahsi Ikeda and Yasunao Aoki with Screenplay by Katsuyuki Sumisawa based on the manga by Rumiko Takahashi. NNS 2000-2004.

Jobless Reincarnation. Directed by Manabu Okamoto and Hiroki Hirano with Screenplay by Manabu Okamoto and Hiroki Hirano based on the manga by Rifujin na Magonote. Tokyo MX 2021-Present.

Kakushigoto: My Dad's Secret Ambition. Directed by Yūta Murano with Screenplay by Takashi Aoshima based on the manga by Kōji Kumeta. Tokyo MX 2020.

Kimba the White Lion. Directed by Eiichi Yamamoto with Screenplay by Osamu Tezuka. Toho 1965-1966.

Laputa: Castle in the Sky. Directed by Hayao Miyazaki with Screenplay by Hayao Miyazaki. Toei 1986.

Little Witch Sally. Directed by Toshio Katsuta and Hiroshi Ikeda based on the manga by Mitsuteru Yokoyama. Toei 1966-1968.

Log Horizon. Directed by Shinji Ishihira and Junichi Wada with Screenplay by Toshizou Nemoto based on the light novel series by Mamare Touno. NHK Educational TV 2013-2014.

Lost. Directed by Jack Bender et al. with Screenplay by J. J. Abrams et al. ABC 2004-2010.

Love Hina. Directed by Yoshiaki Iwasaki with Screenplay by Kurō Hazuki based on the manga of the same name by Ken Akamatsu. TV Tokyo 2000.

Lupin III. Directed by Hayao Miyazaki, Isao Takahata and Masaaki Ōsumi. Yomiuri 1971-1972.

Lupin III: Castle of Cagliostro. Directed by Hayao Miyazaki with Screenplay by Hayao Miyazaki and Haruya Yamazaki based on the manga by Monkey Punch. Toho 1979.

Macross Plus: Directed by Shōji Kawamori and Shinichiro Watanabe with Screenplay by Keiko Nobumoto. Crunchyroll 1994-1995.

Magical Play. Directed by Hiroki Hayashi with Screenplay by Hiroshi Ōnogi. AIC 2001-2002.

Maison Ikkoku. Directed by Kazuo Yamazaki, Takashi Annō, Naoyuki Yoshinaga with Screenplay by Tokio Tsuchiya, Kazunori Itō, Hideo Takayashiki based on manga by Rumiko Takahashi. Fuji TV 1986-1988.

Mazinger Z. Directed by Tomoharu Katsumata based on the manga by Go Nagai. Toei 1972-1974.

Megazone 23. Directed by Noboru Ishiguro with Screenplay by Hiroyuki Hoshiyama. Studio AIC 1985.

Millennium Actress. Directed by Satoshi Kon with Screenplay by Sadayuki Murai and Satoshi Kon. Madhouse 2001.

Mirai. Directed by Mamoru Hosoda with Screenplay by Mamoru Hosoda. Toho 2018.

Mobile Suit Gundam. Directed by Yoshiyuki Tomino with Screenplay by Yoshiyuki Tomino. Nagoya TV 1979-1980.

Mobile Suit Gundam F91. Directed by Yoshiyuki Tomino with Screenplay by Tsunehisa Ito, Yoshiyuki Tomino. Shochiku 1991.

Mobile Suit Gundam SEED. Directed by Mitsuo Fukuda with Screenplay by Chiaki Morosawa. JNN 2002-2003.

Momotaro's Divine Sea Warriors. Directed by Mitsuyo Seo with Screenplay by Mitsuyo Seo. Shochiku 1945.

Mononoke. Directed by Kenji Nakamura Kenji. Toei Animation 2007.

Mushishi. Directed and Screenplay by Hiroshi Nagahama based on the manga by Yuki Urushibara. Fuji TV 2005-2006.

Mushishi: Zoku-Sho. Directed and Screenplay by Hiroshi Nagahama. Fuji TV 2005-2006.

My Last Day. Directed and Screenplay by Barry Cook. Campus Crusade for Christ 2011.

My Neighbor Totoro. Written and directed by Hayao Miyazaki. Toho 1988.

My Neighbours the Yamadas. Directed by Isao Takahata with Screenplay by Isao Takahata. Shochiku 1999.

Mysterious Play. Directed by Hajime Kamegaki with Screenplay by Yoshio Urasawa based on the manga by Yuu Watase. TV Tokyo 1995-1996.

Nadia: The Secret of Blue Water. Directed by Hideaki Anno and Shinji Hicguchi with Screenplay by Hisao Ōkawa and Yasuo Tanami. NHK 1990-1991.

Naruto. Directed by Hayato Date with Screenplay by Katsuyuki Sumisawa and Junki Takegami based on the manga by Masashi Kishimoto. TXN TV Tokyo 2002-2007.

Nausicaä of the Valley of the Wind. Directed by Hayao Miyazaki with Screenplay by Hayao Miyazaki. Toei 1984.

Neon Genesis Evangelion. Directed by Hideaki Anno with Screenplay by Hideaki Anno. TV Tokyo 1995-1996.

New Cutie Honey. Directed by Yasuchika Nagaoka. Discotek 1994-1995.

Oh My Goddess. Directed by Hiroaki Gōda with Screenplay by Kunihiko Kondo and Nahoko Hasegawa based on the manga of the same name by Kōsuke Fujishima. AIC 1993-1994.

Okja. Directed with Screenplay by Bong Joon-ho. Netflix 2017.

Oldboy. Directed by Park Chan-wook with Screenplay by Hwang Jo-yun et al. Show East 2003.

One Piece. Directed by Kōnosuke Uda et al. with Screenplay by Junki Takegami and Hirohiko Kamisaka. Toei 1999-present.

Only Yesterday. Directed by Isao Takahata with Screenplay by Isao Takahata based on the manga by Hotaru Okamoto and Yuko Tone. Toho 1991.

Orange. Directed by Hiroshi Hamasaki and Naomi Nakayama with Screenplay by Yuko Kakihara based on the manga by Ichigo Takano. Tokyo MX 2016.

Otogi Manga Calendar. Directed by Ryūichi Yokoyama. Otogi Production 1961-1962.

Ouran High School Host Club. Directed by Takuya Igarashi with Screenplay by Yōji Enokido based on manga series by Bisco Hatori. Nippon TV 2006.

Overlord. Directed by Kunihiro Wakabayashi with Screenplay by Yukie Sugawara based on the light novel by Kugane Maruyama. Tokyo MX 2015-2022.

Panda! Go, Panda!. Directed by Takahata Isao with Screenplay by Miyazaki Hayao. Tokyo Movie Shinsha 1972.

Parasite. Directed with Screenplay by Bong Joon-ho. CJ Entertainment 2019.

Paradise Lost. Directed by Kenji Kamiyama with Screenplay by Kenji Kamiyama et al. Crunchyroll 2010.

Patlabor. Directed by Mamoru Oshii with Screenplay by Kazunori Ito based on the manga by Masami Yuki. Studio Deen 1988-1989.

Perfect Blue. Directed by Sotashi Kon with Screenplay by Sadayuki Murai based on the light novel *Perfect Blue: Complete Metamorphosis* by Yoshikazu Takeuchi. Madhouse 1998.

Persona 5: The Animation. Directed by Masashi Ishihama with Screenplay by Shinichi Inotsume, Kazuho Hyodo and Noboru Kimura. Tokyo MX 2018-2019.

Phantom Ship. Directed by Noburō Ōfuji. Chiyogami Eiga-sha 1956.

Pinocchio. Directed by Ben Sharpsteen and Hamilton Luske with Screenplay by Ted Sears based on *The Adventures of Pinocchio* by Cario Collodi. Walt Disney 1940.

Pokemon. Directed by Kunihiko Yuyama with Screenplay by Takeshi Shudo. TV Tokyo 1997-present.

Pokémon: Indigo League. Directed by Yūji Asada and Masaaki Iwane with Screenplay by Yukiyoshi Ōhashi and Yūji Asada. TV Tokyo 1998.

Pokémon: The First Movie - Mewtwo Strikes Back. Directed by Kunihiko Yuyama with Screenplay by Satoshi Tajiri et al. Tokyo OLM Inc. 1998.

Pom Poko. Directed by Isao Takahata with Screenplay by Isao Takahata. Toho 1994.

Ponyo on the Cliff by the Sea. Directed by Hayao Miyazaki with Screenplay by Hayao Miyazaki based on *The Little Mermaid* by Hans Christian Andersen. Toho 2008.

Princess Mononoke. Directed by Hayao Miyazaki with Screenplay by Hayao Miyazaki. Toho 1997.

Princess Princess. Directed by Keitaro Motonaga based on the manga by Mikiyo Tsuda. Studio Deen 2006.

Psycho-Pass. Directed by Naoyoshi Shiotani and Katsuyuki Motohiro with Screenplay by Gen Urobuchi et al. Fuji TV 2012.

Rail of the Star. Directed by Toshio Hirata with Screenplay by Hideo Asakura and Tatsuhiko Urahata. Madhouse 1993.

Ramayana: The Legend of Prince Rama. Directed by Koichi Sasaki with Screenplay by Narendra Sharma et al. Toei 1992.

Re:CREATORS. Directed by Ei Aoki with Screenplay by Rei Hiroe and Ei Aoki based on the manga by Daiki Kase. Tokyo MX 2017.

Royal Space Force. Wings of Honneamise. Directed by Hiroyuki Yamaga with Screenplay by Hiroyuki Yamaga. Toho 1987.

Rozen Maiden. Directed by Kou Matsuo with Screenplay by Jukki Hanada based on the manga by Peach-Pit. TBS 2004.

SAC_2045. Altered Carbon: Resleeved. Directed by Takeru Nakajima and Yoshiyuki Okada with Screenplay by Dai Satō and Tsukasa Kondo based on the novel *Altered Carbon* by Richard K. Morgan and TV series *Altered Carbon* by Laeta Kalogridis. Anima 2020.

Sailor Moon. Directed by Junichi Sato, Kunihiko Ikuhara and Takuya Igarashi with Screenplay by Sukehiro Tomita. Toei 1992-1997.

Sazae-san. Directed by Kenji Kodama based on the manga by Machiko Hasegawa. Fuji TV 1969-present.

Serial Experiments Lain. Directed by Ryutaro Nakamura with Screenplay by Chiaki J. Konaka. TV Tokyo 1998.

Seven Deadly Sins. Directed by Tensai Okamura with Screenplay by Shōtarō Suga based on the manga by Nakaba Suzuki. JNN 2014-2015.

Slam Dunk. Directed by Nobutaka Nishizawa with Screenplay by Nobutaka Nishizawa and Yoshiyuki Suga. Toei 1993-1996.

Snow White. Directed by David Hand with Screenplay by Ted Sears based on *Snow White* by The Brothers Grimm. Walt Disney 1937.

Space Battleship Yamato [TV series]. Directed by Leiji Matsumoto, created by Leiji Matsumoto, Yoshinobu Nishizaki and Eichi Yamamoto with Screenplay by Eiichi Yamamoto, Keisuke Fujikawa and Maru Tamura. NNN 1974-1975.

Space Battleship Yamato [film]. Directed by Toshio Masuda and Noboru Ishiguro with Screenplay by Eiichi Yamamoto. Toei 1977.

Speed Racer. Directed by Hiroshi Sasagawa with Screenplay by Jinzō Toriumi based on the manga by Tatsuo Yoshida. Fuji TV 1967-1968.

Spirited Away. Directed by Hayao Miyazaki with Screenplay by Hayao Miyazaki. Toho 2001.

Squid Game. Directed with Screenplay by Hwang Dong-hyuk. Netflix 2017-2021.

Star of the Giants. Directed by Tadao Nagahama with Screenplay by Ikki Kajiwara based on sports manga by Ikki Kajiwara. Yomiuri Television 1968-1971.

Steamboy. Directed by Katsuhiro Otomo with Screenplay by Sadayuki Murai and Katsuhiro Otomo. Toho 2004.

Stein;Gate. Directed by Tatsuya Matsubara with Screenplay by Chiyomaru Shikura et al. 5pb 2009.

Steven Universe. Created by Rebecca Sugar. Cartoon Network 2013-2019.

Superdimensional Fortress Macross. Directed by Noboru Ishiguro with Screenplay by Kenichi Matsuzaki. MBS 1982-1983.

Sword Art Online. Directed by Tomohiko Itō with Screenplay by Yukie Sugawara et al. based on the novel series of the same name by Reki Kawahara. Tokyo MX 2012.

Tenchi Universe. Directed by Hiroshi Negishi with Screenplay by Ryoe Tsukimura based on the manga by Hitoshi Okuda. TV Tokyo 1995.

That Time I Got Reincarnated as a Slime. Directed by Atsushi Nakayama et al. with Screenplay by Fuse based on the manga by Fuse. Tokyo MX 2018-2019.

The Big O. Directed by Kazuyoshi Katayama with Screenplay by Chiaki J. Konaka and Kazuyoshi Katayama based on the manga by Hitoshi Ariga. Wowow 1999-2000.

The Bubblegum Crisis. Directed by Katsuhito Akiyama et al. with Screenplay by Toshimichi Suzuki. AIC 1987-1991.

The DoorMan. Directed by Ōten Shimokawa. Tenkatsu 1917.

The End of Evangelion. Directed with Screenplay by Hideaki Anno and Kazuya Tsurumaki. Toei Company 1997.

The Faraway Paladin. Directed by Yuu Nobuta and Akira Iwanaga with Screenplay by Tatsuya Takahashi based on the manga by Kanata Yanagino. Tokyo MX 2021-Present.

The King of Eden. Directed by Kenji Kamiyama with Screenplay by Kenji Kamiyama et al. Crunchyroll 2009.

The Legend of the White Snake. Directed by Taiji Yabushita with Screenplay by Taiji Yabushita and Shin Uehara based on *Legend of the White Snape*. Toei 1958.

The Matrix. Directed and Screenplay by The Wachowskis. Warner Bros 1999.

The Promised Neverland [TV series] Directed by Mamoru Kanbe with Screenplay by Toshiya Ono and Kaiu Shirai based on the manga by Kaiu Shirai. Fuji TV 2019-2021.

The Promised Neverland [film]. Directed by Yūichiō Hirakawa and Jun Shiozaki with Screenplay by Noriko Goto based on the manga by Kaiu Shirai. Toho 2020.

The Sky Crawlers. Directed by Mamoru Oshii with Screenplay by Chihiro Ito based on the novel series by Hiroshi Mori. Production I. G. 2008.

The Tale of Princess Kaguya. Directed by Isao Takahata with Screenplay by Isao Takahata and Riko Sakaguchi based on *The Tale of the Bamboo Cutter* by an unknown author. Toho 2013.

The Thief of BaghdadCastle. Directed by Noburō Ōfuji. Jiyu Eiga Kenkyusho 1926.

The Vision of Escaflowne. Directed by Kazuki Akane with Screenplay by Hiroaki Kitajima, et al. TV Tokyo 1996.

The Wallflower. Directed by Shinichi Watanabe from the manga of the same name by Tomoko Hayakawa. Nippon Animation 2006-2007.

The Whale. Directed by Noburō Ōfuji. Chiyogami Eiga-sha 1952.

The Wind Rises. Directed by Hayao Miyazaki with Screenplay by Hayao Miyazaki based on both the novel *The Wind Has Risen* by Tatsuo Hori and the life of Jiro Horikoshi. Toho 2013.

Three Tales. Directed by Keiko Kozonoe with Story by Hirosuke Hamada et al. NHK 1960.

Titanic. Directed and Screenplay by James Cameron. Paramount Picture 1997.

To Your Eternity. Directed by Masahiko Murata and Kiyoko Sayama with Screenplay by Shinzo Fujita based on the manga by Yoshitoki Oima. NHK Educational TV 2021-Present.

Tokyo Ghoul. Directed by Shuhei Morita with Screenplay by Chūji Mikasano based on the manga by Sui Ishida. Tokyo MX 2014.

Tokyo Godfathers. Directed by Satoshi Kon with Screenplay by Keiko Nobumoto and Satoshi Kon. Sony Pictures 2003.

Tokyo Revengers. Directed by Koichi Hatsumi with Screenplay by Yasuyuki Muto based on the manga by Ken Wakui. MBS 2021-Present.

Tower of God. Directed by Takashi Sano with Screenplay by Erika Yoshida. Crunchyroll 2020-present.

Trigun. Directed by Satoshi Nishimura with Screenplay by Yosuke Kuroda based on the manga by Yasuhiro Nightow. TV Tokyo 1998.

Triton of the Sea. Directed by Yoshiyuki Tomino with Screenplay by Yoshiyuki Tomino based on the manga by Osamu Tezuka. Asahi Broadcasting Company 1972.

UFO Robot Grendizer. Directed by Tomoharu Katsumata with Screenplay by Go Nagai based on the manga by Go Nagai. Toei 1975.

Urotsukidōji. Legend of the Overfiend. Directed by Hideki Takayama with Screenplay by Shō Aikawa. Shochiku 1989.

Urusei Yatsura. Directed by Mamoru Oshii with Screenplay by Takao Koyama, Kazunori Ito and Michiru Shimada based on a manga of the same name by Rumiko Takahashi. Kitty Films 1981-1986.

Victory Gundam. Directed by Yoshiyuki Tomino with Screenplay by Akira Okeya, Hideki Sonoda, Kazuhiko Godo, Minoru Yokitani and Sukehiro Tomita. TV Asahi 1993-1994.

Welcome to the N.H.K. Directed by Yūsuke Yamamoto with Screenplay by Satoru Nishizono based on the manga by Tatsuhiko Takimoto. Chiba TV 2006.

Wonder Woman. Directed by Patty Jenkins with Screenplay by Allan Heinberg (Warner Bros 2017).

Yashahime: Princess Half-Demon. Directed by Teruo Sato and Masakazu Hishida with Screenplay by based on the manga by Takashi Shiina and Katsuyuki Sumisawa. NNS 2020-2022.

Your Name. Directed by Makoto Shinkai with Screenplay by Makoto Shinkai. Toho 2016.

YuYu Hakusho. Directed by Noriyuki Abe with Screenplay by Yukiyoshi Ohashi based on the manga by Yoshihiro Togashi. Fuji TV 1992-1994.

General Internet and Webpage Sources

"1st Anti-Fascist Congress Attended by Military Attaches from 26 States—Defense Ministry". *TASS* 02nd September 2022. https://tass.com/defense/1501587.

"Agape". *Encyclopedia Britannica.* https://www.britannica.com/topic/agape.

Bibliography

"Akemi's Anime World". *waybackmachine.* https://web.archive.org/web/20070707043344/http:/animeworld.com/howtodraw/faces.html#top.

"All Aboard the Steampunk Anime Train! Choo-Choo!". *MyAnimeList.* https://myanimelist.net/featured/1299/Top_10_Best_Steampunk_Anime___Let_Off_Some_Steam_.

"Anime". *Britannica.* https://www.britannica.com/art/anime-Japanese-animation.

"Anime Industry Report 2021 Summary". The Association of Japanese Animations. https://aja.gr.jp/info/1919.

"Anime Market Size, Share and Trends Analysis Report by Type (T.V., Movie, Video, Internet Distribution, Merchandising, Music) by Region and Segment Forecasts 2021-2028". *Grand View Research.* https://www.grandviewresearch.com/industry-analysis/anime-market.

"Anime Market Size, Share and Trends Analysis Report By Anime Type (T.V., Movie, Video, Internet Distribution, Merchandising, Music) by Region (MEA, Japan) and Segment Forecasts 2022-2030". *Grand View Research.* https://www.grandviewresearch.com/industry-analysis/anime-market#:~:text=b.-,The%20global%20anime%20market%20size%20was%20valued%20at%20USD%2024.80,USD%2026.89%20billion%20in%202022.

"Anituber". *Urban Dictionary.* https://www.urbandictionary.com/define.php?term=Anituber.

"Best of Persona 5". *Youtube.* https://www.youtube.com/watch?v=joVwwQlu134.

"China's Economy Could Overtake U.S. Economy by 2030". *Chosun Ilbo.* http://english.chosun.com/site/data/html_dir/2022/01/05/2022010500491.html.

"Content Industry Current Status and Direction of Future Development". *Ministry of Economy, Trade and Industry.* https://www.meti.go.jp/english/policy/mono_info_service/content_industry/pdf/20160329001.pdf.

"Contradictories and Contraries". *Encyclopedia Brittanica.* https://www.britannica.com/topic/contradictories-and-contraries.

"Cool Japan Initiative". *Cabinet Office Intellectual Property Headquarters.* https://www.cao.go.jp/cool_japan/english/pdf/cooljapan_initiative.pdf.

"Cool Japan Proposal". *Cool Japan Movement Promotion Council.* https://www.cao.go.jp/cool_japan/english/pdf/published_document3.pdf.

"Cyberia: Life in the Trenches of Hyperspace by Douglas Rushkoff". *Publishers Weekly.* https://www.publishersweekly.com/9780062510105.

"Demand for Anime Content Soars". *Parrot Analytics.* https://www.parrotanalytics.com/press/demand-for-anime-content-soars/.

"Did Nuclear Weapons Cause Japan to Surrender?". *Carnegie Council for Ethics in International Affairs.* https://www.carnegiecouncil.org/education/008/expertclips/010.

"Dragon Ball Super: Broly (2018)". *Box Office Mojo.* https://www.boxofficemojo.com/title/tt7961060.

"Dragon Ball Super: Super Hero". *Box Office Mojo.* https://www.boxofficemojo.com/title/tt14614892.

"Evangelion, Misogyny, and Sexuality: The Women of Evangelion in Relation to Shinji and the Audience", *controlaltdelete-my-existence.* https://www.tum

blr.com/controlaltdelete-my-existence/640625310518427648/evangelion-misogyny-and-sexuality-the-women-of.

"Fan Service". *Urban Dictionary*. https://www.urbandictionary.com/define.php?term=fan%20service.

"Fertility Rate, Total (Births per Woman)—Japan". *The World Bank Group*. https://data.worldbank.org/indicator/SP.DYN.TFRT.IN?locations=JP.

"Game within a Game". *TV Tropes*. https://tvtropes.org/pmwiki/pmwiki.php/Main/GameWithinAGame.

"Hayao Miyazaki". *Britannica*. https://www.britannica.com/biography/Miyazaki-Hayao.

"Hello Kitty Cosplay". *Pinterest*. https://www.pinterest.com/liz26donovan/hello-kitty-cosplay/.

"How Evangelion Impacted the Industry?". *TV Tropes*. https://tvtropes.org/pmwiki/posts.php?discussion=kqk9rhs9hw4ro10t9gvf63x2&page=1.

"Human Instrumentality Project". *Evangelion Wiki*. https://evangelion.fandom.com/wiki/Human_Instrumentality_Project.

"Infinity". *Youtube*. https://www.youtube.com/watch?v=0jm8nnHqx80.

"Isomorphic". *Merriam-Webster*. https://www.merriam-webster.com/dictionary/isomorphic#:~:text=%3A%20being%20of%20identical%20or%20similar,isomorphic%20crystals.

"Japan's Animation Industry Failing to Cultivate Next Generation of Talent". *Nippon* 10th August 2017. https://www.nippon.com/en/currents/d00337/.

"Japan: Religious Affiliations in 2019". *Statista*. https://www.statista.com/statistics/237609/religions-in-japan/.

"Layer 09". *Serial Experiments Lain Wiki*. https://sel.fandom.com/wiki/Layer_09.

"Low Wages in the Anime Industry". *YouTube*. https://www.youtube.com/watch?v=dZgQCAgRLC4&t=2s.

"Marriage in Japan". *U.S. Embassy and Consulates in Japan*. https://jp.usembassy.gov/services/marriage/marriage-in-japan/.

"Number of Suicides Increase in 2022". *Nippon.com* 27th March 2022. https://www.nippon.com/en/japan-data/h01624/#:~:text=The%20number%20of%20suicides%20in,from%20the%20National%20Police%20Agency.

"Otaku". *Anime News Network*. https://www.animenewsnetwork.com/encyclopedia/lexicon.php?id=22.

"Otaku: Japan's Anime-Obsessed Enthusiasts". *NBC News* 20th August 2006. https://www.nbcnews.com/id/wbna14415584.

"Phantom Thieves of Hearts". *Heroes Wiki*. https://hero.fandom.com/wiki/Phantom_Thieves_of_Hearts#:~:text=Sick%20of%20the%20deception%2C%20hypocrisy,Kazuya%20Makigami%20and%20Futaba%20Sakura. "Population Ages 65 and Above, Total—Japan". *The World Bank Group*. https://data.worldbank.org/indicator/SP.POP.65UP.TO?contextual=default&locations=JP.

"Reading List". *Lain Official Reading List*. http://www.cjas.org/~leng/readlist.htm.

"Religion and Philosophy in Ancient India". *Indian Culture and Heritage Secondary Course*, 111-126. https://www.nios.ac.in/media/documents/SecICHCour/English/CH.08.pdf.

"Research Material Anime Japan 2020". *Film Hub Midlands*. https://filmhubmidlands.org/app/uploads/2020/02/Anime-Background-research.pdf.

"*Shugen-dō*". *Britannica*. https://www.britannica.com/topic/Shugen-do.

"Tengu Japan's Large Nosed Mountain Goblin". *Japan Experience* 18th February 2013. https://www.japanallover.com/2013/02/tengu/.

"The Growing Anison Scene in Japan". *Trends in Japan*. https://web-japan.org/trends/11_culture/pop160713.html.

"The History of Anime: Part 2". *Evolution*. https://evolutioninjapan.wordpress.com/2021/01/26/the-history-of-anime-1970-to-2010s/.

"The Wired". *Serial Experiments in Lain Wiki*. https://sel.fandom.com/wiki/The_Wired.

"Toei Animation Phils". *Toei Animation Co.* https://corp-toei--anim-co-jp.translate.goog/ja/company/affiliated_companies.html?_x_tr_sl=ja&_x_tr_tl=en&_x_tr_hl=en&_x_tr_pto=sc#a03.

"Top 10 Shojo Properties—Summer 2013". *Icv2.com*. https://icv2.com/articles/comics/view/28057/top-10-shojo-properties-fall-holidays-2013.

"Top 10 Shojo Properties—Fall/Holidays 2013". *Icv2.com*. https://icv2.com/articles/comics/view/28057/top-10-shojo-properties-fall-holidays-2013.

"Types of Isekai". *Royal Roads*. https://www.royalroad.com/forums/thread/107284.

"Typographics". *Serial Experiments Lain Wiki*. https://lain.wiki/wiki/Typographics.

"Wake Up, Get Up, Get Out There". *Youtube*. https://www.youtube.com/watch?v=0jm8nnHqx80

"Weeaboo vs. Otaku: Here's the Difference!". *linguablog* 15th April 2023. https://linguaholic.com/linguablog/weeaboo-vs-otaku/.

"What is Cool Japan Fund?". *Cool Japan Fund*. https://www.cj-fund.co.jp/en/about/cjfund.html.

"*Yamabushi*". *Britannica*. https://www.britannica.com/topic/yamabushi.

Index

A

A.L.I.C.E, 38
Academy Award, 38, 40, 41, 42
Adolf Hitler, 158
aesthetic, xviii, xxiv
affective labor, 245, 254
Afternoon (Magazine), 243
agape-charis, 257, 261, 269
agency, 187
aging society, 245
AI, 75, 79
Akira, 3, 4, 5, 6, 8, 11, 12, 15, 17, 21, 22, 24, 26, 29, 30, 31, 34, 36, 37, 38, 43, 97
Akiyama, Katsuhito, 29
algorithmic governmentality, 74, 78, 81, 86
alienation, 78
Altered Carbon: Resleeved, 49
Amazon, xvii
American Academy Awards Oscar, 37
American transcendentalism, 73, 81, 82, 83, 95, 96, 98
android, 243, 245, 246, 247, 250, 253
angel, xxv
Angel's Egg, 30
Animage, 23, 50
anime, 63
Anime Insider, 50
anime music videos AMVs, 51
anime style, 23, 58
anime-esque, 4, 51, 60
Anison, xix
AniTubers, 50, 51
Anne of Green Gables, 27
Anno, Hideaki
 Anno, xxi, 18, 27, 33, 35
apocalyptic, xxv
"archetype", 77
Armored Trooper Votoms, 28
Art Reflecting the Artist, xxiv
art style, xviii
artificial intelligence, 243, 245, 246, 250
Asia, 3, 17, 53, 57
Astro Boy, 6, 13, 14, 15, 16, 17, 18, 19
Attack on Titan, 42, 97, 279
authenticity, 190
automated grave, 249, 251, 252, 255
Avatar, xx
Avatar: The Last Air-Bender, 58
Azuma, Hiroki, 14, 22, 23, 32, 33, 34, 39, 43, 44, 49
Azumanga Daioh, 49

B

Bambi, 11
BANZAI, xxviii
Barefoot Gen, 30
Bible, xxv
bildungsroman, 95
Bioluminescence, 100
bishōjo, 21, 43
bishōnen, 45, 117, 125, 127
Black Bird, 117, 118, 119, 123, 125, 126, 127, 128, 130, 131, 132
black comedy, xxii
Blast of Tempest, 278
Bleach, 283

Blue Exorcist, 278
Body Change, 173
body techniques, 194
Bolton, Christopher, 8, 28, 29, 36, 43
Bones, 39, 45, 54
Brain Powered, 36
Btooom!, 276, 277
Buddha, 70
Buddhism, xxv, 117, 119, 120, 121, 122, 123
Buddhist, 243, 244, 246, 247, 248, 249, 250, 251, 253, 255
Bulma, 172
Bunraku, 8

C

cafes, xxiv
Candy, 21
cannibalism, 226, 227, 229, 232, 236, 240, 241
Captain Tsubasa, 31
Cartesian Dualism, 82
cartoon, 2
Castle of Cagliostro, 24
Cavallaro, Dani, 2, 5, 6, 8, 29, 48, 56
Cel-animation, 9, 10
China, 55, 57, 60
  Chinese, 55
chiyogami, 9
Christian, 287
Christian Existentialism, 265
Christian themes, xix
Christian theology, 286, 287, 294
Christianity, xviii, xxiii, xxv
church, xxvii
claymation, 49
Clements, Jonathan, 2, 3, 8, 9, 12, 13, 14, 16, 18, 19, 20, 21, 22, 23, 27, 29, 31, 32, 33, 40, 44, 45, 49, 59
Code Geass, 98
cognitive dissonance, xxii, xxiii, xxiv, xxvii
collective personhood, 93
Collective Unconscious, xxvi
Comiket, 50
coming-of-age, xxi, 117, 125, 127, 128, 130
compatibilism, 153, 155, 156
Condry, Ian, 4, 6, 8, 13, 17, 19, 20, 33, 34, 39, 40, 49, 54, 56
consciousness, 174
Cool Japan, 7, 34, 44, 52, 55
cosplay, xix, xxiv
cosplaying, 33
COVID-19, 52, 53
Cowboy Bebop, 38, 277
Crow Tengu. *See* Karasu Tengu
cultural codes, 194
cultural hegemony, 78, 84, 85, 86
cultural norms, 183
cybernetic divinity, 136
cyberpunk, 28, 29, 36, 43

D

Daddy Issues, xxi
Dallos, 32
Death Note, 42, 44
deconstructionism, 80
deconstructivism, 73, 77, 96
Dejiko, 44
Demon Slayer, 41, 42
Demon Slayer the Movie: Mugen Train, 41
Demon Slayer: Kimetsu no Yaiba, 100
Dende, 175
denial, xxvii

Index

Denison, Rayna, 3, 4, 6, 8, 9, 10, 11, 12, 13, 14, 19, 20, 21, 22, 24, 27, 28, 31, 32, 33, 38, 39, 43, 53
Derrida, Jacques, 218, 219
despotic signifier, 78
determinism, 155, 156
dialectic, 83
Disney, 9, 11, 12, 13, 24, 56, 58
domination, 183
doujinshi, 33, 50
Dragon Ball, xxi, xxviii, 31, 153, 154, 155, 156, 157, 159, 160, 161, 162, 163, 164, 165, 166, 167, 168, 169, 170, 171, 172, 173, 174, 175, 176, 177, 178, 179, 180, 257, 258, 259, 260, 261, 262, 263, 266, 267, 268, 269
Dragon Ball GT, 154
Dragon Ball Super, 154, 258
Dragon Ball Super: Broly, 259
Dragon Ball Super: Super Hero, 259
Dragon Ball Z, 31, 153, 154, 155, 156, 157, 159, 160, 161, 162, 163, 165, 166, 167, 168, 169, 170, 171, 172, 173, 174, 175, 176, 177, 178, 180, 257, 258, 259, 260, 261, 262, 263, 266, 267, 268, 269, 281
Dragon Ball Z Kai, 258, 260, 262, 263, 266, 267, 268, 269
"dramaturgical actor", 77

E

Eastern culture, xviii, xxvii
Eastern religion, xxiii, xxvii
Eden of the East, xxii
Edo period, 7
8 Man, 15
eldercare, 245, 254
Emakimono
   picture-scrolls, 7

embodiment, 183, 187, 191
Emerson, 81
encyclopedia, 203, 210
Enlightenment, 74, 76, 82
ephebophilia, xx
epistemology, 74, 75, 76, 77, 79, 80, 83
Erased, 277
Ergo Proxy, 73, 90, 91, 96
eternal recurrence, 79
EVA, xxv
existential angst, xxv, xxvii
existentialism, xxiii, xxv, xxvi, xxvii
extension of the human lifespan, 96
Extropy, 75

F

family dysfunction, xxv
Fan Service, xx
fansubbing, 33, 50
Fate/Zero, xix
female sexuality, 125, 127, 132
Fifteen Years War, 10
Filament, 100
First Great War, 159, 163
folklore, 100
folkloresque, 101
Foucault, Michel, 208
freewill, 155, 156, 173, 176, 177
Freiberg, Freda, 21, 26
Friedrich Nietzsche, 265
friendship, 215, 216, 219, 221
Frieza, 154, 157, 158, 160, 163, 164, 165, 166, 167, 168, 169, 171, 172, 173, 175, 177, 179
Fullmetal Alchemist, xix, xx, 278
funerary, 245, 248, 250, 251
Funimation, 39
Future Boy Conan, 24

G

Gainax, 27, 28, 33, 35, 42
Galaxy Express 999, 18
GeGeGe no Kitaro, 103
gender, 117, 118, 119, 124, 125, 130, 132, 183, 189, 190, 191, 192
gender ambiguity, 244
genre
  subgenre, 271, 272, 273, 287
Getter Robo, 18, 20
Ghibli
  Studio Ghibli, 1, 12, 16, 23, 24, 25, 26, 27, 30, 38, 39, 40, 41, 54
Ghost in the Shell, 36, 41, 49, 97
Ghost in the Shell 2 Innocence, 41
Ghost in the Shell: SAC_2045, 49
Ghost-type Pokémon, 210, 211, 212
Gigantor, 15, 18
Ginyū, 173, 174
glorified body, 160
God, 286, 287
God of High School, 57
godhood, 89, 90, 92, 95, 96
Gohan, 154, 155, 157, 158, 160, 161, 163, 173, 179
Goku, 153, 154, 155, 156, 157, 158, 159, 160, 161, 162, 163, 168, 169, 171, 172, 173, 174, 176, 177, 178, 179
Golgo 13
  The Professional, 38
Gonzo, 39, 54
Gospels, 271, 272, 285, 286, 287
gothic, xviii
Grave of the Fireflies, 27, 30
Great Wars, 158
Gulliver's Travels Beyond the Moon, 16
Gunbuster, 33
Gundam. *See Mobile Suit Gundam*
Gurren Lagann, 41, 42

H

H+, 75
Hard Determinism, 156
harem, 44, 45, 46
Hays Code, 2
healing, 183
Heart Sutra, 247, 248
hegemony, 73, 81, 83
Heidi
  Girl of the Alps
    Heidi, 21, 27
Hell Girl, 44
Hello Kitty, xxiv
Henry David Thoreau, 82
hentai, 31
high schools, xxiv
Hikikomori, xxii
Himitsu no Akko-Chan, 21
Honey and Clover, xix, xxi, xxvii
honor and shame culture, xxi
Horusu
  Prince of the Sun, 16
Hōseki no Kuni, 243, 244, 245, 250, 251, 252, 253, 254, 255
How Do You Live?, 40
How Not to Summon a Demon Lord, 276, 277
Howl's Moving Castle, 3, 4, 5, 6, 8, 11, 12, 17, 21, 22, 26, 29, 31, 34, 36, 37, 38, 40, 43
Hu, Tze-yue, 2, 3, 5, 7, 8, 9, 10, 11, 13, 14, 22, 23, 24, 26, 27, 33, 34, 37, 41, 55, 56, 57
Human Psyche, xxvi
Humanity Plus, 75
hybridity, 117, 118, 119, 125, 127, 131, 132, 253, 254, 255

I

Ichikawa, Haruko, 243
iconography, xviii, xxv, xxvii
idealism, 73, 76, 80, 83, 96
identity, 167, 169, 174, 175, 182
immigration, 246, 255
immortality, 96
In Another World with My Smartphone, 277
India, 55
Indian spiritual, 70
individualism, 82
internet sources, xvii
intersubjective agreement, 77
Inuyasha, 281, 282
isekai, 4, 5, 45, 46, 47, 48, 59, 271, 272, 273, 274, 275, 276, 277, 278, 279, 280, 281, 282, 283, 284, 285, 286, 287, 323
Ishiguro, Noboru, 9, 18, 22, 28, 29, 30
isomorphic, 271, 272, 285, 288

J

J. O. Company, 9
Japan Animation Association JAA, 23
Japan Animation Film Association. *See* Japan Animation Association
Japanese culture, 118
Japanese folklore, 122, 123
Jesus, 271, 272, 285, 286, 287
Joaquim Xirau, 265
Jobless Reincarnation, 276
John Locke, 174
josei, 30
Journey to the West, 154
Jungian, xxvi

K

Kabbalah, xxv
Kabuki, 8
Kaijo no Michi, 105
Kaiō-*sama*, 160, 171
Kaiu Shirai, 225, 226, 227, 228, 231, 233
Kakushigoto, xxii
Kamakura period, 7
Kami, 102, 161
kamikaze attacker, 161
Kamishibai
  picture card story-telling, 7
Kanada, Yoshinori, 22
Kannon, 248
Karasu Tengu, 119, 120, 122, 123
karma, 71, 252
kawaii, xxiv, 21, 26
Kawamori, Shoji
  Kawamori, 18
Ketchum, Ash, 207, 211, 213, 214, 215, 216, 218, 220
Ki, xxi
Kimba the White Lion, 15
Kitayama Film Studio, 9
Kitayama, Seitarō, 8
Kizuna Ai, 51
Kobayashi Shōkai, 9
Kōdaiji, 247
Kon, Satoshi, 32, 38, 41
Kongō, 244, 245, 250, 251, 252, 253, 254, 255
KonoSuba: God's Blessing on this Wonderful World, 46
Kotabe, Yoichi
  Kotabe, 12
Kōuchi, Jun-ichi, 8
Krillin, 160, 161, 162, 163, 171, 172, 179
Kyōgen, 8

L

labor conditions, 55
LaMarre, Thomas, 3, 5, 6, 7, 8, 9, 10, 14, 18, 32, 34, 48
Land of the Lustrous. *See* Hōseki no Kuni
Laputa
  Castle in the Sky
  Laputa, 25
Le Blanc, Michelle, 12, 16, 23, 25, 26, 27, 30, 38, 39, 40
Leibniz, 156
Levi, Antonia, 5, 6
Levy, Tani, 46, 47, 48, 50
linguistic domination, 78
linguistic hegemony, 77
Little Witch Sally, 21
Localization, 205, 207, 214
Log Horizon, 277
"looking glass self", 77
Loss of Innocence, xxi
Lost, 278
love, 257, 260, 261, 262, 264, 265, 269
Love Hina, 44, 45
Lu, Amy Shirong, 6, 46, 48, 51
Ludomusicology, xix
Lupin III, 24
Lyn, xix

M

Macross Plus, 38
MacWilliams, W. Mark, 2, 3, 5, 6, 8, 15, 16, 37, 56, 57, 59
Madhouse, 23, 30, 38, 41, 42, 44, 54
Magical Girl
  Mahō Shōjo, 20
magical girlfriend genre, 31
Magical Play, 49
Maison Ikkoku, 30
manga, 2, 8, 10, 13, 15, 16, 17, 18, 20, 21, 22, 23, 24, 28, 29, 30, 31, 32, 33, 36, 37, 39, 41, 42, 44, 45, 48, 49, 50, 52, 56, 57, 61, 117, 118, 119, 124, 125, 131
manhwa, 57
Manifest Destiny, 83
Martial arts, xx
Masaoka, Kenzō, 10
Matrix, 36
Matsumoto, Leiji
  Matsumoto, 12, 17, 18
Mazinger Z, 18, 19
"McDonaldization", 83
mecha, xx, xxv, xxvi, 1, 4, 18, 20, 25, 35, 38, 42
media franchise, 37
media-mix, 1, 3, 6, 14, 19, 31, 39, 46
Megazone 23, 29
Meiji era, 8
Meiji Seika, 14
memory, 170, 174, 175
Mendlesohn, 272, 273
mental health, xxii, xxiv
meritocracy, 83
Mes, Tom, 38
metamodernism, 79, 80, 81, 83
metamodernist oscillation, 96
metamodernity, 73, 77, 81, 83, 84, 86, 96, 98
metaphysics, xxv, xxvi
meta-subjectivity, 73, 77
Metaverse, xxvi
Mewtwo, 208, 214, 218
Miguel de Unamuno, 265
Millennium Actress, 32, 41
Minakata Kumagusu, 104
Mind Screw, xxv
Mindar, 248, 255
minzokugaku, 104

Mirai, 24, 41
Miyazaki, Hayao
    Miyazaki, 1, 3, 12, 16, 21, 23, 24, 25, 26, 27, 30, 37, 38, 39, 40, 41
Mizuki Shigeru, 103
Mizuko, Ito, 32, 33, 39, 49, 50, 52, 59
Mobile Suit Gundam, 19, 36, 42, 98, 277
    Gundam, 18
Mobile Suit Gundam F91, 36
Mobile Suit Gundam SEED, 41, 42
moe, xxiv, 21, 43, 44
moeyōso, 43
Momotaro's Divine Sea Warriors
    Momotarō, 10
monk, 243, 244, 245, 246, 247, 248, 249, 250, 251, 252, 253, 254
Mononoke, 100
monsters, 101
morality, 251, 252, 253, 255
Mori Masahiro, 246
Mori, Yasuri, 12
Morrissy, Kim, 42, 46, 47, 53, 56
Mountain *Tengu*, 122, 126, 127
mundane. See slice of life
Murata, Yasuji, 9
Mushi Productions, 13
Mushishi, 100
Mushoku Tensei: Jobless Reincarnation, 47
Musicology, xix
My Neighbor Totoro, 25
My Neighbours the Yamadas
    Yamadas, 38, 39
Mysterious Play, 278

N

Nadia
    The Secret of Blue Water, 35
Nail, 168, 175

Nakazawa, Keiji, 30
Namekian, 160, 165, 168, 171
Napier, Susan, 3, 4, 5, 6, 7, 8, 11, 12, 13, 15, 17, 21, 22, 25, 26, 29, 30, 31, 32, 33, 34, 35, 36, 37, 38, 43
Nappa, 156, 157, 158, 159, 160, 161, 162
Narō, 47
Naruto, xx, 42, 43
Natsume's *Book of Friends*, 100
Nausicaä of the Valley of the Wind
    Nausicaä, 24, 30, 101
NEET, xxii, xxiii
neoliberal hegemony, 85
Neon Genesis Evangelion, xviii, xx, xxiv, xxvi, 8, 20, 35, 73, 87, 88, 95, 96, 140
Netflix, xvii, 49, 56, 58
New Cutie Honey, 37
New Testament, 287
Newtype, 50
nichijō. See slice of life
Nick Bostrom, 136
Nietzsche, xxiii, 76, 79, 81, 96
Nihon Manga Eiga Kabushiki Kaisha, 10, 11
Nikkatsu Corporation, 9
Nikkatsu Kitayama, 9
Nirvana, 251
Nō theatre, 8
normativity, 183

O

Objectivity, 202, 209, 210, 212, 219, 221
Occupation period, 10, 11
Odell, Colin, 12, 16, 23, 24, 25, 26, 27, 30, 38, 39, 40
offshore, 22, 56
Ōfuji, Noburo, 9

Oh My Goddess!, 45
Okuno, Takuji, 7, 34, 44
omnipotence, 90, 93, 96
omnipotent, 287
omnipresence, 96
omniscience, 96
One Piece, 37
online streaming, xvii, 39, 48, 49, 53, 54, 56, 58
Only Yesterday, 37
ontologically naturalized, 275, 280, 281, 282, 283, 284, 285, 287
Ontology, 108
Orange, 277
organizational ecology theory, 79
Orientalism, xix, 207, 208
Original Net Animation ONA, 3, 49
Original Sin, xxvii
Original Video Animation OVA, 3, 32
Originary, 218, 219, 220
Osamu Tezuka, 61
Oshii, Mamoru, 28, 30, 31, 32, 36, 41, 42, 43
otaku, xxiii, 1, 32, 33, 35, 39, 43, 44, 47, 48, 49, 50, 51, 52, 59, 60
otaku culture, 75, 87
Otogi Manga Calendar, 12
Ōtomo, Katsuhiro, 29, 30, 41
Ouran High School Host Club, 45
outsourcing, 22, 55, 56, 60
Overlord, 280

P

P.A. Works, 39
P.C.L., 9
Panda! Go, Panda!, 24
panopticon, 78
paper-cut animation, 49
Paradise Lost, xxii

Patlabor, 28
patriarchal discourse, 118, 126, 127, 128, 132
Paul Tillich, 265
penetration of the lifeworld, 97
Pepper (robot), 248, 255
Perfect Blue, 38
Persona 5, xix, xxiv, xxvi, xxvii
personal identity, 174
Phos (character), 252, 253, 254, 255
physical space, 61
Picard, Martin, 43
Piccolo, 155, 156, 158, 160, 161, 168, 169, 170, 171, 175, 179, 257, 259, 261, 262, 263, 264, 265, 266, 268, 269
pictocentricism, 8
Pierrot, 23, 42, 54
Pierrot Anime Studio, 23
Pikachu, 207, 215, 216, 219
Pinocchio, 11, 14
Pocket Monsters, 205
Pointon, Susan, 60
Poitras, Gilles, 2, 4, 6, 8, 10, 12, 13, 15, 16, 17, 19, 20, 28, 30, 32, 33, 34, 35, 38, 39, 41, 48, 49, 54
Pokédex, 202, 203, 204, 206, 210, 211, 212, 214, 215, 217, 219, 220
Pokemon, 39
Pokémon Blue, 203, 206, 214
Pokémon Green, 203, 206
Pokémon Red, 203, 206, 214
Pokémon: Indigo League, 202, 205
Pokémon: The First Movie - Mewtwo Strikes Back, 206, 208, 214, 218
political liberalism, 178
political realist, 163
Pom Poko, 37
Ponyo on the Cliff by the Sea Ponyo, 40

Index 333

posthuman, 139
postmodernism, 83
post-Second World War, 7
Potrais, Gilles, 12
power, 181, 182, 183, 186, 187, 188, 189, 190, 191, 192, 193, 194, 196, 197, 198, 200
pre-established harmony, 156
Primitive Saiyan Philosophy, 157
Princess Mononoke
Mononoke, 3, 5, 13, 15, 25, 30, 32, 33, 34, 37, 38, 39
Princess Princess, 44
Production I.G, 28, 43, 49, 54
Professor Oak, 203, 204
Psycho-Pass, 73, 92, 94
punk, xviii
puppet animation, 49

Q

queer, 183
queer theory, 183

R

Raditz, 155, 156, 157, 158, 159, 160, 162, 171, 179
Rail of the Star, 30
raito noberu, 47
Ramon Llull, 264
"rational capitulationism", 76
Re: Zero Kara Hajimeru Isekai Seikatsu, 46
Re:CREATORS, 284
recluses, xxii
refashioning, 117, 118, 119, 126, 131, 132
reincarnation, 274, 282
religion, 202, 221
religious studies, 190
rental priest, 248, 252, 254

resistance, 183
resurrection, 286
reverse harem, 45
Rintora, 18
Royal Space Force: Wings of Honneamise, 28
Rozen Maiden, 44

S

Said, Edward, 207, 208
Sailor Moon, 21, 37
Saint Augustine, 264
Saiyan, 155, 157, 158, 159, 162, 163, 168, 171, 172, 179
Sakurakouji Kanoko, 117, 119, 125, 126, 127, 128, 129, 130, 131, 132
samsara, 79
Sazae-san, 16
Scouter, 159, 160
seinen, 19, 22, 30, 244
self, 190
self-determination, 82, 96
self-realization, 95, 96
Serial Experiments Lain, 73, 89, 90, 95, 96
Seven Deadly Sins, xix
sexual identity, 183
sexual orientation, 191
Shadows, xxvi
Shashin Kagaku Kenkyūsho, 9
Shimokawa, Ōten, 8
Shin Nihon Dōga Sha. *See* New Japan Animation Company, *See* New Japan Animation Company
Shingon, 244
Shinkai, Makoto, 41, 320
Shinto, 117, 119, 121, 122, 126
Shochiku, 10
shōjo, 4, 21, 26, 31, 36, 43, 244
shōjo manga, 117, 118, 123, 124, 125, 126, 128, 129

shōnen, 4, 20, 21, 22, 28, 31, 35, 37, 48
Shonen Jump, 50
Shōsetsuka ni Narō, 47
shōshikōreika. *See* aging society
Shōwa period, 7
Slam Dunk, 37
slave morality, 76
slice of life, 44, 46, 47
Slice of Life, xxi, xxvii
Snow White, 11
social constitution of reality, 77
social engineering, 74
social reality, 77, 93, 98
social space, 63, 64
Soft Determinism, 155
Son Gohan, 257, 258, 259, 261, 262, 263, 264, 266, 268, 269
Son Goku, 257, 258, 259, 260, 261, 262, 263, 266, 267, 268, 269
South Korea, 22, 55, 56, 57, 60
Space Battleship Yamato, 17, 22
space opera, 17
Speed Racer, 15
Spirited Away, 40, 41, 103
spontaneity, 166
Star of Giants, 31
stateless, 5, 6, 17, 59, 60
Steamboy, 41
steampunk, 17, 18, 24, 25, 35
Steinberg, Marc Aaron, 3, 13, 14, 15
Steins;Gate, 282
Stuckmann, Chris, 6, 15, 29, 32, 33, 36
Suan, Steve, 3, 4, 51, 55, 56, 58, 60
subaltern, 77, 86
subcontracting, 55
substantially bound, 175
suicide, xxi, xxii, xxiii, xxv
Sunrise, 22, 36, 38, 39, 42, 54
Sunrise Anime Studio, 22

Superdimensional Fortress Macross, 28, 30
supernatural, 117, 121, 122, 125, 126, 132, 202, 210, 212, 221
supernatural powers, xx
surrealism, xxv
Suzuki, Toshio, 24, 29
Sword Art Online, 46, 73, 94, 95, 96, 277

T

Tajiri, Satoshi, 203
Takahashi, Ryosuke
Takahashi, 18
Takahata, Isao
Takahata, 12, 16, 23, 24, 26, 27, 30, 37, 38, 39, 41
Taoism, xxv
Team Rocket, 207, 212, 214, 215, 216, 217, 219
technology, 202, 213, 217, 218
teen problems, xxiv
Tenchi Universe, 277
tengu, 117, 118, 119, 120, 121, 122, 123, 126, 127, 128, 129, 131, 132, 323
Tenkatsu, 8, 9
Tensei Shitara Slime Datta Ken, 46
Tezuka, Osamu
Tezuka, 1, 12, 13, 14, 15, 16, 18, 22
Tezuka's Curse, 14
Thailand, 55
That Time I Got Reincarnated as a Slime, 279
The Big O, 284
The Bubblegum Crisis, 29
The Doorman, 8
The Electric Tale of Pikachu, 206, 212
The Faraway Paladin, 276

Index

The History of Trunks, 176
The King of Eden, xxii
The Legend of the White Snake, 12
The Matrix, 74
the Patriot Act, 76
The Phantom Ship, 16
the Philippines, 55
The Promised Neverland, 279
The Sky Crawlers, 42, 43
The Tale of Princess Kaguya, 41
the Temptation, 287
The Thief of Baghdad Castle, 9
the Trinity, 286
the Virgin Birth, 286, 287
The Vision of Escaflowne, 37, 45
The Wallflower, 45
The Whale, 16
The Wind Rises, 40
thirdspace, 63, 65
Three Tales, 12
Titanic, 38
To Your Eternity, 277
Toei, 1, 11, 12, 13, 16, 18, 21, 22, 24, 31, 37, 54, 55, 319
Toei Animation. *See* Toei
Toei Dōga, 11
Tōhō, 10, 11
Tokkōtai, 161
Tokyo Ghoul, 42
Tokyo Godfathers, 41
Tokyo Motion Picture Distribution Company. *See* Toei
Tokyo Revengers, 277
Tomino, Yoshiyuki
 Tomino, 13, 18, 19, 22, 36
Tono Monogatari, 104
totalitarian, 158, 164, 165, 166, 167
totalitarian movement, 158
Tower of God, 57
traditional culture, xxi, xxiv
traditions, 183
transcendence, 143

Transcendentalism, 73, 81
transformation, 166, 167, 168, 169
transhumanism, 73, 74, 75, 76, 77, 78, 79, 81, 82, 83, 86, 89, 90, 91, 93, 95, 96, 97, 135
Transhumanist Statement, 75
Trigun, 277
Triton of the Sea, 22
Tsugata, Nobuyuki, 7, 8, 9, 10, 11, 13, 14, 15, 16, 20, 24, 27, 34, 35, 36, 60
tsukijin, 244, 245, 250, 251, 252, 253, 254, 255
2001 A Space Odyssey, 250
typology, 271, 272, 279

U

Ubermensch, xxiii
UFO Robot Grendizer, 22
Ukiyo-e
 woodblock print image, 7
union, 175
Urotsukidōji: Legend of the Overfiend, 31
Urusei Yatsura, 31
Urushibara Yuki, 100
utilitarian, 76
utilitarianism, 76
Utsushi-e
 Edo anime, 7

V

Vegeta, 154, 156, 157, 158, 159, 160, 161, 162, 163, 166, 167, 168, 169, 171, 172, 173, 176, 177, 179, 257, 259, 261, 262, 266, 267, 268, 269
Victory Gundam, 36
VTubers, 50, 51

W

War on Terror, 76
Watanabe, Shinichiro
   Watanabe, 38
Waters, 100
Weberian ideal types, 77
Webtoons, 57
weeaboo, xxiii
Welcome to the N.H.K., xxii, xxiii, xxiv
Wells, Paul, 3, 6, 7
Western, xviii, xxii
Western animation
   Western cartoons, 2, 3, 4, 5, 14, 58
Westernization, 86
When a Cat Faces West, 100
Wonder Woman, 279
World War I, 158
World War II, 153, 161, 178
World Wars, 158
Worthy Opponent, 266, 267

X

Xian'er, 247, 248

Y

Yamabushi Tengu. *See* Mountain Tengu
Yamada, Naoko, 60
Yamaguchi, Yasuo, 9, 12, 13, 15, 18, 34, 39, 49
Yamamoto, Sanae, 9, 10, 16
Yamamoto, Sayo, 60
Yanagita Kunio, 104
Yashahime, 277
Yasuhiko, Yoshikazu
   Yasuhiko, 22
yokai, 100
Young Adult fiction, 118, 124, 128
Your Name, 41
YouTube, 21, 50, 51, 56
YuYu Hakusho, 278

Z

Zarbon, 167

www.ingramcontent.com/pod-product-compliance
Lightning Source LLC
Chambersburg PA
CBHW072119290426
44111CB00012B/1714